RUMORS OF RESISTANCE

RUMORS OF RESISTANCE

STATUS REVERSALS AND HIDDEN TRANSCRIPTS IN THE GOSPEL OF LUKE

AMANDA C. MILLER

Fortress Press

Minneapolis

RUMORS OF RESISTANCE

Status Reversals and Hidden Transcripts in the Gospel of Luke

Cover design: Alisha Lofgren

Library of Congress Cataloging-in-Publication Data is available

Print ISBN: 978-1-4514-6935-6

eBook ISBN: 978-1-4514-8427-4

The paper used in this publication meets the minimum requirements of American National Standard for Information Sciences — Permanence of Paper for Printed Library Materials, ANSI Z329.48-1984.

Manufactured in the U.S.A.

This book was produced using PressBooks.com, and PDF rendering was done by PrinceXML.

For Alec, who's been there since the first word of the first chapter
and
For Lukas, who's turned our story upside down
ἠγαλλίασεν τὸ πνεῦμά μου

CONTENTS

Preface and Acknowledgements

The focus of *Rumors of Resistance*, originally my PhD dissertation, grew out of my mutual passions for music, particularly its power to convey both help and hope for a variety of people, and for the Bible and its powerful call to social and spiritual transformation of faith communities and of the world. These twin interests led me first to the Magnificat, then to other ancient songs of status reversal, and finally to the development of this reversal imagery in the Gospel of Luke.

My research has also been shaped, informed, and enriched along the way by various conversations about and experiences with issues of oppression and redemption. Specifically, I am interested in exploring how we might right the injustices of this world, yet refrain from creating new prejudices and boundaries in their place. One central inspiration for this task has been the congregation of Tabernacle Baptist Church, Richmond, VA, particularly our sisters and brothers from Burma. They came to the United States as refugees from widespread ethnic oppression, some quite literally fleeing in the night and not knowing until months later whether children and other family members had made it to safety as well. Yet in spite of all this, they remain kindhearted, gracious, optimistic, and faithful, and have become treasured members of Tabernacle and the Richmond community. They are passionate in their desire for change, for an end to the oppression of their people, and for justice to be done in their home country. Yet they almost always express this passion without harmful bitterness or a desire for vengeance on those who have wronged them. I am humbled and blessed by the example of my Karen, Chin, Karenni, Lesu, and Kachin sisters and brothers, and my work in this project is the better for my having known them.

I also wish to thank my professors at Central Baptist Theological Seminary (Shawnee, KS) and Union Presbyterian Seminary (Richmond, VA). David M. May first inspired me to pursue a graduate degree in biblical studies and modeled teaching the New Testament as a ministry. And deep gratitude must be extended to the scholars who have walked with me from the beginning of this study: John T. Carroll, Frances Taylor Gench, and Warren Carter.

They have offered me valuable insight, thoughtful critique, and endless encouragement, and for that I cannot thank them enough.

My colleagues at Belmont University have been a great help and support as I have juggled the last steps of this project and the first steps of my life as a teacher. I am grateful for their encouragement, flexibility, advice, and understanding.

Finally, my family and friends have been an immeasurable help throughout the past several years. In particular, my parents, Roy and Emily Smith, have always had an unshakeable belief that I could and would accomplish whatever I wanted to, and I would not be where I am today without that confidence. And of course, I could never have completed this project without my husband, Rev. Alec Miller, and our son, Lukas. For all the support, conversations, advice, debates, snuggles, laughs, encouragement, dinners cooked, and dogs walked, I can only say, with all my love, thank you, thank you, and thank you again.

Abbreviations

AB	Anchor Bible
AJT	*Asia Journal of Theology*
Ann.	Tacitus, *Annales*
ANRW	*Aufstieg und Niedergang der römischen Welt: Geschichte und Kultur Roms im Spiegel der neueren Forschung*
Ant.	Josephus, *Jewish Antiquities*
Ant. rom.	Dionysius of Halicarnassus, *Antiquitates romanae*
BDAG	Danker, F. W., W. Bauer, W. F. Arndt, and F. W. Gingrich. *Greek-English Lexicon of the New Testament and Other Early Christian Literature*
BDB	Brown, F., S. R. Driver, and C. A. Briggs. *A Hebrew and English Lexicon of the Old Testament*
BETL	Bibliotheca ephemeridum theologicarum lovaniensium
BibIntS	Biblical Interpretation Series
BRev	*Bible Review*
BZNW	Beihefte zur Zeitschrift für die neutestamentliche Wissenschaft
CahRB	Cahiers de la Revue biblique
CBQ	*Catholic Biblical Quarterly*
Did	*Didaskalia*
Ep.	*Epistulae*
Epigr.	Martial, *Epigram*
EvT	*Evangelische Theologie*
ExpTim	*Expository Times*
Fin.	Cicero, *De finibus*
Geogr.	Strabo, *Geographica*
GNS	Good News Studies
Greg	*Gregorianum*
Hist. nat.	Pliny the Elder, *Naturalis historia*
Hist. rom.	Cassius Dio, *Roman History*
HvTSt	*Hervormde teologiese studies*
JBL	*Journal of Biblical Literature*
JQR	*Jewish Quarterly Review*
JR	*Journal of Religion*
JSNT	*Journal for the Study of the New Testament*
JSNTSup	Journal for the Study of the New Testament: Supplement Series

JSOTSup	Journal for the Study of the Old Testament: Supplement Series
JTS	*Journal of Theological Studies*
J.W.	Josephus, *Jewish War*
LCL	Loeb Classical Library
LEH	Lust, J., E. Eynikel, and K. Hauspie, *Greek-English Lexicon of the Septuagint*
LNTS	Library of New Testament Studies
LXX	Septuagint
MT	Masoretic Text
Neot	*Neotestamentica*
NIB	*The New Interpreter's Bible*
NICNT	New International Commentary on the New Testament
NJPS	*Tanakh: The Holy Scriptures: The New JPS Translation according to the Traditional Hebrew Text*
NovT	*Novum Testamentum*
NovTSup	Supplements to Novum Testamentum
NRSV	New Revised Standard Version
NTS	*New Testament Studies*
NTT	New Testament Theology
OBT	Overtures to Biblical Theology
Off.	Cicero, *De officiis*
Op.	Hesiod, *Opera et dies*
Or.	Dio Chrysostom, *Orations*
PRSt	*Perspectives in Religious Studies*
PTMS	Princeton Theological Monograph Series
RST	Regensburger Studien zur Theologie
Sat.	Juvenal, *Satirae*
SBLDS	Society of Biblical Literature Dissertation Series
SBLSP	*Society of Biblical Literature Seminar Papers*
SBLSymS	Society of Biblical Literature Symposium Series
SemeiaSt	Semeia Studies
SNTSMS	Society for New Testament Studies Monograph Series
Socr.	Dio Chrysostom, *De Socrate*
SP	Sacra Pagina
Spec.	Philo, *De specialibus legibus*
WBC	Word Biblical Commentary

Introduction

In the opening chapter of the Gospel of Luke, the evangelist introduces a subversive image—that of a world turned upside down through status reversal—through the words of a surprising character, a sexually compromised, unmarried girl named Mary. This unlikely mother-to-be sings an unlikely song better suited to the celebration of a victorious army than to a private meeting between a once-barren pregnant woman and a pregnant virgin (Luke 1:39-56). Yet still Mary says of her God,

> He has shown strength with his arm,
>> he has scattered the arrogant because of the thoughts of their hearts.
> He has thrown down rulers from thrones,
>> and lifted up the lowly.
> The hungry he has filled with good things,
>> and the rich he has sent out empty. (Luke 1:51-53)[1]

From this opening declaration, Luke[2] continues to develop throughout his Gospel the idea of divinely initiated inversion between rich and poor, powerful and powerless, social insider and social outsider. The Lukan Jesus opens his public ministry with a reprise of the Magnificat's upward reversals for the poor and oppressed (4:16-30). Later, he repeatedly defines his teaching and healing work, and the reign of God that it proclaims, by this same theme of status reversal (for example, 6:20-26; 7:18-23; 13:30; 14:7-24; 18:9-14). Finally, Jesus' shameful death as a condemned traitor, even though he is, according to the Gospel narrative, the Son of God, sets up the crowning enactment of status reversal, as Jesus first humbles himself and is then exalted by God through resurrection and ascension.[3]

---

1. Unless otherwise noted, all translations of the New Testament, Hebrew Bible, and the Dead Sea Scrolls in this book are my own.

2. I use the name "Luke" throughout this book to refer to the third evangelist as a term of convenience, while acknowledging that we do not know who actually composed the Gospel of Luke and the Acts of the Apostles.

3. John O. York, *The Last Shall Be First: The Rhetoric of Reversal in Luke*, JSNTSup 46 (Sheffield: Sheffield Academic Press, 1991), 172. For a comparison of Jesus' ascension with the deification of the Roman emperors, see Gary Gilbert, "Roman Propaganda and Christian Identity in the Worldview of

The prominence of status reversal imagery in the Gospel of Luke has contributed significantly to its reputation for championing the cause of the poor, weak, and oppressed to a greater extent than many other New Testament authors. This same Gospel, however, has also been characterized as favorably disposed toward the Roman Empire, or as a peacemaker between church and empire. These characterizations seem to be in conflict with each other, for it is difficult to appease a powerful oppressor while at the same time convincing the oppressed that one is on their side. More recently, Steve Walton has argued that Luke presents both positive and negative aspects of the imperial order, maintaining an objective "critical distance" from the Roman ruling powers.[4] This study will explore that tension, arguing that it is evidence of what political anthropologist James C. Scott calls the "hidden transcript of resistance," common to groups under material, personal, and ideological domination and humiliation. He suggests that we "interpret the rumors, folktales, songs, gestures, jokes, and theater of the powerless as vehicles by which, among other things, they insinuate a critique of power while hiding behind anonymity or behind innocuous understandings of their conduct."[5]

In the following chapters, I will consider the subversive dynamics of some of Luke's prominent status-reversal texts: the Magnificat (1:46-55), the Nazareth proclamation (4:16-30), and the parable of Lazarus and the rich man (16:19-31). Through the tools of intertextual comparison, sociological analysis, and contextual interplay with historical and literary settings, I will explore the role of these texts of status reversal in Luke's developing vision for living as Christian communities in the midst of imperial power. In this study, I will argue that the reign of God as espoused by the Gospel of Luke utilizes, among other strategies of imperial negotiation, a significant resistance to some of the dominant values and practices of the Roman Empire. Central to that vision is the challenge issued to readers and hearers from all levels of social status to confront and transform their prejudicial or dominating attitudes and actions in light of the reversals proclaimed in these texts.

Luke-Acts," in *Contextualizing Acts: Lukan Narrative and Greco-Roman Discourse*, ed. Todd Penner and Caroline Vander Stichele, SBLSymS (Atlanta: Society of Biblical Literature, 2003), 243–47.

4. Steve Walton, "The State They Were In: Luke's View of the Roman Empire," in *Rome in the Bible and the Early Church*, ed. Peter Oakes (Carlisle: Paternoster, 2002), 33–35.

5. James C. Scott, *Domination and the Arts of Resistance: Hidden Transcripts* (New Haven: Yale University Press, 1990), xiii.

ROME, REVERSALS, AND THE GOSPEL OF LUKE

One common view of Luke's political perspective, which continues to be predominant today, is that the author was attempting to present his Christian communities as acceptable to the Roman Empire, and at the same time affirming the cultural and political status quo. Yet there is also general acknowledgement that Luke gives prominent place to Jesus' teachings on status reversals that celebrate divine shattering of the earthly status quo. As both of these seemingly contradictory aims are central to our study, they must be examined in more detail.

THE ROMAN EMPIRE AND THE GOSPEL OF LUKE

For some time, the conciliatory relationship between Luke and Rome was treated as a foregone conclusion. Henry Cadbury made the case in 1927 for reading Luke-Acts as a two-pronged defense of Christianity, arising from a need to explain why its great leaders Jesus and Paul were innocent despite the numerous charges brought against them in Roman courts, and from a need to argue that Christianity was a *religio licita* like Judaism.[6] Three decades later, Hans Conzelmann proposed only a slight tweak to this theory, arguing that Luke was motivated by the problem of the delay of the parousia. In Conzelmann's reading, the evangelist sought to forge a permanent settlement between the church and the Roman Empire by emphasizing the Jewish role in the various Christian trials, and minimizing the Roman one.[7]

Philip Esler and Paul Walaskay offer other modifications of essentially the same understanding. Using socio-redaction criticism, Esler identifies Luke's general strategy not as apologetic aimed at pagan Romans, but as legitimation aimed at Roman Christians who might be questioning their decision to join the new movement.[8] This legitimation tactic sought to assure community members that they could continue working for the Roman military or administration and still remain faithful Christians.[9] Walaskay, on the other hand, surveys various Lukan passages that would not endear the church to a loyal Roman.[10] He concludes not that Luke wanted to make the church acceptable to Rome, but

6. Henry J. Cadbury, *The Making of Luke-Acts*, 2nd ed. (Peabody, MA: Hendrickson, 1999), 308–16. It should be noted that the Roman practice of authorizing certain foreign faiths as *religio licita* is generally considered exaggerated or entirely fictitious today.

7. Hans Conzelmann, *The Theology of St. Luke*, trans. Geoffrey Buswell (London: Faber and Faber, 1960), 138–40.

8. Philip Francis Esler, *Community and Gospel in Luke-Acts: The Social and Political Motivations of Lucan Theology*, SNTSMS 57 (Cambridge: Cambridge University Press, 1987), 16–17.

9. Ibid., 210.

that he wanted to convince the church to make its peace with living in the empire, by portraying Rome in the best possible light.[11]

While much work has been done on the signs of resistance to Rome that are found in historical Jesus research, the Q texts, and various New Testament authors,[12] only a few scholars have ventured to argue that the Gospel of Luke was anything other than conciliatory toward that first-century superpower. One notable exception is Richard Cassidy's 1978 work *Jesus, Politics, and Society: A Study of Luke's Gospel.* Cassidy examines Jesus' social stance, his interactions with Palestinian and Roman rulers, and his trial and death, and concludes that Luke presents a Jesus who, although not advocating armed revolt, was openly critical of Roman officials and vassals, and especially of the imperial policy's reliance on violence, exploitation, and social hierarchy.[13] Although Cassidy's work draws attention to significant features of the Lukan presentation of Jesus, he tends to explain away passages that conflict with his thesis by arguing that the revolutionary parts of Luke-Acts override the conciliatory ones. In the end, this approach fails to make a convincing argument based on the entirety of Luke's work, in the same way that scholars who read Luke as friendly to Rome must sideline the subversive reversal texts by various (and in my opinion questionable) means in order to make their own interpretations work.

Recently, however, scholars have begun to approach Luke's perspective on the Roman Empire in a more balanced way. Steve Walton, in an essay from 2005,[14] surveys the positive *and* negative imperial interactions in Luke-Acts, concluding that Luke offers "critical distance" from the Roman Empire, which allows him to evaluate both its strengths and its weaknesses.[15] Gary Gilbert also presents a persuasive argument for a conflicted, multivalent relationship

10. Paul W. Walaskay, *"And So We Came to Rome": The Political Perspective of St. Luke*, SNTSMS 49 (Cambridge: Cambridge University Press, 1983), 16–22.

11. Ibid., 14.

12. See, e.g., Warren Carter, *Matthew and Empire: Initial Explorations* (Harrisburg, PA: Trinity, 2001); Carter, *John and Empire: Initial Explorations* (London: T&T Clark, 2008); William R. Herzog, *Jesus, Justice, and the Reign of God: A Ministry of Liberation* (Louisville: Westminster John Knox, 2000); Richard A. Horsley, ed., *Hidden Transcripts and the Arts of Resistance: Applying the Work of James C. Scott to Jesus and Paul*, SemeiaSt (Atlanta: Society of Biblical Literature, 2004); and Horsley, *Jesus and Empire: The Kingdom of God and the New World Disorder* (Minneapolis: Fortress Press, 2003).

13. Richard J. Cassidy, *Jesus, Politics, and Society: A Study of Luke's Gospel* (Maryknoll, NY: Orbis, 1978), 61–62.

14. Walton, "State," 1–41.

15. Ibid., 35. See also Peter Oakes, "A State of Tension: Rome in the New Testament," in *The Gospel of Matthew in Its Roman Imperial Context*, ed. John Riches and David C. Sim, JSNTSup 276 (London: T&T Clark, 2005), 86–88.

between Lukan Christianity and the Roman Empire, mainly through analysis of Luke-Acts in relation to other literature and propaganda of the time.[16] Another significant voice in this conversation is that of C. Kavin Rowe, who examines the conflict between Rome and the Lukan communities at the "level . . . of the ordering principles of thought and their concomitant relation to praxis."[17] The work of these and a few other scholars[18] yields significant insights for this project and its approach to the relationship between the Gospel of Luke and the Roman Empire, namely, that (1) a more nuanced (and likely more realistic) view of Lukan imperial negotiation is required, (2) with particular attention to the time of the evangelist and his earliest reading communities, (3) as situated through "thick" description of their social, historical, and cultural setting.

The need for nuance in our treatment of this topic is demonstrated clearly by Steve Walton's concise review in two areas: (1) Luke's positive engagements with the Roman Empire (for example, John the Baptist's teaching that allows Roman retainers to keep their positions as long as they execute their work fairly [Luke 3:10-14]; the positive portrayal in Luke-Acts of Roman centurions and other officials [Luke 7:1-10; 23:46-47; Acts 10:1-48]; Paul's respect for the Roman legal system and its repeated declarations of his innocence [e.g., Acts 22:22-29; 23:26-30; 25:1—26:32]);[19] and (2) the negative portrayal of imperial practices in Luke-Acts (such as corrupt officials like Felix who seek bribes [Acts 24:24-27]; Pilate's execution of Jesus even when he believes him to be innocent [Luke 23:13-25]; the social and economic trouble caused by Paul's evangelism [for example, Acts 19:23-41]).[20]

The work of Rowe deepens this understanding of the complexity of Luke-Acts and its attitude toward Rome.[21] In his book *World Upside Down: Reading*

16. Gary Gilbert, "Luke-Acts and Negotiation of Authority and Identity in the Roman World," in *The Multivalence of Biblical Texts and Theological Meanings*, ed. Christine Helmer and Charlene T. Higbe, SBLSymS (Atlanta: Society of Biblical Literature, 2006), 83–104; and Gilbert, "Roman Propaganda," 233–56.

17. C. Kavin Rowe, "Luke-Acts and the Imperial Cult: A Way Through the Conundrum?," *JSNT* 27 (2005): 298. See also his monograph: C. Kavin Rowe, *World Upside Down: Reading Acts in the Graeco-Roman Age* (Oxford: Oxford University Press, 2009).

18. Note in particular Yong-Sung Ahn, *The Reign of God and Rome in Luke's Passion Narrative: An East Asian Global Perspective*, BibIntS 80 (Leiden: Brill, 2006); David Rhoads, David Esterline, and Jae Won Lee, eds., *Luke-Acts and Empire: Essays in Honor of Robert L. Brawley*, PTMS (Eugene, OR: Wipf & Stock, 2011); and Kazuhiko Yamazaki-Ransom, *The Roman Empire in Luke's Narrative*, LNTS 404 (London: T&T Clark, 2010).

19. Walton, "State," 20–23.

20. Ibid., 23–26.

21. Rowe, "Luke-Acts," 288.

Acts in the Graeco-Roman Age, he draws upon such texts as the conflict between the apostles and the Ephesian worshippers of Artemis (Acts 19:18-40) to show that the Christian mission was not entirely innocuous in its effect upon the social, political, and economic world of the imperial provinces.[22] But he also argues that "the Christian mission as narrated by Luke is not a counter-state. It does not . . . seek to replace Rome or to 'take back' Palestine, Asia, or Achaia."[23] He cites as support Paul's multiple trials and acquittals before Roman officials such as Claudius Lysias (Acts 21:27—23:30), Felix (Acts 24:1 27), and Festus and Herod Agrippa II (Acts 25:1—26:32).[24]

The work of Gary Gilbert illustrates yet again, through slightly different methods, the multifaceted relationship between Luke and Rome. In an essay entitled "Luke-Acts and Negotiation of Authority and Identity in the Roman World," he compares Luke to writers of the Second Sophistic like Plutarch and Dio Chrysostom, who generally lived comfortably within the empire and even praised Rome at times, but also used their writings to modify or reject the imperial claim to superiority.[25] Like these Greek authors, Gilbert argues, Luke also gave tacit (partial) approval to Rome and its dealings with early Christians, but still urged his readers to develop an identity distinct from and superior to that dictated by Rome, thereby rejecting its major imperial claims.[26] Gilbert's work is especially suggestive in that it holds together the entirety of Luke-Acts, both the parts that appear accommodating and those that appear resistant, rather than forcing it to align with one extreme or the other. In the words of Peter Oakes, there is, for Luke as for other residents of the Roman provinces, a "tension between appreciation and resentment. . . . Luke's Rome is a mixture of efficiency, openness, justice, cruelty and corruption."[27]

Another commonality between the studies discussed above is that they work on the historical and literary level of the evangelist and his earliest audiences, an approach that I will follow in this project. Although there is certainly value in reflecting upon the possible impact of Jesus' teachings in early-first-century Palestine, the identification of specific passages as earlier or more likely "authentic" (that is, stemming from Jesus' historical career) is fraught with uncertainties and, more importantly for this project, breaks up the narrative arc of the Gospel of Luke and the Acts of the Apostles. Rowe refers

---

22. Rowe, *World Upside Down*, 42–49, 51.

23. Ibid., 87.

24. Ibid., 64–83.

25. Gilbert, "Luke-Acts and Negotiation," 96–97.

26. Ibid., 104.

27. Oakes, "State of Tension," 88.

to Acts as a "culture forming narrative" that seeks to construct "an alternative total way of life . . . that runs counter to the life-patterns of the Graeco-Roman world."[28] We will gain clearer insight into the Lukan narrative and its effects if we study the finished product and its possible implications in the life of the earliest reading communities. It is this focus on the context of the Gospel's composition that allows Gilbert to understand Luke-Acts as "a counter-discourse that . . . seeks to constitute an understanding of being a Christian in the Roman world."[29] Warren Carter employs a similar focus on the imperial context of the evangelists and their audiences in his significant work on imperial negotiation in the Gospels of Matthew and John.[30] In this project, I will approach the Gospel of Luke in the same manner, as a complete narrative composed for Christian communities seeking, in Gilbert's apt phrase, "to develop . . . a sense of place within the Roman world."[31]

Flowing from this decision to focus on the compositional stage of the Lukan narrative is another pertinent method also observed in the work of Rowe, Gilbert, Carter, and others. A perceptive account of the impact of Luke's narrative on its earliest audiences must be informed by an accurate understanding of the sociocultural world in which they lived. This contextual study must go beyond overt references to Rome in the text or a brief survey of the emperors and imperial officials at the time of the Gospel's composition. These are important elements, but they are only starting points in developing a complete understanding of Luke's sociohistorical context. The Roman Empire was, as Carter says, "the foreground, not the background, of late first-century daily life."[32] As such, there is much insight to be gained from close attention to the political, economic, social, and religious context in which Luke and his readers lived their everyday lives. Walton, for example, discusses the administration of the Roman Empire and Christianity's place within it before commencing with his survey of positive and negative imperial interactions in Luke-Acts.[33] Carter devotes multiple chapters to the topic of Roman presence and culture in both his books on imperial negotiation and the Gospels.[34]

---

28. Rowe, *World Upside Down*, 4.

29. Gilbert, "Luke-Acts and Negotiation," 87. See also Rowe's focus on general Christian readers of Luke-Acts in the late first century (*World Upside Down*, 11).

30. Carter, *Matthew and Empire*; and Carter, *John and Empire*.

31. Gilbert, "Roman Propaganda," 237.

32. Carter, *John and Empire*, x.

33. Walton, "State," 13-16.

34. Carter, *Matthew and Empire*, 9–53; and Carter, *John and Empire*, 3–89.

Within such wide-ranging contextual knowledge, a sharper focus on more specific areas has also proven fruitful. To understand Luke-Acts in its Roman context, Gilbert effectively employs a narrower lens, that of the literature and propaganda that were well-known at the time. He argues that Luke adapts Roman imperial propaganda (found in literature, laws, imperial images, architecture, inscriptions, coins, games and other public spectacles) to support the Gospel's claims about God and God's place in the world.[35] Gilbert also compares Luke's quest to provide Christian identity in the midst of the empire to the literary work of the Greek authors of the Second Sophistic and their reaction to the growing literary voice of Roman power.[36] Rowe, in a similar manner, grounds much of his work in a specific area of the Lukan social context—a detailed understanding of the imperial cult and the conflict caused by the competing claim that Jesus, not the emperor, is "Lord of all" (Acts 10:36).[37]

Such meticulous engagement with the world of the Roman provinces contributes significantly to these scholars' deeper, more nuanced readings, as discussed above. The current scholarship on the imperial engagement of Luke (and the other evangelists) makes clear that this sort of "thick" sociohistorical description must be an important part of any discussion on imperial negotiation in the biblical text. In this study, I will consider carefully the Roman imperial setting of Luke's Gospel and its earliest audiences throughout the following chapters. I have chosen, like Gilbert, to focus on one theme and type of literature, specifically texts of status reversal, in order to explore in some detail how these passages might have been understood in their ancient context.

STATUS REVERSAL AND THE GOSPEL OF LUKE

Images of status reversal, where the reigning world order is turned upside down and inside out, can be found in all three Synoptic Gospels, particularly in the example of Jesus' own life, death, and resurrection, and more explicitly in short, antithetic aphorisms attributed to him. Jesus offers such provocative declarations as the following: "Indeed, some are last who will be first, and some are first who will be last" (Luke 13:30; cf. Matt. 19:30; 20:26; Mark 10:31); "For those who want to save their life will lose it, and those who lose their life for my sake will save it" (Luke 9:24; 17:33; cf. Matt. 10:39; 16:25; Mark 8:35; John 12:25); " For all who exalt themselves will be humbled, and those who humble themselves will be exalted" (Luke 14:11; 18:14; cf. Matt. 23:12). In Luke, however, this idea

---

35. Gilbert, "Roman Propaganda," 236–37.

36. Gilbert, "Luke-Acts and Negotiation," 87–90.

37. Rowe, "Luke-Acts," 280–94. See also his continuing argument in Rowe, *World Upside Down*, particularly 92–136.

of a "great reversal" has been developed to a significantly more extensive degree. Indeed, Allen Verhey argues that the idea of social reversal is central to both Lukan theology (especially Christology) and Lukan ethics.[38]

In his book *The Last Shall Be First: The Rhetoric of Reversal in Luke*, John O. York presents the fullest available survey of reversal as a Lukan theme.[39] He divides the relevant Gospel pericopes into either explicit or implicit examples of bi-polar reversal (that is, with both downward and upward reversals) and also situates them within a first-century Mediterranean context. He discusses our three focal stories (Luke 1:46-55; 4:16-30; 16:19-31) in some detail, as well as related texts such as the beatitudes and woes in the Sermon on the Plain (6:20-26); the anointing of Jesus by the sinful woman, whom Jesus treats as more honored than his Pharisaic host (7:36-50); the parable of the humble tax collector and the self-justifying Pharisee (18:9-14); and Jesus' instructions for table fellowship (14:7-24). York focuses specifically on the function of the reversal texts not in a hypothetical earlier form, but in the Gospel itself, "in the progression of Luke's message" and "as the repetition of a particular theme."[40] At the end of his survey he concludes that the reversal pattern in Luke is related as much to social issues of status (honor and shame) as it is to physical and material conditions, and that the mixture of present and future reversals in the Gospel supports the "already-not yet" eschatology of Luke, as well as its two-pronged message of hope for those of little status and of warning to the elite.[41] One of my goals in the following chapters is to explore in much more detail this pairing of hope and warning in the status reversals.

A contentious interpretative issue about Luke's status reversals is whether they are to be taken literally or figuratively. Consistent with the conclusions from York sketched above, the reversals proclaimed in the Third Gospel are multifaceted, involving not only the material state of wealth or poverty, but also social values like status, power, honor, and shame. But the frequent attempts by Luke's interpreters throughout history to spiritualize the reversals are simply not convincing. Rather, this approach seems to have offered, in both ancient and modern times, a way to domesticate the deeply unsettling reversals into something less threatening to the status quo. Taking the Magnificat as a test case, we find that Cyril of Alexandria, as early as the fifth century CE, was arguing that the formerly rich and powerful, and now deposed, rulers

---

38. Allen Verhey, *The Great Reversal: Ethics and the New Testament* (Grand Rapids: Eerdmans, 1984), 94.

39. York, *Last Shall Be First*.

40. Ibid., 40.

41. Ibid., 182–83.

mentioned in Luke 1:51-53 were the demonic powers, Greek philosophical schools, and Pharisees and other Jews who did not believe in Jesus[42]—that is, anyone who did not subscribe to faith as Cyril himself saw it. Such an interpretation expediently gave all the blessings of status reversal to Christians and all the downward reversals to their opponents. In a contrasting interpretation, though, Albert the Great (thirteenth century CE) identified the Magnificat's proud rulers as those who use their power in an unacceptable manner—to oppress the poor, glorify themselves, and rule as tyrants.[43] Although these are ancient interpretations of only one Lukan status-reversal text, a similar debate continues today. To illustrate again with the Magnificat, an array of interpretations can be found in recent biblical scholarship, ranging from a call for military revolution to a celebration of those who are spiritually humble, and many readings in between.[44]

The literal-figurative debate has played out in Lukan scholarship particularly with regard to the issues of poverty, wealth, and use of possessions in the Gospel and Acts, beginning with the 1977 work *The Literary Function of Possessions in Luke-Acts*, by Luke Timothy Johnson. Looking specifically and solely at the literary level, Johnson maintains that in the narrative world of the third evangelist, one's right use of possessions and wealth is symbolic of acceptance of Jesus as Messiah and prophet. It also imbues one with the authority to assume a leadership role in the new Christian community, while at the same time serving as evidence of proper submission to such leaders.[45] Johnson does not, however, in any way deny that the extensive Lukan teachings on poverty and wealth have a literal meaning as well as a symbolic one:

> Luke takes with great seriousness both the literal problem and opportunity presented by men's [*sic*] actual use of and attitude towards possessions. . . . It is precisely this profound appreciation of the literal role of possessions that enables Luke to perceive the

42. *Commentary on the Gospel of Luke*, 1:51. See further Edouard Hamel, "Le Magnificat et le Renversement des Situations: Réflexion théologico-biblique," *Greg* 60 (1979): 56.

43. Hamel, "Le Magnificat," 56.

44. See, e.g., J. Massyngberde Ford, *My Enemy Is My Guest: Jesus and Violence in Luke* (Maryknoll, NY: Orbis, 1984), 19–23; Raymond E. Brown, *The Birth of the Messiah: A Commentary on the Infancy Narratives in the Gospels of Matthew and Luke*, new updated ed. (New York: Doubleday, 1993), 350–55; David Peter Seccombe, *Possessions and the Poor in Luke-Acts* (Linz: Studien zum Neuen Testament und Seiner Umwelt, 1982), 74–83; and Joel B. Green, *The Theology of the Gospel of Luke*, NTT, ed. James D. G. Dunn (Cambridge: Cambridge University Press, 1995), 88.

45. Luke Timothy Johnson, *The Literary Function of Possessions in Luke-Acts*, SBLDS 39, ed. Howard C. Kee and Douglas A. Knight (Missoula, MT: Scholars, 1977), 166–70, 202–3.

> metaphoric possibilities to be found in the language of possessions
> for expressing the conditions of men's [*sic*] hearts.[46]

This assertion, unfortunately, is often overlooked by later scholars who build on Johnson's work in an effort to argue for entirely symbolic interpretations of Lukan reversals.[47] David Peter Seccombe, for example, takes the symbolism one step further and maintains that Luke followed Isaiah in equating the poor with Israel in an hour of need;[48] this effectively eliminates, in Seccombe's reading, any application of the Third Gospel to the literal poor and disadvantaged.[49]

Other voices in the debate, however, caution against such a strict separation between spiritual and social or material matters. Walter Pilgrim notes the impossibility of separating body and soul; it is a dangerous false dichotomy today, and would have been alien to the worldview of Jesus or Luke.[50] Unlike Seccombe, Pilgrim advocates a social and political understanding of the Gospel's reversals and concludes (with York) that Luke offers both comfort to the poor (that their place in God's reign is assured) and challenge to the rich (that they must work alongside God to help the less fortunate if they want to participate in this new reign).[51] In a similar manner, Joel Green observes that salvation in Luke includes both spiritual matters (repentance, forgiveness of sin) and earthly concerns (empowering the disadvantaged, reconciliation across social boundaries, healing).[52] The perspectives of Green and Pilgrim are particularly fruitful as readings of Luke's text and time, and they also align well with the direction of my own research.

In addition to the works noted above, which come from the discipline of biblical studies, the field of anthropology offers insight into the theme of status reversals. The work of James C. Scott shows that such reversals are an exceedingly common characteristic in the culture and traditions of subordinated peoples. He maintains that such texts of inversion appear "in nearly every major cultural tradition in which inequities of power, wealth, and status have been pronounced."[53] They attempt to counteract dignity-depriving public ideologies

---

46. Ibid., 159.

47. E.g., Gary T. Meadors, "The 'Poor' in the Beatitudes of Matthew and Luke," *Grace Theological Journal* 6, no. 2 (1985): 306–7; and Seccombe, *Possessions and the Poor*, 16–17.

48. Seccombe, *Possessions and the Poor*, 39.

49. Ibid., 228.

50. Walter E. Pilgrim, *Good News to the Poor: Wealth and Poverty in Luke-Acts* (Minneapolis: Augsburg, 1981), 14.

51. Ibid., 160.

52. Green, *Theology*, 136, 152.

53. Scott, *Domination*, 80.

that depict the status quo as inevitable or divinely ordained, and the subordinated as inherently inferior to the elite.[54] He regards status reversals as one of many ways in which non-elites make subtle public declarations of their disagreement with the status quo, which casts them as "less than" in some way. In Scott's view, these statements constitute a major part of the "hidden transcript of resistance."[55] The connection of status reversals with the resistant folk culture of subordinated groups is central to this study.

Anthropological and sociological study also contributes another consideration to the spiritual-material debate, the location of the interpreters themselves. In the context of modern-day scholarship (particularly in Europe and North America), they are often ensconced in privilege within the status quo and thus greatly endangered by the disruptive demands of true status reversal. The vehement espousal of spiritualized and therefore "safe" readings of the Lukan reversals by wealthy and elite readers, even today, reinforces the conviction that there is something deeper, more threatening, and more potentially transformative at work here, alongside the more conciliatory strategies of imperial negotiation. If these passages are indeed part of a strategy of hidden resistance by non-elites, as I will argue, this deeper meaning must include an element of real social commentary and change, or at least the desire for such. Otherwise it would not have to be hidden, nor would it create the need for such passionate (and sometimes convoluted) opposition from the socially and materially comfortable.

UNEXPLORED TERRITORY IN THE STUDY OF ROME, REVERSALS, AND THE GOSPEL OF LUKE

Although good work nuancing Luke's attitude toward the Roman Empire has emerged in the last several years, as demonstrated above, there is much more still to be done. An approach that forces Luke to be either completely accommodating or completely resistant has too often dominated investigation into the work of the third evangelist. My project will attempt to correct this tendency by a reading that takes seriously the more subversive side of Luke, yet keeps it in conversation with the multiple strategies of negotiation evident in the Gospel. The insightful contributions outlined above are essays or journal articles, with the exception of Rowe's monograph *World Upside Down*, which focuses almost exclusively on the book of Acts. Thus there is a need for more

---

54. Ibid., 199. See also his sections on "Symbolic Inversion, World-Upside-Down Prints," 166–72; and "Rituals of Reversal, Carnival and Fêtes," 172–82.

55. Ibid., 172. The work of Scott will be discussed in full detail in chapter 1 below.

detailed and sustained attention to the complexities of the imperial-Christian dynamic as it is portrayed in the Gospel of Luke.[56]

Another area that has yet to be developed to its full potential is the sociological role of status reversals in Luke's narrative and in the earliest audiences' historical context. How might the subversive underpinnings of such a theme affect our understanding of Luke's various recommendations for approaching the imperially sanctioned status quo? The application of sociological and anthropological models to biblical texts is in general well accepted, although not without cautions. Critics of the method raise two principal concerns: (1) social scientific criticism is reductionist and discounts religious, theological, and individual factors; and (2) it is anachronistic to apply modern models to ancient peoples.[57] The former is certainly a possible temptation, but one that this project will avoid by attending closely to similar themes in other religious literature and by placing the study's sociocultural conclusions into the context of the larger narrative. Indeed, this sort of integration with other interpretative strategies is where social scientific criticism can make its most valuable contributions.[58] Religion hardly exists and functions within a vacuum devoid of social, political, and cultural structures and should not be treated as if it does. In light of this unavoidable fact, the advantages outweigh the concerns of anachronism because it is better by far to apply consciously a carefully chosen sociological model than to impose unconsciously one's own cultural norms and values on the biblical text.[59]

---

56. The recent monograph by Ahn, *The Reign of God and Rome in Luke's Passion Narrative*, approaches the text from a similar perspective as mine, specifically arguing that the entire text of Luke (not only the conciliatory or only the resistant passages) needs to be considered equally (89), and that its religious and political aspects should not be separated from each other, nor the Jewish authorities from the Roman authorities (90). We reach similar conclusions about Luke's (albeit ambivalent) resistance to the values of the Roman Empire (211–12), but the focus of his study is exclusively on the passion narrative, specifically Luke 19:45—21:38, while my work looks at one theme, that of status reversal, as it develops through the Gospel narrative. Yamazaki-Ransom, on the other hand, studies in his book *The Roman Empire in Luke's Narrative* both the Third Gospel and the book of Acts. His work covers a broader scope than my own, but with a different lens, specifically Luke's portrayal of Roman officials, including Roman procurators and Herodian rulers (3–4). His research interest, however, is quite different from my own in his focus on the function of these portrayals to "illuminate the theology, Christology, and ecclesiology of Luke-Acts" (200). My study will maintain a central interest in the political, social, and economic ramifications of the proclamation of status-reversal texts in the midst of the Roman Empire.

57. Stephen C. Barton, "Historical Criticism and Social-Scientific Perspectives in New Testament Study," in *Hearing the New Testament: Strategies for Interpretation*, ed. Joel B. Green (Eugene, OR: Wipf & Stock, 1995), 74–75; and Esler, *Community and Gospel*, 12.

58. Naomi Steinberg, "Social-Scientific Criticism," in *Dictionary of Biblical Interpretation*, Vol. 2 K–Z, ed. John H. Hayes (Nashville: Abingdon, 1999), 481.

Scholars are coming to realize that early Christianity was much more immersed in the cultural and political world, and consequently was much more sociopolitical, than has been previously recognized.[60] This is true for the work of the third evangelist as much as for Jesus, Paul, and the other Gospel authors. But most of the concentrated application of Scott's model to the New Testament has focused on the earliest historical sources: Mark, Q, and Paul.[61] There has been little application of sociopolitical models like that of Scott (discussed briefly below and extensively in chapter 1 of this work) to the Gospel of Luke, perhaps because of Luke's entrenched reputation of (only) sympathy towards Rome.[62] The time is ripe, then, to reconsider these two areas of Lukan research, the theme of status reversal and the complex view of the Roman Empire, in conjunction with each other and in light of the historical and social context of the world of the Roman provinces. The tools employed in this task will be intertextual literary analysis, the sociological work of Scott on resistance strategies of subordinated groups, and contextual studies of stratified societies in general and of the Roman Empire in particular.

METHODS OF ANALYSIS AND INTERPRETATION

The following chapters comprise a close, focused study of three specific texts from the Gospel of Luke that proclaim coming or present status reversals (such as the poor and lowly being lifted up while the rich and powerful are thrown down): Mary's song known as the Magnificat (1:46-55), Jesus' initial proclamation at Nazareth and the response it provokes (4:16-30), and the parable of Lazarus and the rich man (16:19-31). Status reversals are, of course, present and even prominent in passages other than the three that will serve as a focus for this study.[63] In the end, though, three were selected for manageable detailed analysis, and I chose the three specified passages for several reasons. First, they all contain special Lukan material not found in the other Gospels; this preempts the argument that such texts were so universally accepted in the Jesus tradition that Luke could not conceivably leave them out.[64] Second, they are sizable pericopes with clear, bold, and carefully constructed proclamations

59. Esler, *Community and Gospel*, 15.

60. Todd Penner, "Contextualizing Acts," in Penner and Vander Stichele, *Contextualizing Acts*, 19.

61. See, for example, the essays in Horsley, *Hidden Transcripts*. Several of these will be discussed in chapter 1 below.

62. A similar point is made by Warren Carter, "James C. Scott and New Testament Studies: A Response to Allen Callahan, William Herzog, and Richard Horsley," in Horsley, *Hidden Transcripts*, 91–93.

63. For a full survey, see York, *Last Shall Be First*, 40–162.

of explicit status reversal, and generally occur at pivotal points in the Gospel. Finally, all three focus on reversals that are not merely religious or spiritual, but also social, political, and economic, with all the ramifications that such reversals entail.

Each Lukan reversal passage will be examined through three interrelated areas or spheres in order to elucidate its role in the Gospel, especially with regard to the Gospel's influence on its audiences' relation to the cultural norms, social systems, and ruling authorities of the day. My reading strategy is similar to Vernon K. Robbins's socio-rhetorical criticism, which is grounded in a conviction that texts are best understood when studied through several different lenses, both diachronic and synchronic. Specifically, he defines socio-rhetorical criticism as examination of a text at four levels (or textures, in his terminology): inner texture (rhetorical workings of the pericope itself), intertexture (allusions to other literature), social and cultural texture (unseen social norms working behind the text), and ideological texture (authorial purpose in including the passage).[65] Within this model, there is some flexibility with regard, for example, to what comparative literature one uses and what sociological and anthropological models are engaged. For my particular research concerns, Robbins's inner texture, the rhetorical study of the text, is more illuminating when considered in concert with the other three areas, particularly the final two, leaving three areas of inquiry in which the rhetoric of the text is engaged throughout. Although they are differentiated from one another in theory, in practice the inevitable overlap and interplay between these various spheres add to the dynamic reading of the Gospel.

INTERTEXTUALITY

The first consideration of this project is an intertextual comparison of the Lukan reversals with older or contemporaneous texts that have either similar forms or similar themes of reversal, or sometimes both. The goal of this comparison is not to posit sources, direct influence, or even direct contact, but to examine other settings within the cultural milieu of the Lukan reading communities in which status reversals were declared and celebrated. Interplay between different texts that reinterpret one another through a dialogical relationship, as posited by Julia Kristeva,[66] will be important in this area of inquiry, as well as the larger

64. For an example of this perspective, see Luise Schottroff, "Das Magnificat und die Älteste Tradition über Jesus von Nazareth," *EvT* 38 (1978): 304–6.

65. Vernon K. Robbins, "Socio-Rhetorical Criticism: Mary, Elizabeth, and the Magnificat as a Test Case," in *The New Literary Criticism and the New Testament*, ed. Elizabeth Struthers Malbon and Edgar V. McKnight, JSNTSup 109 (Sheffield: Sheffield Academic Press, 1994), 171.

context and concepts invoked by each textual quotation or allusion.[67] Audience understanding and attribution of meaning will also be considered alongside possible authorial intention and interpretation.[68] These techniques will allow us to better understand Luke's use of the imagery of reversal, particularly where he has nuanced the theme in a unique way.

A strong connection between Luke-Acts and the Hebrew Bible is already acknowledged among Lukan scholars,[69] as the evangelist frequently quotes and alludes to the Septuagint. Luke's narrative goes to great lengths to demonstrate Christianity's continuity with the faith of Israel, expressing a theological conviction "that God who brought salvation to his people in the Old Testament continues to do this, especially through Jesus Christ."[70] Themes of status reversal are no exception to this close relationship with the Hebrew Bible, as we can see, for example, in the quotation from Isaiah 61 and 58 in Luke 4:18-19, and in the similarities between the Magnificat and Hannah's song (1 Sam. 2:1-10). Thus the Hebrew Bible and Septuagint will be important resources in this sphere of inquiry. Other comparative literature, however, must be considered as well. My study will include texts that are pertinent to each of the three passages examined based on significant thematic or formal parallels, including examples from the Jewish Apocrypha and Pseudepigrapha, the Dead Sea Scrolls, and Greco-Roman literature.

SOCIOLOGICAL ANALYSIS

The second sphere to be examined, the social constructs influencing and expressed by status reversal themes, is central to my study and will form the backbone of its thesis. Primarily, I will consider how Scott's model of hidden resistance enlightens our understanding of the Gospel text. In interpretative work that views Luke as wholly conciliatory toward the Roman Empire, scholars often cast Luke as a pragmatist who sought to enable Christianity to survive in the midst of imperial power.[71] This move, some maintain, might

---

66. Steve Moyise, *Evoking Scripture: Seeing the Old Testament in the New* (London: T&T Clark, 2008), 138–39.

67. Warren Carter, "Evoking Isaiah: Matthean Soteriology and an Intertextual Reading of Isaiah 7–9 and Matthew 1:23 and 4:15-16," *JBL* 119 (2000): 505.

68. Moyise, *Evoking Scripture*, 135–36. See also Carter, "Evoking Isaiah," 505n8, particularly his description of the "authorial audience."

69. See, e.g., the various essays in Craig A. Evans and James A. Sanders, *Luke and Scripture: The Function of Sacred Tradition in Luke-Acts* (Minneapolis: Fortress Press, 1993).

70. Robert F. O'Toole, *The Unity of Luke's Theology: An Analysis of Luke-Acts*, GNS 9, ed. Robert J. Karris (Wilmington: Michael Glazier, 1984), 17.

have been motivated by the delay of the parousia[72] and a desire to "blunt the apocalyptic appeal" of anti-Roman sentiments in certain Christian communities.[73] Such assessments of the Gospel's political views, though, often struggle to explain the subversive nature of the status reversal texts that are so central to its narrative, and are seldom able to incorporate them satisfactorily into their arguments.[74] Scott's model can provide part of a solution to this quandary. Much scholarly attention has been given to open rebellion and armed revolt on the part of subordinated peoples, and when these factors are absent, non-elites are often viewed as passive and accepting of their domination.[75] But Scott argues that multiple layers actually lie between these two extremes, and in these layers the dominated are well able to express their resistance to the status quo in which they live.[76] I will show that this form of resistance, more subtle than open revolt, is present in the Gospel of Luke, as one of several different strategies for imperial negotiation. Such resistance is evidenced by the status reversal texts, among other factors.

This second sphere, then, will explore the selected passages in Luke to illuminate how they may have communicated resistance to the imperial status quo. I will first consider the reversal text itself (divided into segments as appropriate to each passage) in light of Scott's model, and then apply a similar method to the immediate literary setting in which the reversal text is located, for example, Mary's visit to Elizabeth, during which she proclaims the Magnificat (Luke 1:39-45), or Jesus' dispute with the Pharisees that prompts his telling of the parable of Lazarus and the rich man (16:14-18). The sociocultural analysis based on Scott's model in this section of each exegetical chapter (chapters 3–5) will also be enriched by insights from studies of agrarian societies, aristocratic empires, and the Roman Empire in particular. Dennis Duling wisely cautions that Scott's general theory must be balanced by contextual specificity.[77] Thus I will incorporate Gerhard Lenski's in-depth study of social stratification,[78] John

---

71. Conzelmann, *Theology*, 138–40; and Walaskay, *"And So We Came to Rome,"* 66–67.

72. Conzelmann, *Theology*, 14; and Walaskay, *"And So We Came to Rome,"* 14.

73. Walaskay, *"And So We Came to Rome,"* 67.

74. A fuller survey of scholarly views on Luke and empire can be found above.

75. E.g., the exclusive focus of Stephen L. Dyson on military revolts in his two articles: "Native Revolts in the Roman Empire," *Historia* 20 (1971): 239–74; and "Native Revolt Patterns in the Roman Empire," in *ANRW* 2.3, ed. Joseph Vogt, Hildegard Temporini, and Wolfgang Haase (Berlin: Walter de Gruyter, 1975), 138–75. For an example in biblical studies, see Seyoon Kim, *Christ and Caesar: The Gospel and the Roman Empire in the Writings of Paul and Luke* (Grand Rapids: Eerdmans, 2008). He concludes that since the Lukan Jesus does not advocate an overthrow of Roman rule (95), complete submission with no alteration of existing political, social, or economic structures is the only alternative (114, 123).

76. Scott, *Domination*, 18–20.

H. Kautsky's treatment of aristocratic politics,[79] and a wide variety of classical Roman studies.[80] Another important question is raised by Scott's observation that the reversals envisioned by oppressed peoples usually take one of two forms, either total inversion (where the formerly subordinated become the dominant rulers and vice versa), or leveling (which envisions a world entirely devoid of status distinctions).[81] The task of determining which of these types of reversal is espoused within the Lukan narrative will be explicitly addressed in my sociological analysis, as well as engaged throughout the study.

CONTEXTUALITY

The third and final sphere of this project's research method has two major components: literary context and historical context, or, more specifically, each reversal text's relation to the rest of the Gospel narrative and to the earliest Lukan audiences.[82] First, I will engage the literary context of each status reversal passage by putting the insight gained from careful attention to the intertextual and sociological dimensions of the text into conversation with the entire Gospel and the Lukan ethic, worldview, and theology—especially its complex approach to the Roman Empire. The hidden resistance revealed in the diachronic examination of these three passages will be incorporated at this stage into a synchronic reading of the wider Gospel narrative. Specifically, I will consider how each pericope relates to other status reversal texts both before and after it in the Lukan narrative, as well as how its subversive imagery interacts with, enhances, and even transforms the larger themes and more commonly recognized negotiation techniques of the Gospel and Acts. The development elsewhere in Luke-Acts of themes, events, and characters that are central to

---

77. Dennis C. Duling, "Empire: Theories, Methods, Models," in *The Gospel of Matthew in Its Roman Imperial Context*, ed. John Riches and David C. Sim, JSNTSup 276 (London: T&T Clark, 2005), 73.

78. Gerhard E. Lenski, *Power and Privilege: A Theory of Social Stratification* (1966; repr., Chapel Hill: University of North Carolina Press, 1984).

79. John H. Kautsky, *The Politics of Aristocratic Empires* (Chapel Hill: University of North Carolina Press, 1982).

80. E.g, Peter Garnsey and Richard Saller, *The Roman Empire: Economy, Society and Culture* (Berkeley: University of California Press, 1987); Janet Huskinson, ed., *Experiencing Rome: Culture, Identity, and Power in the Roman Empire* (London: Routledge, 2000); Christopher Kelly, *The Roman Empire: A Very Short Introduction* (Oxford: Oxford University Press, 2006); Jerry Toner, *Popular Culture in Ancient Rome* (Cambridge, MA: Polity, 2009); and C. R. Whittaker, "The Poor," in *The Romans*, ed. Andrea Giardina (Chicago: University of Chicago Press, 1993), 272–99.

81. Scott, *Domination*, 80–81.

82. The question of who these earliest reading communities may have been is treated in detail in chapter 2 of this study.

status reversal texts will illumine their meaning and function in the focal pericopes.

The second part of this section of each chapter will consider the social and historical context of the communities of Jesus-followers who were the earliest readers of Luke's Gospel. It will engage the models of hidden resistance and imperial stratification at the level of the Lukan audiences, asking how, in their own situation of imperial domination, they might have heard, evaluated, and responded to the messages of reversal and resistance as proclaimed and enacted by the Lukan Jesus. The exact geographical, social, and historical location of the third evangelist's community (or communities) has proven notoriously difficult to pinpoint with any confidence.[83] But much insight can still be gained from a focus even on general Christian readers in the Hellenistic cities within Roman-controlled Greece and Asia Minor, and I shall fruitfully engage that sociocultural milieu in this final step of my analysis. In this, I follow Rowe's commitment to engaging fully with the "cultural encyclopedia" of the late-first-century Roman world in order to understand better the biblical text of Luke-Acts as written within that world.[84] Reading from the perspective of "Christian readers of various kinds in the late first century"[85] is a general specification, certainly, but also, as we shall see, an effective one that sheds new light on the status-reversal texts considered in this project. This final section of the analysis of each focal passage will add yet another illuminating layer to the developing understanding of Luke's diverse tactics of imperial negotiation, an area that is too often absent in discussions of the Luke-Rome relationship, as well as in treatments of wealth and poverty in Luke-Acts and of the Lukan theme of status reversal.

OUTLINE OF THE STUDY

Chapters 1 and 2 will provide a firmer methodological and contextual foundation for my work with the Gospel of Luke. Chapter 1, "Hidden Transcripts, Models of Empire, and the Gospel of Luke," undertakes an extended exploration of the sociological models engaged especially in the second sphere of my research method. I begin with an overview of the influential models of empire that provide insight into the Lukan communities'

---

83. See, e.g., Joseph A. Fitzmyer, *The Gospel According to Luke I–IX*, AB 28 (Garden City, NY: Doubleday, 1981), 57; and Luke Timothy Johnson, "On Finding the Lukan Community: A Cautious Cautionary Essay," in *SBLSP* 1979, vol. 1, ed. Paul J. Achtemeier (Missoula, MT: Scholars, 1979), 87–100. See further the discussion in chapter 2 below.

84. Rowe, *World Upside Down*, 8–9.

85. Ibid., 11.

everyday experience of living under Roman rule, specifically Lenski's model of social stratification in agrarian societies[86] and Kautsky's study of politics and power in aristocratic empires.[87] Then I survey in detail the theory of hidden transcripts of resistance, as laid out by Scott in his 1990 book *Domination and the Arts of Resistance: Hidden Transcripts*. This section gives an overview of his argument for public and hidden transcripts and the various levels of resistance employed by subjugated peoples, with special focus on the role played in such resistance by imagery, texts, and festivals of status reversal. All three of these models are illustrated with specific examples from the Roman imperial world. The final part of chapter 1 presents a review of previous scholarship applying these imperial models, particularly that of Scott, to the New Testament Gospels, and shows how this monograph builds upon that work.

Chapter 2, "The Context of Luke and His Reading Communities," establishes the historical context of the earliest audiences reading Luke and their possible social composition. The tense and paradoxical relationship between Rome and the Greek East is addressed as part of a "thick" description of the full social, economic, religious, and political environment in which Luke and his readers lived. I also consider the social diversity that most likely existed within the early Christian communities, and perhaps particularly within those known to the third evangelist. The contextual work done in this chapter will provide an important grounding for the third sphere of inquiry in the next three chapters, as that section of each chapter will consider the likely reactions of Christians of various status levels to the reversals proclaimed in our focal texts.

In chapters 3 through 5, which form the main body of this study, I apply the research methods outlined above to three especially significant status reversal texts from the Gospel of Luke. Mary's song, traditionally known as the Magnificat (Luke 1:46-55), will be the focus of chapter 3. Intertextual comparisons (the first area of inquiry) are made with women's victory songs in the Hebrew Bible and Apocrypha, hymns from the Dead Sea Scrolls, and Greco-Roman reversal texts, and I will demonstrate that the Magnificat is a later development of this ancient victory song tradition. The second sphere closely attends to the personal and communal status reversals inherent in both the text of Mary's song and its narrative setting of her meeting with Elizabeth. The Magnificat is Luke's initial declaration of God's vision for the world. Status reversals comprise a significant part of that vision, and of the upcoming ministries of John and Jesus, the children about to be born, who will begin to

---

86. Lenski, *Power and Privilege*, particularly pp. 189–296.

87. Kautsky, *Politics*.

make it a reality. The final section on contextuality examines how these status reversals in Luke 1:46-55 introduce and foreshadow the work of Jesus, whose very life will be a story of status reversal. Study of the wider literary context shows the development of the theme throughout the Gospel, and study of the social world of Luke's audiences explores the possible impact of singing such a song of reversal within a mixed group of Jesus-followers.

Chapter 4 delves into the important and complex pericope narrating Jesus' controversial return to his hometown of Nazareth and his teaching in the synagogue there (Luke 4:16-30). We find in this passage extensive development and nuancing of the role of status reversals among the various imperial negotiation strategies of Luke. Particular attention is given to the challenges posed to the non-elite beneficiaries of status reversal. While the Magnificat was inconclusive on the question of whether its reversals involved inversion or social leveling, Jesus' declaration of "the year of God's favor" (Luke 4:19) is uncompromising in its call for non-elites to work alongside repentant elites in creating alternative social communities that give concrete expression to the reign of God. In the process, these non-elites must reform their own ideas of hierarchy and superiority. The intertextual treatment in chapter 4 focuses on Jesus' quotations of Trito-Isaiah in Luke 4:18-19 and on ancient festivals of reversal such as the Hebrew Jubilee and the Roman Saturnalia. The sociological analysis carefully applies Scott's model to Jesus' Scripture reading, the Nazareth congregation's reaction, and finally to Jesus' inflammatory illustrations of prophetic help for non-Israelites (Luke 4:25-27, drawing from 1 Kgs. 17:8-24; 2 Kgs. 5:1-19). The jarring dissonance between Jesus' ideas and those of the Nazarenes is one of the first indications that Luke is indeed proclaiming resistance, but with an unexpected twist. The final, contextual section of chapter 4 explores the possible ramifications of Jesus' readiness to critique both the right of the dominants to rule and the assumption of the subordinates that only they should receive God's help.

As the Nazareth proclamation demonstrates the challenges posed by Lukan status reversal to the non-elites in Luke's audiences, chapter 5 of this project explores the message of these reversals for elite readers and hearers, through close study of the parable of Lazarus and the rich man (Luke 16:19-31). Intertextually, Jesus' parable of stark reversal in the afterlife is compared to Aesop's fables, to an ancient Egyptian tale of underworld reversal, and to the Greco-Roman author Lucian's reflections on the poor, the rich, and their eternal fates (in his narratives *Gallus* and *Cataplus*). As in the Magnificat, Luke takes another common literary form, the story of status reversal after death, and adapts it slightly but significantly in Luke 16, to demonstrate that God's effecting of status reversal is based not simply on morality, but on the clear injustice of conspicuous wealth accumulated at the expense of those of no status, no power, and great poverty. This conclusion will be supported through the second and third spheres of research, as I consider the role of status reversal in the parable itself, in Jesus' dispute with the Pharisees that prompts its telling, in connection with the rest of Luke's Gospel, and in the life of Luke's mixed communities. This parable of status reversal, told near the end of Jesus' ministry and complementing the proclamation at its beginning, makes the case yet again that the Lukan status reversals add a clear resistant strain to his treatment of the imperially endorsed and maintained status quo. But they were resistant in such a way that demanded change, voluntary initiation of downward reversal, and greater equality from all in Luke's audiences, no matter their status as defined by dominant sociocultural values.

The conclusion summarizes findings from the preceding chapters and confirms Luke's careful nuancing of his call for resistance to, and transformation of, imperial values and the Roman social hierarchy. It also includes a survey of other possible connections between the Gospel of Luke and Scott's hidden transcripts of resistance, beyond this project's focus on texts of status reversal. This brief exploration will lead, finally, to consideration of the book's implications for further study of Luke-Acts in the context of the Roman imperial world, and its implications for the life of the church and for other interested readers of Luke's Gospel today.

Moving Forward

I anticipate that this project will have important ramifications both inside and outside of the relatively small sphere of Lukan scholarship. The model of hidden resistance enables one to discern strategies for negotiating power imbalances that are evident in various times and places throughout history, and is thus enlightening not only for the study of Luke and other biblical books, but also for church history, missiology, modern-day groups that are forced to exist under domination and oppression, and all of us as we negotiate life in our own imperial contexts. The seeds of this project began in my own reflections and ruminations on contemporary issues of domination and subordination, and how I (as a Christian, a minister, and a professor) ought to participate in, support, question, and reform today's prevailing systems of power. This process addresses issues that range from the personal (how do I as a woman in traditionally male fields like ordained ministry and theological education navigate the various levels of acceptance and rejection with which I am faced?), through the group (how long can or should a group retain the label "oppressed" in settings where strides forward are being made and they are being treated equitably?), to the global level (how to deal with and eventually prevent situations where the power balance has been reversed to the extent that the formerly weak are now oppressing others?). Since its inception, the church has been engaged in a constant balancing act between weakness and power, between the margin and the center, between gaining influence and selling out. A better understanding of the way in which this tension played out in the Lukan communities will give communities of faith today an important resource to ponder, question, adapt, reflect upon, and learn from. It is to this ultimate end that I hope my project will make a meaningful contribution.

1

Hidden Transcripts, Models of Empire, and the Gospel of Luke

As outlined in the previous chapter, this project will make extensive use of various models from sociology, anthropology, and political science. Such models, while always in need of contextual specificity,[1] provide an important basis for better understanding the world of an ancient text like the Gospel of Luke, which is far removed in time, space, culture, and worldview from the lives of today's readers and interpreters. Luke was not written, nor did Jesus and the disciples live, in a religious vacuum separate from the social, political, and cultural structures of their day, and they should not be treated as if they did. While there may be some concern over the possibly anachronistic application of modern models to ancient peoples,[2] carefully chosen social-scientific models yield great insight into the biblical text and help modern readers minimize the unconscious imposition of our own cultural norms and values. Thus I will consider in some detail here the work of three social scientists who illuminate issues of power, empire, and resistance in societies similar to and including the Roman Empire.

Gerhard Lenski examines the history of social stratification, the problem of "who gets what [resources] and why."[3] Particularly important for the study of biblical texts in general and Luke in particular is Lenski's extensive two-chapter treatment of agrarian societies, of which the Roman Empire was one.[4] John

---

1. Dennis C. Duling, "Empire: Theories, Methods, Models," in *The Gospel of Matthew in Its Roman Imperial Context*, ed. John Riches and David C. Sim, JSNTSup 276 (London: T&T Clark, 2005), 73.

2. Stephen C. Barton, "Historical Criticism and Social-Scientific Perspectives in New Testament Study," in *Hearing the New Testament: Strategies for Interpretation*, ed. Joel B. Green (Eugene, OR: Wipf & Stock, 1995), 74–75; Philip Francis Esler, *Community and Gospel in Luke-Acts: The Social and Political Motivations of Lucan Theology*, SNTSMS 57 (Cambridge: Cambridge University Press, 1987), 12.

3. Gerhard E. Lenski, *Power and Privilege: A Theory of Social Stratification* (1966; repr., Chapel Hill: University of North Carolina Press, 1984), 2–3.

H. Kautsky focuses more narrowly on the politics of the imperial ruling strata, the aristocracy that lives off the labor of those of lower status.[5] While he does not consider Rome, with its numerous and thriving merchants, to have been a pure aristocratic empire,[6] much of his work still enlightens relevant aspects of its imperial politics. Finally, James C. Scott's discussion of subordinated peoples' hidden resistance to their situation of domination will be engaged fully, with a special focus on the role played in such resistance by imagery, texts, and festivals of status reversal. I will close the chapter with a survey of the initial efforts of New Testament scholarship to apply Scott's theory to the Gospels in a systematic manner, as these studies undergird the role of the hidden transcript in the status-reversal passages that are the focus of this project. All of these models will prove invaluable in enhancing our understanding of the Lukan community's everyday setting, experience of the Roman Empire, and likely range of responses to the Gospel's status reversals.

Gerhard Lenski and Social Stratification

Gerhard Lenski's extensive study *Power and Privilege* deals first with the causes of social stratification, the nearly universal process by which human societies distribute scarce valuable resources to various groups and members.[7] Although we can argue interminably about whether such stratification is good or bad, natural or human-initiated, the reality is that it exists in essentially every human society, and especially in the Roman Empire of Jesus, Luke, and the New Testament. The very word "empire" is based on the Latin verb *imperare* (to command) and is regularly defined as a hierarchical system of absolute authority and unequal power relations based on military might.[8] The Roman Empire was certainly such a political entity, with supreme power ascribed to the emperor and his local representatives. Additionally, it controlled so many territories and their attendant resources that the economic surplus, and the power inequality caused by its unequal distribution,[9] were both massive. Lenski provides valuable insight on how this distribution of power, privilege, and wealth was determined in general, and specifically in agrarian societies like the Roman Empire.

---

4. Ibid., 189–296.

5. John H. Kautsky, *The Politics of Aristocratic Empires* (Chapel Hill: University of North Carolina Press, 1982), 24.

6. Ibid., 33–39.

7. Lenski, *Power and Privilege*, ix–x.

8. Duling, "Empire," 51.

9. Lenski, *Power and Privilege*, 46, 85.

The human drive to live with others in a social system is an inescapable reality of both history and our everyday lives. But at the same time, individuals and individual groups have their own interests that they seek to fulfill. Lenski argues forcefully that the behavior of any single person is determined by self-interest; even cooperative actions usually have some self-serving result (he gives the example of "antagonistic cooperation" in team sports, where individual players cooperate with their teammates only because they cannot play the game and experience the satisfaction of victory without one another).[10] In a similar manner, the goals of a society, usually dictated by the ruling group, seek the consolidation of as many valuable resources as possible. Actions that result in survival, health, status, and the wealth that provides these commodities are regularly condoned and undertaken even when they harm others (either of another group or the lower members of the society itself).[11] Extensive intra-group sacrifice, for example, seldom translates to a similar willingness to help those outside the group, thus allowing Lenski to argue that even such cooperation has a selfish motive of personal gain through group preservation.[12] He concludes that the two major aims of any human society (or at least its dominant group) are to maintain the political status quo and maximize the production of resources.[13]

The Roman Empire, for example, claimed to benefit all over whom it ruled, but in reality (as in Lenski's model), the benefits accrued mainly to the elites. Augustus's *Res Gestae*, an autobiographical narration of his reign, extensively details the many benefits and services he extended to the people who came under his rule; they were expected to offer in turn their unconditional loyalty and deference.[14] Also a good illustration of this claim to benefaction is a statement from Cicero (c. 60 BCE): "The province of Asia must be mindful of the fact that if it were not part of our empire it would have suffered every sort of misfortune that foreign wars and domestic unrest can bring. . . . Let Asia not grudge its part of the revenues in return for permanent peace and tranquility."[15] There is evidence that Augustus's patronage did indeed help several provinces of Asia Minor recover from long years of civil war,[16] and the vast task of supplying

10. Ibid., 26–27.

11. Ibid., 41.

12. Ibid., 28–29.

13. Ibid., 41–42.

14. Peter Garnsey and Richard Saller, *The Roman Empire: Economy, Society and Culture* (Berkeley: University of California Press, 1987), 149.

15. Quoted in Craige B. Champion, ed., *Roman Imperialism: Readings and Sources, Interpreting Ancient History* (Malden, MA: Blackwell, 2004), 261.

the city of Rome with sufficient food meant that grain farmers throughout the provinces had a ready-made market for their produce.[17] Even some modern classical scholars seem convinced that the benefactions provided by the elites eased the tension of the extensive social, economic, and political inequality that was the hallmark of the Roman Empire.[18]

Upon closer inspection, however, this "peace and tranquility" proves to be at best an ambiguous benefit for the empire's non-elites. The emperor, according to Pliny the Younger's speech around the turn of the first century CE, was accountable primarily to the elites and the furthering of their interests.[19] Local provincial elites were the true beneficiaries of Roman rule because it was in the interest of the empire to allow them to maintain power and increase their wealth and status.[20] The basic pattern of life was subsistence-level existence for the vast majority of the population, while those of high status cemented their place with an ever-increasing share of the available wealth, land, and power.[21] The wages of a basic laborer and the income of a senator stood roughly at a ratio of one to two hundred, and even in the military, an elite tribune made four hundred times what a common legionary did, and over six times the pay of a centurion.[22] The elite portion of the tax burden demanded by Rome from Asia Minor and elsewhere was almost certainly passed on to non-elites at a level they could ill afford, effectively stripping many peasants of their best resources and forcing them into extensive indebtedness.[23] One scholar calculated that at least 10 percent and maybe as many as 44 percent of loans made went into default, with the debtor then losing land, property, and on occasion even the

16. See, e.g., David W. J. Gill, "Achaia," in *The Book of Acts in Its Graeco-Roman Setting*, ed. David W. J. Gill and Conrad Gempf, *The Book of Acts in Its First Century Setting* (Grand Rapids: Eerdmans, 1994), 441; and Paul Trebilco, "Asia," in Gill and Gempf, *The Book of Acts in Its Graeco-Roman Setting*, 299–300.

17. Phil Perkins, "Power, Culture and Identity in the Roman Economy," in *Experiencing Rome: Culture, Identity, and Power in the Roman Empire*, ed. Janet Huskinson (London: Routledge, 2000), 209.

18. E.g., Garnsey and Saller, *Roman Empire*, 148.

19. Christopher Kelly, *The Roman Empire: A Very Short Introduction* (Oxford: Oxford University Press, 2006), 33–34.

20. Ibid., 46–48.

21. Garnsey and Saller, *Roman Empire*, 43, 51–52; and Ramsay MacMullen, *Roman Social Relations: 50 B.C. to A.D. 284* (New Haven: Yale University Press, 1974), 38–39, 42.

22. C. R. Whittaker, "The Poor," in *The Romans*, ed. Andrea Giardina (Chicago: University of Chicago Press, 1993), 278.

23. Michael H. Crawford, "Rome and the Greek World: Economic Relationships," in Champion, *Roman Imperialism*, 98; Garnsey and Saller, *Roman Empire*, 98; Keith Hopkins, "Conquerors and Slaves: The Impact of Conquering an Empire on the Political Economy of Italy," in Champion, *Roman Imperialism*, 117–18; and MacMullen, *Roman Social Relations*, 33–34.

entire family's freedom, to the (usually elite) lender.[24] Basically, in the words of Ramsey MacMullen, "Rome wrung ultimately from the provincial peasants all that could be economically extracted."[25]

What we find, though, in the life of Jesus and the work of the third evangelist, particularly in the status reversals that are the focus of this study, is the opposite of Lenski's conclusions about societal maintenance: a celebration of and call to *de*stabilize and even overturn the political and economic status quo. The Jesus movement was only one among many groups that exhibited some knowledge of and resistance to this disconnect between propaganda and reality.[26] Hostility toward local elites was often linked to resentment of Roman taxes. Residents of Dyme in Achaea, for example, had to be subdued militarily when they called for a cancellation of all debts and attempted to burn the city loan records.[27] Moreover, formal complaints were sometimes lodged against those with social and material resources who were more than willing, through excessive rent or tax, the purposeful ruin of crops, and even physical injury, to exploit those who lacked such resources.[28] Thus it is clear that non-elites were well aware of the inequality and vulnerability of their position in the Roman social order.

In contrast, the Lukan community is presented with a Jesus who breaks from Lenski's basic model of preserving the status quo, as he deliberately helps those outside his own social group, even assisting a centurion, one of the occupying Roman force (7:1-10), and going so far as to sacrifice his own life so that repentance and forgiveness might be extended "to all nations" (24:47). From the very start, then, we must consider the Gospel of Luke as a story and a message that would have raised some eyebrows among its Roman-era audience, accustomed as they were to a sharply stratified power differential—offending some, perhaps resonating with others, and most likely doing a little of both at the same time.

In Lenski's analysis, human societies tend toward a repetitive political cycle wherein a new elite group seizes power by force and violence, and then tries to legitimize its rule "by right" instead of "might."[29] This transformation is usually

---

24. Jerry Toner, *Popular Culture in Ancient Rome* (Cambridge, MA: Polity, 2009), 24–25. For a discussion of loan records and evidence that a high proportion of debtors were farmers, see MacMullen, *Roman Social Relations*, 51–52.

25. MacMullen, *Roman Social Relations*, 36.

26. Warren Carter, *Matthew and Empire: Initial Explorations* (Harrisburg, PA: Trinity, 2001), 50–51.

27. Crawford, "Rome and the Greek World," 98.

28. MacMullen, *Roman Social Relations*, 8–11.

29. Lenski, *Power and Privilege*, 59.

gained through ideological changes such as revamped laws and (sometimes forced) endorsement of the new ruling group by other institutions (educational, media, religious, etc.), changes that require cunning and intelligence rather than the original military power.[30] Thus, with power consolidated and its rule presented as natural or divinely sanctioned, the new elite group is able to dictate how status, wealth, and privilege are to be distributed, and the majority of non-elites are essentially powerless to change it. In the Roman Empire, this legitimizing "myth of supernatural power" was centered upon the person of the emperor as the carrier of divine will and favor for the entire realm.[31] Augustus began cementing his rule almost immediately by, among other things, combining elements from various Trojan, Greek, and Roman myths to create a legendary divine ancestry for both himself and the city of Rome.[32] His effort was augmented by deferential authors like Virgil, whose *Aeneid* proclaims Rome's natural, divinely given right to rule through the mouth of Jupiter himself. Rome, according to Virgil's account, is "destined to rule Earth's peoples . . . to pacify, to impose the rule of law, to spare the conquered, to battle down the proud."[33] The truth of this claim to just rule, of course, is up for much debate. For one thing, Rome's "rule of law" generally left the non-elites with only the bare necessities of resources, so that, according to Lenski, their lives were too consumed with survival to have time to engage extensively in elite politics.[34] Again, however, Luke seems to break with this assessment. The Gospel, and the status reversals in particular, envision a new ideology that is centrally concerned with a change in the status quo in all aspects of society: political, religious, economic, and social.

One weakness of Lenski's model stems from his modern worldview, which separates these realms from one another; in the first-century world they were all inextricably entwined. Modern scholars often assert Luke's complacency with Roman rule or advance an apolitical reading, based on this erroneous separation and on the fact that he never calls for overt military rebellion.[35]

---

30. Ibid., 52–55.

31. J. Rufus Fears, "The Cult of Jupiter and Roman Imperial Ideology," in *ANRW* 2.17.1, ed. Hildegard Temporini and Wolfgang Haase (Berlin: Walter de Gruyter, 1981), 7–9.

32. Janet Huskinson, "Élite Culture and the Identity of Empire," in Huskinson, *Experiencing Rome*, 102.

33. Quoted in Kelly, *Roman Empire*, 21.

34. Lenski, *Power and Privilege*, 54.

35. See, e.g., the discussion of Seyoon Kim, *Christ and Caesar: The Gospel and the Roman Empire in the Writings of Paul and Luke* (Grand Rapids: Eerdmans, 2008), 95–100: "For in [Luke's] report there is no promise, call, or action by Jesus for an overthrow of Roman imperial rule. . . . Jesus does not advocate even nonviolent passive resistance to it" (95); and François Bovon, *Luke 1: A Commentary on the Gospel of Luke 1:1–9:50*, trans. Christine M. Thomas, Hermeneia, ed. Helmut Koester (Minneapolis: Fortress Press,

Such assumptions result in a view of the evangelist as having solely religious concerns,[36] or in a reading that equates a nonretaliatory stance with offering full approval to the imperial order and negates the political ramifications of the Gospel's focus on social justice.[37] In reality, the third evangelist very possibly functioned for his audiences as Lenski's "rebellious intellectual" who provides "the catalytic agent, the counterideology, which is necessary for every successful social revolution."[38] His role is that of a visionary who develops the picture of a new social order and leaves it up to the audience to support and implement it. Notably, Luke treats centurions well in his work (Luke 7:1-10; 23:44-47; Acts 10:1—11:18), as well as minorities like Samaritans (Luke 10:25-37; Acts 8:4-25) and eunuchs (Acts 8:26-40). Such groups, particularly members of the military willing to transfer their loyalty away from the ruling powers, are especially important to social revolutions.[39] Thus we see perhaps some ambiguity in Luke's vision here: violence and extensive wealth are not condoned, but it is necessary to have access to both power and material resources to carry out real social change.

Finally, before moving to the specifics of agrarian social systems, we must address one more general aspect of Lenski's model: status inconsistency. Any given individual has varying ranks in different "class systems" (in Lenski's terminology), such as political power, property, occupation, ethnicity, and religious establishment. Cultures as a whole struggle to define which of these should be valued more highly,[40] and individuals tend to view themselves in terms of the system that accords them their highest possible position. Others, meanwhile, are more likely to evaluate them by their lower positions instead, leading to status inconsistency.[41] A member of an ethnic minority, for example, in a highly skilled, high-status occupation, or a merchant with plenty of wealth but little social standing, is likely to experience some kind of conflict as a result of these divergent rankings. Roman freedpersons (manumitted slaves) are

---

2002), 9: "Luke wants to . . . quell Roman fears about the Christian mission. Luke is convinced that the gospel is politically innocuous; on the contrary, the ethical attitude of the Christians can only work to the advantage of their pagan neighbors."

36. As in John Nolland, *Luke 1–9:20*, WBC 35a (Dallas: Word, 1989), xxxii–xxxiii.

37. As in John K. Riches, "The Synoptic Evangelists and Their Communities," in *Christian Beginnings: Word and Community from Jesus to Post-Apostolic Times*, ed. Jürgen Becker (Louisville: Westminster John Knox, 1993), 236–37.

38. Lenski, *Power and Privilege*, 71.

39. Ibid., 71–72. For examples of native revolt leaders with experience in the Roman military, see Stephen L. Dyson, "Native Revolts in the Roman Empire," *Historia* 20 (1971): 255, 264.

40. Lenski, *Power and Privilege*, 81.

41. Ibid., 87–88.

perhaps one of the clearest examples of this phenomenon. Some of them gained great wealth using skills learned from their elite masters, but the stigma of slavery lowered their honor and status for life,[42] as well as opening them up to jealousy and mockery from both above and below.[43] This kind of treatment made such people prime candidates to be leaders in social change, as they possessed resources like wealth, status, and leadership skills often denied to other non-elites, but also a certain measure of grievance with the status quo.[44] This dissatisfaction, combined with the experience of at least some level of prejudice, also led those who did not fit easily into Rome's hierarchy to have greater empathy for the unfortunate, such as the Greek foreigner who is the only person from the Roman era memorialized on his tomb as a "lover of the poor."[45] I will show in the following chapters that the depiction of Jesus and other Lukan figures as having such status inconsistency would likely have resonated with, and perhaps motivated, a community of readers and hearers in similar situations.

Probably the piece of Lenski's work that is best-known in the area of biblical scholarship is the chart reproduced here, a visual representation of status groups in agrarian societies, by number and amount of power and privilege.[46]

Indeed, Lenski's two extensive chapters on agrarian societies, of which the Roman Empire was one of the largest and best documented, provide valuable insight into the daily life and cultural experience of the first-century writers, readers, and hearers of the New Testament writings. The primary characteristic of any agrarian society was its use of the plow, which enlarged farming from small plots to entire fields. This technological advance, combined with the development of transportation and military technology like wheels, sails, and cavalry, generated a surplus of valued resources both tangible and intangible that grew exponentially, along with the level of power and status inequality.[47] Dominant agrarian societies tended to grow into "conquest states" that subjugated other ethnic and religious groups to their central power; the Roman Republic and later Empire is a prime example.[48] Power in all its forms (economic, political, religious, and cultural) became concentrated in urban

---

42. Garnsey and Saller, *Roman Empire*, 120; and Valerie Hope, "Status and Identity in the Roman World," in Huskinson, *Experiencing Rome*, 130, 138.

43. Hope, "Status and Identity," 143–44. The first-century author Petronius sharply parodied the stereotypical wealthy but gauche freedperson through the character of Trimalchio (Huskinson, "Élite Culture," 103–4).

44. Lenski, *Power and Privilege*, 88.

45. Whittaker, "The Poor," 296–97.

46. Lenski, *Power and Privilege*, 284.

47. Ibid., 190, 193.

48. Ibid., 195–96.

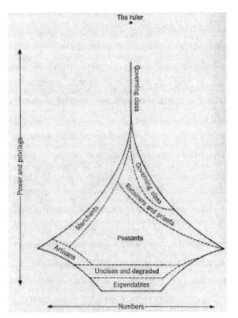

Figure 1: A graphic representation of the relationship among classes in agrarian societies.

centers, as economic surplus, specialized goods, and artisans skilled in all occupations gathered in the cities in order to serve the elites who were based there.[49] This was particularly true in the Greek East, where, even under Roman rule, Hellenistic city-states maintained a level of self-governance (through local elite magistrates loyal to Rome) and influence over their surrounding rural territories.[50] Thus, with insight drawn from sociohistorical and sociological analysis, one would expect an urban audience of Luke's Gospel to be a diverse gathering of people, coming from a wide variety of levels on Lenski's diagram of stratification. Most likely every individual heard the story of Jesus with somewhat different understandings, based on her or his unique standing in the community.[51]

49. Ibid., 200, 205.

50. Garnsey and Saller, *Roman Empire*, 28.

51. Lenski's model regrettably does not account for gender to any significant degree. Many married women likely shared their husbands' status, but there are also accounts of widows or single women at all social levels with their own standing and independent resources. Particularly as resources like money and power increased, some women wielded considerable prestige and political power (Garnsey and Saller, *Roman Empire*, 135). Claudia Capitolina, e.g., from a Roman senatorial family, is recorded as a major patron of a synagogue in Asia Minor (Margaret Williams, "Jews and Jewish Communities in the Roman Empire," in Huskinson, *Experiencing Rome*, 312). For further information, see also Bernadette J.

At the pinnacle of Lenski's stratification model is, of course, the ruler (in our case, the Roman emperor) and the elite governing class (senators, governors, procurators, local elites or decurions). This small proportion of the population controlled governmental responsibilities and almost all of the land and its surplus produce (either directly through a proprietary right or indirectly through taxes and tariffs).[52] Land ownership provided the elites with the security of prestige and wealth that could be passed down generationally, while public office offered ample opportunity for political and economic advancement. In the imperial provinces, local elite hierarchies were modeled on that of Rome and mirrored its constant jostling for status and competitive "benefaction."[53] Required of city magistrates, these charitable donations of public buildings, entertainment, food, and other civic services served more to legitimize and cement the domination of Rome and its local elite collaborators than they did to provide significant lasting help to the non-elite citizenry.[54]

Essential to maintaining this status quo that so favored the ruler and governing elites was the retainer group, which served the political elite as servants, petty officials, professional soldiers, and personal retainers; for this service they received a (small) share in the economic surplus and a status ranking slightly above that of the common "masses."[55] One of the most important characteristics of retainers was their complete dependence upon the elites' pleasure and approval (quite unlike the modern concept of a middle class). Retainers were used by the elites to carry out and maintain their exploitation of the vast majority, acting as buffers and mediators who implemented the actual transfer of surplus and absorbed much of the non-elites' hostility in the process.[56] Loyalty to the elites and thus to the status quo was necessary to maintain one's retainer status and maximize personal power and prestige, and conversely, the defection of the retainers to the non-elites would greatly endanger the security of those of highest status. Thus, in the Gospels, Jesus engages repeatedly and intensely with retainers like Pharisees[57] and centurions,[58] who are embedded in the Roman status quo, and whose positive or

Brooten, "Early Christian Women and Their Cultural Context: Issues of Method in Historical Reconstruction," in *Feminist Perspectives on Biblical Scholarship*, ed. Adela Yarbro Collins, Biblical Scholarship in North America (Chico, CA: Scholars, 1985), 65–91; and Carolyn Osiek, Margaret Y. MacDonald, and Janet H. Tulloch, *A Woman's Place: House Churches in Earliest Christianity* (Minneapolis: Fortress Press, 2006), 17–49, 194–219.

52. Lenski, *Power and Privilege*, 214–16, 220–21.

53. Hope, "Status and Identity," 137.

54. Garnsey and Saller, *Roman Empire*, 33; and Whittaker, "The Poor," 294–95.

55. Lenski, *Power and Privilege*, 243–44.

56. Ibid., 246.

negative reaction to his vision of the reign of God had potentially far-reaching ramifications.

Like the retainer group, merchants and priests in agrarian societies had a wide range of wealth and power somewhere between the elite rulers and the numerous peasants. The merchant group, of course, dealt in trading goods mostly to the elite, with whom they had a complicated love-hate relationship. Merchants usually had some sort of humble beginning (whether as a "landless" younger son of the elites or perhaps as an ambitious peasant with some capital) and took an unusually large chunk of the economic surplus away from the elites,[59] but at the same time the two groups were dependent upon each other for the provision of luxury goods.[60] Most importantly, however, and unlike the retainers, they enjoyed a certain amount of freedom from elite rule; merchants were in market relationships with those of higher status, rather than under their direct authority as employees.[61]

Lenski's "priestly class," those in roles as religious leaders, also occupied a mixed position in agrarian societies. They had something of a privileged role, especially in the higher echelons, but were also, in theory at least, supposed to serve a deity rather than the ruler and elites.[62] The relationship between political and religious authorities was both naturally symbiotic and naturally contentious because of the constant struggle over which authority (ruler or deity) was ultimately higher.[63] Priestly influence therefore varied greatly across, and even within, individual societies. Rome attempted to solve this problem by making the ruler and deity essentially identical.[64] As a result, the public imperial cult was completely enmeshed with politics, and its priests were appointed public officials, usually elites serving a limited term of office at the pleasure of Rome and its representatives.[65]

57. On the Pharisees' role as retainers for the ruling elite and their status as political and social leaders, see Anthony J. Saldarini, *Pharisees, Scribes and Sadducees in Palestinian Society: A Sociological Approach* (Wilmington: Michael Glazier, 1988), 41–42, 277–97.

58. As professional soldiers of non-elite status, centurions are one of the most common examples of retainers in the New Testament. For the placement of centurions and other military personnel in Lenski's hierarchy, see Warren Carter, *John and Empire: Initial Explorations* (London: T&T Clark, 2008), 66; and Duling, "Empire," 65.

59. Lenski, *Power and Privilege*, 248–49.

60. Ibid., 255.

61. Ibid., 250.

62. Ibid., 266.

63. Ibid., 261.

64. Fears, "Cult of Jupiter," 9; and James Rives, "Religion in the Roman Empire," in Huskinson, *Experiencing Rome*, 267.

Even the Jerusalem high priesthood had become, by the turn of the era, a political office awarded as a favor to elite insiders; Josephus records instances of both Julius Caesar and Herod the Great appointing favorites to the job (*J.W.* 1.199 and 1.437). This was one way that an elite seeking to legitimize his or her rule of military force obtained that especially useful witness of religious support. But at the same time, religious traditions often portray the deity or deities as fundamentally opposed to tyranny and inequality of the kind that the elites want endorsed. This image is found, for example, in the ancient Persian code of Hammurabi, the Levitical law code (for example, Lev. 19:9-18; 25:8-55), the Hebrew prophets (for example, 2 Samuel 11–12; Micah 2–3; Isa. 10:1-4; 11:1-9; 42:1-9), and many of the early Christian traditions (for example, Mark 9:33-37; 10:17-31; James 2:1-17; 5:1-6; Revelation 18).[66] Certainly Luke and the other Gospels, drawing upon teaching from both the Torah and the Prophets, portray Jesus as a leader focused on divine justice and with a comprehensive vision of a new society. As a result, he comes into serious, and in the end violent and fatal, conflict with the local elites of Jerusalem, whose true loyalty is shown to be with Rome and its rulers, rather than with the Hebrew ancestral traditions of equality and social justice. Religion, like everything else in the Roman world, involved public power negotiation.[67] And when an individual's dissenting private belief began to affect his public identity or increase her social power, conflict with Roman rule became almost inevitable.[68]

The great majority of agrarian people fell into the large peasant and somewhat smaller artisan groups. Their work shouldered almost the entire burden of supporting the state and its elite rulers through taxes and forced labor that left them nothing except subsistence resources.[69] Peasants were mostly farmers, while artisans were craftspeople (sometimes peasants who had lost their land) who sometimes organized into guilds that could wield a measure of power for themselves.[70] In general, though, life as a peasant or artisan meant significantly lower levels of status, wealth, and power; degradation by the elites; and a limited exposure to alternate societal orders. The massive income difference between a laborer and an elite in the Roman Empire has already been delineated above. In addition to this inequality, more subtle domination tactics were masterfully employed by the imperial elite. Even in a relatively

---

65. Rives, "Religion," 249, 255.

66. Lenski, *Power and Privilege*, 263–64.

67. Kelly, *Roman Empire*, 30; and Rives, "Religion," 266.

68. Rives, "Religion," 258.

69. Lenski, *Power and Privilege*, 266–68.

70. Ibid., 280.

peaceful region like Asia Minor, Roman military might, and the willingness to use it, served as an ever-present reminder of subjugation for provincials (peasant and elite alike): "Though rarely deployed, the threat of Roman retaliation for perceived provincial resistance hung like a storm cloud over the towns of empire."[71] Every day, the sharp stratification of imperial life took its toll on the physical and mental health of those of lower status. Modern studies have shown that stratified societies produce exponentially more intense social stressors on those of lower status.[72] Thus we can conclude that the mental health of Roman non-elites would ordinarily have decreased rapidly under the burdens of heavy manual labor, subsistence living, extensive debt, poor living conditions, and violent treatment—burdens that the elites did not have to shoulder because those of lower status did.[73] Even the stress of status negotiation and its accompanying public insults took its toll; there is evidence that this was keenly felt by many Roman non-elites to be the worst part of being poor and having low status.[74]

A few factors had the potential to improve the peasant's lot to a limited extent, either in perception or in reality. When these factors were present, they could increase the level of non-elite acceptance of the ruling order in some cases. Elite benefaction in the form of public buildings, occasional food handouts, and sponsorship of games and entertainment served both to nominally benefit the people and to reinforce the Roman order. The games, especially, reproduced Rome's view of the world in miniature: seating arrangements visually represented the imperial hierarchy for all in attendance; battle reenactments illustrated Roman military power; and the humiliation and execution of criminals and captives ridiculed any possible rule, law, or worldview except that of Rome.[75] Non-elites with slightly higher status, such as urban artisans, generally benefited more from this elite patronage, and therefore were more likely to be supportive of the status quo.[76] More actual benefit and opportunity for status improvement for all non-elites were found, Lenski notes, when the ruling group's military force was dependent upon the service of average peasants. In this situation, elites tended to treat the peasants somewhat

---

71. Kelly, *Roman Empire*, 59–60.

72. Toner, *Popular Culture*, 58.

73. Ibid., 62–74.

74. MacMullen, *Roman Social Relations*, 111. MacMullen points to the example of non-elites being invited to elite feasts for the sole purpose of being humiliated and set apart from the "real" guests by substandard food, insulting seat placement, and public shaming.

75. Toner, *Popular Culture*, 114–17. See also Garnsey and Saller, *Roman Empire*, 117; and Kelly, *Roman Empire*, 79–82.

76. Whittaker, "The Poor," 297–98.

better.[77] It is no coincidence that military service was perhaps the surest way for a non-elite man to improve incrementally his status in the Roman Empire; a common soldier, for example, could be promoted to centurion and thus gain power, increased income, and potentially land (that most precious of resources in an agrarian economy).[78] Also, as discussed above, the presence of a religious system with social justice values had potential to benefit the peasant and artisan groups.[79] But despite these slight benefits, people of non-elite status still existed in what was essentially a state of oppression and exploitation. The effects of this domination and non-elite resistance to it will be examined in much greater detail in the discussion of Scott's model below.

Finally, the groups with the least status, power, and privilege were the degraded and expendable, including those in unacceptable but necessary professions (such as tanners, prostitutes, and miners) and those with no real means of survival except wits, crime, and charity (thieves, beggars, itinerants, and bandits).[80] These were segments of society that the dominant groups were unwilling to support because to do so cut into the elite share of the surplus without adding anything to it. These groups grew mainly as a result of the downward mobility that was quite extensive in agrarian societies, with some younger siblings of larger families potentially falling several steps down the status scale.[81] Upward mobility was also possible (although seldom for the degraded and expendable), but usually only one step up per generation; and even then, it only occurred in relatively rare cases of good fortune, exceptional skills or intelligence, or a combination of the two.[82] Interaction with these "lowest of the low" groups is, as we shall see, an important part of the stories of Jesus and the earliest Christian communities.

I have not yet addressed the place of slaves in agrarian empires, and they do not appear in the chart included above. Lenski's model regards them as peasants with legal rights and freedom that are more restricted than normal.[83] In the eastern Roman Empire, slaves played a minor role compared to their large numbers in Italy and Rome itself; land in the Greek and Asian provinces was worked mostly by free peasants, tenants, and day laborers.[84] Thus slavery

---

77. Lenski, *Power and Privilege*, 275.

78. Garnsey and Saller, *Roman Empire*, 124.

79. Lenski, *Power and Privilege*, 276–77.

80. Ibid., 280–81.

81. Ibid., 290.

82. Ibid., 291.

83. Ibid., 288–89.

84. Kelly, *Roman Empire*, 111.

will not be a major issue in our discussion, focused as it is on the reception of Luke in the Greek East, but a brief statement is in order. Roman slaves are difficult to categorize as a single group because they varied so greatly in wealth, living conditions, and amount of power. They ranged from the valued imperial or elite household adviser with great wealth and influence, to the lowest farm laborer, and everything in between.[85] What they did have in common was a legal status that denied them freedom and a social stigma that remained even if they were fortunate enough to be manumitted. They were sometimes regarded as "speaking tools," subject to abuse and ill treatment at their masters' whims, with only the barest legal recognition of their humanity.[86] This juxtaposition led to significant status inconsistency for many slaves and freedpersons, which will be suggestive for our consideration of the perception of Luke and its status reversals in urban Asia Minor.

JOHN H. KAUTSKY AND ARISTOCRATIC POLITICS

While Lenski provides an excellent overview of social stratification in an agrarian society like Rome, John H. Kautsky's *The Politics of Aristocratic Empires* offers a more focused study of elite ruling groups and their origins, values, and governing role. He defines *aristocracy* as "a ruling class in an agrarian economy that does not engage in productive labor but lives wholly or primarily off the labor of peasants."[87] This, of course, necessitates the presence in such a society of a significantly larger group of non-elite producers, or peasants. Kautsky's work has strong areas of connection with Lenski's agrarian models, but he identifies many of Lenski's examples, including Rome, as "commercialized" (that is, incorporating things like private land ownership, a significant merchant class, and slavery) rather than "pure" or "traditional" aristocratic empires like medieval Europe or the Ottoman Empire.[88] This comparison yields some valuable insights for our work with the Roman Empire.

An aristocracy can arise out of its own indigenous populations, as some community members begin to take on the specialized role of protection or, loosely, government, while others cultivate and provide basic necessities. This seems to be the case with the Roman Republic.[89] Much more often, however, and during most of Rome's imperial era, aristocratic societies originated by way

85. Garnsey and Saller, *Roman Empire*, 119; and Hope, "Status and Identity," 140.

86. Garnsey and Saller, *Roman Empire*, 116; and Toner, *Popular Culture*, 70–71.

87. Kautsky, *Politics*, 24.

88. Ibid., 20.

89. Ibid., 57, 61–62.

of conquest, as one group subdued another by force and demanded tribute or booty, which is in Kautsky's view essentially a form of taxation whereby the conquerors are able to obtain enough resources to live comfortably.[90] The aristocracy was then maintained largely through hereditary inheritance and intermarriage. Who actually "owns" the land is relatively unimportant in a traditional aristocracy; the economic surplus (minus subsistence resources for the peasants) is paid to the elite, whether the peasants pay taxes on land they own or act as tenants and pay the elite landlord in kind.[91] Eventually, the surplus goods can be extracted without violence, although the threat of it remains. The elites specialize in war and war-like endeavors because therein lies their main power to exploit the greater population; they are also then able to claim that they provide the service of protection and physical security to the peasants, in return for their surplus goods.[92] This was the basic argument for the *pax romana* in Roman literature like the *Res Gestae*, Augustus's "explanation and justification of the conquest of the known world."[93] Similarly, Virgil claims in the *Aeneid* that Jupiter destined Rome to rule all nations in order to bring the great benefit of Roman civilization to the world's lesser peoples.[94] As I will demonstrate in the upcoming discussion, however, this public transcript claim is almost always a partial truth or faulty rationalization.

Kautsky maintains that there is a sharp divide between the aristocrats and the peasants, but overstates the case when he argues that they represent two different cultures. The "government" of the former over the latter consists mainly of warfare and taxation;[95] this is amply demonstrated by Rome's preference for localized government focused on those very two areas.[96] Provincial administration under the empire employed only about ten thousand bureaucrats to support a population roughly equivalent to the modern United Kingdom (which today requires about five hundred thousand employees).[97] Local elites, naturally, supported this minimalist approach to governing, as it allowed them to maintain their own prominence and power as local gentry.[98]

---

90. Ibid., 52–53.

91. Ibid., 100.

92. Ibid., 100, 111.

93. Richard Miles, "Communicating Culture, Identity and Power," in Huskinson, *Experiencing Rome*, 41.

94. Fears, "Cult of Jupiter," 42.

95. Kautsky, *Politics*, 6, 144–55.

96. Garnsey and Saller, *Roman Empire*, 20.

97. Kelly, *Roman Empire*, 44.

98. Ibid., 44–45.

But contrary to Kautsky's argument that there was little to no interaction and thus little to no conflict between aristocrats and peasants,[99] local elites and their subordinates in the Roman Empire actually did have a sizable amount of contact and conflict with each other. Archaeological work done on a typical Italian villa, for example, indicates that the living spaces of the elite owner and the peasant (or slave) laborers were actually attached to each other, and the owner likely had significant involvement in the estate's work.[100] Patron-client relationships also by necessity involved regular interaction of elite and non-elite, so that the requisite favors, honor, and loyalty could be exchanged.[101]

Despite this interaction, elite culture was still vastly different from that of the non-elite. While conflict is often rife between empires and within the ruling group of a single society, Kautsky observes that the aristocratic system itself tends toward stability.[102] The individual ruler might change, or the noble family wielding the most power at any given moment, but this has only minimal impact on the people as a whole, and does not change elite values. As mentioned above, military skills and their attendant ideals of service, duty, honor, and glory are ranked above almost anything else. Money is not something with which the elites were to concern themselves because their income is practically guaranteed; riches are then regarded as existing solely to be spent in a conspicuous display of immense wealth and nobility.[103] Connected to this is the aristocratic elite's claim to inherent superiority over the laboring peasants, townspeople, and even merchants who have to work in some way for survival.[104] Every part of an aristocratic society was set up to favor the elites over the non-elites, such as marriage customs designed to maintain the purity of noble blood,[105] and a justice system always stacked toward the elites who administered it, offering them lower penalties for major crimes but unbelievably stiff punishments to any commoner who dared to commit a crime against an aristocratic victim.[106] Under Roman law, the testimony of elite and non-elite was weighted differently, and penalties increased in severity as one's status decreased. This inequality intensified even further when the social

---

99. Kautsky, *Politics*, 73.

100. Perkins, "Power, Culture and Identity in the Roman Economy," 188–91.

101. See the discussion of patron-client relations in Garnsey and Saller, *Roman Empire*, 151–52.

102. Kautsky, *Politics*, 247.

103. Ibid., 188.

104. Ibid., 200–1.

105. Ibid., 205–10.

106. Ibid., 199.

hierarchy became more entrenched, pushing the common people deeper into subservience.[107]

Such a biased values system will play an important role in our study, especially as we consider how a Roman elite in the Lukan community, sharing some or all of these values, might react to the gospel. Kautsky makes the interesting observation that "ethical" religions like Christianity and Islam have to forsake some of that character when they are adopted by aristocrats, who must conquer and dominate others to keep their honor intact.[108] If Luke really was an attempt to reconcile Rome and Christ,[109] we might expect to see examples of such accommodations. Instead, however, the third evangelist and the characters in his narrative make bold claims of justice and of good news for the poor and oppressed (for example, Luke 4:16-21). Such declarations of God's favor for peasant girls like Mary (1:28-33, 42-45, 47-49) and hungry beggars like Lazarus (16:22, 25) surely struck a discordant note for elites whose daily lives and culture were designed to testify to their superiority. Jesus, in seeming agreement with standard aristocratic practice, maintains that excess wealth should indeed be spent rather than hoarded (Luke 12:13-21); but his suggested outlets for all that surplus extracted from the peasants were not servants, military campaigns, and other conspicuous luxuries. Rather, in a turn that must have been shocking to elite ears, he advocated "consuming" one's resources by sharing them with others, especially the poor who cannot reciprocate (an idea Kautsky calls entirely unthinkable and untenable in an aristocratic worldview[110]). For Jesus, extreme charity becomes an alternate way of "displaying" one's wealth in accordance with one's spiritual faith. Even more shockingly, all who want to follow Jesus are to engage in this alternate form of benefaction, not only the elite (see, for example, Luke 6:27-36; 14:7-14). As we shall clearly see in the following chapters, the Lukan theme of status reversal quickly redefines the ideals of service, honor, and glory so central to the elite value system.

Finally, a word is needed about Kautsky's treatment of the other 90 percent (or more) of the population in an aristocratic empire: peasants, merchants, and townspeople. In this area, his assessment suffers greatly from a limited view of how deeply peasants, slaves, and other non-elites are able to think, feel, and imagine. Peasants, in his estimation, are accustomed to paying taxes and so care little for where such taxes go, especially if compliance allows them to live in

---

107. Garnsey and Saller, *Roman Empire*, 111, 118.

108. Kautsky, *Politics*, 177.

109. See the discussion in the introduction above.

110. Kautsky, *Politics*, 193–94.

peace.[111] He makes the common argument (strongly refuted by Scott's model, discussed below) that aristocrats and peasants live entirely separate from each other, that they cannot imagine life any other way, and that neither group, therefore, has the inclination to change or agitate against the system. While there is some truth in the vast divide between elites and non-elites and the longevity of many aristocratic empires (whether traditional or commercialized), Kautsky's dismissal of conflict between elite and non-elite in "pure" aristocratic economies is too quick. His argument that most "class conflict" is due to commercialization and thus diluting of the "pure" model is not convincing. The status reversal imagery found not only in the New Testament but also throughout ancient (as well as modern) literature makes it clear that non-elites can indeed imagine themselves living a better life, no matter how far removed they may be from those ruling over them. They may be nearly powerless, but they can and do find ways to seek change within the system. Even Kautsky acknowledges that, at the least, they protest new or sudden increases in tax or labor demands[112] and attempt to use cunning to withhold part of their produce.[113]

Non-elites also learn the power of community and seize any opportunity for change that presents itself. Kautsky notes that an increase in commercialization can create an environment ripe for peasant revolt and social change: merchants serve as an example of non-elites improving their situation, and also provide a market where peasants could spend surplus resources to enhance their own quality of life.[114] The critical mass of townspeople (anyone not peasant or aristocratic) also increases along with commercialization, and Kautsky's model greatly underestimates the influence of this group. He observes correctly that the townspeople were much more varied in occupation and lifestyle than either the peasant or the aristocrat, interacted with a wider range of people, and thus had a broader intellectual horizon than most peasants. But contrary to his assertion, it does not automatically follow that they also lacked a central ideology and identity.[115] Merchants, artisans, and sometimes even thieves often organized themselves in some way. Craftspeople and vendors would come together to form guilds, which provided not only training, work standards, and insurance for members' widows and orphans, but also, and more importantly, a sense of community and voice, and a political arena

111. Ibid., 73, 252–53.
112. Ibid., 308.
113. Ibid., 275.
114. Ibid., 289–90.
115. Ibid., 330–31.

separate from that of the aristocrats.[116] Called *collegia* in the Roman world, such associations were available only to those non-elites with enough status and resources to afford the entry fees, and the elites were able to maintain some control of them through benefaction.[117] The coexisting independence and mimicry of the Roman *collegia* is important to note. These associations made elites nervous about their potential to turn revolutionary.[118] But at the same time, their members aped elite hierarchy and did not seek practical material benefits like holidays or lower taxes, but instead lobbied for a modest level of elite values, such as public honor and social prestige.[119] *Collegia* were an important beginning place, even with their ambivalence toward elite Roman values, for movements of social change, such as the early Jesus movement and others, to gain a foothold and some momentum to orchestrate social change beneficial to both peasants and townspeople, and perhaps even to the elites as well. For more in-depth exploration of this most important area, then, we must turn to the work of James Scott.

James C. Scott and Hidden Resistance

Sociology and anthropology have generally paid attention only to open rebellion and armed revolt on the part of subordinated peoples; if these are not present, the people are assumed to be passive and accepting of their domination.[120] James C. Scott, however, takes issue with this conclusion and offers a cogent counterargument in his book *Domination and the Arts of Resistance: Hidden Transcripts*. Through a historical comparison of subordinated groups like African-American slaves, peasants from various times and places, the Indian caste system, and others, Scott shows that multiple layers lie between the extremes of unquestioning submission and military revolt. Within these intermediate gray areas, the dominated are well able to express their dissatisfaction with the status quo in which they live. This, we shall see, is the type of resistance that we find in several different forms in the Gospel of Luke.

116. Ibid., 333–34.

117. Toner, *Popular Culture*, 109; Whittaker, "The Poor," 287.

118. Toner, *Popular Culture*, 107–8.

119. MacMullen, *Roman Social Relations*, 74–75; and Toner, *Popular Culture*, 108.

120. E.g., the exclusive focus of Stephen L. Dyson on military revolts in his two articles: "Native Revolts in the Roman Empire," 239–74; and "Native Revolt Patterns in the Roman Empire," in *ANRW* 2.3, ed. Joseph Vogt, Hildegard Temporini, and Wolfgang Haase (Berlin: De Gruyter, 1975), 138–75. For an example in biblical studies, see Kim, *Christ and Caesar*; he concludes that since the Lukan Jesus does not advocate an overthrow of Roman rule (95), complete submission with no alteration of existing political, social, or economic structures is the only alternative (114, 123).

Scott focuses his work specifically on similar behaviors and characteristic reactions among groups from different times and places who face similar types of domination (what anthropologists call a distant or macrocomparison[121]). The systems of domination examined by Scott must meet several criteria: institutionalized means of extracting labor, goods, and services from a subject population; assumptions about innate superiority and inferiority reinforced through daily indignities visited upon those of lower status by those of higher status; public rituals that uphold the hierarchy; and a decent number of "offstage" opportunities for subordinates to form their hidden transcript.[122] Such a definition of domination can be seen clearly in the situation of first-century Palestine (the narrative world of Luke's Gospel). The non-elites of Judea, Galilee, and Samaria were under multiple layers of Roman authority in the guise of Herodian client kings, the Jerusalem aristocracy, and Roman officials like procurators, prefects, and soldiers. The power of the elites and their right to levy taxes were assumed and hereditary in many instances,[123] and were demonstrated in numerous and often humiliating ways. This included public ceremonies like sacrifices for the well-being of the emperor (and through him, the entire empire) in the Jerusalem Temple, as well as everyday experiences such as the common person's inability to provide for a family's basic needs or, as in Luke 18:2-8, a widow's inability to get the justice she deserves from those who claim to provide it.

It is more difficult to ascertain whether or not the context of Luke's author or audience fits this description of domination, not least because any conclusions about such a context can only be hypothetical. But certainly, as will be discussed in detail in chapter 2 of this work, Luke's Gospel was read in, transmitted by, and quite possibly originated among the Hellenistic cities of Rome's eastern provinces in Greece and Asia Minor. In this context, positing a Christian audience of mixed Jews and Gentiles of various economic strata, some connections can be made. This is a group certainly under the domination and taxation of Rome, the first century's superpower, and existing in a highly stratified society with limited opportunity for upward social mobility. Rome's presence was felt wherever one went, especially through the imperial imagery

121. Andre Gingrich, "When Ethnic Majorities Are 'Dethroned': Towards a Methodology of Self-Reflexive, Controlled Macrocomparison," in *Anthropology, by Comparison*, ed. Andre Gingrich and Richard G. Fox (London: Routledge, 2002), 229; cf. Esler, *Community and Gospel*, 10–11.

122. James C. Scott, *Domination and the Arts of Resistance: Hidden Transcripts* (New Haven: Yale University Press, 1990), 21.

123. Kautsky observes that elite aristocrats typically viewed peasants as resources that went with the land, and thus such taxation and exploitation was simply the natural order of things (*Politics*, 110).

located in all municipal buildings, from temples to the council house, and from baths to theaters.[124] The empire operated on the assumption that Rome (in the person of the emperor and in the divinely chosen Roman people) was destined to rule the entire known world. Dennis Duling writes, "In short, the Romans believed that they were God's chosen people and that if their leaders, especially the emperor, maintained the appropriate virtue and piety their mandate to rule the world was a mandate from heaven."[125] Although not all, and probably not even most, of those hearing Luke's Gospel were subjugated to the same extent as African-American slaves or Indian untouchables, there were likely at least a few community members from the lowest (and some of the higher) social strata, and all would have been affected in some way by imperial domination. The Greek East's Hellenistic culture as a whole occupied an ambiguous place in the Roman hierarchy. Its arts and philosophy formed the basis for the empire's own culture, but Romans also looked down on the Greeks as extravagant, degenerate, self-indulgent, and too proud to admit completely Rome's superiority.[126] Overall, there can be little doubt that "the Roman Empire was the foreground, not the background, of late first-century daily life," and as such cast its shadow over every aspect of life for all those living in it.[127] In such a context, the intimate gatherings of Jesus-followers would have provided an ideal safe location for voicing, refining, and sharing a hidden transcript. Thus the emergence of an alternative reality like that presented by the Gospel of Luke and its possible effects among urban imperial groups will be an important touchpoint for further exploration throughout this study.

The foundation of Scott's model rests on the existence of a "public transcript," that is, what is openly said and done in interactions between subordinates and their dominants, often misleading and aimed at preserving appearances,[128] alongside "hidden transcripts" of both the subordinate and the dominant that are developed and expressed "offstage," in safe places among one's equals.[129] The public transcript is of course controlled and dictated mostly by the dominant elites, "to affirm and naturalize the[ir] power . . . and to conceal

---

124. S. R. F. Price, *Rituals and Power: The Roman Imperial Cult in Asia Minor* (Cambridge: Cambridge University Press, 1984), 109–10.

125. Duling, "Empire," 73–74.

126. Huskinson, "Élite Culture," 98–100; and Janet Huskinson, "Looking for Culture, Identity and Power," in Huskinson, *Experiencing Rome*, 9, 15.

127. Carter, *John and Empire*, x.

128. Scott, *Domination*, 2.

129. Ibid., 4. Although the focus of his work is on the hidden transcripts of the subordinated people, Scott is also careful to maintain that the dominant have their own hidden transcripts different from their public faces (although theirs is admittedly less of a liability if it is revealed): "If subordination requires a

or euphemize the dirty linen of their rule."[130] This control of the public rituals and unspoken rules of everyday life is an important part of the dominant group's hold, allowing them to obscure their unsavory actions and stigmatize others, sometimes fatally.[131] For example, in the "show trial"[132] of Jesus in the Gospel narratives, the elite public transcript turns a social revolutionary into a full-fledged traitor. Likewise, any gathering of subordinates that is not authorized by the elites is a potential threat and is therefore designated as a "mob," with all that term implies.[133] For example, Emperor Trajan wrote to Pliny the Younger, who was governing in Asia Minor, about the danger of trade guilds and other non-elite associations: "We must remember that it is associations like these which have been responsible for the political disturbances in your province, particularly its towns. If people assemble for a common purpose, whatever name we give them and for whatever reason, they soon turn into a political club."[134] It is easy to imagine the threat of such an assessment hanging over the heads of the members of the unauthorized Lukan community and other early Christian groups.

In the face of this overwhelming, ever-present public transcript, non-elites generally have to exert great self-control to keep up the facade of compliance, and thus the ability to absorb insults and humiliation becomes an important survival skill.[135] A particularly brutal or humiliating slight to a subordinate's human dignity and self-esteem, however, sometimes breaks through that control, and the hidden transcript is brought out into the open. In the Lukan narrative, Jesus reached this breaking point at the end of his extended engagement with the Jerusalem elite in chapters 19–21. As his actions became more openly threatening, the challenge could be ignored no longer. The

credible performance of humility and deference, so domination seems to require a credible performance of haughtiness and mastery" (11).

130. Ibid., 18.

131. E.g., designating revolutionaries as "criminals" and declaring any non-orthodox beliefs to be "heresies" (Ibid., 55).

132. Defined in William R. Herzog, *Jesus, Justice, and the Reign of God: A Ministry of Liberation* (Louisville: Westminster John Knox, 2000), 240–41, as a type of political theater where the guilt of the accused is already determined by the judges, unlike an actual fair trial. The purpose is not legal at all, but rather a political attempt to humiliate an enemy of the state.

133. Scott, *Domination*, 63.

134. Quoted in Toner, *Popular Culture*, 107.

135. Scott draws an interesting comparison between the aristocrat's duel, where any insult has the potential to lead to mortal combat, and African-American culture's "dirty dozens," where insults are traded back and forth and the one who can keep his or her temper the longest is declared the winner (*Domination*, 136–37).

Jerusalem elites, aided by the power of Satan (often connected to Roman power in the first-century texts that articulate resistance to the empire),[136] took action against Jesus (Luke 22:1-6; cf. verse 53 ["This is your hour, and the power of darkness!"]). Scott notes the import of such an event: "The first open statement of a hidden transcript, a declaration that breaches the etiquette of power relations, that breaks an apparently calm surface of silence and consent, carries the force of a symbolic declaration of war."[137] At such times, it becomes especially clear that outward compliance with the status quo is not a true reflection of the actual opinions and feelings of those being subordinated and oppressed. It is sometimes argued that eventually non-elites will conform to the mask of submission that they wear everyday and come to accept the status quo.[138] The alternate point of view, though, is demonstrated again and again; eventually the pressure of wearing such a mask builds up into a kind of explosion, which often reveals some of the hidden transcript and the non-elites' true opinions.[139]

Most of what is recorded in history either comes from the public transcript or reports of armed revolt against the dominant group. Scott regards such open revolt as the most extreme option the subordinates have of protesting against their lot in life, but not their only option.[140] There are in reality three more levels of possible action (termed "resistance" by Scott, but what we might better designate as "negotiation") that usually precede the stage of violent

136. See, e.g., Revelation's imagery of Rome and its rulers as grotesque beasts brought forth by the devil (e.g., chapter 13); 2 Esdras (4 Ezra, chapters 3–14), which portrays Rome as an eagle with "most evil little wings" and "malicious heads" about to be devoured by the Lion of Judah (11:36-46); and the canonical temptation accounts that pinpoint the devil as the origin of all earthly power (Matt. 4:8-9; and even more explicitly Luke 4:5-7). Also significant is the fact that both Luke and John portray Judas Iscariot's betrayal of Jesus to the Roman-allied chief priests as a direct result of his possession by Satan (Luke 22:1-6; John 6:70-71; 13:2, 26-27; 18:3).

137. Scott, Domination, 7-8. The publicness of these "explosions" is particularly important: anti-communist heckling of the Romanian president on live television (204); the jubilant celebration of slaves when a particularly harsh master finally died (208); Frederick Douglass's refusal to accept a beating from his master and the ensuing physical fight between them (208-9); public picketing against long-accepted gender restrictions in the modern American workplace (209); the commandeering of a director's limousine by striking factory workers in Communist Poland (210-12); and the open declaration and practice of heterodox religious beliefs during the English Civil War by protest groups like the Diggers, Levellers, and Quakers (225-26).

138. Ibid., 10. Kautsky's recurring argument (Politics, 73, 252-53, 273-74, 316-19, 335-37) that non-elite peasants and townspeople do not have the ability, will, or desire to envision and pursue a different existence than the one they have always known is an example of this perspective.

139. Scott, Domination, 9.

140. Ibid., 19.

action or outburst. The safest course of action is appeal to the public transcript, which inevitably claims that the dominant group is actually looking out for the good of their subordinates, and demand that this promise be fulfilled.[141] A succinct version of the basic public transcript in agrarian societies, and the reality it conceals, is found in Kautsky: aristocrats claim to give peasants the right to work the land (even though the peasants are the ones who make it produce for the benefit of the aristocrats); and to provide protection, justice, and physical security for the supposedly peace-loving and militarily inexperienced commoners (although there is no freedom to accept, reject, or question this "security" and "justice").[142] This kind of power negotiation may well be part of the subtext in, for example, the Lukan Jesus' many Sabbath controversies with the Pharisees, when he demands proof that they put the welfare of the people first as dictated in Torah (Luke 6:9; 13:15-16; 14:3-5).[143] Most of the time, Scott argues, there is an expectation in this negotiation tactic that the basic system itself will be preserved, as that is the only hope for success.[144] Most urban riots in Rome and its eastern provinces were not against Roman rule itself, but were the people's reaction to hunger, hardship, or even a lack of entertainment (all benefits that were to be provided by the local elites).[145]

Despite this relative conservatism, calling for adherence to the public transcript also has some subversive power: it can potentially reveal the inconsistencies and downright untruths in the elite version of events. One of its biggest strengths is the ability to appeal to those whom Scott calls "sincere elites," who truly believe that they are working for the good of non-elites and themselves alike. This subtle negotiation can persuade such members of the ruling group to improve living conditions for their immediate subordinates, but in some cases it can do even more. Sincere elites by definition have faith in the system of domination. If, however, they can be convinced of its flaws, the power of their disillusionment has far greater potential to threaten the status quo than that of a cynic who never bought into it at all.[146] Luke, it would seem, is

---

141. Ibid., 18.

142. Kautsky, *Politics*, 111–12.

143. There is also perhaps a similar challenge in Luke 22:24-27 regarding the Gentile rulers' claim to be benefactors of the people. See the preface of Frederick W. Danker, *Luke*, 2nd ed., Proclamation Commentaries, ed. Gerhard Krodel (Philadelphia: Fortress Press, 1987), for an argument that the Gospel of Luke portrays Jesus as the Great Benefactor, in sharp contrast to the many false benefactors of the first-century world.

144. Scott, *Domination*, 92.

145. Paula James, "The Language of Dissent," in *Experiencing Rome: Culture, Identity, and Power in the Roman Empire*, ed. Janet Huskinson (London: Routledge, 2000), 298–99. See also Toner, *Popular Culture*, 35–36.

well aware of this dynamic and willing to use it, especially with lower elites and retainers. Thus we meet in chapter 7 a centurion who is clearly characterized by Luke (though not by Matthew; cf. Matt. 8:5-13) as a sincere retainer: as a centurion, he has negotiated the Roman hierarchy with at least some success, and yet he is also reputed to be a friend to the people of Capernaum (Luke 7:2-5). Jesus commends him for his surprising faith and willingness to accept Jesus' authority and power as greater than that of Rome (7:6-9). The fact that he came to Jesus for aid in the first places implies a lack of confidence in the system in which he is currently embedded. A few chapters later, Jesus challenges another retainer, a lawyer, to enact the public transcript's rhetoric of loving God and loving neighbor above all (10:25-37). This is a person connected with the elites who can at least recognize genuine mercy when he sees it; whether or not he accepts Jesus' challenge to "go and do likewise" is left to the audience's imagination (10:36-37).

The next negotiation tactic in Scott's model stops short of armed revolt, but ideologically undergirds such action when it actually occurs. It is the development of a hidden transcript, with its strong dissent to what is publicly done to and proclaimed about the subordinated population.[147] It is here that the subordinated espouse among themselves a different worldview refuting all three levels of their domination through action, speech, and belief: "At its most elementary level, the hidden transcript represents an acting out in fantasy—and occasionally in secretive practice—of the anger and reciprocal aggression denied by the presence of domination."[148] Material appropriation such as taxation and forced labor is combatted by dawdling, foot-dragging, holding part of the product back, and other evasive techniques. Even more important, though, is the hidden transcript's resistance against public subjugation: it forms a coherent, community-endorsed counterideology that enables the dominated to fight against the daily rituals of public humiliation and powerlessness with which they are faced. This provides an outlet for their suppressed anger, indignity, and shame, and validates their humanity and worth through group resonance.[149] Under Roman rule, "simply asserting one's self-worth was a way to resist the dehumanizing effect of the dominant culture" and "to resist the anonymity to which society mostly condemned the non-elite."[150] This was done, for example, through burial clubs, taking pride in one's trade (however humble), and even

146. Scott, *Domination*, 105–7.

147. Ibid., 18.

148. Ibid., 37–38.

149. Ibid., 118–19.

150. Toner, *Popular Culture*, 167.

flaunting socially unacceptable preferences like sexual deviance or dislike of wifely submission.[151] We must also note, however, that the world envisioned in the hidden transcript has strong and sometimes alarming echoes of the oppressive world that gave it birth. Such imperial mimicry can certainly be seen in the New Testament (for example, in Revelation's unambiguous declaration of a rival rule and emperor to Rome's), and when it appears, it is both similar to and different from the oppressive Roman regime in significant ways.[152] We must be aware of both the comparisons and the contrasts in this study of Luke.

The actual content of this hidden transcript is practically impossible to recover, as it is by definition hidden, seldom written down, and dependent upon socially marginal "carriers," such as popular prophets or lower-status traveling preachers, to disseminate it.[153] As a document used mainly "in-house," Luke likely contains more pieces of the actual hidden transcript than most public records, but it is my argument that the Lukan community was mixed enough in status, wealth, and loyalties that the evangelist may still have felt a need to disguise and protect much of the Gospel's resistant message to some degree.[154] What can be recovered, though, is a more nuanced type of negotiation with the status quo, one that lies somewhere between appeal to the public transcript and development of a hidden transcript. This is found in the places where "a partly sanitized, ambiguous, and coded version of the hidden transcript is . . . present in the public discourse of subordinate groups," usually protected by double meanings or anonymity and thus allowing for generally recognizable (but unpunishable) resistance to the humiliation of subjugation.[155]

Acts of deference can only be taken as outward expressions of acquiescence and do not necessarily indicate the attitude behind such an action—as anyone who has worked under a difficult boss can attest.[156] The widespread popularity of the imperial cult in Asia Minor, then, should not be understood simply as pure enthusiasm for Roman rule on the part of all the people. It is more likely that, at least in part, embracing the emperor as a divine appointee and a god-in-waiting was a power-negotiation technique.[157] It allowed the local elite of the Hellenistic city-states, and even the non-elite citizens, to save face, for there was less shame in being conquered by a demigod than by a mere human

---

151. Ibid., 167–69.

152. Carter, *John and Empire*, 79–81.

153. Scott, *Domination*, 124.

154. See chapter 2 below.

155. Ibid., 19–20.

156. Ibid., 24.

157. Rives, "Religion," 266.

being. Joining Rome in this way "could provide a language for comprehending absolute power. . . . The celebration of a special connection with a superhuman emperor both reinforced the privileged position . . . and confirmed the superior status of their cities."[158] Often this seeming submission was accompanied by reasons other than pure loyalty and by subversions of the dominant imagery; Richard Miles asserts,

> The authorized reading will always be ranged against the power of its receivers to generate new interpretations. By creating new meanings, the languages and images of the ruler can also be a source of power for the ruled. So through the same set of channels we are able to witness not only the configuration of different forms of power, but also *resistance* to it.[159]

This is why Lukan reversal texts must not be explained away or sidelined in a discussion of the purpose and theology of Luke-Acts. They are hints that there is more going on beneath the surface than Luke's apparent deference to Rome might indicate. Scott writes, "By recognizing the guises that the powerless must adopt outside the safety of the hidden transcript, we can, I believe, discern a political dialogue with power in the public transcript."[160]

To safely declare or imply the hidden transcript in public, it must be given some form of disguise, either of the messenger (through anonymity of some kind) or of the message itself (through ambiguous or veiled meaning).[161] To begin with the former, Scott's discussion of spirit possession is relevant for New Testament studies. He calls it "a quasi-covert form of social protest," wherein the spirit is the one speaking subversive ideas rather than the actual person. One study of ecstatic religions found a correlation between episodes of spirit possession and unjust treatment by a superior.[162] Such observations add an interesting facet to the more charismatic experiences of Jesus and his followers: demon possession, particularly the fact that the demons know the truth about Jesus' identity before anyone else; speaking in tongues, which was regarded by many early Christian groups as speaking a higher form of truth; and prophecy, which mediates between God and the world, as exhibited in Luke-Acts by

---

158. Kelly, *Roman Empire*, 30. For more discussion of ambiguity toward Roman rule and the imperial cult, see Toner, *Popular Culture*, 178–84.

159. Miles, "Communicating Culture," 36. Emphasis in original.

160. Scott, *Domination*, 138.

161. Ibid., 139–40.

162. Ibid., 141.

Mary, Elizabeth, Zechariah, Simeon, Peter, Stephen, and Jesus himself, to name just a few. These ideas about spirit possession are consistent with the beliefs of the larger Roman world, particularly among the non-elite. Mental illness of any kind, along with other unexplainable events, was usually attributed to demonic spirits from the underworld.[163] This madness, however, was not always entirely negative; when attributed to a more positive supernatural force, it was sometimes regarded with fearful awe as divine inspiration, and was used as a safe place to express socially unacceptable or threatening ideas.[164]

Gossip, rumors, anonymous threats, and seemingly spontaneous mob action are other methods of disguise that protect the identity of the messenger. While some of these might seem relatively innocuous, it is worth noting that the Roman emperors had an entire order of officials whose sole job was to report the rumors that were circulating at any given time.[165] Rumors of a socioreligious nature, particularly of imminent liberation at the hands of a higher power, were especially powerful in their ability to express the hopes of the oppressed, while allowing them to avoid individual punishment for expressing such a desire for change.[166] The political religion of Rome justified imperial rule and claimed to offer collective community benefits, but the Jesus movement and other non-Roman cults offered individual experience, ethics, and a more prominent role for non-elites.[167] Religious ideas proved, in the end, to be a more insidious type of resistance than armed revolt, one that could not be entirely eliminated through Rome's great military power. Jerry Toner writes, "Religions such as Christianity showed that the people were capable of imagining a new social order . . . a potentially threatening message" that "needed to create a new social space where it had greater freedom to express itself."[168]

Sometimes, though, the messenger cannot or does not want to hide, and in this case the resistance of the hidden transcript must be disguised through ambiguity, double meanings, and insider language. The development of non-elite popular culture, which is separate from and yet related to that of the elites, provides one important place to carry out this task. Toner writes of the interdependence and negotiation that was continually occurring between elite and non-elite: "Popular culture in ancient Rome was not just about folklore;

163. Toner, *Popular Culture*, 79.

164. Ibid., 85.

165. Scott, *Domination*, 144.

166. Ibid., 148.

167. Garnsey and Saller, *Roman Empire*, 170–71; and Toner, *Popular Culture*, 173.

168. Toner, *Popular Culture*, 174.

it was about how people sometimes mocked, subverted and insulted their superiors; how they manipulated the elite to get something of their own way; and how they saw through the ideologies by which the powerful sought to dominate them."[169] Because a society retains in its collective memory only what is meaningful for its members and their life situation, this folk culture generally comes to reflect the values of the group, and its inherent symbolic and metaphorical nature lends itself to the disguise of ambiguity.[170] What is most important is that the double meaning strikes a delicate balance: it must be pointed enough that elite and subordinate alike understand at least some of the resistance, yet still hidden enough that there is nothing explicit for which the speaker could be punished.[171] The predominance of oral tradition in folk culture is an advantage here, in that the message can be tailored to each individual situation, either clarifying the subversiveness in safe places or presenting it more innocuously in a dangerous setting. The master of such wit and cunning in folklore is the trickster hero, the Brer Rabbit figure who subtly humiliates his "betters" to their faces yet always manages to escape without harm.[172] For much of his ministry, Jesus himself plays the trickster role as he outwits and outmaneuvers the various traps set for him by Jerusalem elites and their retainers.

A particularly important part of this non-elite culture of hidden resistance for our study is the presence of status reversals in the songs, legends, plays, prayers, and poems of the oppressed. Such reversals are examples of millennial imagery and what Scott calls "symbolic inversion," and they appear "in nearly every major cultural tradition in which inequities of power, wealth, and status have been pronounced."[173] They are a major component of hidden transcripts that attempt to counteract public ideologies depicting the status quo as inevitable or divinely ordained, and the subordinated as inherently inferior to the dominant groups.[174] The prominence of such themes in the Gospel of Luke, through poetry, parables, teaching, and actions, is a powerful indication that the third evangelist is espousing a worldview and theology that are not simply compliant with Roman rule. Despite their possible metaphorical interpretation, it is exceedingly difficult to deny the subversive possibilities of such a

---

169. Ibid., 10.

170. Scott, *Domination*, 157–58.

171. Ibid., 156.

172. Ibid., 162.

173. Ibid., 80.

174. Ibid., 199. See also the sections on "Symbolic Inversion, World-Upside-Down Prints," 166–72, and "Rituals of Reversal, Carnival and Fêtes," 172–82.

proclamation of the divine overthrow of earthly rulers (Luke 1:52) or the casting of woe upon the rich, happy, and well-thought-of (6:24-26).

Scott discusses the example of "world-upside-down" broadsheets of the sixteenth and early seventeenth centuries, which were popular for their depictions of a topsy-turvy world where children spanked parents, the poor gave alms to the rich, and the king walked on foot leading a peasant on horseback.[175] In addition to such statements and illustrations of inversion, we find another expression in festivals of role reversal like Carnival, Passover, and the Roman Saturnalia. During Saturnalia, for example, everyone wore the attire of a freedperson, enhancing the slaves' status and decreasing that of the citizens so that all were equal at least for a week.[176] Various contemporaneous reports indicate that masters and slaves dined together (sometimes with the master serving), that non-elites were allowed to freely criticize the ruling group, and even that slaves administered government and justice for a day or two.[177]

The innocuous interpretation of such ideas is that they are simply imaginative and playful, carried out for the sheer fun of fantasy, or that they allow social tensions to be vented in essentially harmless ways.[178] Robbins, for example, employs this latter argument in his socio-rhetorical reading of the Magnificat, in an attempt to show that Mary's song upholds the hierarchy of the status quo, rather than a different social order.[179] But the effort to which authorities generally go to suppress the dissemination of such ideas clearly argues against their harmlessness,[180] as do the riots and full-blown revolts that have begun at festivals of role reversal like Saturnalia,[181] Carnival,[182] or

175. Ibid., 167–72.

176. H. S. Versnel, *Transition and Reversal in Myth and Ritual: Inconsistencies in Greek and Roman Religion II*, Studies in Greek and Roman Religion 6 (Leiden: Brill, 1993), 158.

177. Ibid., 149–50. See also the extensive treatment of Saturnalia and its influence on non-elite entertainment throughout the year in Toner, *Popular Culture*, 93–122.

178. Scott, *Domination*, 167–68. Similar explanations were offered for festivals of role reversal such as the ancient Roman Saturnalia and Bona Dea festivals, and the Christian pre-Lenten Carnival. For a detailed treatment of the Roman festivals, see Versnel, *Transition and Reversal*, chapters 3 and 5, respectively.

179. Vernon K. Robbins, "Socio-Rhetorical Criticism: Mary, Elizabeth, and the Magnificat as a Test Case," in *The New Literary Criticism and the New Testament*, ed. Elizabeth Struthers Malbon and Edgar V. McKnight, JSNTSup 109 (Sheffield: Sheffield Academic Press, 1994), 199.

180. Scott, *Domination*, 168.

181. E.g., riots against Emperor Julian occurred when he visited Antioch during the Saturnalia celebrations. See the discussion in Toner, *Popular Culture*, 95–96.

182. E.g., the 1580 Carnival in Romans, France, in which the reversals proclaimed in a non-elite-sponsored procession were so threatening to the city rulers that they assassinated the non-elite leader and started a small civil war, a trend that continued for the next few centuries; and the fear of a Russian czar

Passover.[183] I would argue that the extensive effort to spiritualize the Lukan reversals (even by Christian interpreters from ancient to modern times) is another indicator of their potential power to effect social change.[184] The descriptive words used in them are often capable of either literal or spiritualized interpretation (for example, hunger for food or spiritual hunger, and the dual meaning of ἄφεσις as release from monetary debt and forgiveness of sins), and for that reason are well suited to the hidden transcript. The ambiguity would have allowed a threatened proclaimer of such status reversals to claim the less threatening meaning in a dangerous situation, while still retaining some measure of resistance in the face of power. If there were no real message of social change in these New Testament reversals, there would be no need for the passionate and often convoluted arguments for metaphorical and spiritualized interpretation undertaken by modern readers ensconced within today's status quo.[185]

IMPERIAL MODELS AND THE NEW TESTAMENT

The relevance of the work of Lenski, Kautsky, and other imperial theorists is already well established in the field of biblical scholarship, particularly for literature from the Roman era. Life in the first century was circumscribed and controlled by outside forces largely unspoken by the biblical writers and thus unfamiliar to the modern North American reader; it is therefore necessary to educate oneself in such intangible cultural assumptions in order to deepen understanding of the biblical text. In most ancient cities, for example, autocratic kings collected taxes and ruled with a small, select group of family and fellow

in 1861 of announcing unpopular new laws during the Carnival season. See the discussion in Scott, *Domination*, 179–81.

183. E.g., the Jerusalem crowd's anger at Archelaus's continuance of his father's oppressive, pro-Roman policies which led to a massacre of Passover pilgrims; and a mid-first-century Passover protest-turned-riot in reaction to the presence of disrespectful Roman soldiers in the temple, both related in Josephus's *Ant.* 17.204-7; 20.106-11. See the discussion in Richard A. Horsley, *Jesus and Empire: The Kingdom of God and the New World Disorder* (Minneapolis: Fortress Press, 2003), 46–47.

184. See my discussion in the introduction above.

185. Gary T. Meadors, e.g., argues that the term "poor" in the Lukan beatitudes actually refers to the pious, with the express purpose of making Luke fit into his own preconceived theological conclusions ("The 'Poor' in the Beatitudes of Matthew and Luke," *Grace Theological Journal* 6, no. 2 [1985]: 310). David Peter Seccombe, meanwhile, concludes that Luke followed Isaiah in equating the poor with Israel in an hour of need, and awkwardly attempts to argue that this is the implication of all Luke's references to the poor and needy (*Possessions and the Poor in Luke-Acts* [Linz: Studien zum Zeuen Testament und Seiner Umwelt, 1982], 39). This, for him, effectively eliminates any possible application to the literal poor and disadvantaged (16–17, 228).

elites; guilds limited competition and controlled pricing on most constructed goods; and elite patriarchal families dominated religion and social order.[186] This was the context that birthed most of the New Testament documents, with their proclamation of new economic interactions, a new definition of status and honor, and a new vision of what it meant to rule justly. Lenski's model of agrarian social stratification is still one of the best resources for understanding the cultural context of first-century Palestine and other regions ruled by the Roman Empire,[187] and is often reproduced and adapted for the biblical world.[188] The various social groupings of ruling elites, retainers, peasants, artisans, and degraded and expendables help organize biblical characters for modern readers, and Kautsky helps us understand how that elite 2 percent ruled everyone else so effectively for so long. Many an introduction to Rome's imperial system makes use of these two models,[189] and they have proven to be fruitful resources for any study interested in the historical and cultural context of the New Testament period.

Social-scientific biblical criticism specifically focused on Scott's model, on the other hand, is still in comparatively early stages. Brief references to *Weapons of the Weak, Domination and the Arts of Resistance*, or "hidden transcripts" appear with some frequency in works dealing with Jesus, Rome, and other dominant powers, but these are not systematic applications.[190] When Scott is put into intentional conversation with the New Testament, though, it has proven fertile ground for the study of both the Gospels and Paul's letters. I will survey a few essays on this topic in order to identify where the initial forays have been made and how further work, including this book, can expand and improve upon them. General conclusions about the presence of a hidden transcript in the New Testament will provide the foundation for the following chapters.

Focused research on Scott and New Testament literature most frequently addresses the earliest historical sources (Mark, Q, and the authentic Pauline epistles).[191] Richard A. Horsley states that documents such as Mark and Q are

---

186. Duling, "Empire," 56.

187. T. Raymond Hobbs, "The Political Jesus: Discipleship and Disengagement," in *The Social Setting of Jesus and the Gospels*, ed. Wolfgang Stegemann, Bruce J. Malina, and Gerd Theissen (Minneapolis: Fortress Press, 2002), 251.

188. See, e.g., a first-century Palestinian version of Lenski's chart, as constructed by Richard L. Rohrbaugh, in "Ethnocentrism and Historical Questions about Jesus," in Stegemann, Malina, and Theissen, *The Social Setting of Jesus and the Gospels*, 36.

189. E.g., Carter, *John and Empire*, 52–58; and Carter, *Matthew and Empire*, 9–19.

190. Greg Carey, "Symptoms of Resistance in the Book of Revelation," in *The Reality of Apocalypse: Rhetoric and Politics in the Book of Revelation*, ed. David L. Barr, SBLSymS 39 (Atlanta: Society of Biblical Literature, 2006), 169–80; Duling, "Empire," 70–73; and Horsley, *Jesus and Empire*, 114.

unusual in that they seem to preserve the hidden transcript itself, rather than merely remnants of it (as in Luke, in his view),[192] while Paul's letters, in his opinion, provide a window into the process of developing hidden resistance.[193] Scott helps to widen the lens of biblical scholarship beyond the religious and theological, and this is vitally important because religion and theology interact constantly with culture, politics, and economics. Domination occurred at all of these intertwined levels: the Jerusalem elite based in the temple, the Herodians and their supporters, and the magnates of Greco-Roman cities throughout Greece and Asia Minor (all three of which cooperated with Roman domination to maintain their own power and status).[194] Since Jesus and his followers had no access to official elite politics, we must look to the informal yet highly effective hidden transcript, and its advantageous connecting of religious, emotional, political, and material aspects of life under domination.[195]

The three essays on the Gospels in *Hidden Transcripts and the Arts of Resistance* (by Allen Dwight Callahan, William R. Herzog II, and Horsley himself) in general hold to the pattern of focusing on historical conditions in first-century Palestine, Markan pericopes, and historical Jesus research. Callahan's article, entitled "The Arts of Resistance in an Age of Revolt," exhibits considerable caution about the application of Scott's approach to the Gospels. Focusing on the various Jewish resistance movements and military uprisings around the turn of the Common Era, Callahan argues that the actions of Jesus and other popular prophets of the first century were not a matter of silent or hidden resistance, but open revolt against their Roman overlords.[196] While there were certainly public movements to resist the empire, they were not nearly as widespread as Callahan implies. Additionally, the existence of open rebellion does not negate the existence of hidden resistance. Indeed, Scott points out that the hidden transcript is what typically nourishes and undergirds non-elite public declarations and actions against the status quo.[197]

191. See, e.g., these two books edited by Richard A. Horsley: *Hidden Transcripts and the Arts of Resistance: Applying the Work of James C. Scott to Jesus and Paul*, SemeiaSt (Atlanta: Society of Biblical Literature, 2004); and *Oral Performance, Popular Tradition, and Hidden Transcript in Q*, SemeiaSt (Atlanta: Society of Biblical Literature, 2006).

192. Richard A. Horsley, "Introduction: Jesus, Paul, and the 'Arts of Resistance': Leaves from the Notebook of James C. Scott," in Horsley, *Hidden Transcripts*, 14.

193. Ibid., 19.

194. Ibid., 3–4.

195. Ibid., 21.

196. Allen Dwight Callahan, "The Arts of Resistance in an Age of Revolt," in Horsley, *Hidden Transcripts*, 39.

197. Scott, *Domination*, 207–12.

Herzog's essay, "Onstage and Offstage with Jesus of Nazareth: Public Transcripts, Hidden Transcripts, and Gospel Texts," examines two main components of the Synoptic tradition in light of Scott's work: stories about Jesus eating with tax collectors and sinners, and the question of whether it is lawful to pay taxes to the Roman emperor (Mark 12:13-17; cf. parallels in Matt. 22:15-22; Luke 20:20-26). In the case of the former, Herzog contrasts the Jerusalem elites' "great tradition" (by his definition, purity regulations from the Torah) to Jesus' acting out of the "little tradition" embraced by peasants.[198] The Pharisees are presented as retainers aligned with the ruling authorities and their oppressive great tradition, and as a table fellowship group that sought to keep temple-level purity regulations in their own everyday meals.[199] Jesus' own table practices, then, are viewed by the establishment as impure, but by the common people as inclusive. Herzog writes, "At table with outcasts, Jesus was acting out an alternative political vision for the renewal of Israel, which included the ingathering of those who were made outcasts by the elite reading of the great tradition."[200]

This interpretation of Jesus' table fellowship with sinners and tax collectors as a ritual of reversal is helpful in highlighting political and economic implications, along with theological ones, but the domination that is here resisted by Jesus has an even wider scope than Herzog allows. He focuses on the issue of Torah purity laws as a mainly religious question, and on the argument that the Jerusalem elites emphasized them in order to maximize the distance between elites who could afford to keep them and peasants who could not.[201] As Warren Carter notes in his response, however, Herzog does not give enough attention to Roman complicity in the Jerusalem elites' oppressive practices, or to the complexity of the great tradition beyond the purity laws.[202] The multiple references in the Synoptic Gospels to Jesus eating with "tax collectors and sinners" (Mark 2:16; Matt. 9:11; Luke 5:30; 15:1) or to his befriending them (Matt. 11:19; Luke 7:34) never invoke the purity codes, and scholars like Amy-Jill Levine[203] and Paula Fredriksen[204] have repeatedly and persuasively pointed

198. The terminology of great tradition and little tradition is related to and even roughly coordinated with the language of public and hidden transcripts.

199. William R. Herzog, "Onstage and Offstage with Jesus of Nazareth: Public Transcripts, Hidden Transcripts, and Gospel Texts," in Horsley, *Hidden Transcripts*, 44–45.

200. Ibid., 46.

201. Ibid., 43.

202. Warren Carter, "James C. Scott and New Testament Studies: A Response to Allen Callahan, William Herzog, and Richard Horsley," in Horsley, *Hidden Transcripts*, 86–87.

203. See, e.g., *The Misunderstood Jew: The Church and the Scandal of the Jewish Jesus* (New York: HarperCollins, 2006), 144–49.

out that applying these laws to Gospel texts is a problematic and unsupported reading of the social world of first-century Palestine. They argue that it is unclear how stringently, if at all, the centuries-old Levitical code was followed in the first century, and by how many people.

Jesus' practice of open table fellowship was indeed a ritual of reversal, as Herzog asserts, but the reversal expressed resistance to the larger situation of imperial colonization that rendered tax collectors as collaborators and many "sinners" as expendable people of low status and little concern. The table fellowship debate between Jesus and the Pharisees is not a matter of great tradition versus little tradition, but a conflict between different opinions on imperial negotiation and hidden transcripts. Both Jesus and the Pharisees were trying to figure out how best to form the identity of their people in the world of Roman domination, but they had differing ideas about how to go about that daunting task. Herzog himself points out that the Pharisaic emphasis on temple-level holiness in daily life was consistent with their status as a colonized people seeking to maintain their unique identity in one of the few areas of daily life where they could still exert control.[205] This suggests a group seeking refuge from domination in old traditions, rather than one dedicated wholeheartedly to the status quo of the Roman-allied Jerusalem elites—although it must also be remembered that as retainers, the Pharisees likely had some level of vested interest in perpetuating the system.[206] Jesus' vision of the hidden transcript in Luke, on the other hand, resists multiple types of domination, even the status divisions that often occur within the subordinate groups themselves.[207] His followers are to open their communities willingly to all persons subordinated to Rome, even if they have placed themselves outside the pale of traditional non-elite society, and he wants the Pharisees also to embrace this vision of resistance.

Herzog's application of hidden resistance is more compelling in his discussion of the second pericope, Mark 12:13-17. He recognizes that this text not only probes the relationship between civic and religious duties, but also represents an attempt at lethal political entrapment; the Herodians and Pharisees are trying to goad Jesus into revealing the hidden transcript that chafes at paying taxes to Rome and its elite allies.[208] Herzog's addition of the hidden transcript model to the more commonly applied honor-shame dynamic enhances and deepens what is at stake in this question.[209] The denarius coin

---

204. "Did Jesus Oppose the Purity Laws?" *BRev* 11, no. 3 (June 1995): 18–25, 42–47.

205. Herzog, "Onstage and Offstage," 45.

206. Scott, *Domination*, 27n13.

207. Ibid., 26.

208. Herzog, "Onstage and Offstage," 52.

portrayed the emperor as the divine ruler and high priest; its payment in the Roman tribute tax was regarded by some first-century Jews as collaboration with Rome. It was certainly idolatrous in its proclamation of another god besides Yahweh, and significantly, it is found in the possession not of Jesus but of his elite questioners, marking them as complicit in Roman domination.[210] Jesus, in the role of trickster folk hero, must answer their question while somehow both proclaiming his resistance to elite domination and escaping punishment; otherwise he will either betray his beliefs and his God or openly identify himself as a dissident. The Markan Jesus does this with a simple antithetical aphorism stating that the idolatrous coin should be given back to Caesar, but in reality the things that truly matter belong to God and are given to God. This coded message of resistance does not keep the peasants from paying the tax, but it does allow them to view it as a defiant self-cleansing of idolatrous Roman domination, instead of as acquiescence to their subordination.[211]

The final Gospel essay in *Hidden Transcripts and the Arts of Resistance*, by Richard Horsley, is entitled "The Politics of Disguise and Public Declaration of the Hidden Transcript: Broadening Our Approach to the Historical Jesus with Scott's 'Arts of Resistance' Theory." It takes a wide-angle view of hidden resistance in Mark and Q, the earliest sources detailing Jesus' teaching and actions. For Horsley, the work of Scott is instrumental in demonstrating how Jesus could be a "figure fully engaged in political-religious conflict" without leading an actual military revolt.[212] He identifies in the Gospels three of Scott's four techniques for addressing a situation of domination: cultivating the hidden transcript in private, implying it in public through anonymity and disguise, and declaring it in the face of power (i.e., at the Jerusalem temple event).[213] Jesus began his work in relatively safe places, teaching and healing in fields, villages, and the synagogue, but eventually his reputation spread. Horsley notes that Scott's treatment of rumors coheres with the Gospels' portrayal of Jesus' message of the liberating reign of God and its resonance with the hidden transcripts of the Galilean and Judean peasantry. Jesus' mission "resembles other

---

209. For analysis of the pericope using the honor-shame lens, see, e.g., Bruce J. Malina and Richard L. Rohrbaugh, *Social-Science Commentary on the Synoptic Gospels*, 2nd ed. (Minneapolis: Fortress Press, 2003), 198–201.

210. Herzog, "Onstage and Offstage," 54–55.

211. Ibid., 58–59.

212. Richard A. Horsley, "The Politics of Disguise and Public Declaration of the Hidden Transcript: Broadening Our Approach to the Historical Jesus with Scott's 'Arts of Resistance' Theory," in Horsley, *Hidden Transcripts*, 62–63.

213. Ibid., 63. I would add that Jesus also demonstrates the fourth kind not mentioned here, appealing to the public transcript; see the above discussion of Scott's model.

peasant movements that spread through rumor, movements where subordinated peoples' long-suppressed yearning for liberation that had been cultivated in their hidden transcript suddenly, in response to a rumor or a prophet's promise and miraculous actions, bursts forth in rapidly spreading collective anticipation that the hour of deliverance is at hand."[214] For Horsley, this coherence also lends some historical credibility to Mark's version of events.[215]

The only specific pericopes on which Horlsey focuses are the Q/Luke version of Jesus' Sermon on the Plain, particularly the beatitudes and woes, as a renewal of the Mosaic covenant (Luke 6:17-49),[216] and most importantly in his reading, Jesus' direct confrontation of the Jerusalem temple system during Passover week (Mark 11:15-19; Matt. 21:12-17; Luke 19:45-48; John 2:13-25). I agree with Horsley that this is probably the most blatant and explicit resistance to the status quo recorded in the Gospels. It was a public symbolic action carried out during a politically charged festival; Passover celebrated the freedom of the Israelites, but it was also a public ritual of subordination to the Jerusalem elites who controlled the Temple, and to the Roman conquerors who controlled them.[217] Although Horsley goes too far in arguing that this direct confrontation is what made Jesus' teaching and social renewal into a lasting movement,[218] it was certainly a defining moment of Jesus' ministry and a declaration of a well-formed or "cooked" (in Scott's terminology) hidden transcript, "not an impulsive expression of blind fury but a measured symbolic action and a formal prophetic pronouncement."[219] Horsley gives only passing attention, however, to the fact that the account of this and other events in Jesus' life is refracted through the lens of each individual evangelist, and that the symbolism of the temple incident has therefore been well processed and "cooked" in varying ways by several different communities. This insight has great potential to deepen our understanding of the ways in which Jesus' hidden transcript resonated with the resistance techniques and philosophies of his later followers.

The respondents to the essays in *Hidden Transcripts and the Arts of Resistance*, Warren Carter (the Gospels) and Susan M. Elliott (Pauline literature), offer important observations and cautions about the application of Scott's model to New Testament literature. One of Carter's most significant points is that the Gospel-focused studies do not go very far, if at all, beyond the level of

214. Ibid., 71.
215. Ibid., 73.
216. Ibid., 67.
217. Ibid., 74–76.
218. Ibid., 73.
219. Ibid., 78.

Jesus himself and the earliest sources. The imperial world, however, is clearly still present during the composition of Matthew, Luke, and John, and, as the somewhat later book of Revelation amply demonstrates with its anti-imperial and imperially imitative rhetoric, the passage of time does not necessarily yield subordinate compliance.[220] Another aspect of the model of hidden resistance that needs further attention from biblical scholars is the strong social pressure for conformity even among members of the non-elite subordinate groups. Carter demonstrates that the reign of God, as presented in some pericopes in the Gospels, is at times just as demanding of compliance with its hidden transcript as the Roman Empire is with its public transcript.[221] This is a nuance that needs to be considered carefully.

Elliott also makes some important points that will be engaged throughout this study. Chief among these is her assertion that a variety of hidden transcripts are espoused by different groups of non-elites; some of these might even advocate forgiveness and transcendence as the best way to deal with domination.[222] Her point is well taken. Competing hidden transcripts are likely preserved within the same biblical book, and perhaps even espoused, approved of, and engaged by the same community of Jesus-followers. Finally, Elliott issues some important cautions: (1) Scott's work is preliminary and general, and thus must be evaluated carefully in each context;[223] (2) interpreters need to distinguish between actual resistance and simple anger or resentment, and between resistant behaviors that are helpful and those that are potentially self-destructive; and (3) it is incumbent upon every interpreter to decipher the hidden transcript that actually exists within the text, rather than trying to make the resistance discerned in New Testament writings conform to our own ideas about how one should react to domination and oppression.[224]

These essays and the critical responses of Carter and Elliott have laid out various connections between Jesus, the Gospels, and the imperial negotiation techniques of the hidden transcript; and their conclusions will undergird our more focused study of the Gospel of Luke. But we will also move beyond them, to the level of Luke's author and audience. The prominence of the "Great Reversal" theme in the New Testament—and its use by the third evangelist

220. Carter, "James C. Scott," 91.

221. Carter, "James C. Scott," 85.

222. Susan M. Elliott, "Hidden Transcripts and Arts of Resistance in Paul's Letters: A Response," in Horsley, *Hidden Transcripts*, 168.

223. Dennis Duling also notes that the generality of Scott's macrocomparative theory must be balanced by careful contextual specificity ("Empire," 73).

224. Elliott, "Hidden Transcripts," 169–70.

in particular—is well documented in scholarship.[225] But its role in turning the status quo on its head has been overlooked, explained away, or denied for too long. In the following chapters, I will build upon the groundwork laid here to elucidate the place of specifically Lukan status reversals in the Gospel narrative and the way in which such social upheavals might have been heard and understood by first-century readers and hearers from all levels of imperial society.

225. See, e.g., Allen Verhey, *The Great Reversal: Ethics and the New Testament* (Grand Rapids: Eerdmans, 1984); and John O. York, *The Last Shall Be First: The Rhetoric of Reversal in Luke*, JSNTSup 46 (Sheffield: Sheffield Academic Press, 1991).

2

The Context of Luke and His Reading Communities

The author and setting of the Gospel of Luke have been, over the years, notoriously difficult to place. There is general agreement that the author was Hellenistic and urban, but beyond that most discussions of Lukan context tend to conclude with statements such as the following: "As for the place of the composition of the Lucan Gospel, it is really anyone's guess. . . . In the long run, it is a matter of little concern, because the interpretation of the Lucan Gospel and Acts does not depend on it."[1] While I acknowledge the imprecise nature of this search and lack of clear evidence for a specific locale, I cannot agree with Joseph Fitzmyer that it is immaterial to our study of Luke-Acts. On the contrary, for this project the early settings in which the Third Gospel was written, and even more importantly, heard and read, will be central to our understanding of what the status reversals might have meant to those first audiences. Luke, like all biblical narratives, is a "cultural product . . . a representation of the values and contexts within which it was generated," which both reflects and challenges the world of its composition.[2] The hierarchy and system of domination that characterized Roman rule colored every part of daily life, including the writing and reception of New Testament literature, and the placement of its readers and writers within the imperial provinces and their status groups will deepen our understanding of the text by clarifying something of its import in such a context.

Certainly there are limits to the search for a Gospel community.[3] But even small insights into the character and context of author or audience, when

---

1. Joseph A. Fitzmyer, *The Gospel According to Luke I–IX*, AB 28 (Garden City, NY: Doubleday, 1981), 57.

2. Joel B. Green, *The Gospel of Luke*, NICNT, ed. Gordon D. Fee (Grand Rapids: Eerdmans, 1997), 11–12.

coupled with historical inquiry, have great potential for illuminating the text. We will begin with a few significant textual clues that point to Luke's own contextual assumptions. In several passages, rural Palestinian situations are adapted for urban Hellenistic ears: for example, the turf roof of Mark 2:4 becomes a tile one in Luke 5:19, and house foundations replace rock and sand in the parable of the wise and foolish builders (Luke 6:48-49; cf. Matt. 7:24-27). Additionally, a change of Semitic titles to their Greco-Roman counterparts (e.g., ῥαββουνί in Mark 10:51 to κύριος in Luke 18:41; and γραμματεύς in Mark 12:28 to νομικός in Luke 10:25) is another indication of Luke's Hellenistic setting, although it need not indicate a solely Gentile audience, as Fitzmyer argues.[4]

These characteristics strongly imply a context in non–Palestinian, Greek-speaking cities, but that does not negate the possibility of a significant Jewish presence. Archaeological evidence from synagogues in Asia Minor shows a high degree of assimilation among Hellenistic Jews, from a predominance of the Greek language in their names and everyday dealings to Greek-style education, awards, and official titles.[5] Luke's affinity for and familiarity with city settings is confirmed by the centrality of Jerusalem in both the Gospel and Acts, and the urban focus of the Acts mission narrative. Luke-Acts contains by far the most uses of the word πόλις (city) in the New Testament, as much as the rest of the books combined.[6] But no single city can really be identified as a likely setting for Luke-Acts's origination on the basis of the biblical text alone.

Later extracanonical sources attempted to fill this gap and offer some answers. The earliest copy of the full Gospel (late second or early third century) attributes it to Luke, usually thought to be the physician mentioned as Paul's companion in Col. 4:14 (cf. Philem. 24 and 2 Tim. 4:11). An ancient prologue, dated to either the third or the second century CE,[7] further identifies Luke as a native of Syrian Antioch who wrote the Gospel "in the regions of Achaea."

---

3. See, e.g., the arguments in Luke Timothy Johnson, "On Finding the Lukan Community: A Cautious Cautionary Essay," in *SBLSP 1979*, vol. 1, ed. Paul J. Achtemeier (Missoula, MT: Scholars, 1979), 87–100.

4. Fitzmyer, *Luke I–IX*, 58–59. A similar conclusion is drawn, without specific support, by Luke Timothy Johnson, *The Gospel of Luke*, SP 3, ed. Daniel J. Harrington (Collegeville, MN: Liturgical, 1991), 3.

5. See the discussion in Margaret Williams, "Jews and Jewish Communities in the Roman Empire," in *Experiencing Rome: Culture, Identity, and Power in the Roman Empire*, ed. Janet Huskinson (London: Routledge, 2000), 316–22.

6. Richard L. Rohrbaugh, "The Pre-Industrial City in Luke-Acts: Urban Social Relations," in *The Social World of Luke-Acts*, ed. Jerome H. Neyrey (Peabody, MA: Hendrickson, 1991), 125. See also 129–37 for his sociological understanding of the preindustrial urban system.

Other cities with a proposed Lukan connection include Ephesus,[8] Philippi,[9] and other Macedonian locales.[10] Obviously, this is not a puzzle that we can solve with any certainty, but even the general context of a city in Roman-controlled Greece or Asia Minor, when examined in some detail, is helpful. It is possible to identify some "'typical' aspects of urban life in a Greco-Roman city" and glean some insight into Luke and Acts.[11] Many scholars argue that Luke was writing for an audience wider than a single community of Jesus-followers.[12] Whatever he intended, it is certain that Luke's work did indeed circulate widely among Greek-speaking Christians, and thus it becomes vital for us to consider how the surrounding culture influenced what they read and heard. Among other aspects of the Gospel of Luke, the status reversals on which I am focusing illustrate that the author had a keen awareness of and interest in the constant status competition that characterized the daily lives of both himself and his audience. My goal in this chapter, then, is to elaborate upon the Gospel's Hellenistic milieu and its author's and audiences' experience within it.

THE GOSPEL OF LUKE IN THE HELLENISTIC CITIES

Roman domination in the Greek East was, in many ways, a different experience than it was in other provinces or in Italy itself. Many of the city-states there were involved with Rome in some fashion well before Augustus and the establishment of the empire, through support of one side or another in Rome's civil wars, and often to the Hellenistic city's detriment. For example, Pompey, Brutus, Cassius, and Mark Antony all demanded money and troops from the cities of Asia Minor;[13] Corinth was destroyed by Roman forces in 146 BCE;[14]

7. See, respectively, R. Alan Culpepper, "The Gospel of Luke: Introduction, Commentary, and Reflections," in *NIB*, ed. Leander E. Keck, vol. 9 (Nashville: Abingdon, 1995), 6–7, referencing R. G. Heard; and Fitzmyer, *Luke I–IX*, 38–39.

8. Culpepper, "Gospel of Luke," 9.

9. John Nolland, *Luke 1–9:20*, WBC 35a (Dallas: Word, 1989), xxxix.

10. François Bovon, *Luke 1: A Commentary on the Gospel of Luke 1:1—9:50*, trans. Christine M. Thomas, Hermeneia, ed. Helmut Koester (Minneapolis: Fortress Press, 2002), 8–9.

11. Halvor Moxnes, "The Social Context of Luke's Community," in *Gospel Interpretation: Narrative-Critical and Social-Scientific Approaches*, ed. Jack Dean Kingsbury (Harrisburg, PA: Trinity, 1997), 168.

12. See, e.g., Stephen C. Barton, "Can We Identify the Gospel Audiences?" in *The Gospels for All Christians: Rethinking the Gospel Audiences*, ed. Richard Bauckham (Grand Rapids: Eerdmans, 1998), 187; Johnson, "On Finding," 91; and John K. Riches, "The Synoptic Evangelists and Their Communities," in *Christian Beginnings: Word and Community from Jesus to Post-Apostolic Times*, ed. Jürgen Becker (Louisville: Westminster John Knox, 1993), 233–34, both of whom base this conclusion on the presence and content of the prologue; and Johnson, *Gospel of Luke*, 3, because of the length and complexity of Luke-Acts.

and Athens suffered a significant loss in prestige and wealth when it supported Antony in his losing battle with Octavian.[15] One scholar goes so far as to classify the Greek East as "bankrupt" at the end of Rome's civil wars.[16] But Octavian, later Emperor Augustus, expended a considerable amount of effort and resources to secure the support of local Hellenistic elites through patronage, debt cancellation, and other financial aid. In 20 BCE, for example, after an inspection of the province of Asia, he issued monetary gifts to cities in need of aid, although at the same time he increased the tribute owed by others.[17] Augustus also outlawed extortion by his provincial procurators and other administrators, according to Cassius Dio.[18] He is hailed by an Ephesian inscription as "a god made manifest and the common savior of human life."[19] In a similar manner, Strabo writes that Augustus's successor Tiberius aided the Asian city "Sardis and many others" after they suffered extensive earthquake damage.[20]

Thus by Luke's time the *pax romana* had proved to be quite beneficial to the prosperity of the area[21]—or at least to that of its elites, whose privileged position now required significant cooperation with imperial rule. The Roman Empire's policy of minimal provincial government meant that they would happily help the local nobles maintain their power and control of city governance, as long as the Greek leaders accepted and advanced Rome's rule over them.[22] The ready compliance of Hellenistic city magistrates meant that Asia Minor was one of the most peaceful areas of the Roman Empire, with a minimal military presence and relatively little imperial intervention into city life and politics.[23] The local elites seemed to accept and even promote the domination of Rome's "peace" in order to preserve the stability of their political and economic system.[24] As a

---

13. Paul Trebilco, "Asia," in *The Book of Acts in Its Graeco-Roman Setting*, ed. David W. J. Gill and Conrad Gempf, *The Book of Acts in Its First Century Setting* (Grand Rapids: Eerdmans, 1994), 296–97.

14. David W. J. Gill, "Achaia," in Gill and Gempf, *The Book of Acts in Its Graeco-Roman Setting*, 448.

15. Ibid., 441.

16. Anthony D. Macro, "The Cities of Asia Minor under the Roman Imperium," in *ANRW* 2.7.2, ed. Hildegard Temporini and Wolfgang Haase (Berlin: Walter de Gruyter, 1980), 659–60.

17. Trebilco, "Asia," 297–98.

18. *Hist. rom.* 53.15.4–6.

19. Quoted in Warren Carter, *John and Empire: Initial Explorations* (London: T&T Clark, 2008), 59.

20. *Geog.* 13.2.8. See also Trebilco, "Asia," 298.

21. Trebilco, "Asia," 299–300.

22. Macro, "Cities of Asia Minor," 661.

23. Christopher Kelly, *The Roman Empire: A Very Short Introduction* (Oxford: Oxford University Press, 2006), 44–47.

24. Lorna Hardwick, "Concepts of Peace," in Huskinson, *Experiencing Rome*, 349–50.

result, they would have been the face of power most directly seen, and therefore resented, by the non-elites, but they also would have been a group in position to extend patronage to any new social and religious movement if they so chose. This, then, is the world into which Luke was taking his message of a new savior inaugurating a new world order; little wonder that there was a need for Jesus-followers to exhibit both a degree of circumspection in declaring such a gospel and a cautious willingness to work within the system for at least a time.

Underneath the apparently peaceful, stable surface of the Greek East, though, things were, as always, more complicated than it would seem at first glance. Social hierarchy and its attendant status negotiation were constantly present in the daily lives of those under Roman rule, from the lowest peasant to the emperor himself,[25] and this competition flourished in the cities of Asia Minor. Pliny the Younger famously wrote of a banquet where the host divided his guests by status and served them food and wine of varying quality, as he deemed appropriate to each attendee's place in the social hierarchy.[26] Pliny himself was scornful of this practice, but other contemporaneous writings would suggest that it was not uncommon (for example, Juvenal, *Sat.* 5.24–155; Martial, *Epigr.* 9.2). Valerie Hope writes that "by using both publicly acknowledged social and legal factors and his own more personal criteria the host was able to create his own social hierarchy which was given physical expression at the dinner table."[27] Publicly, seats in the amphitheater were also distributed according to social status, and even certain types of clothing were restricted to the elites.[28]

Non-elites, with low status and few resources with which to increase it, competed mostly with one another for status and honor, finding some measure of satisfaction in at least having more than their neighbors. The acceptance of a "limited good society" in which one person's gain or good fortune meant someone else's loss or bad fortune likely motivated such a tensive environment. One mark of this competition is the prevalence of curses invoked upon one's social competitors in an attempt to curb a run of a good luck that was deemed "more than their fair share."[29] We also find evidence of

25. Valerie Hope, "Status and Identity in the Roman World," in Huskinson, *Experiencing Rome*, 127, 150. See also the treatment of Roman social hierarchy in Peter Garnsey and Richard Saller, *The Roman Empire: Economy, Society and Culture* (Berkeley: University of California Press, 1987), 107–25.

26. *Ep.* 2.6, as quoted in Hope, "Status and Identity," 125.

27. Hope, "Status and Identity," 128.

28. Ibid., 126. See also Kelly, *Roman Empire*, 79–80. He gives the example that in the Roman Colosseum, 60 percent of the fifty thousand seats were given to the well-off, 20 percent to the urban poor, non-citizens, and slaves, with the remaining 20 percent at the very top allowed to women (80).

people attempting to portray an image of higher status than they actually possessed. Martial writes of non-elites sitting in seats reserved for lower elites,[30] and Pliny the Elder notes that slaves and freedpersons sometimes wore gold-plated iron rings in an attempt to convey equestrian status.[31] Elites, meanwhile, fought amongst themselves for ruling power, government offices, imperial favor, and public honor. Rome effectively utilized this tensive system to cement its rule through the enthusiastic participation of local elites; they went to great lengths to outdo one another in proving their affinity for all things Roman and honoring this new overlord, and in the process they helped legitimize their own subordination.[32]

This phenomenon of status competition also moved beyond individuals to the cities themselves, which had a hierarchy of their own, with Rome and provincial capitals at the top, followed by Roman colonies, self-governing cities, and lower-ranked towns.[33] Citizens of Hellenistic cities in particular tended to exhibit great civic pride and a burning desire to present their city as superior to all others. The competition for preeminence among the Asian cities of Ephesus, Smyrna, and Pergamum is preserved in Dio Chysostom's exhortations for them to view one another with goodwill rather than as competitors for superiority.[34] Ramsey MacMullen gives as a further example graffiti from a tavern in southern Italy proclaiming Pergamum as the "golden city," with another "competitively patriotic hand" maintaining that Rome deserved that title instead.[35] In such an environment of constant competition and self-promotion, Luke's teachings about humbling oneself (14:7-11; 18:9-14) and about giving and lending without reciprocation (6:27-36) become quite interesting to consider. To many in the audience, they likely seemed perplexing and even discordant. At the same time, however, some Hellenistic hearers might have welcomed or at least been intrigued by the prospect of a break from the constant struggle in which persons of all social levels were

29. Jerry Toner, *Popular Culture in Ancient Rome* (Cambridge, MA: Polity, 2009), 14–15.

30. *Epigr.* 5.8, 14.

31. *Hist. nat.* 33.6.23. See further Hope, "Status and Identity," 149–50.

32. Garnsey and Saller, *Roman Empire*, 33; and S. R. F. Price, *Rituals and Power: The Roman Imperial Cult in Asia Minor* (Cambridge: Cambridge University Press, 1984), 62.

33. Phil Perkins and Lisa Nevett, "Urbanism and Urbanization in the Roman World," in Huskinson, *Experiencing Rome*, 215.

34. *Or.* 34.48. See also Trebilco, "Asia," 33.

35. Ramsay MacMullen, *Roman Social Relations: 50 B.C. to A.D. 284* (New Haven: Yale University Press, 1974), 60.

Plutarch and his readers did; the message of the Third Gospel offered them a unique identity, distinct from all that dictated value and shame in the imperial order. For the residents of Asia Minor and Greece in particular, "being ruled by Rome was a complex experience that created ambiguity in the articulation of that experience," and thus we should not be surprised when we find (as we often do) visions of destruction or social upheaval alongside messages of appeasement or collaboration.[47]

Much of this power, identity, and status negotiation played out in the arena of the imperial cult, which was widespread in the provinces of Greece and Asia Minor, where we have situated the Gospel of Luke. Thus a brief consideration of its role in the lives of people and cities is in order. The imperial cult is often considered in biblical studies to have been worship of the emperor, and thus an essentially religious matter, but this is only partly true. It is better characterized as a multifaceted power negotiation that affected the interdependent areas of politics, economics, and social relations just as much as it did religion; one author calls it "a matter of hotly contested social prestige."[48] Roman religion in general focused on the rituals of prayer and sacrifice to establish contact and a type of patron-client relationship between deities and mortals, in which the gods receive honor and their human clients receive divine favor in return.[49] It was a community affair as much as or more than an individual undertaking, at least as far as the imperial government was concerned: "Public religion was . . . the sum of the rituals employed by public representatives to maintain good relations between the community and its gods."[50] The imperial cult, then, was not focused on personal worship of a particular living emperor, but rather on communal loyalty to the image of the emperor as symbolic of the whole concept of the Roman Empire and its divine right to rule. This perspective clarifies the enormity of a Christian's decision on whether to participate in imperial religion, and the far-reaching consequences of such a decision.[51]

In Asia Minor, imperial worship was particularly widespread and well entrenched. Pergamum, apparently on its own initiative, established an imperial temple dedicated to Augustus as early as 29 BCE, immediately after Octavian's

47. Toner, *Popular Culture*, 187.

48. Kelly, *Roman Empire*, 28. He goes on to note that "religious imagery and religious language were an inseparable part of Roman political vocabulary" (30).

49. James Rives, "Religion in the Roman Empire," in Huskinson, *Experiencing Rome*, 247, 258.

50. Ibid., 253.

51. The commands in 2 Pet. 2:13-17 to accept all human authorities and to honor the emperor suggest that some Christians did, in fact, participate in the imperial cult without feeling that it compromised their belief in Jesus. See also Rom. 13:1-7 and Rev. 2:14-15, 20.

victory over Antony,[52] and it eventually became the center of Asia Minor's provincial cult, to which all cities sent offerings and representatives. Such a level of cultic organization, higher than the standard municipal efforts, was unique to the Asian provinces, and illustrates the local elites' interest in the imperial cult and the high level of social prestige it garnered in their value system.[53] The chief priest of this provincial cult served a year-long term, but carried the high honor associated with the office for the rest of his life.[54] After this early beginning in Pergamum, local elites made imperial worship a central part of their status competition and endowed temples, statues, offerings, and festivals at an impressive rate. The provincial assembly of Asia, for example, utilized the imperial cult as part of its negotiation with Rome; in 9 BCE they changed the local calendar so that the year began on Augustus's birthday.[55] More than eighty imperial sanctuaries and temples are archaeologically attested in over sixty cities of Asia Minor. Ephesus alone had four temples, imperial statues in multiple public buildings and in the streets, fountains and gates dedicated to imperial dynasties, and various other altars, porticos, and gymnasia associated with one imperial family member or another.[56] The priests of such sanctuaries were among the most prominent figures in the Hellenistic cities, and their presence and status brought honor to both themselves and the city as a whole.[57]

We must be cautious, however, in assuming that this enthusiastic endorsement of imperial worship meant a wholehearted acceptance of the emperor's divinity and Rome's god-given superiority. Recent, more nuanced study of the literary, sociological, and archaeological evidence indicates instead that imperial worship was one among many methods that the Hellenistic cities used to make sense of their subjugation to Rome. The worship of living emperors "could provide a language for comprehending absolute power. . . .

---

52. Garnsey and Saller, *Roman Empire*, 164–65.

53. Perkins and Nevett, "Urbanism and Urbanization," 219; Price, *Rituals and Power*, 56; and Rives, "Religion," 266.

54. Macro, "Cities of Asia Minor," 681–82.

55. Carter, *John and Empire*, 60.

56. Price, *Rituals and Power*, 135–36. Colin Miller rightly notes that not all of these can be dated to the first century CE, when the New Testament authors were writing (Colin Miller, "The Imperial Cult in the Pauline Cities of Asia Minor and Greece," *CBQ* 72 [2010]: 316–19). The evidence, however, is likely more extensive for Luke's time in the 80s or later, than for Paul's time (which is his specific focus). Additionally, his repeated argument that the presence of other deities in Pauline cities makes the imperial cult "marginal" (316, 323, 325, 331) overreaches. Certainly the imperial family was not worshipped exclusively in the polytheistic cities of Greece and Asia Minor, but that does not entirely neutralize its influence. A lack of personal devotion (321) says nothing about the imperial cult's sociopolitical import.

57. Price, *Rituals and Power*, 62–63.

To worship a god offered local grandees a way of recognizing their inferiority without any loss of face."[58] It must also be remembered that the flourishing imperial cult did nothing to diminish worship of beloved local deities, such as Artemis of Ephesus. This goddess was central to the city's identity, and its citizens claimed great honor and pride in how widely she was worshipped and how famous her temple was. An inscription from the second century CE states that "with the improvement of the honouring of the goddess, our city will remain more illustrious and more blessed for all time."[59] Indeed, Roman rulers were often linked with traditional local deities, rulers, and legends, through festal processions, art, and architecture, in an attempt to soften the blow of Roman rule and also to assert some continued relevance and prestige for the subjugated city's gods and therefore for the city itself.[60] Examples from first-century Ephesian architecture include a peristyle celebrating the cults of Artemis (the local patron goddess) and Augustus (the new representative of Roman order), and a Basilika Stoa dedicated to Artemis, Augustus, Tiberius, and the city of Ephesus itself.[61]

As is evident in the discussion above, much of our information about the Greek and Asian provinces, and about the empire as a whole, necessarily comes from an elite perspective. It is simply the nature of the field, due to the available literary and archaeological evidence. But the vast majority of the people in Ephesus, Philippi, or Aphrodisias were not elites; they were artisans, peasants, merchants, soldiers, and slaves. They were also not, as elite rhetoric often implied, an undifferentiated mass.[62] The "poor" (all non-elites) of the Greco-Roman world covered a wide range of occupations, economic levels, and political status and influence. For this reason, I make reference throughout the following chapters to the seven levels of the Roman-era Poverty Scale (PS) established by Steven J. Friesen,[63] and modified by Bruce W. Longenecker

58. Kelly, *Roman Empire*, 30. Interestingly, several decades earlier, Price made a similar argument for the origination of ruler cults in Asia Minor: that they were the Greek citizens' way of coming to terms with domination by an external power (*Rituals and Power*, 29–30).

59. Trebilco, "Asia," 327. See further 236–48.

60. Perkins and Nevett, "Urbanism and Urbanization," 219–20; and Kelly, *Roman Empire*, 23–26, who describes in some detail the examples of an elaborate Ephesian procession and certain marble porticos in Aphrodisias, both donated by local aristocratic patrons and both entwining their city's Greek origin myths with Roman imperial imagery.

61. For these and other examples, see Carter, *John and Empire*, 60–64.

62. Bruce W. Longenecker, *Remember the Poor: Paul, Poverty, and the Greco-Roman World* (Grand Rapids: Eerdmans, 2010), 43.

63. Steven J. Friesen, "Poverty in Pauline Studies: Beyond the So-Called New Consensus," *JSNT* 26 (2004): 323–61.

as an Economy Scale (ES).[64] Friesen first divided the superwealthy elites into three categories (PS1–3), and the much more numerous non-elites into four categories (PS4–7) ranging from the relatively rare level of one with moderate surplus resources (PS4) to the unfortunately large number of individuals living below subsistence level (PS7). He then attempted to estimate the percentage of each level in a typical Roman city (defined as ten thousand or more people).[65]

PS1	Imperial elites	imperial dynasty, Roman senatorial families, a few retainers, local royalty, a few freedpersons
PS2	Regional or provincial elites	equestrian families, provincial officials, some retainers, some decurial families, some freedpersons, some retired military officers
PS3	Municipal elites	most decurial families, wealthy men and women who do not hold office, some freedpersons, some retainers, some veterans, some merchants
PS4	Moderate surplus resources	some merchants, some traders, some freedpersons, some artisans (especially those who employ others), and military veterans
PS5	Stable near-subsistence level (with reasonable hope of remaining above the minimum level to sustain life)	many merchants and traders, regular wage earners, artisans, large shop owners, freedpersons, some farm families
PS6	At subsistence level (and often below minimum level to sustain life)	small farm families, laborers (skilled and unskilled), artisans (esp. those employed by others), wage earners, most merchants and traders, small shop/tavern owners
PS7	Below subsistence level	some farm families, unattached widows, orphans, beggars, disabled, unskilled day laborers, prisoners

Figure 2: Friesen's Poverty Scale for the Roman Empire

64. Bruce W. Longenecker, "Exposing the Economic Middle: A Revised Economy Scale for the Study of Early Urban Christianity," *JSNT* 31 (2009): 243–78; and Longenecker, *Remember the Poor.*

65. Friesen, "Poverty," 340–41.

Longenecker strongly supports Friesen's gradated scale and its valuable nuancing work, but adjusts the proposed percentages for the non-elite groups of ES4–7. He argues convincingly that Friesen's estimate of only 7 percent of the typical urban population belonging to the level 4 "middling" group is much too low, due to the erroneous binary understanding of the poor as a massive undifferentiated group.[66] Individuals with moderate resources would also have congregated in urban areas, providing even more reason to consider a higher rather than lower estimate of their numbers.[67] Thus I will follow here the 2010 revised percentages of Longenecker's Economy Scale (cited with Friesen's original Poverty Scale numbers for reference):[68]

Friesen's 2004 Urban Percentages	Longenecker's 2010 Revised Urban Percentages
PS1–3: 3%	ES1–3: 3%
PS4: 7%	ES4: 15%
PS5: 22%	ES5: 27%
PS6: 40%	ES6: 30%
PS7: 28%	ES7: 25%

Figure 3: Comparison of Friesen's Poverty Scale and Longenecker's Economy Scale

Friesen and Longenecker are both working with the urban Pauline communities of Jesus-followers in view, as is Wayne A. Meeks in his book on a related topic, *The First Urban Christians*. Considering Luke's very similar setting in the urban centers of Asia Minor and Greece, the Economy Scale will be invaluable in helping us identify with more precision the Lukan characters, author, readers, and hearers. Meeks has argued that the Pauline groups usually comprised "a fair cross-section of urban society," with particular prominence given to members with some measure of status inconsistency.[69] Friesen and

66. Longenecker, *Remember the Poor*, 45, 320.

67. Ibid., 51. For the extended discussion supporting Longenecker's revised estimates, see 317–32; and Longenecker, "Exposing," 251–64.

68. Longenecker, *Remember the Poor*, 52–53. Longenecker does, however, delineate a few cautions about his increased percentage on the middling group, ES4. It was not a middle class as we would think of it today, due to the members' lack of status and wealth security. Additionally, the presence of a larger middling group does not in any way negate the massive poverty and economic exploitation inherent in the imperial world, nor does it necessarily increase the number of Jesus-followers with an ES4-level surplus (56–57). Cf. Friesen, "Poverty," 341–47.

69. Wayne A. Meeks, *The First Urban Christians: The Social World of the Apostle Paul*, 2nd ed. (New Haven: Yale University Press, 2003), 72–73. He remains uncommitted on whether those with high status inconsistency were attracted to Christianity in larger than usual numbers, or whether they gravitated

Longenecker both acknowledge the presence of some ES4 members in Pauline communities, based on the sparse information we have on named individuals in the letters such as Erastus (Rom. 16:23), Phoebe (Rom. 16:1-2), and Gaius (Rom. 16:23; 1 Cor. 1:14).[70] But they agree, against Meeks, that there is little indication of even lower elites in the Jesus-followers addressed by Paul. Paul himself was an itinerant artisan, no higher than ES5,[71] and Longenecker notes that Paul's repeated instruction to his readers to work with their own hands (for example, 1 Cor. 4:11-13; 1 Thess. 4:11-12) indicates an audience of individuals mostly living near subsistence level (ES5–6).[72] First Corinthians 11:22, with its reference to the literal "have-nots" (τοὺς μὴ ἔχοντας), also indicates the clear presence of ES7 individuals among the Corinthian Jesus-followers.[73]

With regard to the Lukan groups of Jesus-followers, we can posit with relative confidence a comparable community makeup, characterized by a mixture, somewhat unusual for the time, of various ethnicities, occupations, religious backgrounds, levels of wealth, citizenship, and status. Asia Minor in particular, with its complex layering of cultures both Roman and Hellenistic, native and imported, elite and non-elite, provided a rich diversity in its communities,[74] and this is reflected in the work of Luke and its potential influence upon its audiences. In the second section of this chapter, I will first explore the pieces of information we can glean about the relationships and social connections of the third evangelist and the Gospel's dedicatee Theophilus. Then I will widen the focus to consider a few salient characteristics of artisan culture and the relationships between elites and non-elites, as they relate to social, political, and religious negotiation of the imperial world.

Social Diversity in the Reading Communities of Luke

The prefaces to Luke (1:1-4) and Acts (1:1-2) provide a starting point for our discussion of the Lukan communities, as they identify at least two members of them: the dedicatee Theophilus and the anonymous author. Loveday

---

toward leadership positions and thus were more visible in the community, and thus more likely to receive literary mention. There has been some critique of Meeks's use of the modern idea of status inconsistency; see, e.g., Rohrbaugh, "Pre-Industrial City," 127–28. But even in Roman classical studies, status inconsistency has proven to be a useful and accurate category for analysis; see Hope, "Status and Identity," 146–50.

70. Friesen, "Poverty," 348–57; Longenecker, *Remember the Poor*, 236–46.

71. Friesen, "Poverty," 350.

72. Longenecker, *Remember the Poor*, 253–58.

73. Friesen, "Poverty," 349; Longenecker, *Remember the Poor*, 256–57.

74. Huskinson, "Élite Culture," 108.

Alexander's 1993 work *The Preface to Luke's Gospel* argues that Luke 1:1-4 finds its closest parallels in Greco-Roman scientific and technical writings (like those of the physician Galen, among others), not classical historiography or biography (the usual comparisons). The evangelist's style, she concludes, is "literate but not literary" and establishes a connection between Luke's Gospel and rabbinic schools, medical instruction, and the artisans' apprenticeship system.[75] He was educated, to be sure, in the standard written Greek of official and technical documents,[76] and evidently had leisure to undertake an extensive two-volume writing project. But his main heroes, the carpenter Jesus and the leather-worker Paul, are certainly not elite and would hardly have interested most aristocratic readers.[77] Also, it would be inaccurate to picture Luke as a professional author similar to Virgil or Plutarch, who were both members of the middle or lower elite (ES2–3). As a member of a new socioreligious movement with at least some values counter to the prevailing Roman propaganda, Luke's sociopolitical situation was far messier and more uncertain than any faced by the aristocratic writers even of the Second Sophistic.[78] Thus we can cautiously posit that Luke had status similar to that of a relatively well-off artisan (mostly likely ES5, perhaps the lowest end of ES4): a non-elite with a measure of wealth, social connection, and education, and likely considered by himself and others to be a peer and full community member alongside the mostly non-elite audience of Jesus-followers.[79] Incidentally, this conclusion fits well with the traditional identification of Luke as a physician, although it certainly does not provide conclusive proof.[80]

Theophilus, of course, is the other mysterious character in the preface, the one to whom the Third Gospel was dedicated and also perhaps its patron. The meaning of his name, "lover of God," has symbolic significance, and thus could be posited as "represent[ing] a wider Gentile-Christian readership."[81] It seems most likely, however, that he was indeed a real person of at least some

75. Loveday Alexander, *The Preface to Luke's Gospel: Literary Convention and Social Context in Luke 1.1-4 and Acts 1.1*, SNTSMS 78, ed. Margaret E. Thrall (Cambridge: Cambridge University Press, 1993), 210–11.

76. Ibid., 170–71.

77. Ibid., 177.

78. Milton Moreland, "The Jerusalem Community in Acts: Mythmaking and the Sociorhetorical Function of a Lukan Setting," in *Contextualizing Acts: Lukan Narrative and Greco-Roman Discourse*, ed. Todd Penner and Caroline Vander Stichele, SBLSymS (Atlanta: Society of Biblical Literature, 2003), 294–95.

79. Green, *Gospel of Luke*, 35–36.

80. Alexander, *Preface*, 174, 177.

81. Johnson, *Gospel of Luke*, 28.

acquaintance with Luke. Publication of written works in the first century was accomplished almost entirely through social networks: elite circles; patron-client relationships; technical schools; and family, friends, and business associates.[82] The main purpose of dedication within a preface seems to have been the opportunity to reach a wider audience through various means. It was "linked very often with a desire to 'fix' a fluid tradition by depositing a definite form of the text in the care (and probably in the library) of a patron."[83] Not only would a work in this way be preserved for future reference and copying, but the patron could also provide a space for public performance and discussion of the work and introduce the author into his or her various networks of acquaintance. There is no indication that the dedicatee was ever assumed to be the only intended reader.[84]

The κράτιστος (most excellent) title given to Theophilus (1:3) was commonly used for Roman and local elites, but it could also be honorary, particularly in dedications of this type; such a writing might be dedicated to a son, a peer, a colleague, a courtier, or even the emperor.[85] Thus we are rightly cautioned against easy assumptions. But considering the above information, I would argue that Theophilus was of a different and probably higher social status than Luke, at the upper end of ES4 or the lower end of ES3. As a local elite or an ES4 individual with relatively high status and an economic surplus, his knowledge, promotion, and recommendation of the Gospel would be most effective in reaching many circles that the artisan Luke alone could not. I am also in agreement with Alexander that he was already a follower of Jesus, likely a member and benefactor of a house church who could offer Luke both a library in which to deposit his book and a venue for further oral teaching about the Way.[86] If Theophilus was acting in this way as a patron for Luke's work, there is some irony in employing a hierarchical patron-client relationship, standard practice in the imperial social system, in order to preserve and publicize a writing in which subversive status reversals play such a central role. As Longenecker notes, the upper echelons of ES4 almost certainly shared with the elites "a commitment to the enhancement of the civic environment that the Roman imperial order cultivated . . . [and] play[ed] a critical role in oiling the civic mechanisms of the Greco-Roman world."[87] Thus Theophilus,

---

82. Loveday Alexander, "Ancient Book Production and the Circulation of the Gospels," in Bauckham, *The Gospels for All Christians*, 99–100.

83. Ibid., 103.

84. Ibid., 98, 104; and Alexander, *Preface*, 57.

85. Alexander, *Preface*, 188–90; and Green, *Gospel of Luke*, 44–45.

86. Alexander, *Preface*, 192, 198.

in supporting Luke's work, was making a significant break with the commonly held views of his status and economic group.

So even considering only the evangelist Luke and the dedicatee Theophilus, we have represented already two different statuses and social groups. The community itself was probably an expanded version of this small sample of diversity. I have argued above that Luke was likely someone with the status and resources of a stable, moderately successful artisan, and his heroes Jesus and Paul were craftspeople as well. No doubt many members of the early Christian gatherings in Asia Minor would have easily identified with such characters, developed as they were using a popular novelistic style, by an author who experienced that life alongside his fellow artisans. Luke, along with many other New Testament authors, showed a higher than usual respect for manual labor and the pride many craftspeople took in their work.[88] Elites generally looked down on the need to work physically for a living, and thus would not understand such pride in an artisanal craft.[89] Cicero's writings indicate that he regarded physical labor as coarsening to the body and the mind.[90] In another example, the honor and credit from a sculpture donated to the city went to the patron who paid for the work, rather than the individual artist, who was seldom even mentioned.[91] But archaeological evidence has revealed that the opposite was true for those who actually did work with their hands, as mention of the deceased's trade or occupation is a frequent feature on non-elite grave markers. Inscriptions from Rome, for example, reveal localized clusters of different craftspeople such as engravers, goldsmiths, tailors, and clothing sellers. MacMullen writes of these graves, "City-dwellers in surprising number specify on their tombstones both their occupation and the place where they pursue it, in the form 'So-and-so, butcher on the Viminal.'"[92]

This pride in one's workmanship is likely another indicator of the artisan-level status of both the author and audience of the Third Gospel. Vernon Robbins, in fact, argues that Luke-Acts presents Christian activity as a type of artisanal work that is "embedded in a way of life in the eastern Roman

---

87. Longenecker, *Remember the Poor*, 332.

88. Alexander, *Preface*, 185.

89. John H. Kautsky, *The Politics of Aristocratic Empires* (Chapel Hill: University of North Carolina Press, 1982), 345.

90. *Off.* 1.150. See also MacMullen, *Roman Social Relations*, 114–15.

91. Huskinson, "Élite Culture," 117–18. She observes that very few artists from the Roman imperial period are named or recorded in any way. One example that is known is a negative one: Zenodorus, the sculptor of the infamous colossus of Nero (Pliny the Elder, *Hist. nat.* 34.18).

92. MacMullen, *Roman Social Relations*, 70.

empire," emphasizing the setting of holy work not in the temple alone, but in the common household and its mundane everyday life.[93] This can be seen, for example, in John the Baptist, the priest's son who performs the redemptive work of the temple in the middle of the wilderness (Luke 3:1-20), and in Jesus' teaching and healing work, which takes place from its earliest days in synagogues (4:16-30, 31-37, 42-44) and in the humble homes of non-elites (4:38-41).[94] Thus it seems clear that Luke would have been a document that resonated with the many in Christian gatherings who were part of ES5-6, what was sometimes called the "good" or "honest" poor,[95] those able to survive at or just above subsistence level through a trade or steady employment—an existence that avoided the immediate threat of destitution, but one immensely far away from the extravagant wealth of the elite.

The local non-elite artisans, merchants, and craftspeople were not alone in the communities that read Luke's text. It is possible that the Gospel's audiences also included at least a few ES4 and lower ES3 members who could provide meeting places, food, money, and other resources for worship, and could assist the lowest status members who lacked even the bare necessities (ES7). Certainly Luke includes in his narratives various reflections on the proper use of wealth and status (Luke 12:13-21; 14:7-24; 16:1-31; 18:18-30; see also Acts 2:43-47; 4:32-37) and several stories of Jesus' and the disciples' relationships with the wealthy and powerful (Luke 7:1-10; 8:1-3, 40-56; 19:1-10; see also Acts 8:26-40; 10:1-48; 16:11-15; 17:4, 12). Paul Bemile concludes from the diverse Lukan material on poverty and wealth "that Luke is addressing a very complex audience with different social and political conditions."[96] F. Gerald Downing pictures, imaginatively but not without some historical basis, a dinner setting for the reading of Luke-Acts, with a mixed audience of men, women, children, slaves, citizens, and freedpersons: people of varying status, social location, and life experience.[97] Halvor Moxnes draws a similar conclusion: "Within the city culture of the Eastern Mediterranean, we can envisage Luke's community as a

93. Vernon K. Robbins, "Luke-Acts: A Mixed Population Seeks a Home in the Roman Empire," in *Images of Empire*, ed. Loveday Alexander, JSOTSup 122 (Sheffield: Sheffield Academic Press, 1991), 213.

94. Ibid., 213–15. See also John H. Elliott, "Temple versus Household in Luke-Acts: A Contrast in Social Institutions," in *The Social World of Luke-Acts*, ed. Jerome H. Neyrey (Peabody, MA: Hendrickson, 1991), 211–40.

95. C. R. Whittaker, "The Poor," in *The Romans*, ed. Andrea Giardina (Chicago: University of Chicago Press, 1993), 279–80.

96. Paul Bemile, *The Magnificat within the Context and Framework of Lukan Theology: An Exegetical Theological Study of Luke 1:46-55*, RST 34 (Frankfurt: Peter Lang, 1986), 201.

97. F. Gerald Downing, "Theophilus's First Reading of Luke-Acts," in *Luke's Literary Achievement: Collected Essays*, ed. C. M. Tuckett, JSNTSup (Sheffield: Sheffield Academic Press, 1995), 94–95.

group of nonelite persons who are culturally and ethnically mixed but who also include among them some who come from the elite periphery."[98]

And the diversity did not stop there. In the first-century Roman Empire, including the cities of Asia Minor, there was a significant increase in social dislocation from trading, slavery, and military resettlement, leading people of various ethnicities to seek new social groups to replace those left behind in their homeland.[99] Undoubtedly some found their new "families" in the urban communities of Jesus-followers, as did Jesus' disciples who left their families and occupations behind (Luke 5:1-11; cf. 11:27-28; 14:25-33). And even though these communities were urban, there was likely some rural presence as well, both from the displacement already mentioned and from regular interaction between city and country. Many rural villages and areas in the Greek East were connected to a particular city and considered to be a part of its economic, political, and religious life.[100] The exchange of food between rural providers and urban consumers meant that the residents of cities, villages, and towns likely interacted on a more frequent basis than is usually posited.[101] Dealing with such a pluralistic context was no doubt a significant challenge for the early Christian communities, and one that the Gospel of Luke was well situated to address.[102]

When we consider how the Gospel would be read in this pluralistic context, one of its most striking characteristics is the many challenges that it presents to a variety of social groups and their closely held assumptions. In imperial agrarian economies, little of the elite affluence that increased so dramatically under Roman rule trickled down to the non-elites. The elites learned the correct level of taxation that allowed peasant survival and maximum production, but also maximum profit for themselves.[103] This state of affairs led to a steady undercurrent, and occasional eruption, of resentment toward the local elites. Pliny the Younger and Emperor Trajan, for example, exchanged letters about the tendency of non-elite associations and *collegia* to become politically active, and about the unrest caused by such groups in the Bithynian cities of

---

98. Moxnes, "Social Context," 174.

99. Moreland, "Jerusalem Community," 300.

100. Garnsey and Saller, *Roman Empire*, 28.

101. Jim Grimshaw, "Luke's Market Exchange District: Decentering Luke's Rich Urban Center," *Semeia* 86 (1999): 40. In this article, Grimshaw makes a solid case for social interaction between city and country, based on the exchange of food. I am, however, less convinced by his conclusions that Luke had no desire for economic restructuring or status reversal, merely a slightly more just hierarchy (46–47).

102. Johnson, *Gospel of Luke*, 9. Although Johnson defines "pluralistic" mainly as a mixture of Gentile and Jew, I think his observation about Luke's function in a nonhomogeneous community is insightful.

103. Kautsky, *Politics*, 105–6. Only the rare case of an exceptionally productive year has the chance of increasing the peasant's standard of living (108).

Nicea and Nicomedeia (*Ep.* 42–43).[104] Yet Luke encouraged all followers of Jesus to live in community with one another, regardless of their status (for example, 7:36-50; 10:25-37; 15:1-32; 19:1-10; cf. Acts 2:42-47; 4:32-37).

The evangelist also questioned prevailing elite and non-elite notions about benefaction (for example, Luke 6:27-36; 14:7-24; 22:24-27). Although some biblical scholars claim that Lukan charity is really nothing more than conventional Greco-Roman euergetism and patron-client relationships,[105] what the Gospel and Acts actually undertake is a comprehensive redefinition of the concept. The benefactors in civic euergetism were generally individuals from ES4 and above, and the recipients at ES5 and above. The proposed Christian charity practices, conversely, call for those from ES4–5 to share with beneficiaries from ES6–7 (people ignored by typical Greco-Roman benefaction).[106] A Hellenistic elite would not have seen his or her gifts to the city and its residents as philanthropic or charitable in our modern understanding of the concepts; the benefaction was utilitarian, yet another way to use one's wealth to gain honor, prestige, and the power of political office.[107] It was also generally given more often and more liberally to the "good" poor who were thought to be deserving, certainly not to the destitute members of ES7 like widows, beggars, foreigners, orphans, and those with physical disabilities.[108] But Jesus, as portrayed by Luke, acted to help representatives of these very groups and restore them to community as part of his ongoing mission and that of his followers (Luke 6:6-11; 7:11-17; 8:26-39, 40-56; 13:10-17; 14:1-6; 21:1-4). He also advocated a sharing of possessions that seeks the good of those less fortunate rather than the advancement of one's reputation, and that purposefully avoids public recognition and honor as much as possible (for example, 14:12-24).

Some of Luke's sharpest challenges, however, are reserved for the evangelist's own peers, non-elites of ES5–6 such as artisans and farmers. For one thing, they are called upon to participate in this new form of benefaction, or communal charity, as much as the elites are (Luke 6:27-36). Such mutual participation in Christian "benefaction" might have seemed unduly taxing to a group that was fiercely protective of what little wealth or status they had gathered for themselves. Non-elites under Roman domination would likely have been inclined to face their world and its complex problems with a trust in their own individual cunning over community aid, as exhibited in non-elites

---

104. Macro, "Cities of Asia Minor," 690–91.

105. Downing, "Theophilus's First Reading," 105; and Riches, "Synoptic Evangelists," 237.

106. Longenecker, "Exposing," 271.

107. Macro, "Cities of Asia Minor," 684–85.

108. Whittaker, "The Poor," 295, 298.

seeking magical solutions in the form of both blessings on themselves and curses on their neighbors and in their general view of all resources as limited goods, and therefore something for which they must compete.[109] Another possible negotiation technique for peasants and artisans was to turn responsibility and blame over to those with more status and resources available to address the issue (that is, their ruling elites). In times of hardship, non-elites commonly expressed their clear dissatisfaction with elite patrons' failure to provide grain, olive oil, and even entertainment, through urban riots.[110]

Luke, however, as indicated above and as will be demonstrated further in the following chapters, encouraged all members of the Christian communities, no matter their status, to take an active role in improving their own quality of life, and that of their peers and of anyone with fewer resources than themselves. Some of the ES5–6 artisans who made up the bulk of the early urban churches would possibly have been resistant to Luke's vision of an upside-down social order. The poorest of the poor, on the other hand, were often willing to take risks, for they had nothing to lose and everything to gain; the richest were also willing, as they could lose much and still have plenty. Tacitus noted this tendency to recklessness in a letter from Tiberius to the Senate, wherein the emperor urges caution and self-control on both the very poor and the very rich, for the good of the whole empire.[111] The "good" poor, though, might have been more hesitant to embrace unorthodox leanings, as the status quo gave them at least a few patronage benefits and limited financial security.[112]

Perhaps some of the best examples of this non-elite dedication to and mimicry of the status quo are the *collegia*, trade guilds, and other associations that provided those who could afford to join them with an imitation of elite honor and power. The poorest were kept out by membership fees, thereby creating hierarchy among the dominated. The individuals with more resources who could and did join received elite patronage, reserved seats in the city amphitheater, and festival days on the official municipal calendar: all markers of elite-approved "worth."[113] In some respects, these *collegia* had certain similarities to early Christian gatherings, such as a strong sense of kinship often symbolized by a sacred ritual of table fellowship.[114] But in their primary values, the vast

---

109. Toner, *Popular Culture*, 11–15.

110. Paula James, "The Language of Dissent," in Huskinson, *Experiencing Rome*, 298–99.

111. *Ann.* 3.54, referenced in Toner, *Popular Culture*, 13.

112. Whittaker, "The Poor," 298.

113. MacMullen, *Roman Social Relations*, 76; and Whittaker, "The Poor," 297–98.

114. MacMullen, *Roman Social Relations*, 77.

differences between associations and early Christian groups assert themselves most clearly. Ramsay MacMullen identifies the major aims of *collegia* thus:

> What is interesting about crafts associations . . . is the focusing of their energies on the pursuit of honor rather than of economic advantage. . . . They cared a lot more about prestige, which the members as individuals could not ordinarily hope to gain but which, within a subdivision of their city, competing with their peers, they could deal out according to a more modest scale of attainments.[115]

The members of these *collegia* clearly showed a strong desire to imitate elite culture and values in miniature, requiring monetary fees to join, seeking public status through monuments and elite patronage, and arranging the guild membership in a strict hierarchy of offices and rankings.[116] The challenge regarding benefaction and honor-seeking addressed by Jesus and Luke to such non-elite groups would actually be quite similar to that posed to the elites: the replacement of public honor and status competition as one's primary value and motivator. Along with the poorest of the poor and the richest of the elite, Luke, as we shall see in chapters 3–5, entreats his fellows in the artisan group, through visions of status reversal and acts of justice and mercy, to transform their priorities and participate in the formation of communities that adhere to God's values rather than to those of Rome.

Conclusion

In this chapter, I have argued that the historical and social context of the earliest audiences of the Gospel of Luke is critical to achieving a deep and nuanced understanding of the narrative's effect upon these reading communities. I surveyed the complexities and ambiguities of life in the Hellenistic cities of Greece and Asia Minor, and the social diversity that seems to have been present specifically in the gatherings of Jesus-followers. This latter fact is particularly significant in the following chapters of this project, which study the three focal pericopes and their images of status reversal. In the diverse communities that Luke was addressing, the ramifications of these subversive texts must have been complex and multivalent, depending upon the particular ethnic, social, religious, or economic group (or groups) with which one identified. Thus with

---

115. Ibid., 76–77.
116. Ibid., 74–75; and Whittaker, "The Poor," 287, 297.

this foundational and contextual work in mind, let us proceed to consider our first text of status reversal, the Magnificat (Luke 1:46-55).

3

Mary, the Magnificat, and the Powers That Be

The Magnificat, or Mary's song, found in Luke 1:46-55, is the first of several poetic or hymnic texts in the birth narratives of the Third Gospel.[1] It is among the most widely studied pericopes in Luke, and a well-beloved staple in the musical repertoire of many Christian traditions. It has also, however, been a favorite rallying cry of revolutionary and dissident groups throughout history, such as the medieval Peasant Revolt,[2] communist-leaning farm workers in Central America,[3] and the urban poor in Peru.[4] Paul Bemile, in his extensive monograph on the Magnificat and its place in the Gospel of Luke, calls this text "the hermeneutical key to the interpretation of Luke's two-volume work."[5] This is the focus of our first foray into the status reversals of the Gospel of Luke.

In this poem, a pregnant Mary offers a song of praise to God after being received by Elizabeth, who honors Mary as the mother of her Lord (Luke 1:43) and proclaims her both εὐλογημένη and μακαρία (1:42, 45). In the first half of the song (1:46-49), Mary exalts God as her σωτήρ, Savior (a title frequently given to Augustus and later emperors[6]) and ὁ δυνατός, the Mighty One (an occasional title for God in the Divine Warrior tradition, e.g., Zeph. 3:17; Ps.

---

1. Portions of my argument in this chapter are also found in Amanda C. Miller, "A Different Kind of Victory: 4Q427 7 I–II and the Magnificat as Later Developments of the Hebrew Victory Song," in *What Does Scripture Say?: Studies in the Function of Scripture in Early Judaism and Christianity*, ed. Craig A. Evans and H. Daniel Zacharias (London: T&T Clark, 2012), 192–211.

2. David Flusser, *Judaism and the Origins of Christianity* (Jerusalem: Magnes, 1988), 131–32.

3. Ernesto Cardenal, *The Gospel in Solentiname*, trans. Donald D. Walsh, rev. ed. (Maryknoll, NY: Orbis, 2007), 15–19.

4. Robert McAfee Brown, *Unexpected News: Reading the Bible with Third World Eyes* (Philadelphia: Westminster, 1984), 84–85.

5. Paul Bemile, *The Magnificat within the Context and Framework of Lukan Theology: An Exegetical Theological Study of Luke 1:46-55*, RST 34 (Frankfurt: Peter Lang, 1986), 168.

44:4-6 [ET 45:3-5]).[7] Specifically, God has executed a reversal on her behalf; she who acknowledges her own lowliness (ταπείνωσις) and her status as a slave (δούλη) is now blessed (μακαριοῦσίν) by all generations (Luke 1:48). If the song stopped there, it would not pose quite the same problem for those who regard Luke as a supporter of the Roman status quo. But Mary does not stop; instead, verse 50 reorients the song from Mary's individual situation toward the divine mercy given to all those who show God fear and reverence. She not only expresses her joy at the gracious love of God, but also addresses that love's implications for liberation and politics.[8] The following verses reveal a God of stark reversals with a strong preference for the hungry and humble, and a bias against the rich and powerful rulers:

> He carried out strength with his arm;
>> he scattered the arrogant because of the thoughts of their hearts.
> He threw down rulers from thrones,
>> and lifted up lowly ones.
> Hungry ones he filled with good things,
>> and rich ones he sent out empty. (Luke 1:51-53)

Herein lies the real problem. How are we to understand Luke's choosing to include a vision of God deposing rulers and upending social hierarchy in a work that is supposed to be conciliatory to Rome and its culture? Conzelmann ignores Luke 1–2 completely,[9] assuming them to be outside the original Gospel (a theory that is much less widely accepted today). In a similarly dismissive manner, Werner H. Kelber acknowledges the poem's possible subversiveness, but simply regards it as an exception, something that Luke allowed to slip into his Gospel but does not really espouse.[10] It seems highly unlikely, though, that

---

6. Gary Gilbert, "Roman Propaganda and Christian Identity in the Worldview of Luke-Acts," in *Contextualizing Acts: Lukan Narrative and Greco-Roman Discourse*, ed. Todd Penner and Caroline Vander Stichele, SBLSymS (Atlanta: Society of Biblical Literature, 2003), 237–39. The Priene inscriptions, e.g., praise Augustus as the Savior "who has made war to cease and who shall put everything in peaceful order" (240).

7. Stephen Farris, *The Hymns of Luke's Infancy Narratives: Their Origin, Meaning, and Significance*, JSNTSup 9 (Sheffield: JSOT Press, 1985), 119; and Douglas Jones, "The Background and Character of the Lukan Psalms," *JTS* 19 (1968): 23.

8. Gustavo Gutiérrez, *A Theology of Liberation: History, Politics, and Salvation*, trans. Caridad Inda and John Eagleson, rev. ed. (Maryknoll, NY: Orbis, 1988), 120.

9. E.g., he begins his survey of Lukan geography with John the Baptist's adult ministry in Luke 3, eliminating the Bethlehem and Jerusalem scenes; see Hans Conzelmann, *The Theology of St. Luke*, trans. Geoffrey Buswell (London: Faber and Faber, 1960), 19.

an author consciously striving to be careful and compose an orderly narrative (Luke 1:1-4) would be satisfied with such a final product. J. Massyngberde Ford argues that the Magnificat, and the infancy narratives as a whole, came from a non-Lukan source that has been included only as a contrast to Jesus' entirely new view of loving one's enemies.[11] But it makes little sense that Luke would portray characters like Zechariah, Elizabeth, Mary, Simeon, and Anna so positively if he actually disagreed with their theology and hopes. These explanations that advocate separating the Magnificat and other reversal texts from the larger context of Luke or minimize their legitimacy do a great disservice to the whole of Luke-Acts and fail to embrace the complexities of its perspective.

Raymond Brown also separates the birth narratives from the rest of the Gospel, although to a lesser degree than Ford, by attributing them to a hypothetical Jewish group called the *Anawim*. This group, he argues, developed the idea that the small "true remnant" of Israel could be saved only by piety, faithfulness, and utter dependence on none but God; thus their material poverty, while present, is not as important as their attitude of humility before God.[12] This interpretation has reinforced the tendency in Western Christianity to spiritualize these reversals as being symbolic or metaphorical rather than literal.[13] This debate was discussed at greater length in the introduction of this study, so here I will simply reiterate that while there are indeed examples from early Jewish literature of a spiritualized understanding of the poor and lowly, the wider Lukan literary context for the Magnificat strongly supports the argument for a literal understanding of its status reversals.

The rich in verse 53 of the song are contrasted not with the spiritualized poor, but with the hungry (a condition of physical need), and in the rest of the Gospel Jesus tends to act out reversal principles very literally by healing the sick (as in Luke 4:38-41; 5:12-26; 6:6-11; 8:40-56; 18:35-43), helping the poor and exhorting his listeners to do the same (as in 4:11-17; 6:20-49; 16:19-31;

10. Werner H. Kelber, "Roman Imperialism and Early Christian Scribality," in *Orality, Literacy, and Colonialism in Antiquity*, ed. Jonathan A. Draper, SemeiaSt (Atlanta: Society of Biblical Literature, 2004), 144.

11. J. Massyngberde Ford, *My Enemy Is My Guest: Jesus and Violence in Luke* (Maryknoll, NY: Orbis, 1984), 28.

12. Raymond E. Brown, *The Birth of the Messiah: A Commentary on the Infancy Narratives in the Gospels of Matthew and Luke*, new updated ed. (New York: Doubleday, 1993), 351–53.

13. See, e.g., David Peter Seccombe, *Possessions and the Poor in Luke-Acts* (Linz: Studien zum Neuen Testament und Seiner Umwelt, 1982), 71–83. Cf. Gary T. Meadors, "The 'Poor' in the Beatitudes of Matthew and Luke," *Grace Theological Journal* 6 no. 2 (1985): 305–14, which presents a similar argument about the Lukan beatitudes and woes.

18:18-30), and incorporating those of low status back into community (as in 7:36-50; 8:26-39; 13:10-17; 14:7-24; 19:1-10). The portrayal of the earliest communities of Christ followers in Acts 2–4 also offers a concrete example of the Magnificat's vision for the reign of God, where distinctions of poor and rich are eliminated.[14]

The main problem with spiritualizing interpretations of Mary's song and other texts of status reversal is that it imposes on the text a false dichotomy that separates body from soul, social and political from religious, in a way that is not faithful to the text or its cultural environment—significantly, a cultural environment in which the vast majority of the people lived in varying degrees of poverty. A better explanation must be sought, one that approaches the Magnificat and related reversal pericopes as vital considerations in the Gospel of Luke.

On the other end of the spiritual-literal spectrum, no one is more attuned to the liberating implications of Mary's song than those actively engaged in struggling against their current situation of economic, political, ethnic, or spiritual subjugation. Groups as diverse as Western feminists and Latin American *campesinos* have recognized in this text a revolutionary strain that has inspired their own visions. Their insights need to be noted, and noted well, by those of us who live more comfortably with our surrounding culture and thus seek to explain away that revolutionary strain. As we proceed in our study of the Magnificat and its potential to encourage resistant negotiation of the reality of empire, the voices of people who experience comparable domination in our own time must be considered. Theologian Dorothee Sölle, for example, in the following poem reinterprets Mary's words in light of the feminist movement:

> It is written that mary said
> he hath shewed strength with his arm
> he hath scattered the proud
> he hath put down the mighty from their seats
> and exalted them of low degree
> Today we express that differently
> we shall dispossess our owners and we shall laugh
> at those who claim to understand feminine nature
> the rule of males over females will end
> objects will become subjects
> they will achieve their own better right[15]

14. Bemile, *Magnificat*, 196–98.

Even more striking are the readings of Latin American and African interpreters, from farmers and laborers to theologians and professors. They read out of their own oppressive situations, from what Leonardo Boff calls "a privileged hermeneutical locus for the reading of Mary's Magnificat and for becoming hearers of its message."[16] Such readers have perspectives that are much closer to the first-century experiences of a Galilean peasant or an urban artisan of Asia Minor than anything most Western scholars like myself can even imagine. One source of such discussions is Ernesto Cardenal's transcription of the Sabbath conversations of the Solentiname congregation in Nicaragua. Regarding the Magnificat, their conclusions are clear; in the words of a woman named Andrea, "[Mary] recognizes liberation. . . . We have to do the same thing. Liberation is from sin, that is, from selfishness, from injustice, from misery, from ignorance—from everything that's oppressive. That liberation is in our wombs too, it seems to me."[17] Especially intriguing for our study is these "uneducated" and "unofficial" interpreters' grasp of nuance, even in their most revolutionary ideas. In a discussion about whether "the proud" automatically equates to "the rich," some argue that even a poor person can become "an exploiter in his heart" if she or he yearns to be rich and acts in a correspondingly exploitative manner.[18] Others regard God's humbling of the arrogant, rich, and powerful as an act of liberation not only for the lowly, poor, and powerless whom they oppress, but also for the arrogant, rich, and powerful; the exploiters must be liberated, according to Solentiname resident Olivia, "from their wealth. Because they're more slaves than we are."[19]

Of course, not all non-Western interpreters speak with the same voice, even when under similar conditions of domination. Ghanaian scholar Paul

---

15. Dorothee Sölle, *Revolutionary Patience*, trans. Rita Kimber and Robert Kimber (Maryknoll, NY: Orbis, 1977), 52.

16. Leonardo Boff, *The Maternal Face of God: The Feminine and Its Religious Expressions*, trans. Robert R. Barr and John W. Diercksmeir (San Francisco: Harper & Row, 1987), 190.

17. Cardenal, *Gospel in Solentiname*, 16.

18. Ibid., 17–18.

19. Ibid., 9. A similar idea is expressed by Boff, *Maternal Face*, 199: "God flings the proud of heart to earth, in the hope that they will be converted, delivered from their ridiculous vaunting and flaunting, to become free and obedient children of God and brothers and sisters to others. . . . God's method of offering them salvation is to topple them from their positions of power." And from the point of view of one who is comparatively wealthy and privileged: "To the degree that I stand in the way of liberation I must be challenged—by the oppressed and by God. But to the degree that I can begin, in however timid ways, to be used by God in a liberating process initially so threatening to folks like me, I too am liberated" (Robert McAfee Brown, *Unexpected News*, 16).

Bemile clearly understands the texts of status reversal in the Gospel of Luke as concrete and liberating for the poor and lowly. But he concludes his extensive study of the Magnificat with a strong critique of Latin American liberation theologians who, in his opinion, take its reversal message too far, namely into the realms of violence, revolution, and class warfare.[20] Bemile reads the Magnificat solely as a celebration of *God's* action in carrying out reversal and salvation for those who are, like Mary, sufficiently humble to receive it.[21] This is a far different reading from, for example, this sentiment from Gustavo Gutiérrez: "The future of history belongs to the poor and exploited. True liberation will be the work of the oppressed themselves; in them, the Lord saves history."[22] We are well reminded, then, that the work of imperial negotiation and the development of dominated people's hidden transcripts, both today and in the time of Jesus and Luke, are part of a complex process with many different facets and opinions. It is with this in the forefront of our mind that we now approach the text of the Magnificat and its images of status reversal.

It should be noted as we begin that Vernon K. Robbins applied his version of socio-rhetorical criticism (on which my method is based) to the Magnificat in the essay "Socio-Rhetorical Criticism: Mary, Elizabeth and the Magnificat as a Test Case." Through the methodological modifications I have made and through different intertextual and sociocultural comparisons, however, we come to quite divergent conclusions. Whereas he focuses his intertextual study on Mary's ταπείνωσις and that word family's connection with humiliated virgins in the Hebrew Bible,[23] I explore instead, in my first sphere of inquiry, the tradition of songs of victory and reversal in the Hebrew Bible, the Apocrypha, and Greco-Roman literature. Similarly, Robbins employs the sect typology of Bryan Wilson and the social-scientific models of kinship, honor and shame, and limited good to illumine the text's social and cultural context.[24] I focus my second section on James C. Scott's model of hidden transcripts of resistance, supplemented by Lenski, Kautsky, and various works from the field of Roman studies. I will then conclude with a consideration of the Magnificat's relationship to the rest of Luke-Acts and especially its ramifications and reverberations among Luke's earliest audiences in the cities of Greece and Asia

---

20. Bemile, *Magnificat*, 239–40.

21. Ibid., 240–41.

22. Gutiérrez, *Theology of Liberation*, 120.

23. Vernon K. Robbins, "Socio-Rhetorical Criticism: Mary, Elizabeth, and the Magnificat as a Test Case," in *The New Literary Criticism and the New Testament*, ed. Elizabeth Struthers Malbon and Edgar V. McKnight, JSNTSup 109 (Sheffield: Sheffield Academic Press, 1994), 182–85.

24. Ibid., 185–87.

Minor. Robbins's examination of the pericope's inner rhetorical workings, its echoes and allusions to other literature, the unseen social norms working behind it, and the author's purpose in including it leads him to conclude that Mary's song introduces Lukan ideas that are picked up, taken over, and changed by the men in the rest of the story, ultimately in service to the continuance (albeit a reformed one) of the current dominating systems of patriarchy and imperial patronage.[25] In the present study, I will argue for an understanding of Mary's song that takes us in quite a different direction.

INTERTEXTUALITY: SINGERS, PRAYERS, AND PROPHETS

Frequently, a parallel is drawn between the Magnificat and Hannah's song in 1 Sam. 2:1-10. Not only do these two texts espouse similar themes of status reversal, but they are also both sung by young mothers whose sons are poised to do great things in their lives of service to God. Any comparison with Hannah also invites comparison with the other Hebrew victory songs, many of them sung and likely composed by women. In this section, I shall compare Mary's song with other songs of victory and status reversal from the Hebrew Bible, the Apocrypha, the Dead Sea Scrolls, and Greco-Roman literature.

COMPARATIVE TEXTS IN THE HEBREW BIBLE

Carol Meyers sums up the tradition of Israelite victory hymns in this way: "Victories by inferior or helpless Israelite forces . . . are attributed to YHWH by women, who greet the victors, be they human or divine, with songs, dance, and the beat of the drum. . . . Not only do they perform but also they probably compose words to fit the specifics of the occasion."[26] Several distinguishing characteristics and themes of victory songs have been identified: military language and imagery; a setting involving some kind of triumph (in war or otherwise); a reprise of the enemy's threat and the battle's heroes; expression of joy and pride in the show of power; and ultimate attribution of the victory to God's saving actions.[27] The song ordinarily affirms that this story, including the deeds of God and the deeds of the humans through whom God worked, will be remembered by future generations. To this list I would also

---

25. Ibid., 196, 199, 200.

26. Carol Meyers, "Mother to Muse: An Archaeomusicological Study of Women's Performance in Ancient Israel," in *Recycling Biblical Figures*, ed. Athalya Brenner and Jan Willem van Henten, Studies in Theology and Religion (Leiderdorp: Deo, 1999), 72.

27. Sigmund Mowinckel, *The Psalms in Israel's Worship*, trans. D. R. Ap-Thomas (Oxford: Basil Blackwell, 1962), 2:276–77.

add the theme of status reversals, which figure prominently in so many of our examples.

Miriam, one of the few women to be designated in the biblical text as a prophet, provides the quintessential example of the well-attested tradition of women drumming, dancing, and singing in public victory celebrations. At the shore of the Reed Sea, after the lengthy song attributed to Moses and the Israelites, we read that Miriam led the women in a command to the people to praise and glorify God: "Then Miriam the prophet, the sister of Aaron, took a drum in her hand, and all the women went out after her with drums and dancing. Miriam sang to them, 'Sing to the Lord, for he has been greatly exalted indeed; horse and rider he has thrown into the sea'" (Exod. 15:20-21). Similar victory celebrations also appear in 1 Sam. 18:6; Judg. 11:34; and Jer. 31:4; and the tradition gains support from archaeology as well, particularly in the wealth of female terra cotta figurines playing the hand drum.[28] The reversal celebrated in Miriam's short verse, and in the longer Song of the Sea (Exod. 15:1-19), is a total inversion of roles gained through military victory at the hand of the Divine Warrior; the Egyptian charioteers and their horses had just been drowned in the Reed Sea while the Hebrews, so recently enslaved by Pharaoh, emerged free and victorious (Exod. 14:26-31).

Although there is no drumming or dancing narrated in Luke 1, the poetic form of the Magnificat, its attribution to a woman, and its victorious tenor all act to cast Mariam of Nazareth as a prophetic figure in the tradition of her namesake Miriam, and Miriam's musical daughters like Deborah, Hannah, and Judith. Also interesting is the shared name, which in and of itself is not an uncommon coincidence. But Luke 1:46 specifically names the singer of the Magnificat Μαριάμ, using the indeclinable Hebrew form rather than the hellenized Μαρία (preferred by Matthew for the mother of Jesus, as in Matt. 1:16, 18, 20; 2:11; cf. Luke 1:41). As there is great flexibility in usage by the canonical evangelists between these two forms, I am reluctant to overstate the case. But it is quite possible, perhaps even likely, that the Hebraized name Μαριάμ combined with the other connections to invoke an echo of the prophetic authority and vocation of Miriam the Exodus prophet for some members of Luke's audience.[29] If Mariam of Luke is a prophetic heir of Miriam

---

28. Meyers, "Mother to Muse," 66–71. There are various arguments to be made for the original placement of Miriam's song before that of Moses, and even for Miriam's composition of the entire Song of the Sea before a later, and perhaps patriarchal, redactor attributed it to Moses instead. See Carol Meyers, "Miriam, Music, and Miracles," in *Mariam, the Magdalen, and the Mother*, ed. Deirdre Good (Bloomington, IN: Indiana University Press, 2005), 28–30; and Phyllis Trible, "Bringing Miriam out of the Shadows," *BRev* 5 no. 1 (1989): 18–20.

of Exodus, we must also consider her older sisters and their victory celebrations, which were generally militant in tone and content.

The song of Deborah and Barak in Judges 5 is regarded as one of the earliest examples of the Hebrew victory hymn. It is a poetic, and more emotional and colorful,[30] retelling of the story already told in prose (Judges 4), and was probably originally separate from its current setting (as were many other victory songs). As in the book of Exodus, the weaker Israelites had just routed a powerful foreign army and its dangerous chariots (Judg. 4:1-16). Particularly interesting in this text are the prominent roles played by women in battle: Deborah accompanies the Israelite army into battle at the request of its general (Judg. 4:8-10), and the enigmatic Jael welcomes Sisera, the foreign general, into her tent, and then proceeds to kill him with a tent peg (Judg. 4:17-22). After these events are narrated, Deborah and Barak commemorate them in a song (Judg. 5:1-31). It opens with a command to the people to bless God and tell of the mighty divine acts for the people of Israel, and then describes the actions of the people, including Deborah, Barak, the various tribes, and finally Jael's defeat of Sisera.

The events themselves, as narrated by the song, present various situations of status reversal, rather than the open declaration and performative speech found in the Magnificat and other texts we shall consider. Deborah's designation as a "mother in Israel" (Judg. 5:7) is perhaps the female equivalent of the prophetic honorific of "father" given to, for example, Elijah and Elisha (2 Kgs. 2:12; 13:14);[31] an Israelite woman in such a high leadership role is not unheard of, but certainly unusual (for either a historical figure or a literary character). The arrogance of the enemy (a prime evil in reversal texts, as we shall see) is mocked through the irony of the last scene, where Sisera's mother and her ladies imagine him tarrying because of the great spoils of his assumed victory, both girls and material wealth (Judg. 5:28-30). The reality, though, is a harsh inverse: instead of enjoying the women of his vanquished foes, Sisera lies dead at the hand of Jael, and God has given the victory to Deborah and her Israelites. Of particular note is the uniqueness of Deborah and Jael's victory; it is perhaps this fact that prompts its memorialization in

29. Mary F. Foskett, "Miriam/Mariam/Maria: Literary Genealogy and the Genesis of Mary in the Protevangelium of James," in Good, *Mariam, the Magdalen, and the Mother*, 64; and Deirdre Good, "The Miriamic Secret," in *Mariam, the Magdalen, and the Mother*, ed. Deirdre Good (Bloomington, IN: Indiana University Press, 2005), 21.

30. Meyers, "Miriam, Music, and Miracles," 40.

31. Susan Ackerman, "Why Is Miriam Also Among the Prophets? (And Is Zipporah Among the Priests?)," *JBL* 121 (2002): 62.

a victory song, over other, less noteworthy military battles. Meyers writes, "In each instance, the victories—of unarmed, outnumbered, under-equipped, or otherwise disadvantaged Israelites—are attributed to ahistorical, miraculous circumstances, namely divine intervention in human affairs. And female humans respond with poetic song and movement that celebrate redemption."[32]

The song of Hannah (1 Sam. 2:1-10), on the other hand, is not related to a war or battle victory at all, though it bears clear marks of the victory hymn tradition. It is set at the dedication of the boy Samuel to God's service in the temple. His once-barren mother Hannah interprets the situation as God granting her victory. She sings, "My heart exults in the Lord, my horn is lifted high in the Lord; my mouth opens wide against my enemies, for I rejoice in your salvation" (1 Sam. 2:1), and she rejoices that the "bows of the mighty ones are shattered" (2:4) as Yahweh thunders against enemies and gives strength to the anointed ruler of Israel (2:10). The militaristic tone of this song is perhaps surprising, given its hybrid domestic and cultic setting. Whereas Deborah was a rare female military leader, Hannah's main desire in this text is to be a mother.

But Hannah, too, exhibits some characteristics unusual for a woman in ancient literature. She is, for example, one of the few women presented in the Bible as actively participating in cultic activities both with her husband and independently; she is intimately involved in both familial ritual obligations and personal prayer and sacrifice.[33] She approaches God individually and makes a personal vow (1 Sam. 1:9-11); takes an offering to the temple, presumably without her husband (1:24); dedicates her son to God's service (1:25-28); and declares her victory in a poetic prayer to the Holy One and Lord of all (2:1-10). This hymn, in addition to its martial imagery, makes extensive use of reversal imagery in verses 4-9. The contrasts are many and varied: the mighty and the feeble, the full and the hungry, the barren and the fertile, death and life, the poor and the rich, the needy and the princes, the faithful and the wicked. In introducing this section, Hannah singles out the arrogant for special censure: "Do not continue speaking so high and mighty, let arrogance depart from your mouth; for the Lord is a God of knowledge, and deeds will be measured by him" (1 Sam. 2:3).

A comparison of Mary with Miriam, Deborah, Hannah, and their songs is enlightening in several ways. First, the political situations addressed in the Hebrew hymns highlight the Magnificat's parallel strains of political revolution,

---

32. Meyers, "Miriam, Music, and Miracles," 40.

33. Susan Ackerman, "Household Religion, Family Religion, and Women's Religion in Ancient Israel," in *Household and Family Religion in Antiquity*, ed. John Bodel and Saul M. Olyan, The Ancient World: Comparative Histories (Malden, MA: Blackwell, 2008), 148.

something that the church, particularly in Western Christianity, has been reluctant to admit in favor of an approach of caution and balance.[34] As Robert McAfee Brown astutely points out, modern Americans are familiar with singing in the course of their participation in political movements, but when the political songs include elements of prayer, many are less comfortable.[35] But that is exactly what we find in the songs and faith of the Hebrew Bible, for its poets did not conceive of a separation of politics and religion.

Second, the echoes of the songs of Miriam, Hannah, and Deborah sounding in the song of Mary also highlight Mary's prophetic role in Luke. Not only does she proclaim poetic praise in a manner reminiscent of two of the Hebrew Bible's five female prophets, but she also takes her place among biblical women like Hannah, who act "not only as critical actors within the practice of ancient Israelite household and family religion, but also as the theologians who give voice to some of the household and family religion's most constitutive beliefs."[36] The annunciation to Mary even has some parallels with the commissioning experiences of some (male) prophets.[37] Third, the settings of the three songs discussed so far all find Israel in a state of liminality, where there are "ruptures in [the] story."[38] These singing women arise at transition points in the narrative of Israel's historical experience: from slavery to becoming a free people (Exodus), in the midst of decades of oppression (Judges 4–5), and moving towards a monarchy (1 Samuel). There is some sociological evidence to suggest that the instability of such liminal periods, when the usual markers of status and identity are stripped away, provides particularly fertile ground for the rise of women in the nontraditional role of prophets.[39] Mary's story in

---

34. Boff, *Maternal Face*, 197–98.

35. Robert McAfee Brown, *Unexpected News*, 77.

36. Ackerman, "Household Religion," 148–49.

37. Richard A. Horsley, *The Liberation of Christmas: The Infancy Narratives in Social Context* (New York: Crossroad, 1989), 89–90. He relies upon Jane Schaberg's work here in comparing Mary's call to the prophetic commissions of Moses in Exodus 3 and Gideon in Judges 6. See, e.g., the greeting to a favored one of God (Judg. 6:12; Luke 1:28), the offering of a sign of confirmation (Exod. 3:12; Judg. 6:36-40; Luke 1:36-37), and the eventual human agreement (Exod. 4:18; Judg. 6:27; Luke 1:38).

38. Meyers, "Miriam, Music, and Miracles," 30.

39. See the discussion of liminality and rites of passage in Ackerman, "Why Is Miriam," 64–71. The entire nation of Israel, for example, is in a liminal state during its flight from Egypt and its wilderness wanderings. They are slaves no longer, but have yet to make the full rite-of-passage transition to become a free and independent people (68–70). As in almost all such transitions, the primary characteristic of the liminal stage is ambiguity of role, identity, and status (67). We see this flexibility in the biblical narrative on the individual as well as communal level. Thus Moses can go from slave to prince to fugitive to shepherd to leader and miracle worker, and Miriam can easily make the transition from secondary character and slave woman to the typically male role of prophetic functionary (71). A similar pattern can

the Gospel of Luke also fits this profile, as she is at the very center of Israel's transition into the in-breaking of God's reign in the world and gives powerful voice to its new (or renewed) vision and identity.

Finally, I want to draw attention to the matter of public, private, and sacred space, which will be discussed more fully later in this chapter. It is conventional that the singers of victory songs "go out" before the people to sing their songs, indicating the performative nature of the practice.[40] Mary, however, more closely resembles Hannah, for her song is set, within the narrative world at least, in a private setting, and probably witnessed by only a few people. But the Magnificat's connection with a distinct performance genre hints at the possibility of a different setting, both before and after the song was set down in writing by the third evangelist.

COMPARATIVE TEXTS IN THE JEWISH APOCRYPHA AND THE DEAD SEA SCROLLS

For the interpretation of any pericope in the Gospels, there is the important question of the appropriate "canon" of comparative literature, in addition to relevant intertexts from the Hebrew Bible.[41] In the case of Luke, we must consider Greco-Roman literature and non-canonical Jewish works from the second century BCE through the first century CE, plus the Septuagint, which is repeatedly alluded to in the Lukan hymns and the entire birth narrative.[42] These writings and the worldviews they express or presume would have been potentially familiar and relevant to Luke's mixed audience of Jews and Gentiles. For example, Raymond Brown identifies close parallels to the Magnificat in several extracanonical victory hymns from late Second Temple Jewish literature, such as those found in 1 Maccabees, Judith, and the Dead Sea Scrolls.[43] These texts illuminate the developments in the genre of the victory hymn that were occurring immediately prior to the composition of Luke-Acts.

---

be traced in the journeys of Hannah (from barren wife to prophet and mother of Israel's "kingmaker") and Mary (from undistinguished peasant to prophet and mother of Israel's Messiah), and their intersection with Israel's journey as the people of God. See also the discussion of individual and communal liminality from an anthropological perspective in Victor W. Turner, *The Ritual Process: Structure and Anti-Structure* (Chicago: Aldine, 1969), 94–130.

40. E.g., Exod. 15:20; Judg. 11:34; 1 Sam. 18:6; Jer. 31:4. The content and context of Deborah's song (Judges 5) also suggest a public act. See Meyers, "Miriam, Music, and Miracles," 41.

41. Robbins, "Socio-Rhetorical Criticism," 181.

42. For helpful summaries of the exact LXX verses alluded to in the Magnificat, see Helmer Ringgren, "Luke's Use of the Old Testament," in *Christians among Jews and Gentiles*, ed. George W. E. Nickelsburg and George W. MacRae (Philadelphia: Fortress Press, 1986), 230–31; and Raymond E. Brown, *Birth of the Messiah*, 358–60.

The second century BCE song of Judith (Jth. 15:14—16:17), for example, combines those of Deborah and Hannah, taking aspects from each. Like Deborah's hymn, it retells the story of a great and unexpected military victory in which the people of Israel are saved by the hand of a woman, showing a God who "protects the weak through the weak . . . that gets at the mighty oppressor outside, but also at those who would dominate inside the community."[44] The status reversals here, however, are more explicit than in Judges, and more like those in Hannah's song—although to a different purpose. The people are called weak and oppressed, but they are able to terrify the enemy merely with their shouts, and even the low-status "sons of slave girls" are said to help in the victory (16:11-12).

Several texts from the Dead Sea Scrolls also bear scrutiny with regard to the Magnificat. The "hymn of return" sung by the victorious children of light after the great eschatological battle of the *War Scroll* (1QM XIV, 4b-18), although laden with sectarian theology and language, has some significant similarities to the song of Judith, especially in its reversal themes. Statements of reversal are explicitly and prominently featured, but the author followed the example of Judith in nuancing them specifically for the battle setting. The tottering, the feeble, the fearful, and the dumb are lifted up and strengthened so that they might fight in the war (XIV, 5b-7), and again the arrogant are warned of their fate in a classic reversal: "You lift up the fallen ones with your strength, and those who are arrogant in stature you cut down to lay them low" (line 11). In this text, reversals are carried out in the midst of war, and the weak of the community are strengthened for the express purpose of winning the battle. The *War Scroll* hymn intimately connects social reversals with nationalistic fervor, as David Flusser writes: "In this Essene prayer on the day after the victory, the national and social components of redemption form a unity."[45]

Flusser sees these two ideals of Jewish eschatology at the turn of the era being refracted into, respectively, the nationalistic redemption pictured by Luke's Benedictus (1:67-79) and the social reversals that mark the Magnificat

---

43. Raymond E. Brown, *Birth of the Messiah*, 349. In addition to victory and reversal themes, these hymns roughly contemporary to the Magnificat share with it the techniques of Hebrew-style parallelism and a Scrolls-style mosaic or pastiche of scriptural allusions. Cf. Maurya P. Horgan and Paul J. Kobelski, "The Hodayot (1QH) and New Testament Poetry," in *To Touch the Text: Biblical and Related Studies in Honor of Joseph A. Fitzmyer*, ed. Maurya P. Horgan and Paul J. Kobelski (New York: Crossroad, 1989), 188–92; and Ringgren, "Luke's Use," 232.

44. George J. Brooke, *The Dead Sea Scrolls and the New Testament* (Minneapolis: Fortress Press, 2005), 276.

45. Flusser, *Judaism*, 138.

(1:46-55).[46] He is correct that these major themes carry over from the Jewish milieu of the *War Scroll* to figure prominently in Luke's birth and infancy narratives, but such a sharp division between the songs of Zechariah and Mary is oversimplified. In fact, the Magnificat contains at the end hints of nationalistic redemption for Israel and Abraham's descendants (Luke 1:54-55), and the Benedictus concludes with the hope of merciful reversal for those living in darkness and hopelessness (Luke 1:78-79). The major difference between the Scrolls song and the Lukan songs is not the separation of these two concepts, but rather the lack of any overt military action in the salvific vision of the Gospel texts. While this does not entirely blunt what Flusser calls the easily recognizable "social explosive" of the Magnificat,[47] Luke is clearly hinting at a new development in the conception of victory.

Another Scrolls text, fragmentary but intriguing, is a Reworked Pentateuch (4Q365) and its version of Exodus 15.[48] Although only a few words at the beginning of each line are readable, it appears that this sectarian Pentateuch version (dated 75-50 BCE) expands Miriam's two lines in Exod. 15:21 into a full hymn. The few fragments that remain contain tantalizing hints of reversal themes: the spite of God for someone, perhaps an arrogant enemy (6 II, 1); the divine titles of "Great One" and "Savior," so common to victory songs (6 II, 3; cf. Jth. 16:13; Luke 1:46-47, 49); and most particularly, the use of the verb רום (to raise up, exalt) to depict both the singer's praise and the actions of God as one who raises up the lowly (6 II, 6; cf. 1 Sam. 2:7-8, 10; Luke 1:52). No more than a century before the composition of the Magnificat,[49] then, we find that the tradition of women singing about upside-down victories of the weak and lowly against the rich and powerful seemed to be alive and well. George J. Brooke asserts that this expanded Dead Sea Scroll "Song of Miriam" provides further support for the Magnificat's connection with pre-Christian

---

46. Ibid., 137–38.

47. Ibid., 131.

48. Briefly mentioned in Meyers, "Miriam, Music, and Miracles," 31. For a full discussion of this scroll fragment and George Brooke's reading of it, see the chapter "Songs of Revolution: The Song of Miriam and Its Counterparts," in *Dead Sea Scrolls*, 272–81.

49. There is debate among scholars about whether this song and its companion hymn in the birth narrative, Zechariah's Benedictus (Luke 1:67-79), were composed by Mary and Zechariah respectively, composed by Luke himself, or adopted by Luke from an outside source. For a summary of the debate and an argument in favor of outside composition, see Farris, *Hymns*, 14–23, 86–94. I tend to agree with his conclusion that the songs were composed by a Christian person or group, and possibly sung in early worship gatherings. See further discussion below.

Jewish hymns.[50] He also argues, most significantly for our study, that this new song

> took up some of the themes of the Song of the Sea . . . and interlaced those motifs with a perspective which suggests that God's victory is often shame for the proud, the arrogant, and the mighty, victory that is brought about surprisingly through the weak and downtrodden. In an eschatological context in which the mighty in Israel might be considered to be the enemy just as much as any foreign power, these motifs become revolutionary.[51]

The Scrolls text with the greatest relevance to our study of the Magnificat, though, is a poem from the *Hodayot* or *Thanksgiving Hymns*, whose most complete form is found in 4Q427 7 I–II (the version I will reference here). Although it is included in the sectarian *Hodayot* (1QH), this song is usually recognized by scholars as sitting uneasily in such a context.[52] The opening self-glorification section that is so different from the self-abasement typical in the Scrolls community's *hodayot*, the juxtaposition of both individual and communal sections in a single song, and the concern with status reversals have caused most *hodayot* scholars to relegate this particular psalm to a footnote stating that it does not fit well with the rest of the scroll. Eileen Schuller and also John Collins and Devorah Dimant propose that 4Q427 7 was originally independent of the rest of the *hodayot*, and perhaps even of the Scrolls community entirely.[53] Building on this conclusion, I would argue even more specifically that this Scrolls song should be classified with the Magnificat as a later eschatological development of the Hebrew victory hymn for the reasons outlined below.

Both songs are at home in this tradition with their praise of a God both merciful and mighty. Their focus on the action of God can be seen, for example, in the fact that God is the subject of almost all the verbs in the Magnificat.[54] God

---

50. Brooke, *Dead Sea Scrolls*, 277.

51. Ibid., 281.

52. See, e.g., Eileen M. Schuller, "A Hymn from a Cave Four Manuscript: 4Q427 7 i ii," *JBL* 112 (1993): 605–28; and John J. Collins and Devorah Dimant, "A Thrice-Told Hymn: A Response to Eileen Schuller," *JQR* 85 (1994): 151–55.

53. Collins and Dimant, "Thrice-Told Hymn," 155; and Schuller, "Hymn from Cave Four," 627. For the opposite point of view, see Paolo Augusto de Souza Nogueira, "Ecstatic Worship in the Self-Glorification Hymn (4Q471B, 4Q427, 4Q491C): Implications for the Understanding of an Ancient Jewish and Early Christian Phenomenon," in *Wisdom and Apocalypticism in the Dead Sea Scrolls and in the Biblical Tradition*, ed. Florentino García Martínez (Leuven: Leuven University Press, 2003), 390–92.

shows strength and might for the people with his hand in the *hodayah* (line 18) and with his arm in the Magnificat (v. 51). A plethora of synonyms describes this divine power: גדול, כבוד, כוח, גבורה (I, 15-18 and II, 12-16), δυνατός, κράτος (1:49, 51). God is seen as working נפלאות (wonders, I, 18 and II, 12) and μεγάλα (great things, 1:49). But God is also loving, caring, and nurturing to God's people. In the *hodayah*, the חסד and רחם of God are emphasized over and over again in these same passages of praise, along with the divine טוב and צדק, while the Magnificat's word of choice is ἔλεος (1:50, 54). God has acted to help both the individual and the community, but this succor is not entirely universal. Both hymns qualify the extent of God's mercy: it is offered to "those who make fruitful his great goodness" (4Q427 7 I, 23), to "all the children of his truth" (II, 13-14), and to "the ones who fear him" (Luke 1:50). These sentiments fit seamlessly with the theology typically expressed in the victory hymn.

The Magnificat and 4Q427 7 are also connected to one another and to the victory hymn tradition by the prominence of reversals that find their closest parallel with those of Hannah's song in 1 Samuel 2 (see, for example, 4Q427 7 II, 3-11, 1 Sam. 2:6-9, and Luke 1:50-53; 4Q427 7 I, 18-23, and 1 Sam. 2:3-5). By contrast, the reversals in the hymns of Judges, Judith, and the *War Scroll*, while present, are less prominent, and they are implemented mainly for the purposes of the present battle. Even Hannah's reversals employ military imagery: "The bows of the mighty are broken, but the feeble gird on strength" (1 Sam. 2:4). The Magnificat and the *hodayah*, however, seem to have moved beyond these connotations of war and nationalistic concern to a more general idea of God's work in the world.[55] The primary reversal imagery (especially in 4Q427 7 I, 18-21; II, 7-11; Luke 1:51-53) shows God lifting up and raising from the dust the poor, the lowly, and those who have fallen, while at the same time throwing down and lowering the princes, the wealthy, and especially the arrogant and proud. 4Q427 7 exhibits special concern for those who have fallen or stumbled into the earth or dust, and for the way in which God is lifting them up (see I, 19; II, 8,10). The Magnificat expands on this vertical imagery, including also the image of the hungry being filled with good things while the rich are sent away empty (Luke 1:53). Both texts use these status reversals to critique the standard structures of imperial social and economic stratification.

What must be noted about these two hymns, though, is that their reversals are not set in a military context, something that sets them apart from most of

54. François Bovon, *Luke 1: A Commentary on the Gospel of Luke 1:1—9:50*, trans. Christine M. Thomas, Hermeneia, ed. Helmut Koester (Minneapolis: Fortress Press, 2002), 56.

55. C. Hugo Zorilla, "The Magnificat: Song of Justice," in *Conflict and Context: Hermeneutics in the Americas*, ed. Mark Lau Branson and C. René Padilla (Grand Rapids: Eerdmans, 1986), 132.

the other victory songs we have examined. The language of the reversals has some martial overtones, but without an actual battle setting.[56] For example, God's throwing down (καθεῖλεν) the rulers from their thrones (Luke 1:52) can be nuanced not just as deposition, but also as destruction (BDAG, 488). The reference to God's strong arm and hand (Luke 1:51 and 4Q427 7 I) as working wonders on behalf of the lowly and against the powerful echoes divine action to save the Israelites from the Egyptians (Exod. 6:6; Deut. 6:21) and to scatter God's enemies (Ps. 89:10, 13-14). Such scattering (Luke 1:51) is the fate of all who are too arrogant or selfish to live as God commands, whether Israelite or foreigner (Deut. 30:1-5; Ps. 53:1-6). The Scrolls text still contains some hints of destruction for the singer's enemies, but they are fragmentary and, in any case, less explicit than those of other victory songs (for example, a claim that God judges with destructive and eternal anger in I, 21 and II, 10).

This image of God as "divine warrior who . . . delivers people from oppressive powers"[57] comes from the usual battle setting of the victory hymns and mimics imperial definitions of power to a certain extent. But it is employed, in the non-martial literary contexts of the Gospel of Luke and the *hodayah*, to bring about a different type of victory—one that still defeats oppressive powers, but with a greater (although not exclusive) focus on social upheaval than on war and violence. The *hodayah* is situated in a collection of psalms intended for worship and prayer, while the Magnificat celebrates the impending birth of a child who will become a victim of imperially sanctioned violence rather than a perpetrator of it. There seems, then, to be a shift in focus underway. In the Magnificat and 4Q427 7, salvation is in the process of being redefined as a re-envisioning of societal structures in order to restore people's relationship with God and with one another,[58] rather than military victory and the opportunity to lord it over one's enemies. It should not be assumed, however, that the Magnificat's weakening of military destruction for the arrogant and rich in any way lessens the subversiveness of such a message (as will be explored more fully in the following section). Suffice it to say for now that the status reversal proclaimed in Mary's song would have posed just as much a threat to the dominant Jewish and Roman powers in the first century as Hugo Zorilla

56. See Warren Carter, "Singing in the Reign: Performing Luke's Songs and Negotiating the Roman Empire (Luke 1–2)," in *Luke-Acts and Empire: Essays in Honor of Robert L. Brawley*, ed. David Rhoads, David Esterline, and Jae Won Lee, PTMS (Eugene, OR: Wipf & Stock, 2011), 37–39, for a fuller list of vocabulary connections between the Lukan hymns and Jewish texts of liberation.

57. Ibid., 37.

58. See, e.g., Joel B. Green, *The Theology of the Gospel of Luke*, NTT, ed. James D. G. Dunn (Cambridge: Cambridge University Press, 1995), 94.

observes that it would be to modern-day Latin American governments[59]—or indeed, to any hierarchical system.

COMPARATIVE TEXTS IN GRECO-ROMAN LITERATURE

The final body of literature with which we must contend is the works of contemporary Greco-Roman authors, which would undoubtedly have been familiar to Hellenistic urbanites in Luke's earliest audiences. Many community members of higher status were likely well-read, and all would have been familiar with the imperial propaganda (both literary and monumental) that was a part of the overarching culture of the first-century Mediterranean world. Status reversals were a relatively familiar theme in these works, as they were in the Jewish literature discussed above. In Greco-Roman perspective, reversals were often attributed to the gods, but could also be regarded as simply the fickleness of fate or life in general. This latter explanation was more usual in Homer's reversals (usually good fortune giving way to chaos and calamity, rather than the other way around), and in the tragic fate, for example, of Sophocles's Oedipus.[60] For examples of divinely ordained reversals, one can refer to sayings such as Aesop's line in "The Two Chickens and the Eagle": "He raises up the one who is low, he pulls down the one who is high."[61] Another prominent example is Hesiod's hymn to Zeus:

> Muses of Pieria who give glory through song, come hither, tell of Zeus your father and chant his praise. Through him mortal men are famed or un-famed, sung or unsung alike, as great Zeus wills. For easily he makes strong, and easily he brings the strong man low; easily he humbles the proud and raises the obscure, and easily he straightens the crooked and blasts the proud—Zeus who thunders aloft and has his dwelling most high.[62]

Whether these reversals are attributed to fate or to the gods, the earlier Greek literature viewed them as creating a certain level of discomfort and insecurity, as one did not know the gods' reasons for such reversals and thus did not know how to avoid them.[63] Various advice is offered: do all things in moderation;

---

59. Zorilla, "Magnificat," 235.

60. Frederick W. Danker, *Luke*, 2nd ed., Proclamation Commentaries, ed. Gerhard Krodel (Philadelphia: Fortress Press, 1987), 47.

61. Quoted in Edouard Hamel, "Le Magnificat et le Renversement des Situations: Réflexion théologico-biblique," *Greg* 60 (1979): 59.

62. *Op.* I.1-10. Also quoted in Hamel, "Le Magnificat," 59.

recognize that life is simply cruel, so seek at least a good death; or acknowledge that prosperity brings with it its own hazards and try to avoid hubris.[64]

One sees a shift, though, in this idea of random reversals in Roman literature closer to the time of Jesus' life and the composition of Luke-Acts. Propaganda from the reign of Augustus casts the first emperor as the near-divine author of positive reversals and improved status for the Roman people. Virgil's *Aeneid*, for example, speaks of the destiny of Rome (in the person of Augustus) "to rule Earth's peoples . . . to pacify, to impose the rule of law, to spare the conquered, to battle down the proud."[65] Like the God of the Magnificat, the Romans here claim to fight against the arrogant and offer mercy to the humble (or humiliated), but the situations of the respective prophets who speak these sentiments differ dramatically: Mary the nondescript peasant girl versus Anchises, the father of the legendary Aeneas, progenitor of the mighty Roman race. Like the works of Virgil and other imperial literature, Roman prayers and hymns were also expected to espouse and uphold Roman values: "It is the protection and blessing of the state that is the primary objective of every public prayer."[66] We can discern, I think, that Mary's song might have raised a few eyebrows and questions in the minds of Luke's audience over who, exactly, is arrogant, and who is truly fighting against the arrogant on behalf of the humble.

Another relevant text is Horace's "Hymn for a New Age" (*Carmen Saeculare*), composed for Augustus's *saeculum* games in 17 bce and the only extant imperial hymn.[67] Again we find an imperial ideal in the person of Augustus, who is presented as both mighty and compassionate: "May he be victorious in battle over his foes yet merciful once they are down" (lines 49–52). This celebration of a new golden age in the Roman Empire revolves around themes of morality, fertility, social conformity, military victory, and eternal empire and blessings for Rome.[68] This is an unusual hymn because it is not

63. Hamel, "Le Magnificat," 59.

64. Danker, *Luke*, 47–48. He points to the examples of various Greek philosophers extolling the virtues of σωφροσύνη, i.e., moderation, prudence (47); the parallel exhortations of the Greek Herodotus ("One who dies well has lived well") and the Roman Juvenal ("Look at life's last lap") (48); and the warning against the dangers of power and prosperity inherent in Sophocles's story of King Oedipus (47).

65. Quoted in Christopher Kelly, *The Roman Empire: A Very Short Introduction* (Oxford: Oxford University Press, 2006), 21.

66. Frances Hickson Hahn, "Performing the Sacred: Prayers and Hymns," in *A Companion to Roman Religion*, ed. Jörg Rüpke, Blackwell Companions to the Ancient World (Malden, MA: Blackwell, 2007), 245.

67. The original text and an English translation can be found in Horace, *Odes and Epodes*, ed. Niall Rudd, Loeb Classical Library 33 (Cambridge: Harvard University Press, 2004), 262–67.

apotropaic (that is, designed to ward off evil), but rather a straightforward confirmation of the glory of the Roman order.[69] Mary's song plays a similar role, but celebrates a very different order that in fact entirely overturns the Roman hierarchy. Through mimicry and transformation, the Magnificat thus offers a countermelody to these status quo values, an alternative vision of a world not subject to Rome's will or power, where victory is gained through service rather than battle, where social norms are challenged rather than accepted, and where eternal peace and blessing are offered to people of any race and status, not only those born into a certain situation.[70]

Another Augustan writer, Dionysius of Halicarnassus, offers an example of what Danker calls moral reversal, that is, one carried out (as in Luke) based on one's responsibility or irresponsibility in the just use of power and wealth.[71] Dionysius wrote of the problem of the poor who were forced into debt slavery by moneylenders and the responsibility of rich patricians to help them. He even included the speech of a poor plebian accusing senators of being the ὑπερήφανοι (proud, arrogant) who oppress the humble ταπεινοί[72]—the exact vocabulary used in the Magnificat (Luke 1:48, 51-52). Thus we see that Luke was not introducing totally unknown ideas to his Gentile hearers, but rather reinforcing values that were already present in the culture at large.[73] Those familiar with Greco-Roman literature knew about the dangers of hubris, while the Jewish audience knew of prophetic warnings against misuse of their divinely elected status;[74] therefore, both would recognize at least to some degree a caution and a concern with moral conduct in the Magnificat's reversals. Luke again is showing his facility with both Hebrew and Hellenistic cultures, and probably also supplying evidence of his mixed audience, both ethnically and economically.

---

68. Carter, "Singing in the Reign," 41–42.

69. Hahn, "Performing the Sacred," 245.

70. Cf. the readings of Allen Brent, "Luke-Acts and the Imperial Cult in Asia Minor," *JTS* 48 (1997): 427–33; and Carter, "Singing in the Reign," 41–43.

71. Danker, *Luke*, 49.

72. *Ant. rom.* 6.23–29. Referenced in David L. Balch, "Rich and Poor, Proud and Humble in Luke-Acts," in *The Social World of the First Christians: Essays in Honor of Wayne A. Meeks*, ed. L. Michael White and O. Larry Yarbrough (Minneapolis: Fortress Press, 2005), 222–24.

73. Balch, "Rich and Poor," 232. It should be noted, though, that the status reversals reported by Dionysius are in several places encouraged by the rich so that the poor can fight in the military on behalf of a threatened Rome (222, 230–31). This indicates that Luke is transforming the reversal expectations not only of his Jewish but also of his Gentile hearers.

74. Danker, *Luke*, 49.

SOCIOLOGICAL ANALYSIS: THE HIDDEN TRANSCRIPT IN PUBLIC SONG

This particular text has come down to us in the form of a poem recited or, traditionally, sung by Mary, the mother of Jesus. It is not generally regarded, however, as having been composed by either Mary or the author of Luke. There are, to be sure, proponents for each of these two options, but the general martial nature of the song would seem inappropriate to its domestic narrative setting of the meeting between two mothers-to-be if it had been written specifically for this scene by either Mary or Luke.[75] David Flusser, for example, locates the composition of both the Magnificat and the Benedictus among the early followers of John the Baptist,[76] and Douglas Jones argues that they came originally from the worship of the earliest Jewish Christians.[77] This latter option is particularly intriguing for our study, as Luke's evident admiration of the early Jerusalem gathering of Jesus-followers (see, for example, Acts 2:41-47; 4:32-35) might explain how their hymnic compositions made their way into the worship and writings of Christians in the hellenized cities of Greece and Asia Minor. Such ideas are interesting and thought-provoking, but of course speculative in the end. The most important point for our study is that the Magnificat was likely adopted (and possibly adapted) by Luke from some outside source, probably a Jewish Christian (or at least Jewish) group.[78] Thus we will consider the imperial negotiation tactics evident in the song itself (Luke 1:46-55), and in the setting in which Luke places it (1:39-45, and the larger context of the infancy narratives in Luke 1–2).

HIDDEN TRANSCRIPTS IN THE SONG

The reversals in the Magnificat are its most prominent feature, delineated most explicitly in Luke 1:51-53, and a key to establishing this text as part of the hidden transcript of resistance. Scott views such status-reversal imagery, voiced ambiguously but powerfully and publicly, as an important part of the subordinates' counterculture that constructs identity and worth separate from the dominant hierarchy and its values.[79] The central verses of the Magnificat (1:51-53) play a strong role in this project, through celebrating God's actions to scatter the arrogant, cast down rulers, lift up the lowly, offer nourishment to

---

75. Farris, *Hymns*, 21.

76. Flusser, *Judaism*, 148.

77. Jones, "Background and Character," 47–48.

78. For an overview of arguments concerning this assertion, see Raymond E. Brown, *Birth of the Messiah*, 346–55; and Farris, *Hymns*, 86–98.

79. James C. Scott, *Domination and the Arts of Resistance: Hidden Transcripts* (New Haven: Yale University Press, 1990), 172.

the hungry, and send the rich away empty. These sentiments are potentially, if not overtly, subversive, and they have grown out of the Hebrew victory song and Divine Warrior traditions (as discussed above). But they also have unique characteristics that will be illuminated by sociological analysis.

A central question about any given status reversal is the end goal of its vision. Usually those goals will fall into one of two broad categories: either an inverted social order, where the subordinated now rule over their previous oppressors, or a world imagined as devoid of class distinctions, where all are brought to the same social level.[80] The poem recorded in Luke 1:46-55 is difficult to pin down as one or the other. There is certainly strong bilateral reversal as rulers are deposed from their seats of power and the lowly ones are exalted by God, from which inversion could be intuited, perhaps even with a violent bent (at least on the part of God, if not human beings).[81] As I argued in the first section of this chapter, this song is undeniably reminiscent of the victory hymns that celebrated military battles and the death of Israel's (or God's) enemies. John York proposes that the chiastic structure of Luke 1:52-53 intensifies the reversals, and he thus argues for an image of total inversion, rather than leveling.[82]

While I agree with York and others that these two verses are undoubtedly the climax of the Magnificat due to their strong parallelism and chiastic arrangement,[83] there are also hints in the text that soften the inversion and move it slightly toward leveling. It is significant that the speaker of the Magnificat considers herself a slave, and Israel, the honored recipient of divine mercy in verse 54, is also called a servant. The singer makes no claims of lording it over others, as would be expected in a situation of total inversion, where the previously oppressed are now the rulers. Instead she focuses her praise on God's power and mercy having been enacted for her sake. Additionally, explicit images of divine anger and destruction are largely absent from Luke 1:46-55, although there are intertextual echoes of God's powerful acts against Pharaoh and the Egyptians in the exodus, such as, in Luke 1:51, his "strong arm" (Exod. 6:6; Deut. 6:21), and his "scattering" of enemies and the unfaithful (Deut. 30:1-5; Ps. 53:1-6). Some of these intertextual connections, though, portray God's power to redeem, alongside the power to punish or destroy those whom God has scattered with a powerful arm. The oracle in Isa. 52:7-10, for example,

---

80. Ibid., 80–81.

81. So Carter, "Singing in the Reign," 37–38, 42; and Ford, *My Enemy*, 19–23.

82. John O. York, *The Last Shall Be First: The Rhetoric of Reversal in Luke*, JSNTSup 46 (Sheffield: Sheffield Academic Press, 1991), 46n5.

83. Ibid., 50.

speaks of God wielding the divine arm so that Israel will be redeemed and so that all nations will see divine salvation. In a similar manner, Deut. 30:3 states that if the Israelites will repent and return to God, "then the Lord your God will restore your fortunes and have compassion on you, gathering you again from all the peoples among whom the Lord your God has scattered you" (NRSV).

Thus there seems to be, even in the Magnificat's downward reversals and martial language, a small move toward allowing the arrogant, the rich, and the rulers an opportunity to repent from their own false superiority and receive salvation. Such an approach to reversal also delivers the lifted-up lowly ones from repeating the cycle of domination by becoming oppressors themselves.[84] The song is not a pure depiction of leveling, for the inversion imagery is strong. But it is moving in that direction, allowing, for example, the Nicaraguan Solentiname community to read the Magnificat as celebrating equality, "a society with no social classes. Everyone alike."[85] In a similar manner, there is some effort among interpreters to cast the downward reversals in a positive light, as the only way to liberate the oppressors from their spiritually and morally corrosive practices.[86] Joel Green puts it this way: "The Song of Mary . . . celebrated the raising up of the lowly and the bringing down of those of high status, so that both might be able to participate fully in the purpose of God."[87] Certainly there is a change in status for the arrogant, the rulers, and the wealthy, and a judgment on their exploitative ways. But even God is not exempt from the pattern of reversal, for in Luke 1:54, we see the Ruler of All, the Mighty One, stooping down to help the divine servant Israel, when a servant is usually the one to do the serving and helping of his or her master.[88]

Thus our study so far of the Magnificat's intertextual and sociocultural context leaves a mixed impression. The speaker has appropriated the tradition of Hebrew victory hymns, but with an eschatological twist that celebrates God's powerful and merciful action in carrying out status reversals both personal and communal. Total military defeat of the enemy is not the final goal of this song.

---

84. Luise Schottroff, *The Parables of Jesus*, trans. Linda M. Maloney (Minneapolis: Fortress Press, 2006), 87.

85. Cardenal, *Gospel in Solentiname*, 19.

86. So Boff, *Maternal Face*, 199; Joel B. Green, *The Gospel of Luke*, NICNT, ed. Gordon D. Fee (Grand Rapids: Eerdmans, 1997), 102; and Hamel, "Le Magnificat," 70.

87. Green, *Theology*, 88. See also the sentiments of liberation theologians like Boff, *Maternal Face*, 199–200: "God does not invert social relationships out of an anthropomorphic spirit of revenge, so that the dominated may now be dominators, and the poor now become wealthy oppressors. No, God turns social relationships topsy-turvy simply to effect the conversion whereby there will be no more rich and poor as antagonistic classes . . . but brothers and sisters all, dwelling together in the one house of God."

88. Brown, *Unexpected News*, 80–81.

Its victory is defined instead through radical social redefinition and reversal between the arrogant and those who fear God, the rulers and the lowly, the rich and the hungry. But the lack of military destruction does not diminish the subversiveness of this song; indeed, the sociological model of hidden resistance would suggest the opposite. The proclamation of divinely ordained social upheaval directly counteracts all who seek to dominate the singer of this song and others of comparable low status with whom she identifies.

Such reversals pose significant danger to the subordinated group or individual if they are voiced publicly. Thus the Magnificat is also a powerful example of the use of ambiguity in protecting the hidden transcript even as it is made public. Scott writes that reversal traditions "represent the public portion of the reply, the counterculture in a quite literal sense, to a dominant transcript of hierarchy and deference. If it is muted or ambiguous, this is because it must be evasive if it is to be public at all."[89] This ambiguity, if it is to be a viable shield for the speaker, has to allow for either a permissible or a rebellious interpretation. Such texts are boundary testers; they cannot go too far or the speaker will be punished by the dominant group, and they cannot be too veiled or the message will not have its intended effect of voicing resistance.[90] Based on the widely varied interpretations of the Magnificat's reversals that have been advanced,[91] it would appear that the song's author has hit the mark. As only a few of the many examples, some argue that its martial tone issues a call for armed military revolution against Rome,[92] some that it celebrates those who are spiritually humble in their dependence upon God,[93] some that it speaks only of spiritual redemption for Israel,[94] and some that it calls for a social reorganization that puts all people, no matter how lowly or how exalted by human standards, on the same level.[95]

The author of this pericope has cloaked its meaning in several different ways. First, concepts that can be easily spiritualized (arrogance, lowliness) are artfully juxtaposed with those that are more concrete (hunger, wealth, rulers), thereby prohibiting any easy categorization of this text as metaphorical or literal. Much effort has been expended over the centuries to show the reversals

---

89. Scott, *Domination*, 172.

90. Ibid., 153–54.

91. For a brief but interesting survey of examples from the Magnificat's history of interpretation, see Hamel, "Le Magnificat," 55–58.

92. Ford, *My Enemy*, 19–23.

93. Raymond E. Brown, *Birth of the Messiah*, 350–55.

94. Seccombe, *Possessions and the Poor*, 74–83.

95. Green, *Theology*, 88.

of the Magnificat in particular and the Gospel of Luke in general to be spiritual and metaphorical; this makes the case that there is something inherently subversive in such ideas, as indeed social, religious, and political dissidents have recognized over the years. For example, Thomas Müntzer, a revolutionary preacher from the medieval Peasant Revolt, understood Luke 1:52 *very* concretely and used it as his rallying message to cast the mighty rulers of his day off their thrones.[96] Scott summarizes the ultimate effect of status reversal images this way: "When we manipulate any social classification imaginatively—turning it inside out and upside down—we are forcibly reminded that it is to some degree an arbitrary human creation."[97] It is, one might add, a human creation that, in the worldview of the Magnificat author, Almighty God stands ready to overturn.

The timing of this divine overturning, however, provides a second layer of ambiguity to these reversals, and, as in the debate over literal and metaphorical interpretations of the Magnificat, the author's hidden transcript techniques have left modern-day scholars without a clear answer. One factor is the aorist tense of all the finite verbs in Luke 1:51-55, and what nuanced meaning we should perceive in that choice. François Bovon lays out some of the options:

> "Are they ordinary observations of past history, or gnomic attestations of God's usual conduct? Are they ingressive aorists, signaling the beginning of eschatological events? Or are they influenced by the prophetic perfect in Hebrew, and thus pictures of the future? In sum, is this hymn a genuine praise to God for help granted, or a hidden prophecy of hoped-for salvation?"[98]

Or is it, in fact, a declaration of the divine work that is already underway, but not yet complete?

All are possible readings; both author and audience were probably safer that way. Prediction of a future reversal or an assertion that God habitually carries out status reversal is little threat to the ruling elites when their power is secure. But at the same time, the idea that God might be starting to reshape the world, to overturn the status quo, would offer great comfort and encouragement to those subordinated in their current situations. Certainly rumors of impending liberation at the hands of the authorities or a great divinity were common among oppressed groups, as a way to express hope that their subordination

96. Flusser, *Judaism*, 131–32.

97. Scott, *Domination*, 168.

98. Bovon, *Luke 1*, 57.

might be coming to end, and also to avoid punishment for such dangerous ideas by attributing them to some god or prophecy.[99] It seems most likely that a measure of "both-and" should be entertained with regard to the Magnificat's reversals, for Luke draws from past action, present possibility, and future hope in shaping this initial declaration of reversal. He invokes the Septuagintal tradition to show that God has always been a God who works for the poor and meek against the rich and powerful; at the same time, however, the coming of the Messiah is a new and unique effort to effect the salvation of status reversal for the final time. Jesus of Nazareth began the eschatological process, but it is left to the disciples and the readers of Luke's Gospel to continue his work until sometime in the future, when these status reversals will be made true and universal reality.

Moving beyond the most prominent reversals in Luke 1:51-53, there are other indications of the Magnificat's status as a text expressing dissatisfaction with the imperial order and its local elite allies. As is often mentioned, God is addressed in 1:47 as σωτήρ, a title given to Greco-Roman figures like epic heroes, military commanders, and local benefactors, those "who brought some tangible benefit to an individual or community."[100] It was then appropriated by Caesar Augustus, during whose reign, narratively, the Magnificat is depicted as being sung (Luke 2:1). As Gary Gilbert observes, "Recognizing the *princeps* as savior became a personal sign of loyalty to him and to the imperial system he represented."[101] Thus naming the God of Israel as σωτήρ within the Roman Empire was, at a minimum, proclaiming Yahweh as a deity of high status who was actively working for the good of the people rather than for the imperial status quo. Even more, for those first reading audiences in Hellenistic cities, this claim must have brought up echoes of another ruler and god (Caesar) acclaimed as savior in the prayers, inscriptions, and monuments with which they came face to face every day. One such example is the decree in 9 BCE from the Koinon of Asia declaring Augustus to be a divinely given savior who would bring peace to the people.[102] In such a context, the simple phrase ὁ θεός ὁ σωτήρ μου could

---

99. Scott, *Domination*, 147–48. He mentions various slave uprisings in the Caribbean and the United States, which were fueled by rumors that British officials or the king had freed the slaves, granted them mandatory days off, or abolished cruel practices like whipping (147). We might also consider the evidence of ancient apocalyptic texts such as, e.g., Dan. 7:9-18 (a vision of power passing back to the "one like a human being" and "the holy ones of the Most High [vv. 13-14, 18]); Rev. 18:1-24; 19:11-21 (an imagining of Rome's downfall); and the *War Scroll* (1QM) from the Dead Sea Scrolls community.

100. Gilbert, "Roman Propaganda," 237–39.

101. Ibid., 239; see also Gary Gilbert, "Luke-Acts and Negotiation of Authority and Identity in the Roman World," in *The Multivalence of Biblical Texts and Theological Meanings*, ed. Christine Helmer and Charlene T. Higbe, SbLSymS (Atlanta: Society of Biblical Literature, 2006), 100.

102. Brent, "Luke-Acts," 418; and Gilbert, "Roman Propaganda," 240.

easily be transformed into a form of quiet resistance, by offering one's loyalty and trust for salvation to someone besides the emperor.

The personal reversal of the opening stanza should also be noted: a slave woman (δούλή) has her low status (ταπείνωσις) reversed into the honor of divine favor (Luke 1:48). The particular ταπείνωσις (humility or humiliation) of Mary is not childlessness,[103] or even her sexually compromised status as an unwed pregnant woman.[104] Rather, it is the same as that of the wider community she represents, which is also lifted up alongside her (1:52): the daily humiliation faced by those living in conditions of poverty, powerlessness, and low status (cf. Prov. 16:18-19; Sir. 11:12-14).[105] Scott notes that domination usually operates at three different levels: material appropriation, public mastery and subordination, and ideological justification for such inequalities, with the first of these being the main point of the whole process of subjugation.[106] While the hidden transcript repudiates this domination on all three levels, it generally focuses on the supreme indignity of personal humiliation and objectification.[107]

This is exactly what the speaker of this song is addressing: her personal worth has been reversed through the care and notice of the holy, mighty God who chose to do great things for a girl of low status and little significance. She praises the action of God, the highest power of all, to provide her with the justice that those who are supposed to rule justly on earth refuse to supply. Thus there is also a critique of the elites' claim to benevolent care for their inferiors. The power of such a declaration—even in disguise—must not be underestimated, as Scott writes: "It may seem that the heavy disguise . . . must all but eliminate the pleasure it gives. . . . It nevertheless achieves something the backstage can never match. It carves out a public, if provisional, space for the autonomous cultural expression of dissent. If it is disguised, it is at least not hidden; it is spoken to power. This is no small achievement of voice under domination."[108]

The Magnificat, therefore, is firmly established as a hidden transcript text, camouflaging its resistant strains under a cloak of ambiguity that allows those in

103. See, e.g., Raymond E. Brown, *Birth of the Messiah*, 361.

104. See, e.g., Robbins, "Socio-Rhetorical Criticism," 182.

105. Janice Capel Anderson, "Mary's Difference: Gender and Patriarchy in the Birth Narratives," *JR* 67 (1987): 197; Carter, "Singing in the Reign," 31; and Horsley, *Liberation of Christmas*, 89. Cf. Jones, "Background and Character," 22, who argues that the lowliness implied here is Israel's oppression by its enemies.

106. Scott, *Domination*, 111–12.

107. Ibid., 113.

108. Ibid., 166.

power to interpret its reversals innocuously if they so choose—as indeed various Christian interpreters have done over the centuries. Alongside the resistance to imperial power, though, we must also pay attention to the hints of mimicry, schadenfreude (delight in others' misfortunes), and reversed oppression that are indicators of how deeply a system of domination can embed itself in the consciousness even of those whom it dominates. The singer, although she claims to have been lifted up, casts herself as a slave (δούλη) in Luke 1:48, with the only difference being that now God is her master rather than humans. Slavery was, of course, a basic foundational structure of Roman economy and society.[109] Therefore the singer seems to adopt an imperial social designation to define her relationship to God.

From our vantage point today, we might question whether being a slave, even to a holy and liberating deity, is necessarily an improvement in situation. The Central American *campesinos* of Solentiname certainly show significant discomfort with the idea. One young man expresses frustration that "God is selfish because he wants us to be his slaves. He wants our submission. . . . I don't see why Mary has to call herself a slave. We should be free!"[110] In further discussion, other members of the community argue that to be a slave to God is to be a slave of love, and claim that such slavery is actually liberating in its solidarity with the oppressed of today.[111] But as we move into the second part of our sociological analysis, an examination of the imperial negotiation techniques found in the evangelist's incorporation of the song and in the narrative context he provides, their discomfort with the language of empire and domination is an apt reminder of the complexities of imperial negotiation.

HIDDEN TRANSCRIPTS IN THE SONG'S NARRATIVE CONTEXT

Sometimes it is argued that such subversive traditions were included in the final form of Luke only because they were a part of the Jesus tradition. Luise Schottroff, for example, holds that the presence of the Magnificat and the Lukan beatitudes and woes in a Gospel that portrays Christianity as socially acceptable bears witness only to the strength and importance of what she dubs the earliest

109. See further K. R. Bradley, *Slaves and Masters in the Roman Empire: A Study in Social Control* (New York: Oxford University Press, 1987); J. Albert Harrill, *Slaves in the New Testament: Literary, Social, and Moral Dimensions* (Minneapolis: Fortress Press, 2006); Richard A. Horsley, "The Slave Systems of Classical Antiquity and Their Reluctant Recognition by Modern Scholars," *Semeia* 83–84 (1998): 19–66; and Peter Garnsey and Richard Saller, *The Roman Empire: Economy, Society and Culture* (Berkeley: University of California Press, 1987), 116–25.

110. Cardenal, *Gospel in Solentiname*, 16.

111. Ibid., 16–17.

Jesus traditions, and is not necessarily indicative of Luke's personal desires and beliefs.[112] But this reading does not give Luke enough credit. His "great omission" of large sections of Mark (6:45—8:27; 9:41—10:12) shows that he was in no way averse to limiting his use of received tradition, and he was certainly under no obligation to include this song, which appears nowhere else in extant early Christian literature. Luke evidently decided, for his own purposes and in his own community context, to include this song and several other texts with strong reversal themes into his Gospel. As a piece of folk culture or oral tradition, Mary's song was preserved because it was meaningful for some group and their value system,[113] and Luke clearly takes his place in this succession. It is especially interesting that Luke, probably residing and writing outside the land of Palestine, adopted this strongly Jewish song as meaningful for his mixed urban community.

The immediate context in which Luke has placed the Magnificat enhances its character as part of a hidden transcript. We have already discussed the protection that the double meanings and ambiguity of the pericope's reversals would have extended to the one giving voice to such resistance. Luke supplies another shield as well, a type of anonymity, which Scott argues allows the bearer of the message to remain unidentified and thus unable to be punished.[114] Although Mary is named as the speaker, she enjoys protection as a character in a story set in a different place and time, rather than an actual person residing within the Lukan community who could be punished for her insubordination. The setting of the previously discussed Dead Sea Scrolls song 4Q427 7 I–II, on the other hand, provides a counterexample. The Scrolls community was already in a state of declared resistance to the Jerusalem authorities and their Roman overlords, and thus it was able to adopt a reversal hymn into its canon of sectarian psalms and prayers without much consequence beyond what it was already experiencing. Luke, however, couches his song of overthrow and exaltation in a story, to the benefit and protection of both himself and his audiences.

Allen Verhey's work implies that this is a recurring technique for Luke, noting Luke's tendency to make his views known through subtle stories and implication rather than direct commands or legal mandates, on topics such as the correct use of possessions, Jubilee-style debt forgiveness, the role of women in the church, and acceptance of sinners.[115] If the Gospel can lead readers into

112. Luise Schottroff, "Das Magnificat und die Älteste Tradition über Jesus von Nazareth," *EvT* 38 (1978): 304–306.

113. Scott, *Domination*, 157.

114. Ibid., 140.

a commitment to its worldview and methods of imperial negotiation, then the desired actions will likely follow without any overt command. Rather than a frontal attack against the Roman Empire, Luke places a hymn in the mouth of a character of notably low social status, a pregnant peasant girl, and has her prophetically announce the vision that her son will bring about, a world in which current ruling powers are thrown down by the God of Israel who is the true Savior, Mighty One, and giver of justice. C. Kavin Rowe writes, "It is at this level—that of the ordering principles of thought and their concomitant relation to praxis—that conflict could begin to break out. No matter how positive Luke's portrayal of the virtues of the Roman Empire and its people, there is at bottom a rival claim to universal Lordship."[116]

In the case of the Magnificat specifically, it is significant that Luke's story places it in the mouth of a woman. And not just any woman, but a woman from the lower ES5 or ES6, who is "among the most powerless people in her society: she is young in a world that values age; female in a world ruled by men; poor in a stratified economy."[117] Scott notes the work of Lynn Viola and her findings that peasant women often take the lead in protesting against oppression. Punishments were generally lighter for women than for men, and if their women were threatened, the men had a safer, more acceptable reason to intervene.[118] Obviously we are dealing in the Gospel with characters in a story rather than living people in the early urban churches, but Scott's point is still applicable. This is perhaps part of the reason that Mary sings the more subversive reversal song in the birth narratives, rather than Zechariah; she appears to pose less of a threat to the status quo, although Luke's readers would likely have recognized the fallibility of such a judgment. Luke clearly envisions a place for women, particularly those with some means and status, in the support and perhaps also the leadership of the church (see Luke 8:1-3; Acts 1:14; 16:11-15; 17:1-4, 10-12; 18:24-26; 21:8-9). Such women would have been present in the communities of Jesus-followers who received Luke's Gospel, and they undoubtedly dealt with status inconsistency. That constant struggle to define and defend their status would likely have led to both a greater empathy for the poor and powerless and a desire to change the status quo that had created

---

115. Allen Verhey, *The Great Reversal: Ethics and the New Testament* (Grand Rapids: Eerdmans, 1984), 95–97.

116. C. Kavin Rowe, "Luke-Acts and the Imperial Cult: A Way through the Conundrum?" *JSNT* 27 (2005): 298.

117. Luke Timothy Johnson, *The Gospel of Luke*, SP 3, ed. Daniel J. Harrington (Collegeville, MN: Liturgical, 1991), 39.

118. Scott, *Domination*, 150.

their own uncertain situation.[119] Hearing that desire voiced by a woman would almost certainly have had a potent galvanizing effect on some of these women. George Brooke writes with regard to the apocryphal "Song of Miriam" and its kindred like the Magnificat: "Some aspects of God's power are most readily visible when sung about by a woman."[120]

Also important, aside from the song's attribution to Mary, is the narrative setting in which she sings it and the reversals evident there: the mother of the one who will become king has gone to visit the mother of his servant,[121] and she is not a queen but a sexually compromised peasant girl. Elizabeth is the older of the two, with higher status, and thus more honored, yet she is inspired by the Holy Spirit to bless Mary and the child Jesus in her womb (Luke 1:41–42, 45). She designates Jesus with the high honorific title κύριος (1:43), and links Mary with strong Jewish heroines like Jael and Judith, who were also called "blessed among women" (Luke 1:42; cf. Judg. 5:24; Jth. 13:18). Both these titles are significant for our study of imperial negotiation. Rowe draws attention to Luke's consistent naming of Jesus as κύριος, with a culminating confession in Acts 10:36 (οὗτός ἐστιν πάντων κύριος), countering the imperial use of similar titles.[122] Mary's connection with Jael and Judith underscores our previous discussion of the Magnificat's indebtedness to earlier victory songs, but with an important difference. Rather than wielding a weapon herself, Mary is instead blessed for the child she will bear and raise and support in his mission; in the process she herself will be pierced with a (metaphorical) sword (Luke 2:35).[123] There is indeed a new ruler with a new imperial family being birthed here, but his way of being "Lord of all" while on earth will be different from those who have come before.

Finally, I want to discuss briefly the unique setting of the Magnificat, the only scene in the New Testament where we are privy to a conversation between two women alone. The meeting of an older and a younger woman over the matter of their impending motherhood is quite appropriate, and no doubt familiar territory for mothers and other women hearing this story. Both archaeological and textual evidence indicates that rituals, prayers, and magical

119. Gerhard E. Lenski, *Power and Privilege: A Theory of Social Stratification* (1966; repr., Chapel Hill: University of North Carolina Press, 1984), 88; and C. R. Whittaker, "The Poor," in *The Romans*, ed. Andrea Giardina (Chicago: University of Chicago Press, 1993), 297.

120. Brooke, *Dead Sea Scrolls*, 271.

121. York, *Last Shall Be First*, 45n2.

122. Rowe, "Luke-Acts," 291–96.

123. R. Alan Culpepper, "The Gospel of Luke: Introduction, Commentary, and Reflections," in *NIB*, ed. Leander E. Keck, vol. 9 (Nashville: Abingdon, 1995), 55.

practices to assure healthy fertility, childbirth, and lactation were based in a household context, and carried out mostly by women—the pregnant woman herself, her family and friends, and professional women like midwives and herbalists.[124] This scene in Luke is a private event, but most female readers would also have regarded it as a sacred one. The content of the Magnificat, shared here only with Elizabeth, heightens the worshipful atmosphere and moves beyond the usual rituals of childbearing. The song itself, as mentioned earlier, is a victory hymn, from a genre that is almost always a public performance before God and all the people.[125] The publication and dissemination of the Gospel of Luke has now restored the Magnificat to a more public stage, in the alternative communities being formed by Jesus-followers within, yet separate from, the Roman Empire. The evangelist is skillfully playing here with accepted notions of public and private, sacred and secular, center and margins. Slowly, he is bringing the hidden transcript out of the safe place where it was birthed into the danger of the public arena, exposing it to a mixed audience that no doubt included people invested in and benefiting from Roman domination. But only in its unveiling in the Gospel text, and perhaps even in the community's worship, can the reversals envisioned by the Magnificat begin to become reality in the lives of those who will listen and begin to carry them out.

Contextuality: The Magnificat in the Hellenistic Churches

The question remains what role Mary's song of reversal plays in the larger context of the Third Gospel and in the life setting of its first readers and hearers. Stephen Farris argues convincingly that the hymns of the birth narrative function in a manner similar to that of Scripture quotations in the rest of Luke-Acts: to "introduce and encapsulate the true theological significance of the story narrated by the author."[126] If this is the case, then the Magnificat is Luke's opening gambit, powerfully signaling a holistic interpretation of Jesus' imminent entry into the world and foregrounding the theme of status reversal for his reading communities. It is to these contextual implications that I will now turn our attention.

---

124. Carol Meyers, *Households and Holiness: The Religious Culture of Israelite Women*, Facets (Minneapolis: Fortress Press, 2005), 37–38, 55–56.

125. Meyers, "Miriam, Music, and Miracles," 41.

126. Farris, *Hymns*, 88.

THE MAGNIFICAT IN THE SWEEP OF THE LUKAN NARRATIVE

The placement of the Magnificat at the birth rather than the death of Jesus is significant, for it indicates that the celebrated divine actions of reversal are made manifest not only in the cross and resurrection, but also in Jesus' concrete ministry of social justice and community engagement.[127] Its theology encompasses both the spiritually focused celebration of God's work, and significant social upheaval on an individual and corporate level. John O. York argues that this was Luke's opening declaration of his reversal theology, probably surprising at first for most readers, but confirmed again and again throughout the rest of the Gospel.[128] Jesus' declaration of eschatological Jubilee in Nazareth, his beatitudes and woes, his communion with those on society's margins, and his eventual death and resurrection are all foreshadowed here by his mother Mary who, as it turns out, is not nearly as "sweet and innocent" as she is often portrayed. Scott writes, "The first open statement of a hidden transcript, a declaration that breaches the etiquette of power relations, that breaks an apparently calm surface of silence and consent, carries the force of a symbolic declaration of war."[129] Thus with the Magnificat, Mary is not simply singing a sweet pious song. She is issuing forth a shout of challenge.

Indeed, Warren Carter regards the Magnificat, together with its related hymns, Zechariah's Benedictus (Luke 1:68-79), the angels' Gloria (2:14), and Simeon's Nunc Dimittis (2:29-32), as "performative speech, part of the dignity-bestowing, hidden transcript."[130] Of particular importance to the task of restoring the dignity of the subjugated is their special relationship with God (clearly cherished by all the singers in Luke), and God's attendant desire to work alongside these human servants as colleagues. All the songs in the birth narrative allude to an honored person called to cooperate with the Messiah in the labor of God's reign: the slave girl Mary (1:48), John the prophet of the Most High (1:76), and the servant Simeon who has now recognized and proclaimed God's salvation (2:29-30).[131]

With Mary, Luke inaugurates a tension between God as the author and actor of revolutionary reversals and God's desire to share that work with God's human followers.[132] Later reversal texts will continue this trend, as Jesus proclaims the fulfillment of good news to the poor and oppressed and challenges

---

127. Horsley, *Liberation of Christmas*, 113–14.

128. York, *Last Shall Be First*, 166.

129. Scott, *Domination*, 8.

130. Carter, "Singing in the Reign," 35.

131. Jones, "Background and Character," 43.

132. Green, *Gospel of Luke*, 88, 100.

his Nazarene neighbors to accept that this hospitality is to be offered even to Gentiles (4:16-30); as Jesus calls the poor and hungry blessed and at the same time calls upon the people to create a new community where this will be so (6:20-49); and as Jesus entreats his influential hosts to make their banquets reflect those in God's realm, where all are equal, and those of lowest status are accorded the highest places of honor (14:7-24). God's choice to work with Mary is one of the first seeds of a major distinctive of Luke's imperial negotiation, and one that would have been particularly important in his mixed communities. Here, God has chosen a nondescript peasant girl to carry the Messiah and Lord, the Son of God, and she is transformed into a powerful prophet. As the Lukan narrative progresses, her son Jesus will show himself willing to work with anyone who shares his goals: not only Jewish peasants, but also Roman centurions (Acts 10:1-48), corrupt imperial officials (such as the chief tax collector of Luke 19:1-10), and a zealous Pharisee who persecutes his earliest followers (Acts 9:1-19). Certainly the openness of Jesus (and by extension of the early Christian churches) to collaboration with people of every status and ethnicity would have been a source of encouragement, but also real challenge, for the Jesus-followers of urban Greece and Asia Minor. From the most powerful elite magistrate to the lowliest beggar, Jesus wanted everyone to help him bring about his vision of the reign of God and its new world order, where the rulers would come down from their thrones so that the hungry could be filled and those of low status given back their dignity.

Luke places this part of the hidden transcript, with its strong call for status reversal, at the beginning of his work, and he must have had a strong reason for bringing it out into the open so early, so clearly, and so forcefully. The "primacy effect" indicates that this early statement of status reversal would have had significant influence upon how Luke's audiences would have understood the rest of the Gospel.[133] Schottroff notes evidence of four possible functions for such social ideas in the centuries before Jesus' birth: ethical warnings to the upper classes, accusations against the deity in the face of social upheaval, encouragement for fighters in an imminent war, and (only later, closer to the time of Jesus' life and Luke's composition) as a message of hope for the poor and oppressed.[134] In the context of Luke, the first and last explanations seem most pertinent. Walter Pilgrim summarizes his survey of the rich and poor in Luke-Acts with just such a two-pronged conclusion: the two books offer both a word

---

133. See Menakhem Perry, "Literary Dynamics: How the Order of a Text Creates Its Meanings," *Poetics Today* 1 (1979): 53–58, for an extended discussion of this effect in psychology and in literary works.

134. Schottroff, "Magnificat," 300.

of comfort to the poor, in that the reign of God belongs to them, and a word of challenge to the rich, exhorting them to share with the poor so they might also share in God's reign.[135]

This assertion adds an important theological aspect to Schottroff's social insights. In Luke, the reversals are evidence of God's action in the world on behalf of all people, the in-breaking of God's reign into daily life.[136] This again fits well with the model of hidden resistance. It is common for subordinated groups to develop a belief that takes hope from the knowledge that God (or a higher power of some kind) has decreed the imminent end of their oppression and defeat of the evil forces that uphold it. Such a theology allows the people to express more openly their hope for salvation from the powers that be, but at the hand of a deity rather than through their own rebellious action.[137] Songs in particular have been used for many years and by many different groups to negotiate oppressive political situations through fostering communal solidarity, dignity, and hope for a change in the dominant system.[138]

This sociological explanation, however, should not be thought to negate the theological message. The Magnificat is a theological proclamation with strong social and political ramifications, and these ramifications deepen Lukan theology. They strengthen and enhance our understanding of the God of Mary, Jesus, and Luke as a God who does not stand for oppression and offers guidance on how to reverse it. The reversals of the Magnificat and the entire Gospel are, as Verhey reminds us, both ethical and christological.[139] Luke does not allow us to separate theology from sociology, divine mercy for insiders from divine (and human) mercy for all, God's reign in this world from God's reign in heaven. Mary's song focuses on the wondrous actions of God, but the situation in which she proclaims them is a reversal embodied by her own acceptance of divinely favored status while still embracing her humility. This becomes all the more evident as the rest of Jesus' story unfolds.

The child is born and proclaimed to be Savior, Messiah, and Lord (Luke 2:11), but this ruler, declared by the angel Gabriel to be greater than the Roman client-king Herod and the emperor himself (1:30-37), is acclaimed at first only by his mother's reflection in song (1:46-55) and by non-elite shepherds fresh from the field (2:8-20), rather than by nobles and foreign dignitaries.

---

135. Walter E. Pilgrim, *Good News to the Poor: Wealth and Poverty in Luke-Acts* (Minneapolis: Augsburg, 1981), 160.

136. York, *Last Shall Be First*, 93.

137. Scott, *Domination*, 148.

138. See Carter, "Singing in the Reign," particularly 28–29.

139. Verhey, *Great Reversal*, 94.

Simeon prophesies that he will bring glory to Israel, but also light to the Gentiles (2:29-32). It should not surprise us by now that such a declaration of social upheaval does not come easily; instead, Simeon continues, it must face opposition, struggle, and division (2:34). As an adult, Jesus begins to flesh out the reversals of Luke 1:51-53. He prefaces his earthly ministry with an announcement of good news for the poor (4:18-21) and then proceeds to show what this looks like. The beatitudes and woes of 6:20-26 again echo the Magnificat and establish these bi-polar reversals as "part of the value-system of the narrative."[140] Jesus shows the Pharisees and other local leaders that Scripture should be interpreted in a way that favors those in need, the oppressed, and those of lowest status.[141] He teaches in both word and action that cultural notions of honor and greatness must be turned upside down (see especially 9:46-48; 14:7-24; 22:24-30). And in the end, Jesus acts these out in his own person and fate.

With his crucifixion and resurrection, Jesus becomes the central embodiment of God's reversing action as celebrated in the Magnificat, all the way back in Luke's first chapter—but not in the way we might think. York notes that Jesus' entire life is a full reversal. He is the Son of God and the new Davidic ruler (Luke 1:32-35), yet destined by that same God to die a shameful death (9:21-22; 18:31-33; cf. 9:44). Knowing this, Jesus voluntarily humbles himself and thus receives the glory of resurrection.[142] In this reading, though, Jesus shatters contemporary notions of how one goes about being a ruler and king. The elites of the Roman Empire expected their emperor to work assiduously for their benefit and to preserve their prerogatives (Pliny), and to show a proper concern for the maintenance of the imperial social hierarchy (Suetonius).[143] Jesus, however, is a κύριος with the very opposite goals. He acts consistently as benefactor not for the elite and powerful, but for those who are honest about their need for help, and he takes action to tear down the hierarchy and status system so highly valued by many people living in the Roman world. We will explore this aspect of Jesus' ministry more fully in the following chapters.

In connection with the worldview that underlies the Magnificat, Jesus is surprisingly cast as one of the rulers who are thrown down, and, at the same time, one of the lowly ones who are lifted up. The victory and reversal themes

140. York, *Last Shall Be First*, 59–60.

141. Green, *Theology*, 149.

142. York, *Last Shall Be First*, 172.

143. Both quoted in Kelly, *Roman Empire*, 33–34. Cf. Lenski, *Power and Privilege*, 231–41; and John H. Kautsky, *The Politics of Aristocratic Empires* (Chapel Hill: University of North Carolina Press, 1982), 6.

of the Magnificat, as I argued above, were already shifting away from more traditional ideas of destruction of one's enemies and military triumph; Luke's incorporation of this text into his Gospel furthers that movement even more. The rulers, to be sure, must be overthrown, but, as Green has argued, "this is not to say that God's overruling human rulers is God's last word for them. Quite the contrary, God's triumph over those who oppose him is itself a redemptive act, placing his opponents in a position whereby they might elect to join God's project."[144] This is perhaps an idealized vision of Luke's Gospel, but it is not without some basis. We will see in the following chapters of this study that Jesus encourages non-elites to work alongside their (former) oppressors in service of God's reign (chapter 4 on the Nazareth proclamation) and offers sharp warning to elites and their retainers about what will happen if they do not change their ways of conspicuous consumption (chapter 5 on the parable of Lazarus and the rich man). If, on the other hand, elites will follow Jesus' example and *willingly* give up their privilege for the benefit of others, rather than having reversal forced upon them as in Luke 1:51-53, they will find themselves welcomed into the community of faith.

Luke forcefully shows that kingship as envisioned by the Jerusalem leaders, the Herodians, the local Hellenistic gentry, and the Roman Empire is not the same as the kingship practiced by God and Jesus. The ruler of God's βασιλεία is one who has given up his throne to become a servant, very unlike the worldly kings and authorities who engage in "benefaction" for the benefit of their own honor and status (Luke 22:24-27). The disciples' debate about greatness that prompts this particular revelation is significantly situated at the Last Supper, as Jesus prepares to undergo the ultimate humiliation on his path to Lordship. This placement underlines Jesus' new definition of leadership, and also calls upon the disciples to emulate it. They are promised authority within the reign of God (22:28-30), but such authority must, like that of Jesus, take the form of status reversal if it is to be true and lasting authority. Thus remarkably, Luke does not simply pass on a vision of a different world, but instead narrates a story in which the new world is acted out in the life, death, and resurrection of Jesus and calls those who profess to follow him to make these ideas a reality.

---

144. Green, *Gospel of Luke*, 102. Cf. Boff, *Maternal Face*, 199–200; and Cardenal, *Gospel in Solentiname*, 9, 17–18. Robert McAfee Brown draws a similar, although less optimistic, conclusion; the rich, for him, "have a bleak future in [Mary's] scenario. Perhaps those who are rich, if ready to be nonrich, can survive. That will be a choice for them to ponder while there is still time" (*Unexpected News*, 80).

THE MAGNIFICAT IN THE SOCIAL WORLD OF THE LUKAN COMMUNITY

Since we have concluded that Luke, from his very first chapter, is bringing part of the hidden transcript and his own version of imperial negotiation out into the open (although not without some remaining layers of protection), the relationship between Luke and the Roman Empire must be reconsidered and nuanced. Of particular concern for our project are the ramifications of Luke's proposed methods of imperial negotiation for those early Christians in the provinces of Asia Minor and Greece who first received his words. The hidden transcript is crafted to contradict the elites' justification of their domination through appropriation of goods, personal humiliation and subjugation, and ideological inequality.[145] Thus its declaration is a subtle, and sometimes not-so-subtle, threat to the carefully constructed system of the dominant culture, which in the case of Luke includes not only Rome, but also its allies closer to home: in Jesus' life, the Herodian client-kings and the Jerusalem elites, and in the context of Luke's first reading communities, local gentry, city magistrates, and provincial authorities.[146] Rome, though, is clearly at the top of the hierarchy and exercises control (whether direct or indirect) in alliance with the other elites. What might have been the effects of Luke's Gospel on those living with such a worldview?

To be sure, Luke offers no overt encouragement anywhere in the Gospel or Acts to overthrow the Roman emperor or even local Roman-allied authorities. It does not follow, however, that this signifies complete acceptance of the status quo. On the contrary, with the Magnificat, Luke issues a call for change that offers its own criticism of the prevailing hierarchies. Scott points out that most publicly made requests or demands by a subordinated group carry realistic expectations that at least some central features of the domination will remain intact. This says little, he argues, about the group members' actual feelings about the system of domination, simply that they are strategic in their protest.[147] Gilbert makes a similar point in connecting Luke-Acts with the Second Sophistic; both appear to acknowledge that Rome is likely to remain the dominant power of their day, but they also criticize its practices and argue for their own culture's superiority in the end.[148] Thus the practicality of Luke's agenda—enacting new values and a new social system within the Christian

145. Scott, *Domination*, 111.

146. See chapter 2 for a complete treatment of the cultural context of Luke's reading communities.

147. Scott, *Domination*, 92.

148. Gilbert, "Luke-Acts and Negotiation," 96–97. For a fuller treatment of this topic, see Simon Swain, *Hellenism and Empire: Language, Classicism, and Power in the Greek World, AD 50–250* (Oxford: Clarendon, 1996).

community, in the midst of the Roman Empire, without advocating actual political overthrow—does not negate the strength of his convictions. In the Magnificat and its eventual fulfillment in Jesus' personal reversal, which in turn enables greater corporate reversals, we have a vigorous statement of Luke's values. They take what Scott identifies as the most radical step in interrogating a system of domination: not simply to denounce one ruler or a series of authority figures as not fulfilling their proclaimed values, but "to repudiate the very principles by which the dominant stratum justifies its dominance."[149] The social upheaval proclaimed in the Magnificat and demonstrated through action and story in Jesus' life questions the very structures upon which the many levels of Jerusalem, Herodian, Hellenistic, and Roman authority were based, and thus it is a challenge to this system, whether it advocates for political overthrow or not, at the level of "the ordering principles of thought and their concomitant relation to praxis."[150]

The most obvious and prevalent challenge in the Magnificat is probably to the members of the Lukan communities with more wealth and status (ES4 and any possible lower ES3 individuals). They are threatened with being stripped of their closely held power, wealth, and status (Luke 1:52-53) and are sharply criticized for their arrogance in attitude and action.[151] Yet Theophilus was possibly an elite, and he must have accepted this censure to some degree, at least enough to preserve the Gospel and accept its sequel from the same author. Hellenistic elites were in a constant struggle with one another for status and power, and Rome was the beneficiary as they sought to outdo their peers in offering honor to their overlord. As a result, they were actually legitimizing and enabling their own subjugation.[152] This endless jockeying for position probably grated on some of them, particularly those who experienced some level of status inconsistency, and would have increased the attractiveness of a vision like that offered in Mary's song: a God and ruler who turns the social hierarchy on its head and in doing so reveals its arbitrary nature.[153]

---

149. Scott, *Domination*, 92.

150. Rowe, "Luke-Acts," 298.

151. Johnson, *Gospel of Luke*, 42. In ancient thought, the heart was the seat of a person's thoughts and intentions. Therefore the Magnificat's condemnation of the arrogant for "the thoughts/imagination of their heart" likely refers to prideful attitudes of those of high status, who were actually nicknamed "the arrogant" by those whom they ruled. See Ramsay MacMullen, *Roman Social Relations: 50 B.C. to A.D. 284* (New Haven: Yale University Press, 1974), 109–10.

152. Garnsey and Saller, *Roman Empire*, 33; and S. R. F. Price, *Rituals and Power: The Roman Imperial Cult in Asia Minor* (Cambridge: Cambridge University Press, 1984), 62.

153. Scott, *Domination*, 168.

This was also, although it can be easy to miss, a significant challenge for the ES5 artisans, merchants, and prosperous farmers in the Lukan audience. Even though they were non-elites who received little benefit from the Roman status system, they often valued honor and status as much as anyone, as is evident in the miniature hierarchies they constructed for themselves in guilds and other associations.[154] A peek ahead to Luke 4 illustrates the challenge to people of every status that is inherent in the life and work of Jesus; the residents of Nazareth were perfectly happy to accept good news for the poor, captive, and oppressed when they thought they were the main beneficiaries (4:16-22), but turn shockingly violent when asked to imagine the extension of that same reversal to those outside their community (4:28-30).

We should also note the vestiges of imperial domination in the Magnificat that are not shaken even by its vision of a world turned upside down. God still demands ultimate loyalty and awe (Luke 1:50), just as did the Roman emperor. Mary is characterized as a slave (1:48), and Israel as a servant (1:54), maintaining status differences even in the midst of status reversals. There are also remnants of the violent military action of the earlier victory hymns in the references to God as "the Mighty One" (1:49) and the strength of God's arm to scatter, throw down, and send away empty (1:51-53). The idea of domination is so ingrained that it is difficult to shake completely.

The final area I wish to discuss is suggested by the poetic form of the Magnificat. In both Jewish and Greco-Roman traditions, poems were almost always chanted, sung, or set to music in some way, and they were often connected to prayer and worship. Frances Hickson Hahn writes, "For the Romans, at least formally, there was no distinction between prayer and spell and poetry and song; all were intimately linked to one another."[155] Thus we can accurately refer to the song of Mary and consider the role it played in the worship of Luke's communities both before and after its inclusion in the Gospel. John Nolland writes that the Magnificat would have been most relevant and popular in "a worship context in which there was a concern to recapitulate the decisive moments of salvation history" and their eschatological

---

154. MacMullen, *Roman Social Relations*, 74–77; and Whittaker, "The Poor," 297–98. For a more detailed discussion, see chapter 2 above.

155. Hahn, "Performing the Sacred," 236. Cf. Meyers, "Mother to Muse," 53–54; and Francois P. Viljoen, "Song and Music in the Early Christian Communities: Paul's Utilisation of Jewish, Roman and Greek Musical Traditions to Encourage the Early Christian Communities to Praise God and to Explain His Arguments," in *Zwischen den Reichen: Neues Testament und Römische Herrschaft*, ed. Michael Labahn and Jürgen Zangenberg, Texte und Arbeiten zum neutestamentlichen Zeitalter (Tübingen: Francke, 2002), 200.

fulfillment.[156] Music in general was an accepted part of Greek, Roman, and Jewish worship. It expressed emotions too great for words alone,[157] conveyed ethics and morality,[158] drew the attention of the deity to his or her devotees,[159] and structured the rhythm and emotions of a ritual.[160] What role would that music have played in the communities reading Luke, and what effect would the Magnificat in particular have had when it was proclaimed in worship?

The communal worship of the early Hellenistic Christian groups took place mainly in the homes of different community members, often centered around a meal. Traditionally, scholars have envisioned these meetings taking place in the large homes of wealthier members, but most likely we should expand this image. Some groups of Jesus-followers may very well have organized their gatherings within non-elite-controlled spaces like *insulae* (tenement buildings common throughout the Roman world), for example, or the shops of small artisans or merchants.[161] The table fellowship of people from all walks of life and levels of status, meeting in various environments, acted out in a concrete way the "world upside down" envisioned in the Magnificat and other reversal texts, and was therefore a powerful setting in which they could be proclaimed. Christopher Page writes:

> A single house could encompass those who were lowly enough to recognize that the teachings of a carpenter Messiah gave them a unique dignity just as it accommodated those who were elevated enough to recognize that those same teachings called them to a humility and service that could become the core of a new cultic identity as patrons, hosts and community elders.[162]

The music at these meals probably incorporated elements of both Jewish and Greco-Roman traditions and would have included singing and some

156. John Nolland, *Luke 1—9:20*, WBC 35a (Dallas: Word, 1989), 64. See also Seung Ai Yang, "Luke 1:46-55 the Magnificat," in *Prayer from Alexander to Constantine: A Critical Anthology*, ed. Mark Kiley (London: Routledge, 1997), 217.

157. Meyers, "Miriam, Music, and Miracles," 38.

158. Viljoen, "Song and Music," 201.

159. Christopher Page, *The Christian West and Its Singers* (New Haven: Yale University Press, 2010), 41.

160. Friederike Fless and Katja Moede, "Music and Dance: Forms of Representation in Pictorial and Written Sources," in Rüpke, *A Companion to Roman Religion*, 259.

161. Bruce W. Longenecker, *Remember the Poor: Paul, Poverty, and the Greco-Roman World* (Grand Rapids: Eerdmans, 2010), 333–34.

162. Page, *Christian West*, 37.

instrumental accompaniment. Jewish musical practices included antiphonal singing or chanting and performance of a soloist or trained groups, perhaps with a group response of "hallelujah" or "amen."[163] Music and prayer in Roman religion tended to be a more public affair, connected with official sacrifices, ceremonies, and festivals and performed by a (usually male) authority figure. Certainly, though, there were daily rituals in the home, shop, and field in which all people would have engaged.[164] The Christian communities began to produce their own hymnody early in the life of the faith, as is evidenced by texts like the Magnificat. Although there is little known for sure about the musical practices of New Testament–era churches, the earliest postcanonical leaders placed a high value on unison singing in worship, particularly because of its symbolic image of a harmonious and unified church.[165] Clement of Alexandria, writing early in the second century CE, noted a practice in Greek banquets of singing a unison song and advocated co-opting the tradition with a spiritual hymn for Christian meal gatherings.[166]

In this context, we can envision the Magnificat playing a significant role in worship, with equally significant ramifications for imperial relations. Most likely it was or became part of the hymnic repertoire for some of the communities that first read and heard the Gospel of Luke. As Luke presents it, its message of radical reversal of the status quo is powerfully communicated as sung by a young woman of little status. This reversal theme becomes even stronger when we consider the underlying tradition of Israelite women's victory songs contrasted with the Roman practice of public prayer ordinarily delivered by elite male authority figures. The Lukan setting possibly gave rise to performances of the Magnificat by a female soloist, perhaps accompanied by a lute or drum. But the power of Mary's song would be magnified many times over if it were ever sung in unison by the whole community, as seems likely from the strong preference for homophonic singing among early church leaders. The image of elite or wealthy members of some standing in the city declaring alongside a freed slave that rulers will be thrown down, the lowly lifted up, the arrogant scattered to pieces, and the hungry filled with good things, or a successful artisan singing such words alongside a destitute beggar, clearly undercuts the "unshakeable and inevitable" aura of the Roman hierarchy

---

163. Viljoen, "Song and Music," 298.

164. Hahn, "Performing the Sacred," 237–38.

165. Johannes Quasten, *Music and Worship in Pagan and Christian Antiquity*, trans. Boniface Ramsey (1930; repr., Washington, DC: National Association of Pastoral Musicians, 1983), 67; and Page, *Christian West*, 40–41.

166. Quasten, *Music and Worship*, 121.

and its social and political power. For Christians immersed every day in a constant competition for status and honor, "psalmody in the common assembly, or at the shared Sunday meal, was a way for them to celebrate and rediscover the true cosmic order, and their true home, amidst the distraction of life in the cities of the eastern Mediterranean that might gradually induce them to forget they were in exile."[167]

The declaration of Luke 1:46-55 in Christian worship was undoubtedly an example of the hidden transcript offering hope and dignity to those under oppression by open expression in one of their safe places.[168] But Luke has moved the discourse to a different level of challenge by its inclusion in a document made public, or at least semipublic. Now it has the power of a disguised, but still public, declaration of dissent in the teeth of power, "no small achievement of voice under domination."[169] Even the very joy with which Mary (together with Luke's communities of faith, as they echo her song in their own worship) expresses praise of God's power and mercy, such a strong theme in the Gospel of Luke,[170] has an element of dissent. Celebrations such as parades and processions, the usual context in Roman life for a hymn like the Magnificat, were only to be organized by the dominant group, as official gatherings. There is usually an "implicit assumption that subordinates gather only when they are authorized to do so from above. Any *unauthorized* gathering . . . has therefore been seen as potentially threatening."[171] Yet here we have what was certainly an unsanctioned gathering of people celebrating with great joy an upheaval in the order of the Roman world, in the person of a crucified and resurrected poor Galilean artisan. A dramatic image indeed.

Conclusion

The Magnificat is one of the first clear, strong statements of bilateral status reversal in the work of the third evangelist. That this song has a resistant strain is made clear by its connection with Hebrew victory hymns and other songs of status reversal, its resonance with the hidden transcripts of oppressed peoples throughout history, and the ramifications of singing it aloud in the midst of the Roman Empire. The sociopolitical aspects of Mary's song are part of Luke's larger perspective on his world, in which politics and theology cannot

167. Page, *Christian West*, 46.

168. Scott, *Domination*, 120–27.

169. Ibid., 166.

170. Culpepper, "Gospel of Luke," 56.

171. Scott, *Domination*, 61. Emphasis is original.

be separated. Allen Verhey designates this Lukan view of reality as having "a theocratic dimension" that allows the author to criticize and at times even ridicule the powers that be (Roman or otherwise) when they do not adhere to the standard held up by God's lordship and Jesus' lifestyle so defined by status reversal.[172] God's style of ruling God's people, exhibited throughout the history of Israel "to our ancestors, to Abraham and his descendants" (Luke 1:55), is first revealed by Luke in the Magnificat, and subsequently in the life of Jesus and his early followers.

John O. York writes, "The reversal of two opposites or contraries is presented as a series of related divine principles, describing God's action towards humanity through the inauguration of the Kingdom in the presence of his son, Jesus. Repetition of the form expands the characterization of the opposing positions and intensifies the importance of the divine principles."[173] While this study of the Magnificat is only a modest step, it is an important one. It establishes the Magnificat as an important initial declaration of status reversal at the very start of Luke's Gospel, entailing a radical shift in values, especially for those who have much earthly honor and status.[174] Also important, though, is the openness within the Magnificat's narrative context in Luke to reconciliation with the rulers and the powerful who must be lowered from their lofty perches. "Heaven has disrupted the customary patterns of political and religious life, God's sovereign rule has begun to refashion human society, and the coming of God's peace disturbs the powerful."[175] If this is the God professed by Luke, such a deity will not be satisfied with the earthly rulers we meet in his two volumes. We must continue our study of other declarations of status reversal in the Gospel of Luke, in order to understand more fully the new community envisioned by Jesus and by Luke, one that centers on a new definition of status, wealth, and power that is to be embraced by elite and non-elite alike.

---

172. Verhey, *Great Reversal*, 101–2.

173. York, *Last Shall Be First*, 93.

174. Ibid., 182.

175. John T. Carroll, "The God of Israel and the Salvation of the Nations: The Gospel of Luke and the Acts of the Apostles," in *The Forgotten God: Perspectives in Biblical Theology*, ed. A. Andrew Das and Frank J. Matera (Louisville: Westminster John Knox, 2002), 104.

4

The Nazareth Proclamation: Nuancing Resistance

This text, almost universally acknowledged as "programmatic" in the Gospel of Luke, stands at the beginning of Jesus' ministry, just as Mary's song stood at the beginning of his life. Both of these texts send a clear message about the identity of Jesus of Nazareth and the mission he is about to fulfill, and both center on images of status reversal. The prominence of these themes of leveling and inversion marks the presence of previously hidden resistance being made partially public in the theology and worldview of the Gospel of Luke, and a hope that the communities reading the Lukan narrative will embody its alternative social relationships. James C. Scott writes, "When we manipulate any social classification imaginatively—turning it inside out and upside down—we are forcibly reminded that it is to some degree an arbitrary human creation."[1]

Indeed, in both the Magnificat and the Nazareth proclamation, the human and arbitrary nature of the Roman imperial hierarchy is highlighted particularly by the focus on God as the author of the reversals that must transpire in order to transform the empire of Rome into the empire of God—the "year approved by the Lord" (Luke 4:19). The identity of God in Lukan theology is the source of its foundational threats to Greco-Roman social, economic, and ethical ideals.[2] The Magnificat introduced Luke's readers to this concept, but the Nazareth proclamation develops and nuances it significantly. The status reversals defined by Jesus in Luke 4:16-30 begin with traditional non-elite hidden transcripts, but then proceed to challenge their adherents to embrace the

1. James C. Scott, *Domination and the Arts of Resistance: Hidden Transcripts* (New Haven: Yale University Press, 1990), 168.

2. C. Kavin Rowe, *World Upside Down: Reading Acts in the Graeco-Roman Age* (Oxford: Oxford University Press, 2009), 141–42.

basic ideals of equality and justice even more completely.[3] A major function of the Nazareth proclamation is to nuance the Christian communities' definition of status reversal, its intended beneficiaries, and its concrete application in their relationships with one another.

The Nazareth proclamation occurs in the middle of Luke 4, the first chapter that focuses exclusively on the beginning of Jesus' ministry. Chapter 3 belongs mainly to John the Baptist, with Jesus' baptism narrated in only two verses (Luke 3:21-22). It is followed immediately by the tracing of Jesus' ancestry from Joseph back to "Adam, the son of God" (3:38), providing verification of Jesus' true identity for the benefit of the reader (cf. 1:32-35). At the beginning of Luke 4, as one final act of preparation for public ministry, Jesus follows the Spirit into the wilderness to be tested and tempted by the devil (4:13). Only after this does the third evangelist narrate Jesus' return to the familiar region of Galilee (4:14-15), and more specifically to his hometown Nazareth (4:16), to begin his work.[4] There, Jesus uses a synagogue reading from the prophet Isaiah to inaugurate his mission of status reversal: an act empowered by the Spirit, defined by preaching good news to the poor, and designed to transform the world in accordance with God's vision of favor, worth, and acceptability (4:18-21). He then pushes the issue even further by challenging the Nazareth congregation's assumptions about his hometown loyalty and adding the images of Elijah helping a Gentile widow and Elisha healing a Syrian warrior (4:23-27). The Nazarenes' reaction to Jesus' proclamation and its unexpected twists is at first mixed (4:22), and then later, in the climax of the story, decidedly united in anger and attempted violence (4:28-30).

The story of Jesus receiving a less-than-enthusiastic welcome from his neighbors in Nazareth is not, of course, unique to Luke's Gospel. Mark 6:1-6 and Matt. 13:54-58 also record him teaching in the local synagogue, facing questions about his parentage, referencing the saying that prophets are not

3. See also the discussion of Joel B. Green, *The Gospel of Luke*, NICNT, ed. Gordon D. Fee (Grand Rapids: Eerdmans, 1997), 200–3. He argues that Luke tends first to cater to Galilean social expectations and then to parody and reverse them. He also emphasizes the centrality of the image of God to Jesus' cultural ethics: "Jesus thus makes an economic statement grounded ultimately in his vision of a transformed system of social relations, itself grounded in his portrayal of God" (203).

4. It is possible to see this as a symbolic, as well as a literary, event. See François Bovon, *Luke 1: A Commentary on the Gospel of Luke 1:1—9:50*, trans. Christine M. Thomas, Hermeneia, ed. Helmut Koester (Minneapolis: Fortress Press, 2002), 151, and his argument that Galilee is, in the annunciation and in the Nazareth proclamation, the site of origin stories and divine revelation, which serves as starting point for the further revelation and proclamation of salvation to the rest of Judea, Jerusalem, and the world.

acceptable in their hometowns, and ultimately being unable or unwilling to perform significant signs for the people there. Beyond this framework, though, Luke is entirely alone in his narration of the Isaiah reading, the content of Jesus' teaching, the references to Elijah and Elisha, and the violent reaction of the townspeople. Additionally, the Matthean and Markan versions place the Nazareth visit in the middle of Jesus' ministry, not at the beginning as Luke's story does. This change is almost certainly a Lukan narrative device to highlight the significance of this episode.[5] But beyond this conclusion (which itself is an educated guess rather than a certainty), source criticism has not produced a consensus opinion.[6] Our concern in this project, however, is mainly with the final form of Luke 4:16-30 and what it might have meant to the Gospel's earliest audiences.

On this level, scholars have often recognized and studied the theme of reversal in the Nazareth proclamation. Certainly the status reversals in the Isaiah quotation have been noted, particularly for their connections to the traditional Year of Jubilee.[7] But this story also contains a powerful reversal of expectations, specifically the expectations of the Nazarenes about who Jesus was and what it meant for him to proclaim the fulfillment of the Isaiah passage. Using Jesus' illustrations from the lives of Elijah and Elisha, scholars have almost always outlined this conflict in terms of the sometimes difficult relationship between Jews and Gentiles in the time of Jesus, as well as in the time of Luke and his reading communities. Jesus' teaching in the Nazareth synagogue and the angry reaction of its congregation have been interpreted in various ways: as

5. Michael Prior, *Jesus the Liberator: Nazareth Liberation Theology (Luke 4:16-30)* (Sheffield: Sheffield Academic Press, 1995), 87–88.

6. Traditionally, the Nazareth proclamation has been viewed, much like the speeches of Acts, as free composition by the evangelist; see, e.g., Henry J. Cadbury, *The Making of Luke-Acts*, 2nd ed. (Peabody, MA: Hendrickson, 1999), 188–89. Others have argued that it is a conflation of various sources; e.g., Joseph A. Fitzmyer, *The Gospel According to Luke I–IX*, AB 28 (Garden City, NY: Doubleday, 1981), 528; and Robert C. Tannehill, "The Mission of Jesus according to Luke iv 16–30," in *Jesus in Nazareth*, ed. Walther Eltester, BZNW (Berlin: Walter de Gruyter, 1972), 53. More recently, some scholars have suggested a historical basis for Luke's version, perhaps in an oral or written source not available to Mark or Matthew. For various arguments from this perspective, see John Nolland, *Luke 1—9:20*, WBC 35a (Dallas: Word, 1989), 193; Prior, *Jesus the Liberator*, 38, 78, 87–88; Sharon H. Ringe, *Jesus, Liberation, and the Biblical Jubilee: Images for Ethics and Christology*, OBT 19 (Philadelphia: Fortress Press, 1985), 41; and James A. Sanders, "From Isaiah 61 to Luke 4," in *Luke and Scripture: The Function of Sacred Tradition in Luke-Acts*, ed. Craig A. Evans and James A. Sanders (Minneapolis: Fortress Press, 1993), 66–67.

7. See, e.g., Ringe, *Jesus, Liberation*, 34–45; and Robert Bryan Sloan Jr., *The Favorable Year of the Lord: A Study of Jubilary Theology in the Gospel of Luke* (Austin: Schola, 1977), 32–89. See also further discussion below.

a foreshadowing of the Gentile mission undertaken in the book of Acts;[8] as a warning to the Jewish nation not to rely too heavily upon their privileged position as the chosen people;[9] as a challenge issued to the Jewish people to accept Gentiles if they themselves want to be accepted in the reign of God;[10] and as a call for early Christian communities to embrace fully the act of regular table fellowship between Jews and Gentiles.[11]

Certainly all these studies have their merits, for the Jewish-Gentile relationship is an important part of the unexpected inclusiveness that Jesus proclaims in Nazareth to be a part of his mission. But it is not the only significant barrier that is broken down in Luke 4:16-30. Social and economic issues are also prominent in both the Isaiah quotation and Jesus' ensuing comments upon it, something that is recognized much less often in the scholarly body of work. Joel Green argues that the poor to whom the good news is to be proclaimed (4:18) are not only economically destitute, but also

> those who are for any of a number of socio-religious reasons relegated to positions outside the boundaries of God's people. . . . Jesus indicates his refusal to recognize those socially determined boundaries, asserting instead that even these 'outsiders' are the objects of divine grace. . . . God has opened a way for them to belong to God's family.[12]

From this starting point, I will explore in this chapter not only the Jewish-Gentile relationship, but also the various other types of boundaries and divisions addressed in the Nazareth proclamation and delineate how they might have been heard by the Christian churches first reading the Gospel of Luke. I will first turn to intertextual considerations, specifically the compiled quotation of Isaiah 58 and 61 in Luke 4:18-19 and its relationship to the Year of Jubilee and other ancient festivals of status reversal. In the second section, I will consider our pericope in light of Scott's model of hidden transcripts of resistance and elaborate the nuances of the social and spiritual transformation that the biblical text envisages. Finally, I will trace the development of these themes throughout

---

8. Tannehill, "Mission of Jesus," 61–62.

9. David R. Catchpole, "The Anointed One in Nazareth," in *From Jesus to John: Essays on Jesus and New Testament Christology in Honour of Marinus de Jonge*, ed. Martinus C. de Boer, JSNTSup 84 (Sheffield: JSOT Press, 1993), 249; and Tannehill, "Mission of Jesus," 59.

10. Jeffrey S. Siker, "'First to the Gentiles': A Literary Analysis of Luke 4:16-30," *JBL* 111 (1992): 83.

11. Bovon, *Luke 1*, 156.

12. Green, *Gospel of Luke*, 211.

the Gospel of Luke and the Acts of the Apostles, and their possible impact in Luke's earliest reading communities.

INTERTEXTUALITY: ISAIAH AND ANCIENT CELEBRATIONS OF REVERSAL

In the previous chapter, we profitably compared the Magnificat with other songs of victory and reversal from the Hebrew Bible, the Jewish Apocrypha, the Dead Sea Scrolls, and Greco-Roman literature. With regard to Luke 4:16-30, however, the task of intertextual exploration will take a slightly different form. Here, instead of genre comparisons, we must consider several Septuagint passages that the Lukan Jesus quotes, references, and alludes to in his proclamation to the people of Nazareth. Most prominent among these is his extended reading from the final chapters of Isaiah, incorporating parts of Isa. 61:1-2 and one line from Isa. 58:6. I will argue that this quotation invokes not only these specific lines as central to Jesus' ministry and the "year of God's favor" (Luke 4:19), but also the wider context of these chapters from Trito-Isaiah and the Torah texts that they themselves echo (Leviticus 25 in particular).

The citation of Hebrew Bible or, more correctly, Septuagint passages in the New Testament is a complex topic, with many factors that must be considered in order to understand fully each quotation and allusion. Richard Hays identifies five factors that can affect its meaning: the author's intentions in including the quotation, the original audience's understanding of it, the intertextual "fusion" in the text itself, the interpretation of the modern reader, and the interpretation of the modern community of readers. Rather than choosing one or two on which to focus, in his work with Paul's scriptural citations he attempts to "hold them all together in creative tension."[13] Certainly such areas are relevant for Luke's use of Isaiah in our focal text, and the strategy of studying them in concert with one another is an important step. But even these five factors do not offer definitive answers or cover the full complexity of the intertextual relationship. For example, it seems clear that Luke is quite purposeful in the inclusion of both the Isaiah quotation and the Elijah and Elisha examples in Jesus' sermon at Nazareth. But it is impossible to declare with any certainty what exactly those intentions were.[14] And even more significantly, authorial intentions do not completely control the new connections that the audience will make in its reading and interpretation of the text. I will argue,

---

13. Richard B. Hays, *Echoes of Scripture in the Letters of Paul* (New Haven: Yale University Press, 1989), 26–27.

14. See Steve Moyise, *Evoking Scripture: Seeing the Old Testament in the New* (London: T&T Clark, 2008), 128–30, for a discussion of authorial intention and the room that it allows for interpretation of quotations, allusions, and echoes of Scripture.

then, in the following paragraphs not for certainty but for, in the words of Steve Moyise, "hypotheses that explain the literary data, offer a plausible intention or purpose for it, and show that it is not impossible for at least some of the readers to have understood it thus."[15]

The author of the Gospel of Luke demonstrates an extensive familiarity with the Septuagint, and a particular preference for the book of Isaiah.[16] It seems likely that he expected his audience also to be acquainted on some level with these texts, and therefore to understand the larger context and significance of the quotations included in the Gospel. That context, Isaiah 58 and 61 specifically, and the work of Trito-Isaiah in general, is invoked by the verses quoted; although it is not as "loud" as the actual citations, it most likely was present in the thinking of Luke's earliest audiences and therefore contributed to their understanding of Jesus' Nazareth proclamation.[17] Warren Carter argues that particularly in oral cultures like those of the biblical world, brief spoken references often bring to mind larger concepts and stories—"[t]he part summons the whole; the citation echoes a much larger tradition."[18]

Two other observations about intertextuality are pertinent to the following discussion. In addition to this relationship between the quotations, their context, and the audience, especially relevant to Luke 4:16-30 is what Julia Kristeva calls a dialogical relationship between intertexts. In this theory, there is a fluidity to texts' meaning as they cite, allude to, and reinterpret one another.[19] I will demonstrate this type of development of the concept of Jubilee and release in the Hebrew Bible, the Septuagint, and the Gospel of Luke. Finally, Warren Carter's definition of an "authorial audience" is helpful to consider, as I evaluate the group's possible understanding of the imagery of reversal and Jubilee found in Luke 4, Trito-Isaiah, and Leviticus 25. Carter writes that this authorial audience is

> the receptor or audience which the author has "in mind" in writing
> the text . . . a "contextualized implied reader" not so much present
> in the text as presupposed by the text and reconstructed in part by

---

15. Ibid., 140.

16. See, for example, the essays in Evans and Sanders, *Luke and Scripture*, particularly 14–25, 46–69, which focus on Isaiah in Luke.

17. See Moyise, *Evoking Scripture*, 137–38.

18. Warren Carter, "Evoking Isaiah: Matthean Soteriology and an Intertextual Reading of Isaiah 7–9 and Matthew 1:23 and 4:15-16," *JBL* 119 (2000): 506.

19. Julia Kristeva, "Word, Dialogue and Novel," in *The Kristeva Reader*, ed. Toril Moi (New York: Columbia University Press, 1986), 36. See also Moyise, *Evoking Scripture*, 138–39.

textual features and by an examination of the interrelation between the text and the context in which the work was produced. . . . This audience is my creation, constructed out of various historical, literary, and Gospel data. . . . It embraces and overlaps a real audience.[20]

My conceptualization of the Lukan audience is described in chapter 2 above, and it will inform the following intertextual discussion, as well as the sociological and contextual spheres of inquiry. Different audiences will have different levels of recognition and understanding of the scriptural quotations and allusions depending on their traditions and sociocultural experiences.[21] All these factors will come into play as we consider Jesus' scriptural quotation in Luke 4:18-19.

TRITO-ISAIAH

The composite quotation in Luke 4:18-19, taken from Isa. 61:1-2 and Isa. 58:6, is one of the main expressions of status reversal in this pericope, and certainly the most explicit. Robert O'Toole contends that a major theological concern in Luke-Acts is to connect the work of Jesus and the earliest communities of his followers with the faith and history of the Jewish people, to show "that God who brought salvation to his people in the Old Testament continues to do this, especially through Jesus Christ."[22] The story of the Nazareth proclamation shows the strength of this connection, specifically with regard to the theme of status reversal; God is shown here to be working, in the time of Jesus as in the time of the Isaianic prophet, on behalf of the poor, the oppressed, and the captive. But the author of the Gospel of Luke seldom adopts any theme without tweaking and transforming it in light of the life, death, and resurrection of Jesus of Nazareth.[23] Thus I will consider here the original context and content of Trito-Isaiah, especially chapters 61 and 58, and how they function in the Nazareth proclamation pericope.

20. Carter, "Evoking Isaiah," 505n8.

21. Ibid., 505.

22. Robert F. O'Toole, *The Unity of Luke's Theology: An Analysis of Luke-Acts*, GNS 9, ed. Robert J. Karris (Wilmington: Michael Glazier, 1984), 17.

23. For extended discussion of Luke's transformation of the themes of Isaiah, see Peter Mallen, *The Reading and Transformation of Isaiah in Luke-Acts*, LNTS 367 (London: T&T Clark, 2008), particularly 102–33. He concludes that "Luke both affirms and transforms the message of Isaiah in developing certain themes in the narrative. . . . While Luke is faithful to the actual text of Isaiah, his interpretation may be considered subversive from a Jewish perspective, since he applies an inclusive hermeneutic to favourite salvation texts and radically challenges the common Jewish understanding of the Messiah" (199).

The later chapters of the canonical book of Isaiah[24] treat concerns of the post-exilic community in Jerusalem, which was struggling to rebuild the city, the temple, and the identity of its people. Its oracles speak to great hope for a glorious redemption (for example, Isaiah 60–62), but only in the midst of judgment on hypocrisy, injustice, and sin, which were also present in the rebuilding community (for example, Isaiah 58–59). Overall, we find "a picture of a . . . community in which there are rich and poor, those close to the sources of power and those deprived of it—a community in which the poor are exploited by the wealthy as always, a community going about its civic and religious business, and especially a community under severe stress."[25] The Isaianic prophet seeks to emphasize the continued working of Yahweh even in the midst of such struggle, and in Deutero- and Trito-Isaiah, there is a particular focus on the extension of Yahweh's lordship and covenant to all nations.[26] But this overall view stood in some tension with the messy reality of struggles between elites and non-elites, between prophetic and priestly circles, and between returned exiles and the people who had remained in Judah.[27]

The main thrust of Jesus' reading at Nazareth is taken from Isaiah 61, often regarded as the literary and thematic centerpiece of Trito-Isaiah. The vision of redemption for Jerusalem that is presented in chapters 60–62 stands at the center of a large-scale chiasm originally proposed by Norman Gottwald, and the prophet's self-declared mission (Isa. 61:1-3) is at the center of this centerpiece:[28]

---

24. Our central focus here will be Isaiah 56–66, traditionally known as Trito- or Third Isaiah, with an acknowledgment that discussion is still ongoing in the scholarly community about the appropriateness of the three-part division of the canonical Isaiah into First (1–39), Deutero- (40–55), and Trito-Isaiah (56–66). For an overview of the debate, see Joseph Blenkinsopp, *Isaiah 56–66*, AB 19B (New York: Doubleday, 2003), 25–37. He writes, "In subject matter, tone, and emphasis, chs. 56–66 are distinct enough to warrant separate treatment, yet they belong on the same textual and exegetical continuum as chs. 40–55" (30).

25. Ibid., 63–64.

26. Henry Jackson Flanders Jr., Robert Wilson Crapps, and David Anthony Smith, *People of the Covenant: An Introduction to the Hebrew Bible*, 4th ed. (New York: Oxford University Press, 1996), 422.

27. John Bright, *A History of Israel*, 4th ed. (Louisville: Westminster John Knox, 2000), 368.

28. Norman Gottwald, *The Hebrew Bible: A Socio-Literary Introduction* (Minneapolis: Fortress Press, 1985), 508. See also Blenkinsopp, *Isaiah 56–66*, 61; and Wes Howard-Brook, *"Come Out, My People!" God's Call out of Empire in the Bible and Beyond* (Maryknoll, NY: Orbis, 2010), 265.

A Proclamation of salvation for foreigners (56:1-8)
  B Indictment of wicked leaders (56:9—57:13)
    C Proclamation of salvation for the people (57:14-21)
      D Indictment of corrupt worship (58:1-14)
        E Lament and confession over sins of the people (59:1-15a)
          F Theophany of judgment/redemption (59:15b-20)
            G Proclamation of fully redeemed people (60–62)
          F' Theophany of judgment/redemption (63:1-6)
        E' Lament and confession over sins of the people (63:7—64:12)
      D' Indictment of corrupt worship (65:1-16)
    C' Proclamation of salvation for the people (65:17-25)
  B' Indictment of wicked leaders (66:1-6)
A' Proclamation of salvation including foreigners (66:7-24)

Figure 4: Gottwald's Chiastic Outline of Isaiah 60–62

The chapters surrounding the center of the chiasm, though, imply that such redemption is not to be gained easily and without struggle; they include, for example, indictments of corrupt or hypocritical worship (Isa. 58:1-14 and Isa. 65:1-16), and oracles of lament over the people's sin and the ensuing divine judgment (Isa 59:1-20 and chapters 63–64). Significantly, the quotation in Luke draws mainly from the hopeful prophetic commission to "bear good tidings to the poorest" (Isa. 61:1), but also includes a line from Isa. 58:6, part of a chapter-long warning against hypocritical religious rituals that are not accompanied by works of social justice and care for outsiders. These two chapters will receive the bulk of our attention here.

Isaiah 61 is an announcement of eschatological salvation for Zion, a reversal from oppression to liberty and from mourning to praise (Isa. 61:1, 3). The prophet claims a role as herald of this new time that is to be pleasing to and worthy of the Lord, and rejoices in the coming recompense for just and unjust alike (Isa. 61:2, 8, 10). The question arises, though, of who exactly are the just and unjust. Who is to receive liberty and the "oil of gladness," and who is to receive vengeance and judgment? Since this chapter is mainly an oracle of salvation, there is only a hint of such judgment, namely in Isa. 61:2, a line famously left out of Jesus' quotation in Luke 4: "to proclaim a year acceptable and pleasing to the Lord, *and the day of vengeance of our God*" (MT, emphasis mine). There is little else in the chapter, though, that elaborates on this divine נָקָם (a strong word for vengeance and retribution),[29] and it is even

---

29. BDB, 667–68.

softened slightly in the Septuagint, which translates נָקָם with ἀνταπόδοσις, a word more generally used to indicate repayment or reward for work carried out, whether positive or negative (see, for example, Col. 3:24, where it refers to a Christian's reward for faithful service to Jesus).[30] Most of the reversals in Isaiah 61 are one-way positive changes like building up destroyed cities and Israel gaining international honor and wealth (Isa. 61:4-6). A hint of downward reversal does appear, however, in Isa. 61:5-6, for the strangers and foreigners who will apparently become Israel's servants, doing the mundane work of herding and farming while the Israelites are honored as priests who enjoy the "wealth of the nations."

It is possible to see here, then, a measure of nationalism, as Zion gains wealth, honor, and redemption at the expense of all other peoples. Several scholars, however, identify a few strands within Isaiah 61 and the larger text of chapters 56–66 that combat or qualify this nationalism. Wes Howard-Brook calls Third Isaiah a "dissenting voice" to the violence, exploitation, and ethnic exclusion championed in Ezra and Nehemiah.[31] Certainly, as he argues, we read nothing in Isaiah 61 nearly as harsh as Ezra's sending away of all foreign wives and their children (Ezra 10:1-17) or Nehemiah's decree of full separation between Israel and all those of foreign descent (Neh. 13:1-3). Indeed, in the chiasm of which Isaiah 61 is the center, the first and final framing theme is the inclusion of foreigners in Yahweh's salvation:

> And the foreigners who join
>   themselves to the Lord,
>   to minister to him, to love the
>   name of the Lord,
>   and to be his servants,
> all who keep the sabbath, and do
>   not profane it,
>   and hold fast my covenant—
> these I will bring to my holy
>   mountain,
>   and make them joyful in my
>   house of prayer;
> their burnt offerings and their
>   sacrifices
>   will be accepted on my altar;

30. BDAG, 87; see also LEH, 53.
31. Howard-Brook, *"Come Out,"* 264.

for my house shall be called a
    house of prayer
for all peoples.
Thus says the Lord God,
    who gathers the outcasts of
    Israel,
I will gather others to them besides
    those already gathered. (Isa. 56:6-8, NRSV)

and

For I know their works and their thoughts, and I am coming to gather all nations and tongues; and they shall come and shall see my glory, and I will set a sign among them. From them I will send survivors to the nations . . . to the coastlands far away that have not heard of my fame or seen my glory; and they shall declare my glory among the nations. They shall bring all your kindred from all the nations as an offering to the Lord. (Isa 66:18-20a, NRSV)

Thus it seems that the inclusion of foreign proselytes in divine redemption is an important concern for the later Isaianic prophet. The oracle in chapter 61 itself ends on a possibly hopeful note, that God will make righteousness and praise spring up so that they are clearly seen by the nations (Isa. 61:11). This action, over which the prophet rejoices (Isa. 61:10), perhaps implies that the way is left open for the nations to respond to the divine goodness that has been revealed to them.

But it would be a mistake to ignore entirely the issue of judgment and vengeance. Howard-Brook appears to regard the mention of strangers herding and foreigners farming in Isa. 61:5 as a positive inclusion, part of his argument that Third Isaiah stood against the ethnic-exclusion program of Ezra-Nehemiah.[32] Unfortunately, the context does not support such a reading very well. As mentioned above, the foreigners seem to be servants of the Israelites, of lower status, and are clearly not included among the priests and ministers of Yahweh who enjoy great wealth and honor (Isa. 61:6). The day of vengeance is a complement to the year of favor (cf. Isa. 63:4): "To correct a situation of abuse and unjust use of force requires both freedom for the victims and punishment of the guilty."[33] But these two groups, the victims and the guilty,

---

32. Ibid., 265.

are not necessarily preset or ethnically determined in the worldview of Trito-Isaiah. Israelites can face the displeasure of humans and the Lord through their oppressive practices (Isaiah 58; cf. Neh. 5:1-5), while ethnic Gentiles are welcomed into the community of faith if they are willing to adhere to its worship and rituals (as discussed above).

This analysis is significant for Luke's quotation of Isa. 61:1-2, particularly in relation to the identity of the poor, oppressed, and captives on whose behalf God's favor is declared. These acts of status reversal will be discussed in more detail in the second section of this chapter, but we must consider who the beneficiaries may have been and how they were envisioned both by the Isaianic prophet and his community, and by the residents of the Roman Empire reading this oracle placed on the lips of Jesus centuries later. The chapters surrounding Isaiah 61, as considered above, argue that the beneficiaries, indicated by the nationalistic term Zion (Isa. 61:3), are recognized more by their behavior and attitude toward God and their fellow human beings than by their ancestral lineage. They are, above all, the עֲנָוִים (Isa. 61:1, LXX πτωχοῖς), literally the "bowed down": the poorest of the poor, the afflicted, the weak and humble.[34]

The socioeconomic connotation of this word is basic to its meaning, particularly in the prophetic tradition where the "'preferential option for the poor' is perhaps the most significant contribution of the Hebrew prophets to the moral tradition of Judaism and Christianity."[35] The poor are further defined as brokenhearted, captive, and imprisoned. The phrase לִקְרֹא דְרוֹר (LXX κηρύξαι ἄφεσιν), "to proclaim liberty," echoes the Jubilee Year legislation in Lev. 25:10 (LXX διαβοήσετε ἄφεσιν), with its central act of freeing all debt slaves.[36] This connection has led several scholars to posit that the captives to be freed in the year of the Lord are, at least in part, those imprisoned for debt.[37] While the language is too vague to allow for certainty on this point, Neh. 5:1-5 offers another piece of support. The laborers' protest here indicates that they were struggling under famine and debt so crushing that they were forced to sell family members into debt slavery—probably not an uncommon issue in the rebuilding of Jerusalem as the people struggled to establish and adjust to new power structures. Non-elites in the Roman Empire suffered similar problems with huge amounts of debt and defaulted loans leading to the loss of land, family, and status, and issued similar demands for debt remission

33. John D. W. Watts, *Isaiah 34–66*, WBC 25 (Nashville: Thomas Nelson, 2000), 873.

34. BDB, 776.

35. Blenkinsopp, *Isaiah 56–66*, 223.

36. The important parallels between Isa 61:1-2 and the theology of Jubilee are treated in depth below.

37. Blenkinsopp, *Isaiah 56–66*, 224–25; and Fitzmyer, *Luke I–IX*, 532–33.

in their resistance movements.[38] The Spirit-commissioned prophet of Isaiah 61, then, is addressing struggles not only (and perhaps not even most importantly) over ethnicity and nationality, but also over issues of status, money, and power. The author of the Gospel of Luke and his earliest reading communities most likely understood this passage in the light of similar ethnic, status, and power conflicts, a conclusion that becomes even more apparent with the reference to Isaiah 58, to which I will now turn.

In this chapter, from which Luke 4:18 draws the line "to send those who have been oppressed out into release," we find an oracle vastly different from the joyful salvation proclaimed in Isaiah 61. Instead, it is an example of a primary prophetic function: denunciation of the social sin of God's people.[39] The prophet is commanded and commissioned to speak for the Lord: "Declare to my people their rebellion, and to the house of Jacob their sins" (Isa. 58:1b). The people are concerned that their fasting has not been noticed or rewarded by God, but the prophet is quick to point out that their fasting is accompanied by the oppression of non-elite laborers, and by quarreling and physical violence among themselves (Isa. 58:3-4). At least some of those being reprimanded here must be elites, along with perhaps some more prosperous non-elites, since they are the ones most likely to have workers to abuse. Fasting was a standard ritual in times of disaster and struggle, performed in order to coax divine assistance.[40] But God makes it clear that at least some of the problems of the Jerusalem community are of their own making and therefore up to them to correct before God will offer help: "To fast in the name of a 'liberator' God and at the same time to practice the enslavement of persons is supremely incoherent, and Yahweh does not accept it."[41]

The prophet, in the voice of Yahweh, proceeds to detail precisely what kind of "fast" marks a day that is pleasing and acceptable to the Lord (Isa. 58:5, using the same language as Isa. 61:2: רָצוֹן לַיהוָה, LXX δεκτός). Isa. 58:6-12 lists a variety of parallel acts of socioeconomic and political import: correcting injustice, freeing the oppressed (as quoted in Luke 4:18), sharing food and shelter with the hungry and homeless, and refraining from blaming others and speaking evil about them. The concrete socioeconomic nature of the parallels argues strongly for a similarly concrete understanding of the release (ἄφεσις)

38. Jerry Toner, *Popular Culture in Ancient Rome* (Cambridge, MA: Polity, 2009), 23–36.

39. Blenkinsopp, *Isaiah 56–66*, 177.

40. Ibid., 178.

41. José Severino Croatto, "From the Leviticus Jubilee Year to the Prophetic Liberation Time: Exegetical Reflections on Isaiah 61 and 58 in Relation to the Jubilee," in *God's Economy: Biblical Studies from Latin America*, ed. Ross Kinsler and Gloria Kinsler (Maryknoll, NY: Orbis, 2005), 103.

offered here to the oppressed (see also Lev. 25:13-17, 35-43). The message of this oracle is not simply about religious ritual separate from other aspects of life; instead it argues forcefully that the establishment of correct policies toward the poor and needy is itself an act of worship expected of both the leaders and the people.[42]

Several scholars see, as they did in the captives of Isa. 61:1, an allusion to debt slavery and imprisonment—an issue with extensive ramifications for social, economic, and political reform.[43] Also prominent is the individual responsibility and call to action issued here. Isaiah 61 presented an image of eschatological salvation, but Isaiah 58 enjoins the people to work actively toward that salvation in their own communities. Particularly important here is the second person plural declarative statement in the last line of Isa 58:6 that is so often glossed over and missed in English translations: וְכָל־מוֹטָה תְּנַתֵּקוּ, "You shall tear off every yoke!" (LXX πᾶσαν συγγραφὴν ἄδικον διάσπα, "You shall tear up every unjust contract!"—an interesting nod to the possible implication of debt slavery mentioned above).[44] In this chapter, the Isaianic prophet calls for the people of God and especially their leaders to reassess their priorities for worship and community. The physical space of the temple and the outward actions of ritual do not matter to God when people are hungry, in debt, and oppressed. More important than institutional reconstruction, in the view of Third Isaiah, is "a reconstruction of life for God's people," a renewal of liberation for the poor, brokenhearted, and captive.[45]

These two very different yet closely related chapters of Isaiah are brought together in Luke 4:18-19 and put into conversation with each other, as well as with the group gathered in the Nazareth synagogue and the early Christians reading Luke's Gospel. The major portion of the reading is taken from Isa. 61:1-2a, stopping after the first line of verse 2 (thereby including the proclamation of "a year pleasing to the Lord" and omitting "the day of vengeance of our God" and "comfort for all who are mourning"). The only other change in Luke is the replacement of the Isa. 61:1 line "to bind up the ones whose hearts are shattered" with "to send out the oppressed as free people" from Isa. 58:6. Taken together with our study of these two chapters from

---

42. Watts, *Isaiah 34–66*, 841.

43. Blenkinsopp, *Isaiah 56–66*, 179; and Watts, *Isaiah 34–66*, 843.

44. See, e.g., the NRSV and NJPS translations of this line as an infinitive. Cf. Watts, *Isaiah 34–66*, 838–39, who translates as I do.

45. Pablo Richard, "Now Is the Time to Proclaim the Biblical Jubilee," in Kinsler and Kinsler, *God's Economy*, 47.

Trito-Isaiah, the composition and editing of the Nazareth reading enhance our understanding of the entire scene.

Obviously, only a very few lines of each are cited directly (parts of two verses from chapter 61, and only one phrase from chapter 58), but these limited quotations, as discussed above, draw their larger context into the conversation.[46] This premise is strengthened by the other thematic connections that appear between Luke and Trito-Isaiah. In Isa. 61:10, for example, the Spirit-anointed prophet praises God in parallel lines and with language very similar to that of Mary in the Magnificat (Luke 1:46-47), including the phrase ἡ ψυχή μου and the verb ἀγαλλιάω. The reversal themes of comfort for the mourning (Isa. 61:2-3), food for the hungry (Isa. 58:7, 10), good news to the poor (Isa. 61:1), and freedom for the captive and oppressed (Isa. 58:6, 10; 61:1) resurface throughout the Gospel of Luke in the Sermon on the Plain and other places (for example, 6:20-26; 7:11-15, 22-23; 13:16). Additionally, the metaphor of God's salvation coming like the light of dawn overtaking the darkness is a shared theme (Isa. 58:8, 10; Luke 1:78-79; 2:32).

Two catchwords connect Isaiah 58 and 61 with each other and also with Luke 4:16-30: ἄφεσις (prominent in the composite quotation of Luke 4:18-19) to describe what Jesus' mission offers, and δεκτός (Luke 4:19, 24) to describe whom it will serve. In both chapters 58 and 61 of Isaiah (LXX), the oracles attempt to define what is δεκτός, that is, what is acceptable to, favored by, and worthy of the Lord. Isaiah 58 elaborates upon the true "fast" (or worship) that God finds δεκτός (verse 5), which is primarily help offered to the poor, hungry, and oppressed. It has been argued, though, that this was mostly an intracommunity concern.[47] Isaiah 61 proclaims the dawning of a time that is δεκτός, characterized again by good news and help for the poor, captive, and mourning, mostly those of Zion (verses 1-3) but with a small ray of hope for the nations to whom Yahweh's righteousness is revealed (verse 11). But Luke makes a subtle change in focus, defining not only what, but also *whom* God finds δεκτός (namely, "anyone who fears him and does what is right," to borrow phrasing from the definition of δεκτός in Acts 10:34-35). In another change, he also addresses the issue of those who are declared δεκτός by *human beings*—certainly not Jesus as the proclaimer of God's δεκτός year, in the view of his hometown neighbors (Luke 4:24).

46. Carter, "Evoking Isaiah," 506; and Moyise, *Evoking Scripture*, 137–39.

47. Isaiah 58:7, e.g., speaks against hiding "from your own kin" (who presumably are poor and need assistance from their family). See also Watts, *Isaiah 34–66*, 843, where he argues that one of the major problems addressed by chapter 58 is the holding of one's relatives in debt bondage.

In a similar manner, the word ἄφεσις (release) is a central part of Jesus' declared mission in the Isaiah reading, but its meaning is multivalent and constantly evolving. In the Septuagint, release can be from monetary debt, imprisonment, and guilt,[48] and in Luke we find much overlap, with the addition of release from Satanic power and bondage.[49] It is also a central word found in imagery of the Year of Jubilee, appearing fifteen times in the main legislation of Leviticus 25 (verses 10-13, 28, 30-31, 33, 40-41, 50, 52, 54). The concept is subsequently explored and developed further throughout the biblical writings, as in Jer. 34:8-22, Isaiah 61, and certainly, as we will explore in the following section on the Year of Jubilee, Luke 4:16-30. Jesus' message to the worshippers in Nazareth pushes the limits of what the readers of Luke are to understand from the concepts of both ἄφεσις and δεκτός: release is social, spiritual, and physical help given to those who need it, those who are acceptable to Jesus no matter their wealth, status, distinguished lineage, or lack thereof.

In combining Isaiah 61 with Isaiah 58, then, the reading at Nazareth evokes a joyful declaration of salvation, but also something of the prophetic rebuke against worship that has been separated from social justice. Luke's inclusion of the line from Isa. 58:6 invokes that warning and "suggests that in addition to Jesus' message being good news for the poor, it is bad news for the rich. The only chance for the rich is to share their bread with the hungry, to bring the homeless poor into their houses . . . and to satisfy the desire of the afflicted (Isa. 58:7-10)."[50] Also significant is the line from Isa. 61:1, which the line from Isa. 58:6 replaces: "To bind up the ones whose hearts are broken." Although there is no way to know exactly why the author chose to delete this particular clause, it is worth noting that it is the only metaphorical image in Isa. 61:1, envisioning the healing not of a literal wound, but of an inner emotional one (a broken heart).[51]

And of course the conflicts and struggles being addressed by Luke, like those faced by the prophet of the rebuilding Jerusalem community, are not quite as simple as "poor versus rich." In Jerusalem of the sixth century BCE and in Asia Minor of the late first century CE, the people of God needed these prophetic reminders to act with justice in the midst of differences in social status, economic level, and ethnic lineage. The Nazareth congregation reveals, through its rejection of Jesus, a deep-seated resistance to the complexities of

48. Ringe, *Jesus, Liberation*, 65.

49. Green, *Gospel of Luke*, 211–12.

50. Prior, *Jesus the Liberator*, 135.

51. Alessandro Falcetta, *The Call of Nazareth: Form and Exegesis of Luke 4:16-30*, CahRB 53 (Paris: Gabalda, 2003), 39; and Nolland, *Luke 1—9:20*, 197.

offering salvation and justice to all people; they failed, as did those addressed by Isaiah 58, to back up their worship with action. One can also imagine a strong temptation for the early readers of Luke, deeply ensconced in their Hellenistic Roman cities, to feel afraid, intimidated, and even scornful at the prospect of challenging the imperial hierarchy, as Isaiah, Jesus, and Luke enjoin the people of God to do. The proclamation of salvation is a joyous occasion, but it does not come cheaply. It entails deep challenge and commitment to change on both individual and systemic levels.

The rest of Luke's work in the Gospel and in Acts narrates some of the story of bringing this salvation to fruition through the work of Jesus and his earliest followers, but Jesus' initial declaration of that description is found right here, in the Nazareth proclamation and its aftermath. Jesus affirms his commissioning by the Spirit of Lord, which descended upon him at his baptism (Luke 3:21-22), by referencing the commissioning of the prophet of Third Isaiah, who was also anointed with the Spirit of the Lord (Isa. 61:1). It is unusual to anoint with the Spirit, and to anoint a prophet (although this was not without precedent; see 1 Kgs. 19:16). More commonly kings and priests were anointed with oil, in order to consecrate them formally into their official roles.[52] Blenkinsopp interprets the pairing in Isa. 61:1 of spirit possession (usually a short-term state to inspire ecstatic prophecy) and anointing (a permanent consecration) to indicate that the speaker was embarking on a lifelong prophetic mission.[53] Certainly this is the case for Jesus in this famously "programmatic" text. The story of the Nazareth proclamation, as told in Luke 4, co-opts the dual prophetic and messianic (anointed) identity and mission of Trito-Isaiah and tweaks them slightly to define more precisely the vision of Jesus and the work of his followers.

THE YEAR OF JUBILEE AND ITS PARALLELS

The theme of ἄφεσις in the Gospel of Luke, particularly in the Nazareth proclamation pericope, necessitates a consideration of the Year of Jubilee (in the LXX, ἐνιαυτὸς ἀφέσεως, Lev. 25:10). Some authors have argued against this assertion and against the presence of Jubilee imagery in either Isaiah 61 or its quotation in Luke 4:18-19. Michael Prior, for example, defines ἄφεσις, in the Lukan worldview, solely as the forgiveness of sin, because outside of the Isaiah 61 quotation, the concept of release (in his opinion) has no connection with the Jubilee emphasis on liberation from debt and slavery.[54] The problem with

---

52. BDB, 602–3.

53. Blenkinsopp, *Isaiah 56–66*, 222–23.

this argument, of course, is that the Isaiah quotation is in fact included in Luke; it does connect ἄφεσις with Jubilee emphases; and it does so in a prominent place, as Jesus lays out the heart of his mission at the very beginning of his ministry. The Jubilee imagery in Isaiah 61 is well accepted by scholars, with the prophet re-envisioning the year-long festival as an eschatological time of divine salvation.[55] Texts like 11QMelchizedek (11Q13, discussed in more detail below) also show an exegetical connection between Leviticus 25 and Isaiah 61. Thus it is not a great stretch to consider how this Jubilee imagery is employed and engaged in the Gospel of Luke.

Leviticus 25:8-55 is the central legislation related to the Year of Jubilee: "And you shall consecrate the fiftieth year and you shall proclaim liberty [וּקְרָאתֶם דְּרוֹר; LXX διαβοήσετε ἄφεσιν] throughout the land to all its inhabitants" (Lev. 25:10a). This phrase resurfaces in Isa. 61:1, proclaiming liberty to those taken captive (LXX κηρύξαι αἰχμαλώτοις ἄφεσιν), and again in Luke, who follows the Septuagint wording—an example of Kristeva's "dialogical relationship between 'texts'" that creates "an 'intersection of textual surfaces rather than a point (a fixed meaning).'"[56] All three texts interact with one another and affect how each is read and interpreted by the Lukan audiences. The Levitical text continues on with the details of the Year of Jubilee, including each family's return to their ancestral landholdings that have been sold or leased to others (Lev. 25:13-17); the freeing of Hebrews sold into debt servitude (Lev. 25:35-43); and the extension of the sabbatical agricultural fallow year (Lev. 25:11-12, 18-24). It is not known whether the Jubilee was ever fully implemented; 1 Macc. 6:49-54 depicts the sabbatical year practice of letting the land lie fallow, but there is no comparable reference to the Year of Jubilee. John Dominic Crossan argues for the power of the legislation even if it was never practiced. Its inclusion in the canon indicates that it is *something that could be done in this world even if it never were*" (emphasis original), and that caring for the rights of the non-elite is mandated as an important value.[57] Considering the high level of control maintained by elite ruling groups in most agrarian societies, and how much they would stand to lose, enactment of such a festival would have been difficult to implement. How exactly to carry out these reversals seems to be one of the questions with which the Gospel of Luke struggles.

54. Prior, *Jesus the Liberator*, 139–40.

55. Ringe, *Jesus, Liberation*, 31. See also Blenkinsopp, *Isaiah 56–66*, 225; and Watts, *Isaiah 34–66*, 873.

56. Quoted in Moyise, *Evoking Scripture*, 138.

57. John Dominic Crossan, *The Birth of Christianity: Discovering What Happened in the Years Immediately after the Execution of Jesus* (New York: HarperCollins, 1998), 195–97.

Even considering this struggle, the idea of the Jubilee remains unique and revolutionary—although certainly not perfect. A major caveat is that this social equality was extended in Leviticus only to Hebrews; foreigners are not to be released from their debts, are not freed from slavery, and are expected to release any Hebrew debt slaves they may have bought (Lev. 25:44-46, 53-54; cf. Deut. 7:3, 12; Exod. 21:2[58]). At least for the Hebrew people, though, it is a plan that incorporates both worship and economics in order to restore social equality and equilibrium to both humanity and creation.[59] Worshipping a sovereign God who values justice and who freed Israel from slavery is presented as the rationale for not cheating one another (Lev. 25:17), for supporting one's kin who have fallen on hard times (Lev. 25:38), and for freeing Hebrew bondservants (Lev. 25:42-43, 55). These commands become, then, not only acts of social justice, but also acts of worship worthy of Yahweh (cf. Isaiah 58). Sharon Ringe writes, "In the very midst of the Holiness Code with its emphasis on cultic matters, these laws bear witness to the continuing power of the image of God as sovereign over Israel, and . . . [its] ethical consequences. To confess God as sovereign includes caring for the poor and granting freedom to those trapped in a continuing cycle of indebtedness."[60]

The Jubilee Year is presented as a festival of social leveling rather than total status inversion; such an ambitious, revolutionary project was nearly unique in the ancient world and also extraordinarily difficult to sustain or even implement in the first place.[61] A story recounted in Jer. 34:8-22 narrates a partial celebration of Jubilee, but it does not end well, to say the least. Jeremiah exhorts King Zedekiah and the people of Jerusalem to free their Hebrew slaves in accordance with Levitical law. They do so, but only temporarily; almost immediately they "brought them again into subjection as slaves" (Jer. 34:10-11, NRSV). God is understandably angered by this and subverts the tradition by "proclaiming a release" (קְרָא דְרוֹר, LXX καλῶ ἄφεσιν) for the unmerciful people into disaster and famine, rather than the expected redemption and freedom (Jer. 34:17). The command invoked here, to free one's Hebrew slaves (שַׁלַּח חָפְשִׁים, literally, to send [them] out as free persons; LXX ἐξαποστεῖλαι . . . ἐλευθέρους) after a certain period of service, is not unique to the Jubilee legislation; it is also issued in Deut. 15:12 (cf. Exod. 21:2-6), referenced in Jer. 34:14, and included as part of Yahweh's "acceptable fast" in Isa. 58:6. Both the Jeremiah and Isaiah

---

58. But cf. Ringe, *Jesus, Liberation*, 18, where she argues that in Exodus, the word "Hebrew" could possibly refer to any wanderer who is an alien in a foreign land, or someone with the status of a slave.

59. Sloan, *Favorable Year*, 14–15.

60. Ringe, *Jesus, Liberation*, 28.

61. Richard, "Now Is the Time," 48–49.

references indicate that the prescribed release was not happening regularly, if at all, much to the prophets' mutual chagrin.

With the proclamation at Nazareth, Jesus shows himself to share this prophetic concern and shows an interest in addressing it. It is, significantly, the line from Isa. 58:6 echoing Deut. 15:12 that is incorporated into his Nazareth reading, and this inclusion brings another level of nuance to the Sabbatical and Jubilee Year connotations of the Lukan pericope. Both Isaiah 58 and Jesus in Luke 4 broaden the definition of those who need to be sent out into release: not only slaves, but all who are oppressed. The original context of debt slavery, though, seems to continue hovering in the background, and the slaves who worshipped in the Greco-Roman congregations first hearing Luke likely would have been interested in exploring the ramifications of the Sabbatical and Jubilee Year legislation. The scriptural calls for regular, mandated manumission of all slaves, and especially the accompanying Jubilee provisions to re-establish economic independence, were unusual.[62] Roman slaves were manumitted only at their owner's discretion (often after decades of service), had to pay for their freedom, and frequently struggled afterwards to support themselves and gain even a small amount of social status.[63]

In comparison with the Year of Jubilee as outlined in Leviticus 25, Greco-Roman festivals of reversal and acts of debt remission seem rather limited. Saturnalia, for example, was a well-known Roman festival celebrating a "world upside down." Saturn, a distinctive deity, was a Roman god and yet also a foreigner, whose function was "to embody references to an alternative world which, in periods of exception, interrupted the steady course of normal life."[64] The festival that honored him was likewise only an exception to the normal social hierarchy, a temporary reversal, lasting about a week (at its longest) during the month of December.[65] Its status reversals, the hallmark of the celebration, incorporated rituals of both social leveling and total inversion. Saturn represented a golden age before society was divided by rank and status;

62. Ringe, *Jesus, Liberation*, 27.

63. K. R. Bradley, *Slaves and Masters in the Roman Empire: A Study in Social Control* (New York: Oxford University Press, 1987), 82, 87, 97–98; Richard A. Horsley, "The Slave Systems of Classical Antiquity and Their Reluctant Recognition by Modern Scholars," *Semeia* 83–84 (1998): 57; and G. Francois Wessels, "The Letter to Philemon in the Context of Slavery in Early Christianity," in *Philemon in Perspective: Interpreting a Pauline Letter*, ed. D. Francois Tolmie, BZNW (Berlin: Walter de Gruyter, 2010), 157–58. The possible impact of Luke 4:16-30 on slaves in the early Christian communities will be explored further in the third section of this chapter.

64. H. S. Versnel, *Transition and Reversal in Myth and Ritual: Inconsistencies in Greek and Roman Religion II*, Studies in Greek and Roman Religion 6 (Leiden: Brill, 1993), 157. See also 139–43.

65. Ibid., 146.

thus the entire population donned the garb of a freedperson for the festival, and masters and slaves ate and gambled together.[66] At the same time, slaves were also served by their masters, men dressed as women, and a mock king was elected from among the non-elites, offering examples of complete inversion themes.[67] But in the end, all this was temporary, effecting no lasting change. At most it offered a chance to consider what a different social world might look like, and perhaps fostered a hope for future justice—or, from a different perspective, could have demonstrated how ridiculous such a world would be.[68] The Year of Jubilee, in contrast, was designed to be a recurring, permanent readjustment of the status quo, an attempt to level the economic playing field, so to speak. The history of the two festivals, of course, reveals the major limit to such sweeping measures of reform as the Jubilee was designed to be: while we have numerous reports of a regular celebration of the Saturnalia, the Year of Jubilee was perhaps never enacted and remained for the most part merely an inspiring idea.

We find another rough parallel to Jubilee legislation in the practice of royal decrees of amnesty and help for the poor, common in both the Ancient Near East and the Greco-Roman world. Such actions, however, were undertaken to assert and strengthen the ruler's authoritative position, not to change it in any way. Hammurabi (eighteenth century BCE) and several of his descendants, for example, issued decrees of release for those in debt slavery near the beginning of their reigns.[69] Ramesses IV of Egypt was celebrated at his enthronement with the following hymn:

> O happy day: Heaven and earth rejoice,
>   for thou art the great lord of Egypt.
> Those who had fled returned to their towns,
>   those who had hidden showed themselves again;
> Those who had been hungry were fed,
>   those who had been thirsty were given drink. . . .
> Those who were in prison were set free,

66. Toner, *Popular Culture*, 93; and Versnel, *Transition and Reversal*, 158.

67. Toner, *Popular Culture*, 93–94; and Versnel, *Transition and Reversal*, 149–50.

68. Toner, *Popular Culture*, 95–96. See also Scott, *Domination*, 172–82. He argues against this classification of reversal festivals as simply "safety valve" releases that in the end allowed the status quo to remain in place, and instead advances the idea that such celebrations were multivalent. He writes, "A complex social event such as carnival cannot be said to be simply this or that as if it had a given, genetically [programmed], function. It makes far greater sense to see carnival as the ritual site of various forms of social conflict and symbolic manipulation, none of which can be said, prima facie, to prevail" (178).

69. Referenced in Ringe, *Jesus, Liberation*, 23–24.

those who were in bonds were filled with joy.[70]

Augustus also celebrated his own generosity in his autobiographical *Res Gestae*, using chapters 15–24 to enumerate his many gifts of money, building projects, and games and festivals to the Roman plebes and soldiers.[71]

But perhaps the most interesting example comes from Emperor Hadrian. Upon his accession to the imperial throne in 118 CE, he needed to placate and win over the people, who were upset by assassinations late in the reign of his predecessor Trajan. One of the ways he did so was through a "sweeping amnesty for tax arrears" in both Italy and the provinces.[72] This act of debt remission received a highly favorable response from the people, even providing something of a short-lived economic stimulus. It was commemorated in a relief sculpture of the burning of the tax debt tablets, and an inscription identifying him as "the first of all *principes* and the only one who, by remitting nine hundred million sesterces owed to the *fiscus*, provided security not merely for his present citizens but also for their descendants by this generosity."[73] Probably the greatest beneficiary, though, of Hadrian's declaration of amnesty, like those of other monarchs, was Hadrian himself. He gained the favor of the people at least temporarily, but more importantly he garnered extensive honor and acclaim for himself—he was lauded for this and other similar actions as "restorer" and "enricher" of the world.[74] Motivated by a desire to placate the angry non-elite population, he managed to do so without improving their actual living situation in any significant, lasting way, thus maintaining the hierarchical order and his own place at the top of it.

Again, let us consider these royal decrees in comparison with the Year of Jubilee. Yahweh was the only one who was to gain any honor or worship from the implementation of Jubilee, and the social and material benefits were to go to those who needed it most (members of the community who had lost their land, their homes, their resources, and even their freedom), at the expense of those of highest status, with resources to spare. Overall, the theme of Jubilee and its prophetic interpretations by Trito-Isaiah and Jesus stand in contrast

---

70. Quoted in Sloan, *Favorable Year*, 55.

71. The full text of this section can be found in Caesar Augustus, *Res Gestae Divi Augusti*, LCL, ed. Frederick W. Shipley (London: William Heinemann, 1924), 366–85.

72. Dio Cassius, *Hist. rom.* 69.8. See also Anthony R. Birley, *Hadrian: The Restless Emperor* (London: Routledge, 1997), 97–98.

73. Birley, *Hadrian*, 97–98; and Richard Duncan-Jones, *Money and Government in the Roman Empire* (Cambridge: Cambridge University Press, 1994), 13, 17.

74. Birley, *Hadrian*, 99.

to their closest parallels in the world around them. Hadrian's proclamation of debt relief served to maintain and even strengthen the imperial system and his own position. But in the Levitical legislation, in the oracles of Isaiah 58 and 61, and in Jesus' proclamation in Luke 4, the idea of ἄφεσις—of release, of Jubilee—professes to transform the imperial mainstays of slavery and debt into acts of God's salvation for all people.[75]

As authors and readers in various historical contexts revisited the idea of a Jubilee Year, it is not surprising that the concept underwent transformation in their hands. We have already discussed Isaiah 61 in some detail, but here I want to look more closely at its adoption and transformation of the Year of Jubilee. Most prominently, the author of Isaiah 61 conflates the Jubilee Year with God's eschatological reign, particularly as both celebrate "God's transformative intent" to break the oppressive power of social and political institutions.[76] Jubilee themes often received eschatological recasting of this kind in prophetic and apocalyptic literature.[77] An eschatological Year of Jubilee could, on one level, limit its possibilities to transform the present world by encouraging the people to sit back and wait for God to restore social equilibrium, or by continuing to limit the benefits of Jubilee to the people of Israel. It could be an attractive vision for those without the power to effect such a change in reality. The Year of Jubilee was, in fact, a convenient and effective metaphor to represent the freedom of the nation of Israel from the trials of exile.[78] It is even occasionally suggested that the Jubilee legislation was established in the postexilic period in an attempt by the returned exiles (mostly elites) to reclaim their land from the current residents (mostly non-elites who had been left behind by the conquering Babylonians).[79] While the liberation motif and the spirit of the entire text make this scenario an unlikely one, the proposal does serve as a useful reminder about the complexity of the socioeconomic issues involved. Groups of people and even individuals self-identify as "oppressed" or "poor" for various reasons;[80] the question for our study is how this identification plays out in Trito-Isaiah and beyond.

---

75. Warren Carter, "Singing in the Reign: Performing Luke's Songs and Negotiating the Roman Empire (Luke 1–2)," in *Luke-Acts and Empire: Essays in Honor of Robert L. Brawley*, ed. David Rhoads, David Esterline, and Jae Won Lee, PTMS (Eugene, OR: Wipf & Stock, 2011), 39.

76. Ringe, *Jesus, Liberation*, 31–32.

77. Sloan, *Favorable Year*, 10–11. Sloan points to texts such as Daniel 7–12, 11Q13, and *The Book of Jubilees*.

78. Watts, *Isaiah 34–66*, 873.

79. This possibility is mentioned briefly by Croatto, "From the Leviticus Jubilee," 90, but he quickly refutes it (108n7). See also Richard, "Now Is the Time," 48.

Even though an eschatological spin might limit the Jubilee's potential to carry out liberation, it can also expand that potential. Indeed, Trito-Isaiah takes steps in this direction. Isaiah 61 does not encourage anyone to sit idle. Instead, the prophet announces that the time of God, the year of divine favor, has in fact already begun, characterized in part by a divinely ordained personal mission to proclaim good news to the poorest of the poor. This prophetic reinterpretation of the Jubilee Year "calls for and impels a social praxis at all times . . . a prophetic 'time' that is measured not by calendar days or years but by reality."[81] Where the Year of Jubilee sought to rectify socioeconomic inequality every fifty years, its new incarnation in Isa. 61:2 proclaims a more permanent era of divine favor and justice by not reinscribing the specific intervals of time (שְׁנַת־רָצוֹן לַיהוָה; LXX ἐνιαυτὸν κυρίου δεκτόν). The prophet, then, issues a call for social justice to be practiced at all times, and perhaps even for all people. Isaiah 61:11 takes a small step toward the revelation of Yahweh's goodness to all the nations, and both Deutero- and Trito-Isaiah make this point even more strongly elsewhere (see 42:1-9; 56:3-8; 66:18-23).

In the Jubilee, social justice and care for human beings and for the land form a central part of the cultic worship of the Lord, and this combination seems to have appealed to later prophetic figures like those in Isaianic circles.[82] These interpreters of Jubilee, however, made some small (and some not-so-small) steps toward including more people in the liberation of Jubilee than the original legislation envisaged. With such a movement, however, there was bound to be a countermovement.

11QMelchizedek (11Q13) exemplifies this type of countermovement by emphasizing vengeance and severely limiting the beneficiaries of Jubilee reform, and thus provides an excellent foil against which to consider the Lukan interpretation of Jubilee and Isaiah. This document from the Scrolls community is partly a pesher on Leviticus 25 and partly a scriptural mosaic or pastiche. The Year of Jubilee proclaimed in Lev. 25:13 (cf. Deut 15:2, which is also quoted) is interpreted by the presumably sectarian author as the eschatological triumph for which the community had been waiting, and which would vindicate and benefit them alone. Significantly, phrases from Isa. 61:1-2 are sprinkled throughout: "to proclaim liberty for them" (line 6); "the acceptable year" (line 9); "anointed by the spirit" (line 18); and "to comfort the mourning" (line

---

80. Even elites sometimes referred to themselves as poor for rhetorical advantage. See the discussion in Bruce W. Longenecker, *Remember the Poor: Paul, Poverty, and the Greco-Roman World* (Grand Rapids: Eerdmans, 2010), 37–39.

81. Croatto, "From the Leviticus Jubilee," 91.

82. Sloan, *Favorable Year*, 13–14.

20). Isaiah 61:1-2 seems to provide the author an interpretative lens through which to view, for his own time and community, quoted texts from the Torah (Lev. 25:13; Deut. 15:2), the Prophets (Isa. 52:7), and the Writings (Pss. 82:1-2; 7:8-9).[83] The Isaiah pericope "provides the eschatological context for the pesher of the jubilee year [and] suggests the eschatological motifs of favor and vengeance around which the figure of Melchizedek is developed."[84] Like Luke, the Scrolls writer sees themes of Jubilee in Isaiah 61 and interprets the prophetic oracle in his own context as an eschatological fulfillment of Jubilee through an anointed figure (Melchizedek in 11Q13, Jesus in the Gospel of Luke). Luke is not making an unprecedented exegetical leap in connecting Isaiah 61 and Leviticus 25, but is using Scripture in a manner comparable to that of other communities of his time, "as mediated to them by their contemporaries and immediate forebears."[85]

Amidst these similarities in exegetical connection, the eschatological celebration of Jubilee, and the presence of a messianic personality, there are also differences between Luke 4:16-30 and 11Q13 that reveal significant divergence in their understanding of status reversal and what it means to be an alternative community. To begin with, while the author of 11Q13 focuses on Leviticus 25, with only implicit references to Isaiah 61, the third evangelist does the exact opposite.[86] This is a seemingly simple difference, but upon closer examination it is revealing. The Year of Jubilee in Leviticus 25 is an occasional festival, celebrated every fifty years, and thus fits with the future-oriented eschatology typical of the Scrolls community (for example, 11Q13 II, 6-9). Status reversals will come, to be sure, but at the hand of God and only in "the last days" (cf. line 4). The author of Luke, however, has an eschatology that is at least partially realized in the work of Jesus and his followers; thus Jesus can claim that *today* this Scripture has been fulfilled (Luke 4:21). The employment of Isaiah 61 as a focal text by the third evangelist suggests that in Luke's narrative, Jubilee is an ongoing project of God in which humans are called to participate. Croatto has argued that "the prophets did not condition the praxis of solidarity with certain fixed dates (seven or fifty years). Rather they demanded it always. . . . The core meaning of the prophetic message is deeper . . . 'not to cause' [*sic*] slavery, debt to the other, or loss of possessions."[87] In keeping with this prophetic stance,

---

83. Merrill P. Miller, "The Function of Isa 61:1-2 in 11Q Melchizedek," *JBL* 88 (1969): 467.

84. Ibid., 469.

85. George J. Brooke, "Shared Intertextual Interpretations in the Dead Sea Scrolls and the New Testament," in *Biblical Perspectives: Early Use and Interpretation of the Bible in Light of the Dead Sea Scrolls,* ed. Michael E. Stone and Esther G. Chazon (Leiden: Brill, 1998), 37. See also Sloan, *Favorable Year,* 44.

86. Brooke, "Shared Intertextual Interpretations," 49.

the status reversal, or more specifically the social leveling, proclaimed in the Lukan Jubilee, begins with divine activity in the present and is further enhanced through human participation.

Two other related differences between the use of Jubilee imagery by Luke and by the author of 11Q13 are the role of outsiders and the metaphorical or literal nature of the status reversals. As with many Dead Sea Scrolls texts, 11Q13 holds to the exegetical principle of reading all positive prophecies in favor of the community and all negative prophecies or judgment as directed to those outside the community.[88] Isaiah's "year of grace," in 11Q13, is for "the sons of light" and "the nation of the holy ones of God," who will be led by Melchizedek to bring the parallel day of vengeance upon "Belial and the spirits of his lot," who are outside the community and therefore irredeemably evil (lines 8-13). This limited view of the beneficiaries of Jubilee is supported better by Leviticus 25, which offers release only to Hebrews, than by Isaiah 61, which is less committal on this particular issue. Community insiders, in 11Q13, are the only ones who will receive liberty and release, and this liberty is defined specifically as release from "the debt of all their iniquities" (line 6), indicating a focus solely on the cultic and spiritual side of Jubilee, at the expense of its extensive socioeconomic aspects. Another Scrolls document, 4Q521 (4QMessianic Apocalypse), makes a similar exegetical move. Like Isa. 61:1-2, it speaks of offering good news to the poor, freeing prisoners, and giving sight to the blind (lines 5-8), but the עניים (the poor) are placed in parallel construction with the pious, the righteous, and the faithful (lines 5-6). Thus we see in these two Dead Sea Scrolls documents that the language of Isaiah 61 is clearly spiritualized and used to limit access to divine salvation only to the in-group of the community.[89] The lack of this explicitly metaphorical interpretation in Luke strengthens the case for understanding the reversals as concrete changes in favor of the poor and the oppressed. In the midst of the Roman Empire, spiritualizing these dangerous ideas would have been the safer and easier route, but Luke refuses to do so, thus leaving intact their power to inspire the vision of a more just world.

It is evident from this brief survey that the image of the Year of Jubilee has been richly mined, explored, and developed over the centuries by various interpreters of Scripture and their communities of faith. Indeed, this work continues even today. The Latin American *campesinos* of Solentiname note, with considerable irony, that for some contemporary Christians, Jubilee has become a year when people travel to Rome for a papal blessing, rather than a

---

87. Croatto, "From the Leviticus Jubilee," 106.

88. Sanders, "From Isaiah," 60.

89. Green, *Gospel of Luke*, 213.

festival of agrarian and social reform.[90] Luke occupies his own unique place in this line, as is exemplified particularly by the story of the Nazareth proclamation in Luke 4:16-30. As our ensuing exploration into this pericope will show, Luke pushes the idea of a "year approved by the Lord" (Luke 4:19) into territory that should cause as much discomfort to modern readers of Scripture as it likely did to Luke's earliest audience. In the words of James A. Sanders, "Prophetical realism is that dimension within a community which challenges its identity, and challenges it on the basis and authority of the very tradition from which that identity springs."[91] Through an appeal to the prophets Isaiah, Elijah, and Elisha, Luke attempts to issue such a challenge to his communities of faith. The challenge, we will find, is not only to religious beliefs and rituals, but also to the hidden transcripts of elite and non-elite alike, with significant ramifications for our understanding of resistance in the early Christian communities.

Sociological Analysis: An Alternative Hidden Transcript

The one-way status reversal imagery of Isa. 61:1-2 stands at the forefront of the Nazareth proclamation pericope and holds a similarly prominent place in the revelation of Jesus' version of the hidden transcript. It is particularly influential on the concrete application of reversal in the Lukan understanding of Jesus' life and ministry. Upon closer inspection of this pericope, however, we find that it engages with the ethics of resistance in much more depth than the simple presence of status reversals might indicate. Luke 4:16-30 explores the reversal of the multiple types of privilege that are claimed by all sorts of people, non-elites included, and in the process challenges certain aspects of the Nazareth community's hidden transcript of resistance. Jesus' interaction with his childhood friends and neighbors about the Isaiah passage and its connection (in his eyes, at least) to the work of Elijah and Elisha reveals much about Jesus, much about the Lukan audience, and much about communities of faith in general. At every stage of the story, the author adds layers of nuance to the definitions and ramifications of sociopolitical and religious relationships in a time of oppression and stratification. Thus we will explore these layers as the story leads us from the Isaiah reading, through the people's mixed reaction, to Jesus' final illustrations and their resounding effects.

---

90. Ernesto Cardenal, *The Gospel in Solentiname*, trans. Donald D. Walsh, rev. ed. (Maryknoll, NY: Orbis, 2007), 65.

91. Sanders, "From Isaiah," 60.

HIDDEN TRANSCRIPTS IN THE SABBATH READING FROM ISAIAH (LUKE 4:16-21)

As soon as Jesus returns to Galilee after his sojourn in the wilderness, hints about his position as a possible threat to the Roman-backed establishment begin to appear. The introduction to his work in the region (verses 14-15) portrays Jesus as a powerfully charismatic figure, filled with the Spirit and teaching the people to near-universal acclaim. Most interesting is the report (φήμη, from the verb φημί, "I speak") about him that was spreading throughout[92] the region; the immediate impression is of the stir that Jesus creates and the number of people talking about him—in essence the rumors that begin to fly (and continue to fly; cf. Luke 4:37). Rumors tend to flourish when events of great importance to the people are occurring, but reliable information about them is unavailable. The potential power and threat of such rumors has long been recognized by ruling groups; the Roman emperors, for example, maintained an order of officials, the *delatores*, assigned to collect and monitor current rumors.[93] Jesus' teaching was apparently finding some resonance with the experience of the Galilean people, enough to get them excited and talking about him. Additionally, rumors change and are embellished as they spread, generally in such a way that they become "more closely in line with the hopes, fears, and worldview of those who hear and retell [them]."[94] Standing as Jesus did entirely outside the power structure of local elites and the Roman-allied Jerusalem ruling group, he was already a figure of some danger to the status quo when he arrived in Nazareth amidst the highest of expectations, and what ensues there serves only to complicate the situation even further.

In the narrative arc of the Gospel of Luke, the story of 4:16-30 is a prominent public declaration of Jesus' worldview and the program for his ministry and movement. From a hidden transcript perspective, this means that Luke portrays Jesus as making in Nazareth one of the more open and therefore dangerous declarations of reversal and resistance in the entire Gospel. Such an open challenge fractures the power dynamic.[95] He provides Jesus with only a few layers of protective anonymity and ambiguity. One is the

---

92. In this context, κατά seems to indicate broad dispersal (BDAG, 510), emphasizing the pervasiveness of Jesus' developing reputation.

93. Scott, *Domination*, 144.

94. Ibid., 145. Scott illustrates this point with a modern study performed in the United States. Subjects were shown a picture of a white man threatening a black man with a razor. In more than half of the retellings by white subjects, the black man was holding the razor and threatening the white man. "On this basis," he writes, "one must expect rumors to take quite divergent forms depending on what class, strata, region, or occupation they are circulating in" (145).

95. See ibid., 202–27.

absence of explicit downward reversals against the powerful; the reversals are one-way only, benefiting the poor and downtrodden rather than trumpeting acts of judgment on those who cause their poverty. But beyond this, Jesus' dissatisfaction with the status quo makes itself quite plain. The text heavily implies that Jesus himself is the Spirit-anointed messenger of good news to the poor, and that is the message the Nazareth congregation apparently receives. There is perhaps a thin layer of protection in the fact that this identification is not completely explicit. But ultimately, with his words in Nazareth and his future ministry of teaching and healing, Jesus claims an active and central role in bringing about the reversals of the Year of the Lord, and thereby an active and central role in threatening the established social, political, and economic system of Galilee (and, by extension, the Roman status quo in general). He does not protect himself by attributing his hopes solely to God, the distant deity.[96] He will act as God's chosen agent for this work, and he claims this role in the midst of a regular synagogue meeting. Jesus chooses not to take advantage of the anonymity that comes from rumors, gossip, grumbling, or mob action.[97]

Another unusual characteristic of the Nazareth proclamation's status reversals is their imminence, or perhaps better, their immediacy, and therefore the immediacy of their potential threat. Jesus states that the Isaianic reversals are fulfilled *today*—not after death (as in Luke 16:19-31), not at some unspecified future time (as in Luke 6:21, 26; but cf. the present tense of verses 20, 22-24, 26), but now, in the present (σήμερον, a word often associated in Luke with salvation of all kinds; see 2:11; 5:26; 13:32; 19:5, 9; 23:43).[98] This declaration of salvation offered hope to those hearing the Gospel who perceived themselves as poor, captive, and oppressed, and thus offered some incentive to resist or at least question the prevailing social system. As José Severino Croatto notes, Jesus continues a prophetic worldview that demands social justice for all people at all times, not just when it is officially legislated.[99] As such, the Nazareth proclamation would have been deemed dangerous to any listening elites and many of their retainers.

Finally, most unusual and potentially dangerous for a declaration of status reversal is the setting in which Luke places Jesus' initial mission statement. In Luke 6, Jesus is presented as the quintessential carrier of the hidden transcript: a popular prophet, not connected with the Roman-allied leaders, safely disseminating his ideas of resistance in unauthorized gatherings outside of

---

96. Ibid., 148.

97. For further discussion of these tactics of disguise for subordinates' resistance, see ibid., 140–56.

98. Prior, *Jesus the Liberator*, 157–58.

99. Croatto, "From the Leviticus Jubilee," 106.

dominant control and surveillance.[100] But the synagogue meeting was an officially authorized gathering, one allowed by the Jerusalem elites and most likely attended and perhaps controlled by their retainers. Early synagogues served social, political, and legal purposes, as well as religious.[101] It is in this official setting that Jesus challenges the very systems in which the synagogue played a local role. It is perhaps also an indication that Luke wanted to portray Jesus as willing to work from within the status quo to change it for the better, and an encouragement for the Gospel's earliest reading communities to do the same in their own local cities and associations.

Jesus' reading in the Nazareth synagogue is carefully set up, with detailed narration of seemingly insignificant actions like standing, sitting, and rolling and unrolling the scroll. All this serves to build tension and focus the readers' attention on the centerpiece of this first section: the compiled quotation from Isaiah 61 and 58, and Jesus' claim on its prophetic mission of reversal. His anointing by the Spirit is mentioned yet again (cf. Luke 3:22; 4:1, 14), paired in 4:18 with a calling to bring good news to the poor. Scott has found that, among many oppressed groups, such a claim to spirit (or even demonic) possession is a tactic used to express social protest in a manner that enables the possessed individual to disavow personal responsibility and thereby escape punishment.[102] Spirit possession is another possible avenue of protection available to Jesus in this story, but he does not seem to avail himself of it. He openly claims the power and authority of the Spirit of God, but gives no indication of using it to abdicate personal involvement and responsibility (as was the case in the examples cited by Scott). On the contrary, Jesus embraces his new role and maintains his position even in the face of potentially fatal opposition from his childhood friends, neighbors, and perhaps even extended family (Luke 4:28-30).

Jesus is following in the startling footsteps of his mother by bringing the hidden transcript of resistance out into the open, an act that Scott says "carries the force of a symbolic declaration of war."[103] A closer examination of the reversals, however, here in the Isaiah reading and throughout Luke 4:16-30, reveals a difference between Jesus' initial declaration of status reversal and that of Mary's song: a notable lack of military imagery comparable to that found in

---

100. Scott, *Domination*, 120–24.

101. Prior, *Jesus the Liberator*, 108–10. For an overview of authorized versus unauthorized gatherings, see Scott, *Domination*, 58–66, especially 61–63.

102. Scott, *Domination*, 141–42. He cites the examples of "hysteric" women in strongly patriarchal cultures, cases of possession of a servant or slave at times of highest tension and unjust treatment, and cultic rituals of ecstasy or drunkenness (141).

103. Ibid., 8.

the Magnificat. Additionally, the reversals of this pericope are one-way only, as is illustrated in verse 18: the poor receive the message of good news, the captives are released, the blind are given sight, and the oppressed are offered freedom. But there is no corresponding downward reversal or bad news for the rich, the captors, and the oppressors, although it is perhaps easy to infer such an idea from the context.[104] This inference, however, is central to the challenge that Luke issues to his non-elite readers in this particular pericope. As with the Year of Jubilee, the focus of the quote in Luke seems to be on addressing the problems of the poor and indebted in order to restore social equality, rather than taking revenge on the powerful through total inversion. In Nazareth and throughout Jesus' ministry in Galilee (4:14—9:50), Luke portrays Jesus as interacting mainly with non-elites, and perhaps a few local retainers.[105] Most of them need no encouragement to celebrate judgment upon the rich, so there is no need for Jesus to declare it here. But they do need to be freed from their own ideas of privilege, as we will see in the rest of the story.

One aspect of the proclaimed reversals that is shared with the Magnificat and, indeed, with most of the Lukan status-reversal texts, is the holistic nature of the reversals, socioeconomic as well as spiritual. In this passage and throughout the Gospel of Luke, Jubilee release is viewed not only as forgiveness of sins, but also as "encompass[ing] spiritual restoration, moral transformation, rescue from demonic oppression, and release from illness and disability."[106] The guiding line in Jesus' "mission statement" is found in Luke 4:18: "It is to bring good news for the poor that he has sent me."[107] Πτωχός is a term with clear economic implications, but it can also encompass those who are disadvantaged in other ways, particularly those with diminished status and low honor and those who are outsiders in some way (for example, Luke 7:20-23; 14:7-24; 21:1-3).[108] The rest of the compiled Isaiah quotation expands on what it means to proclaim good news to the poor, consistently with words that can have either a literal

104. John O. York, *The Last Shall Be First: The Rhetoric of Reversal in Luke*, JSNTSup 46 (Sheffield: Sheffield Academic Press, 1991), 94. As the Gospel of Luke proceeds, it becomes logical for the reader to expect certain character types (those without honor, wealth, or status) to experience positive divine reversal, while characters who are prestigious, wealthy, and powerful receive the opposite (160).

105. Green, *Gospel of Luke*, 201.

106. Nolland, *Luke 1—9:20*, 202.

107. I am reading the infinitive phrase εὐαγγελίσασθαι πτωχοῖς as dependent upon the following clause ἀπέσταλκέν με, rather than the preceding ἔχρισέν με (a reading suggested by the Hebrew MT). The placement of the infinitive phrase at the beginning of the clause before the finite verb emphasizes it as having primary importance in the sentence.

108. Green, *Gospel of Luke*, 211; and Luke Timothy Johnson, *The Gospel of Luke*, SP 3, ed. Daniel J. Harrington (Collegeville, MN: Liturgical, 1991), 79.

or a figurative meaning. As discussed in the previous chapter, such ambiguous language in hidden transcript texts was common, so as to allow for either the intended rebellious interpretation or a protective innocuous understanding.[109]

Here in Luke 4:18, Jesus offers release (ἄφεσις) for the captives (αἰχμαλώτοις) and the oppressed (τεθραυσμένους), and recovery of sight for the blind (τυφλοῖς). Ἄφεσις, as we have already established, is best understood as a multifaceted concept involving both its "moral" meaning of forgiveness and its "jubilary/financial" meaning of release for debtors and prisoners.[110] The idea of spiritual salvation is not separated in the Gospel of Luke from social justice, nor is individual sin from corporate sin. Similarly, one who is αἰχμάλωτος could be a sociopolitical prisoner of war (Luke 21:24) or one controlled figuratively by an outside force such as sin or evil (Rom. 7:23; 2 Cor. 10:5),[111] although it should be noted that in the Septuagint, this word is used almost exclusively for sociopolitical prisoners (for example, Tob. 1:10; 1 Macc. 10:33).[112] One who is τυφλός might be literally blind (Luke 7:21-22; 18:35; Acts 13:11) or, metaphorically, one who lacks true understanding (for example, Matt. 23:16-26; John 9:40-41).[113] The Hebrew in this phrase is ambiguous; the Septuagint (followed by Luke) translates פְּקַח־קוֹחַ (Isa. 61:1) as opening the eyes of the blind, while the Vulgate renders it as opening up the prisons.[114]

This entire range of meanings enriches the depth of the sweeping change presented here as Jesus' mission, begun with his life and to be continued by his followers. It also provides a significant contrast to the mission of Rome, as envisioned in Virgil's *Aeneid*:

> Roman, remember by your strength to rule
> Earth's peoples—for your arts are to be these:
> To pacify, to impose the rule of law,
> to spare the conquered, battle down the proud.[115]

On the surface, there are similarities. Both passages begin with an overarching goal and elaborate upon it with a list of infinitives. The idea

---

109. Scott, *Domination*, 153–54.

110. See, e.g., Sloan, *Favorable Year*, 118–19.

111. BDAG, 31–32.

112. LEH, 18.

113. BDAG, 1021.

114. Sanders, "From Isaiah," 50.

115. Quoted by Christopher Kelly, *The Roman Empire: A Very Short Introduction* (Oxford: Oxford University Press, 2006), 21.

of bringing down the proud and arrogant is a classic reversal idea found elsewhere in the Lukan reversals (for example, Luke 1:51), although not in the upward-only reversals of the Nazareth proclamation. But the content of Rome's mission is in many ways antithetical to that of Jesus; rather than pacifying and conquering foreigners, Jesus proclaims release for prisoners of war, relief from oppression by the rule of (Roman-dictated) law, and in later parts of the chapter, an acceptance of foreigners as equally worthy of God's grace and favor. At the same time, however, there is also imperial mimicry in the shared hope for the eventual encompassing of all Earth's peoples and the requirement of adopting the correct set of values and beliefs. The significant difference is, I think, in how Jesus goes about (and how Luke advocates) trying to attain these hopes, versus the accepted Roman methods.

In the Nazareth proclamation pericope, Jesus does not make any material change to the people's situation, in keeping with the symbolic nature of most initial declarations of the hidden transcript.[116] But he does make it clear that he will not let the power and pervasiveness of Rome's social and material stratification prevent him from speaking out against its injustice and seeking to change it. The ensuing actions of Jesus to address social and economic issues concretely, as well as spiritual ones, prevent any easy spiritualizing of his words. The reversals and the salvation that they embody address various aspects of human life: economic problems of poverty and indebtedness, social problems of status and discrimination, political problems of oppression, physical problems like blindness and other disabilities, and spiritual problems of sin and inauthentic worship.[117] This holistic type of salvation has found great resonance, today and throughout the history of Christianity, with the oppressed and poor of the world. African scholar Samuel Abogunrin writes, "The ministry of the Church, like that of its Lord, must always focus on the whole person. It is only the gospel as announced by Jesus at Nazareth that can be meaningful in the African context."[118] This is particularly noteworthy for our study because it shows the strong resonance of the Nazareth proclamation with oppressed, colonized, and formerly colonized populations. The power that Abogunrin finds in Luke 4, which he claims for the African people and the African church, is in part the power of the hidden transcript of resistance made public, written down, and

---

116. See Scott, *Domination*, 215.

117. See, e.g., Robert McAfee Brown, *Unexpected News: Reading the Bible with Third World Eyes* (Philadelphia: Westminster, 1984), 93–94; Green, *Gospel of Luke*, 211–12; and Nolland, *Luke 1—9:20*, 197.

118. Samuel O. Abogunrin, "Jesus' Sevenfold Programmatic Declaration at Nazareth: An Exegesis of Luke 4.15-30 from an African Perspective," *Black Theology* 1 (2003): 235.

shared over the years. Even when such public declarations of resistance fail, as Jesus ultimately does at Nazareth, they still contribute to the hidden transcript, serving "to restore a sense of self-respect and personhood" to the speakers and hearers[119] and to "lay down another sedimentary layer of popular memory" to nourish future movements.[120]

Obviously the story of Luke 4:16-30 was meaningful enough to play such a nourishing or inspiring role in the context of the third evangelist and his earliest reading communities, since they preserved it as a defining moment in Jesus' life and ministry. But in the story itself, as narrated in Luke 4, it is clear that this acceptance was far from universal, particularly in Nazareth. Not only did Jesus' challenging views about power and prestige eventually draw the dangerous attention of the Roman-allied Jerusalem elites, but also, as he elaborates upon them, they prove unwelcome to his own peers, his fellow non-elites. Let us look in more detail, then, at the reactions of the Nazareth congregation and their dialogue with Jesus after he pronounces the fulfillment of Isaiah in their very midst.

HIDDEN TRANSCRIPTS IN THE INTERACTIONS OF JESUS AND THE PEOPLE (LUKE 4:22-24)

There is a sense of tension in the story as Jesus finishes the Isaiah reading and sits down to teach. Luke notes that "the eyes of all in the synagogue were fixed upon him" (Luke 4:20b), and one can imagine the pregnant pause before Jesus spoke again.[121] The anticipation was likely heightened even further by the reports about Jesus that preceded his visit to Nazareth (Luke 4:14-15), the passage that he read, and perhaps his personal charisma.[122] Finally, Jesus begins to speak and manages only one sentence before there is an eruption of the audience witnessing, wondering, and chattering to one another about the intriguing words of "Joseph's son" (Luke 4:22). Although it is not often read this way, the text seems to suggest that the people interrupted Jesus before he was finished; Luke says specifically that Jesus *began* to talk (ἤρξατο . . . λέγειν), and the imperfect tense of the people's actions (ἐμαρτύρουν . . .

---

119. Scott, *Domination*, 210.

120. Ibid., 212.

121. The anticipation in the story was perhaps heightened further for Luke's readers by the periphrastic participle ἦσαν ἀτενίζοντες. It seems that the aspectual nuance of periphrastic constructions had waned by the first century CE, but Luke certainly could have been familiar with their earlier use to emphasize the continuing nature of an action. See the discussion in Daniel B. Wallace, *Greek Grammar Beyond the Basics: An Exegetical Syntax of the New Testament* (Grand Rapids: Zondervan, 1996), 647–49.

122. See the interesting discussion of charisma in Scott, *Domination*, 221–24.

. ἐθαύμαζον . . . ἔλεγον) paints a picture of ongoing furor that would have distracted any speaker. As with the rumors about Jesus,[123] most groups of non-elite, subordinated peoples would hear what they hoped to hear in Jesus' interpretation of Isaiah's promise of salvation and reversal of the status quo. Proclaiming its fulfillment *today*, here and now, was all it took to set off the excitement.

One of the most intriguing things about the audience's reaction to the declaration of fulfillment is Luke's use, yet again, of ambiguous words. In 4:22, the issue is not whether we should read them literally or metaphorically, but the fact that each verb can be read as either a positive or a negative reaction: μαρτυρέω can indicate witness for, against, or simply about someone (although "against" is relatively uncommon),[124] and θαυμάζω connotes an extreme reaction that encompasses both being impressed and being disturbed.[125] The question "Isn't this Joseph's son?!" certainly expects an affirmative answer, but the tone could equally be wondering, scornful, disbelieving, excited, or some combination thereof. Unsurprisingly, this choice of words, combined with Jesus' strangely aggressive tone in verses 23-24 and the Nazarenes' violent response in verses 28-30, have led interpreters to read the audience's initial reaction in a wide variety of ways. Some argue that the tone in verse 22 is entirely positive,[126] while others discern a measure of unease, distrust, or confusion mixed in with the audience's excitement.[127] A mixture of emotions—positive, negative, and somewhere in between—is the most realistic possibility and the best interpretation of Luke's ambiguous language. It also leaves room in the story for the readers and hearers to consider their own range of reactions and feelings. How do they, or we, truly react to the proclamation of

---

123. Cf. the above discussion on Luke 4:14-15, and the treatment of rumors in Scott, *Domination*, 144–48.

124. See BDAG, 617–18. There is also a strong legal connotation to μαρτυρέω; see John Nolland, "Impressed Unbelievers as Witnesses to Christ (Luke 4:22a)," *JBL* 98 (1979): 219–29. He argues that those who spread reports about Jesus without fully becoming disciples act as "impartial witnesses" to bolster Luke's case with nonbiased evidence. "Luke wants his readers to see that even people so inimical to the claims of Jesus that they seek his death, nevertheless, cannot but be impressed by the words of this imposing figure" (229).

125. See BDAG, 444–45. John Nolland observes that in the work of Luke-Acts, θαυμάζω is usually used to describe the perceptions of observers who have not yet come to have full belief in Jesus and his mission (*Luke 1—9:20*, 198).

126. E.g., Bovon, *Luke 1*, 154–55; Catchpole, "Anointed One," 239; Green, *Gospel of Luke*, 214–15; and Siker, "'First to the Gentiles,'" 79–80.

127. E.g., Abogunrin, "Jesus' Sevenfold," 238; Prior, *Jesus the Liberator*, 98; and Ringe, *Jesus, Liberation*, 40.

imminent eschatological reversals in favor of the poor, captive, and oppressed? Is the first reaction rejoicing about the benefits one will receive, or gladness that the plight of others will be relieved, or anger and fear that the current status quo will be upset? The reader's attitude toward these reversals and their recipients will become very important as the author nuances his views on resistance to the status quo, and thus the ambiguity of verse 22 offers the audience a moment for reflection on their initial inclinations.

The piece of the Nazareth congregation's reaction most often regarded as negative or at least suspicious is the exclamation about Jesus' local parentage.[128] It can easily be seen as skeptics expressing their doubts about the presumption of a simple Nazareth village boy, a local just like them, claiming to bring in the era of eschatological salvation. This reading is particularly common among interpreters who are not European or North American, such as the congregation of Solentiname, Nicaragua, who identified with Jesus and felt that they too are often doubted and belittled as lowly *campesinos* with no scriptural insight valuable enough to be worth the time of the rich and powerful.[129] A group of South Africans reported similar experiences with resentment of "local kids made good" and understood the question about Joseph's son to indicate that some Nazarenes were disappointed that the vaunted "Messiah" was just someone from down the street.[130] It is also possible to understand this question positively, as an act of pride in the success of one of their own, and also perhaps an anticipation of special privilege because of their prior relationship with Jesus.[131] Both readings, of course, exhibit great surprise at God's chosen agent, and both reveal a worldview that limits the reign of God in ways that are unacceptable to Lukan theology. As with Mary singing the Magnificat, the hope for status reversal in Luke comes here from an unexpected source in an unexpected setting: in Luke 1 from a sexually compromised pregnant teenager singing an unexpectedly subversive song, and in Luke 4 from a local man overstepping the bounds in his home synagogue with (apparently) nothing to back it up.

128. E.g., Abogunrin, "Jesus' Sevenfold," 238; Falcetta, *Call of Nazareth*, 48–49; and Prior, *Jesus the Liberator*, 98. For the dissenting view that this question is a positive reaction claiming pride in Jesus as one of their own, see especially Green, *Gospel of Luke*, 214–15; also Catchpole, "Anointed One," 239; and Siker, "'First to the Gentiles,'" 79–80.

129. Cardenal, *Gospel in Solentiname*, 66.

130. "A South African Example: Jesus' Teaching at Nazareth–Luke 4.14-30," in *Voices from the Margin: Interpreting the Bible in the Third World*, ed. R. S. Sugirtharajah (Maryknoll, NY: Orbis, 1991), 424–26.

131. Green, *Gospel of Luke*, 214–15.

In the midst of the confusion, the anger, and the excitement, Jesus continues on with his teaching, because announcing the fulfillment of the Isaiah passage was only the beginning of what he wanted to say. He seeks in Nazareth to proclaim the in-breaking of God's reign into the world, but he also needs to correct some assumptions about what "the year approved by the Lord" will look like. Its status reversals will likely surprise many elites, but two quick proverbs make it clear that some non-elites may be taken aback as well. The first proverb, a concise command of "Doctor, heal yourself!" is what Jesus imagines that the Nazareth congregation will say to him. The metaphor of the sick doctor is common in ancient literature, appearing in various forms in Greek, Roman, and rabbinic writings.[132] Generally, it seems to be applied in two different ways: as a personal insult or retort to someone who does not follow his or her own advice, or as a rebuke to those with great gifts who refuse to put them at the service of their own people.[133] As S. J. Noorda notes, the context of the proverb (both the question about Jesus' parentage and the clarification about the people of Nazareth wanting signs like those given to Capernaum) seems to solidify that the primary meaning intended here is related to loyalty to one's hometown and benefits for one's own people.[134]

If Jesus truly is the prophet anointed by the Spirit to proclaim eschatological Jubilee and the restoration of a just society, it is not illogical for the Nazarenes to expect him to begin with his hometown—or perhaps even closer to home, with himself. The personal insult facet of the doctor proverb is, I think, implicitly present alongside the call to use one's gifts first at home. Rebeca from Solentiname argues that Jesus can imagine the people throwing this saying at Jesus "because he was poor. Let him liberate himself before he liberates others. They don't understand that he has to be poor to liberate the poor, and he can't do it if he's rich."[135] What can Jesus, as a lowly traveling teacher with no official power or prestige, offer in the way of honor and status reversal? But a full application of the hidden transcript that Jesus has already declared, and with which at least some in the Nazareth congregation

132. The most complete list of parallels is found in John Nolland, "Classical and Rabbinic Parallels to 'Physician, Heal Yourself' (Lk 4:23)," *NovT* 21 (1979): 194–206.

133. S. J. Noorda, "'Cure Yourself, Doctor!' (Luke 4,23): Classical Parallels to an Alleged Saying of Jesus," in *Logia: Les Paroles de Jésus–The Sayings of Jesus*, ed. Joël Delobel, BETL (Leuven: Leuven University Press, 1982), 463. See also R. Alan Culpepper, "The Gospel of Luke: Introduction, Commentary, and Reflections," in *NIB*, ed. Leander E. Keck, vol. 9 (Nashville: Abingdon, 1995), 107; Fitzmyer, *Luke I–IX*, 535; and Nolland, "Classical and Rabbinic Parallels," 207–8.

134. Noorda, "'Cure Yourself,'" 464–65.

135. Cardenal, *Gospel in Solentiname*, 67.

seem to agree, does away with these very distinctions, or at least redefines such ideas as prestige and honor. Jesus hopes to reverse the status quo imposed by the Roman Empire, but he also wants to address the "pretensions of his neighbors who claim a place of privilege at the time of fulfillment that Jesus had proclaimed."[136] Such pretensions are also present in the local rivalry behind the Capernaum barb (4:23b)—an element that would have resonated with the Hellenistic congregations reading Luke. Competition for status, honor, and resources was standard practice not only for individuals, but also for cities in the Greco-Roman world.[137] That pervasive status competition was part of the same social structure that must be transformed by the holistic salvation just outlined, and is yet another form of prejudice and domination from which Jesus offers ἄφεσις. This part of his plan for reversal and resistance, however, will begin to raise real problems in Nazareth and later in Jerusalem.

The second proverb is Jesus' rebuttal to the command to "heal" himself: the stark claim that a prophet is never approved of (δεκτός) by his own hometown, or in his native country (Luke 4:24). Prophets, of course, seldom favor their hometown or country; in fact, they tend to do the exact opposite in calling them to account for their actions before God (clearly displayed, for example, in Isaiah 58, an intertext engaged by Jesus in his Nazareth proclamation, as shown above).[138] Jesus was not called, according to Luke, to bring honor to Nazareth or to himself, but instead to bring God's message of transformation in all its complexity and challenge. Alessandro Falcetta observes that the Lukan Jesus was willing to perform prophetic signs when they were for the sole purpose of helping someone who truly needs it,[139] that is, when they advanced the status reversals he had come to carry out. But in the Gospel of Luke, he always refused to do so when the signs are to "prove himself" to those who do not believe: at Nazareth in this pericope, for the devil (4:1-13), for the insincere crowds (11:29), and for Herod Antipas (23:8-11). This unwillingness to comply fully with the wishes of his non-elite peers, particularly his closest neighbors, would have been threatening to their identity and their own preferred methods of

136. Ringe, *Jesus, Liberation*, 41.

137. See Ramsay MacMullen, *Roman Social Relations: 50 B.C. to A.D. 284* (New Haven: Yale University Press, 1974), 59–61; and Phil Perkins and Lisa Nevett, "Urbanism and Urbanization in the Roman World," in *Experiencing Rome: Culture, Identity, and Power in the Roman Empire*, ed. Janet Huskinson (London: Routledge, 2000), 215.

138. Noorda, "'Cure Yourself,'" 465.

139. Falcetta, *Call of Nazareth*, 73–74.

resistance.[140] Jesus is quite aware of this danger, as shown by his citing of the prophet proverb, and yet he forges ahead.

Thus, in the wake of the Isaiah reading and Jesus' announcement that it has been fulfilled, we see that the initial interchange between the people and Jesus, their first reactions to each other, are already fraught with the implications of long-held hopes, insecurities, expectations, and assumptions, and how they are affected by even a hint of challenge. This homecoming is not proceeding the way the Nazarenes had apparently envisioned it when they first heard the rumors of Jesus' glorious teaching elsewhere in Galilee. But the plot continues to thicken as Jesus finishes his sermon, and so do the nuances of the hidden transcript of resistance as revealed in the Gospel of Luke.

HIDDEN TRANSCRIPTS IN JESUS' FINAL ILLUSTRATIONS (LUKE 4:25-30)

Central to much of the scholarly debate surrounding the Nazareth proclamation is the final part of Jesus' message in the synagogue, in which he again cites scriptural material to communicate his message. This time he draws upon the lives of Elijah and Elisha, specifically examples of each prophet performing a sign or miracle on behalf of a non-Israelite person: for Elijah, a Phoenician widow from Zarephath of Sidon (1 Kgs. 17:8-24); and for Elisha, the Aramean warrior Naaman (2 Kgs. 5:1-19). These stories are, of course, a major factor in many commentators' focus (almost exclusive, in some cases) on this pericope's connection to the Gentile mission and Jewish-Gentile relations.[141] While this is certainly one important aspect of the Nazareth proclamation, it is not the only one. It can also fall too easily into an anti-Jewish reading, whether intentional or not.[142] But when we look beyond the religious and ethnic divide between Jews and Gentiles, we find that the Nazareth proclamation addresses even more boundaries, specifically some that might have been more relevant and meaningful in the urban context of Luke's first reading communities.[143]

---

140. Scott, *Domination*, 130–31.

141. E.g., Prior, *Jesus the Liberator*, 142–48; Siker, "'First to the Gentiles,'" 73–90; and Tannehill, "Mission of Jesus," 51–75.

142. One especially problematic example of this is Heerak Christian Kim, *Intricately Connected: Biblical Studies, Intertextuality, and Literary Genre* (Lanham, MD: University Press of America, 2008), 29–47, in which he argues that Jesus was in disagreement with all Jewish groups of his time and that the message at Nazareth was "intentionally meant to offend the Jews" (38) because Jesus "wanted to set his movement apart from Judaism from the very beginning" (44).

143. See chapter 2 above for a detailed discussion of the communities and context of the Gospel of Luke.

Our initial step must be a closer look at the original stories from 1 and 2 Kings. In 1 Kgs. 17:1, Elijah has brought down a drought upon the land, and God subsequently calls him to wait out the ensuing famine in the land of the Phoenicians, partaking of the hospitality of a divinely chosen widow (1 Kgs. 17:8). When he arrives, the widow he approaches for food and water informs him that she and her son are about to eat their last morsels of bread before resigning themselves to death (1 Kgs. 17:12). Elijah eventually performs two separate miracles on her behalf: the flour and oil never run out, enabling all three of them to survive the famine (1 Kgs. 17:13-16); and when the son falls ill and dies, Elijah raises him from the dead for the sake of the widow who has shown him hospitality (1 Kgs. 17:17-24). One particularly noteworthy aspect of this story is that the help and hospitality go both ways; the great Jewish prophet Elijah offers aid to the nameless and impoverished Sidonian widow, but at the same time she provides him with refuge and hospitality during his exile from Israel. Thus the inclusion of this story incorporates not only a reversal in that God has long chosen to show favor to non-Jews, but also a reversal in that Gentiles have sometimes ministered to Israelites, and that a woman of little status and no resources offered succor to a great prophet.[144] This hints at something that Jesus will make even more explicit in the Sermon on the Plain (Luke 6:20-49): unlike in Roman culture, where charity and benefaction are expected mainly of elites and given only to the "good" poor,[145] God's reign calls for all to use whatever resources they might have to help others.

Jesus also refers to a sign performed by Elisha, but one that differs from the Elijah example in many ways. Naaman is a powerful, high-status elite military leader "in high favor" with his king. He is also afflicted with leprosy (2 Kgs. 5:1). Although the disease was apparently not serious enough to keep him from his post as commander, it likely led to some status inconsistency for this seemingly invincible "mighty warrior,"[146] as Naaman shows himself willing to go to great lengths for a cure. Whereas Elijah meets the non-elite widow (a perfect example of the ES7 poorest of the poor) in *her* territory and stays in *her* home, Naaman

---

144. Craig A. Evans, "The Function of the Elijah/Elisha Narratives in Luke's Ethic of Election," in Evans and Sanders, *Luke and Scripture*, 75.

145. Peter Garnsey and Richard Saller, *The Roman Empire: Economy, Society and Culture* (Berkeley: University of California Press, 1987), 117–18; Anthony D. Macro, "The Cities of Asia Minor under the Roman Imperium," in *ANRW* 2.7.2, ed. Hildegard Temporini and Wolfgang Haase (Berlin: Walter de Gruyter, 1980), 684–85; and C. R. Whittaker, "The Poor," in *The Romans*, ed. Andrea Giardina (Chicago: University of Chicago Press, 1993), 294–95.

146. See the discussion of status inconsistency in Gerhard E. Lenski, *Power and Privilege: A Theory of Social Stratification* (1966; repr., Chapel Hill: University of North Carolina Press, 1984), 86–88.

the elite must travel to Israel and seek out the aid of Elisha, who at first will not even see him in person (2 Kgs. 5:5b-11). Also notable about this story is the prominent role the servants play in obtaining a cure for Naaman. A captive Israelite girl serving Naaman's wife first informs them of the power of Elisha (2 Kgs. 5:2-5), and it is only the intervention of Naaman's servants in Israel that convinces him to swallow his pride and follow the prophet's instructions (2 Kgs. 5:13-14). The kings of Aram and Israel, by contrast, are both powerless to help the situation (2 Kgs. 5:5-7), and Naaman himself is stubborn, arrogant, and chauvinistic (2 Kgs. 5:11-12)—exactly what Galilean and Hellenistic non-elites would have expected from an elite like him.

But in the end, surprisingly, Naaman listens to his servants, receives healing, and then responds properly to this display of Yahweh's power: he humbles himself and submits to God, whom he now recognizes as the only one worthy of worship (2 Kgs. 5:13-17), a decidedly unexpected move from this foreign elite. Significantly, both he and the widow helped by Elijah gain spiritual insight and transformation from the prophetic miracles performed on their behalf. Through the signs of nourishment, life, and healing, these two foreigners, as different as can be on the outside, both recognize the man of God in their midst and also recognize the truth and life that are inherent in the work of Yahweh (1 Kgs. 17:24; 2 Kgs. 5:15-17). They provide the community of Nazareth and the later congregations reading Luke with two examples of Jesus' holistic ἄφεσις, which encompasses welcoming Jesus as one sent from God, social and material aid and justice, and spiritual transformation. Such a vision of the reversal and reform, as professed by the Lukan Jesus, is broad enough to address all the various areas of subordination: material appropriation of resources, public domination and mastery, and the ideological beliefs that justify these inequalities.[147] The Nazareth proclamation, with its echoes of Jubilee, calls for material justice and equality in social status and economic privilege, but it also publicly proclaims a theology that testifies to the worth of all people, not just those deemed worthy by the social systems that people construct. Jubilee for Luke's Jesus is, as Pablo Richard observes, primarily the restoration of the life of a poor and oppressed people.[148] But it is also one open to those who are not poor and oppressed, as long as they are willing to acknowledge Jesus as Lord of all (cf. Acts 10:34-36) and to participate in the mission of restoring life to all (for example, Luke 14:12-24; 16:19-31; 18:18-30; 19:1-10).

Scholars have recognized this facet of crossing boundaries, but they usually limit it solely to the boundary between Jews and Gentiles. Jeffrey Siker, for

147. Scott, *Domination*, 111.
148. Richard, "Now Is the Time," 51.

example, writes, "The 'acceptable year of the Lord' is proclaimed with primary reference to *outsiders*, that is, to the Gentiles, and is addressed to the Jews only insofar as they are able to accept the inclusion of the Gentiles. This is the net effect of 4:25-27 as it functions in the narrative—*reversal*."[149] James A. Sanders speaks of the "divine injustice" of God offering grace to foreigners, as it would have been perceived by the Jewish "in-group of true believers,"[150] and Michael Prior makes the observation, as true today as it was in the first century, that "religious people, in general, find it difficult to allow God to act with a generosity that extends his salvation beyond the narrow confines of their tradition."[151] All of these are certainly true and prescient reflections of possible reasons for the angry and violent reaction of the Nazareth residents (Luke 4:28-30). But such a singular focus on ethnic and religious barriers misses the other barriers that are broken, particularly those that would be more relevant for the communities reading (or hearing) the first copies of this Gospel.

By the late first century, when Luke's narrative was circulating in the cities of Asia Minor, many non-Jews had become followers of Jesus; the "Gentile mission" was almost certainly well-established and widely accepted. It was likely not a major point of conflict anymore, particularly in the Lukan reading communities, which included plenty of Gentiles.[152] But as we know, traditions are preserved because they are meaningful for a group of people: "Either an old tradition met the people where they were, at some point earlier or later, or we do not have it today."[153] François Bovon moves toward stronger resonance with the Lukan communities when he argues that the goal of the Kings illustrations "points not so much to the mission to the Gentiles as it does to the fellowship between Jews and Gentiles."[154] The part of the Nazareth proclamation, though, that was particularly germane to the life experience of people trying to follow Jesus faithfully in the midst of the pro-Roman cities of Asia Minor is, I think, closely related to other aspects of status-crossing fellowship, particularly in the significant challenge posed by the call for believers of varying social statuses to interact as equals. The message in Nazareth calls for the breaking down of divisions based on social status, economic inequality, and political power, as

---

149. Siker, "'First to the Gentiles,'" 83. Emphasis in original.

150. James A. Sanders, "Isaiah in Luke," in Evans and Sanders, *Luke and Scripture*, 24.

151. Prior, *Jesus the Liberator*, 99.

152. E.g., Acts 14:1; 17:1-4; 18:6-8; 19:8-10. See also chapter 2 above for my reconstruction of the first Lukan communities.

153. Craig A. Evans and James A. Sanders, "Gospels and Midrash: An Introduction to Luke and Scripture," in Evans and Sanders, *Luke and Scripture*, 13. See also Scott, *Domination*, 157.

154. Bovon, *Luke 1*, 156.

seen especially in the story of Elijah and the Sidonian widow, and that of Elisha and the Aramean warrior.

In both of these scriptural examples, the foreigner receives grace and favor from the God of Israel (who is, for Luke, also the God of all humanity; see, for example, Acts 10:34-36). But contrary to the usual non-elite hidden transcript, with its schadenfreude for the dominant groups,[155] the Lukan Jesus puts forward for the consideration of his audience a form of resistance based on the image of a God who offers as much grace to an arrogant army commander as to a poor widow whose only son has just died. Miracles are performed for those who need them, no matter their status or ethnicity.[156] It is not, however, an entirely free grace for the elite. Naaman must put forth significantly more effort to encounter God and receive his miracle than does the widow, and he must explicitly renounce any other deity (2 Kgs. 5:17).[157] As we will see in the next chapter exploring the parable of Lazarus and the rich man, and throughout the Gospel of Luke, much is demanded of those who come to the reign of God with many resources in hand. Robert McAfee Brown makes an interesting point that God's "preferential option for the poor," a significant emphasis in liberation theology, is distinctly not God's *exclusive* option for the poor. The nonpoor are included, but ministry to them must always be in context of ministry to the poor.[158] In Jesus' vision for transforming the status quo, help for the truly poor and needy is essentially automatic, but those with power and privilege must be ready to demonstrate their loyalty to the mission of Jesus as proclaimed at Nazareth.

Throughout Jesus' entire speech, the audience in Nazareth is slowly being filled with a growing rage (Luke 4:28), which eventually boils over into attempted violence (4:29-30). To some extent, this extreme anger is

---

155. Scott, *Domination*, 41–42.

156. Falcetta, *Call of Nazareth*, 81–82.

157. But cf. 2 Kgs. 5:18-19, where Naaman asks for and receives Elisha's blessing to bow down to the Aramean god Rimmon when he is in the presence of his master the king. Philip Esler argues that this reference would have comforted a Roman administrator or soldier, in that it would have allowed him or her to continue outwardly paying tribute to Greco-Roman deities when it was required professionally. See Philip Francis Esler, *Community and Gospel in Luke-Acts: The Social and Political Motivations of Lucan Theology*, SNTSMS 57 (Cambridge: Cambridge University Press, 1987), 218. I am not convinced that this reference alone is enough to show decisively that the author of Luke approved of such pagan worship. But it does seem to be true that Luke was aware of the fact that incorporating elites and retainers into his Christian communities would involve some compromises to the hidden transcript of resistance, and that he was willing to consider them. This point will be discussed in the final section of this chapter.

158. Brown, *Unexpected News*, 100.

understandable to groups under domination. Typically, the hidden transcripts of non-elite populations include a great deal of anger and rage toward the dominant elites, because such emotions cannot safely be expressed in public to those who perpetrate the daily humiliations of subordination. Scott writes, "At its most elementary level the hidden transcript represents an acting out in fantasy—and occasionally in secretive practice—of the anger and reciprocal aggression denied by the presence of domination."[159] After generations of being subjugated by various foreign empires, Galilean communities like Nazareth had no doubt developed a deep resentment toward foreign conquerors like Naaman. Yet Jesus employs such a hated figure as a recipient of God's grace and favor. One of the major coping mechanisms used by non-elites in the face of constant daily humiliation was grasping at anything that built up at least a measure of self-worth, hence the popularity of non-elites' burial clubs and funerary monuments in the Roman Empire.[160] One avenue of self-worth claimed by the non-elites of Nazareth was their identity as the chosen people of God, privileged recipients of exclusive divine favor. They were outsiders as far as Rome was concerned, but the closest of insiders in God's eyes. Yet Jesus, using their very own Scriptures, takes away in one moment their claim to privilege, status, and self-worth. This action would have been seen by Jesus' subordinated peers as the highest disloyalty and threat to their group values and agreed-upon hidden transcripts, and naturally would be treated and punished as such.[161] Jesus is threatening not only the Roman system that oppresses them, but also the current Palestinian power structure from which they derive at least some benefit.[162]

But even as this anger is understandable, there is also value in Jesus' critique of those hidden transcripts that allow for salvation only of the local poor and needy, or only of those in a designated in-group. The highly nuanced alternative resistance that is advocated in the Nazareth proclamation offers an option more focused on leveling and social equality than on total inversion and the reversed oppression to which it is prone. This preference for leveling is introduced by Jesus' reading of a Scripture passage inspired by the Year of Jubilee, a festival designed to restore social equilibrium, and then reinforced by the examples of release and salvation offered to elite and non-elite alike. The appeal to Scripture for each of these points has the added benefit of proving the case for leveling from the public transcript itself, and therefore making this

---

159. Scott, *Domination*, 37–38. See also the larger discussion of this topic on 37–44.

160. Toner, *Popular Culture*, 167.

161. Cf. Scott, *Domination*, 130.

162. Brown, *Unexpected News*, 97.

version of resistance more attractive and palatable for sincere elites within the Lukan communities (particularly those with knowledge of and respect for the Hebrew Scriptures).[163]

The nuancing of the hidden transcript apparent in this pericope also serves the valuable purpose of addressing the problem of the prejudice and domination that are found even within the ranks of subordinated groups. Sharon Ringe makes this point eloquently:

> The "poor" in the Gospel are thus all those people without presumption of privilege, to whom Jesus' message comes as good news. There are very few to whom that message is totally good news, because most people claim something that sets them over others—age, or gender, or race, or religion, or ability, or health—even if they are economically poor. . . . The point of these Gospel texts is that the word about God's sovereignty is a word of promise particularly for those who can find no security or hope in the structures of human institutions or the plans of human rulers.[164]

Or, more simply, in the reflections of a South African Black man on the Nazareth proclamation: "Blacks can be just as oppressive as whites."[165] Frantz Fanon makes similar observations about intragroup violence among the colonized as a result of their mixed feelings of both envy and animosity toward the system that oppresses them.[166] This is a sharp message and a deep challenge that the Gospel of Luke issues to non-elites who deal with injustice: to acknowledge that they too engage in unjust acts against others. The hidden transcript here holds in tension one's status as potentially both victim and perpetrator of domination, discrimination, and perhaps even oppression. Here, and elsewhere in Luke, interest centers as much on one's own participation in injustice and how to eliminate it, as it does on one's status as a victim of injustice. To be sure, other texts in the Gospel issue a strong challenge to elites and others who use their extensive power and privilege to benefit only themselves, but Luke 4:16-30 aims its challenge particularly at the non-elite residents of Nazareth and the rest of Galilee. This is a difficult message in any time and place, but in the remainder of this chapter we shall consider its

---

163. Scott, *Domination*, 105–7.

164. Ringe, *Jesus, Liberation*, 59–60. Emphasis in original.

165. "South African Example," 429.

166. Frantz Fanon, *The Wretched of the Earth*, trans. Richard Philcox (1963; repr., New York: Grove Press, 2004), 15–16.

particular difficulties in the midst of the Roman-controlled cities of first-century Asia Minor, likely the context for Luke's first reading communities.

CONTEXTUALITY: THE NAZARETH PROCLAMATION IN THE HELLENISTIC CHURCHES

The story of Jesus' experience in his hometown synagogue is the first fully narrated event of his public ministry in the Gospel of Luke. In this single pericope, the third evangelist establishes many characteristics that come to define Jesus' identity and mission: a holistic ministry that addresses people's social, economic, spiritual, and physical concerns; continuity with Hebrew traditions of divinely ordained status reversal, as outlined in the Jubilee legislation and the work of the Isaianic prophet; and a challenge to people at all levels of economic and social status to consider and address their own participation in dominating practices. I will now examine how this seminal narrative event is developed in the rest of Luke-Acts, and how it may have resonated in the early Christian communities reading the Third Gospel.

THE NAZARETH PROCLAMATION IN THE SWEEP OF THE LUKAN NARRATIVE

The themes of status reversal and resistance to the status quo are already well-established in the Gospel of Luke; indeed, I have spent an entire chapter discussing the Magnificat, which presents similar ideas early on in the narrative. But the Nazareth proclamation, like the Magnificat, holds an important primary place in the story because it is the first time these status reversals are declared openly to a public audience, and the first time they are declared by Jesus himself. Mary sang her song in the private home of Elizabeth and Zechariah (Luke 1:39-56), and Simeon spoke of reversal in the temple, but seemingly only for the ears of Mary and Joseph (Luke 2:27-35). But in Luke 4:16-30, Jesus claims the tradition of reversal that has been attached to him since before his birth and outlines what it means in terms of his life and mission, and by extension his death and resurrection, and the work of his followers.

A major question throughout the books of Luke and Acts revolves around the varying responses of the people with whom Jesus comes into contact. How characters in the story react to Jesus as a visitor sent by God, and to Jesus' role as host and mediator of divine salvation, reveals their openness to God, and these reactions range across a broad spectrum.[167] In Luke, Jesus' every action and his very being attract response, sometimes extreme response.[168] This aspect

---

167. Brendan Byrne, *The Hospitality of God: A Reading of Luke's Gospel* (Collegeville, MN: Liturgical, 2000), 4.

of the narrative is particularly effective in encouraging the audience, from the first century until today, to consider their own feelings about the story that they are hearing and with which characters that response is most closely aligned. In Nazareth, the final reaction of the townspeople is of course resounding and seemingly universal rage (Luke 4:28-30), but their earlier actions exhibit mixed feelings, including amazement, wonder, excitement, and confusion (4:20-22). They have an "almost but not quite" experience, an interaction with Jesus in which a character or group engages positively at first but finds him- or herself unwilling to embrace the full import of Jesus' teaching and worldview—here in our pericope, the ramifications of his inclusive hidden transcript of resistance.

Such "almost but not quite" stories are not uncommon in the work of Luke, and they seem to challenge the reader to take the final step that the characters in the story could not. John Nolland observes that Luke often stresses the public's reactions to the ministry of Jesus; even when they do not become disciples, they still play a role in Luke's narrative, as "impartial witnesses" to Jesus' true identity.[169] Many Lukan "opponents," for example, answer Jesus' inquiries about love, release, and grace correctly, but the question of whether they then choose to act upon that conclusion is left unanswered: for example, Simon the Pharisee (Luke 7:36-50); the lawyer to whom Jesus tells the parable of the Good Samaritan (10:25-37); the rich ruler (18:28-25); and even Peter, who confesses that Jesus is the Messiah (9:20) but still denies him in the end (22:54-62). The story of Zacchaeus, one character who *does* fully embrace Jesus' plan for reversal with decisive action (notably, action that works to correct social and economic injustice; 19:1-10), illustrates the dramatic change that accompanies full acceptance of the good news proclaimed by Jesus—the obstacle that the Nazareth congregation and others of the "almost but not quite" stories could not get past. It is thus made clear in Luke 4:16-30 and throughout the Gospel that the grace and salvation offered to all people are freely given, but they demand a similar generosity and inclusiveness from their recipients. The "almost but not quite" episodes also demonstrate how difficult this level of generosity can be.

The sojourn of Jesus in Capernaum (Luke 4:31-44), immediately following the Nazareth proclamation, is an interesting foil, with both differences and similarities, to our focal pericope.[170] Here, Jesus does perform the signs that he refused to do in Nazareth, namely exorcisms and healings (4:33-35, 38-41), thus demonstrating that the ἄφεσις proclaimed at Nazareth includes release from

---

168. Green, *Gospel of Luke*, 221.

169. Nolland, "Impressed Unbelievers," 225–26.

170. Tannehill, "Mission of Jesus," 55.

demonic oppression. Jesus' miraculous works and continued teaching elicit the same amazed and wondering reaction in Capernaum as did his words of prophecy in Nazareth (4:22, 32, 36), but in Capernaum he becomes a decidedly more popular figure. When Jesus goes off by himself, the crowds follow and try to force him to stay among them (4:42). Thus we see that even though Capernaum reacts more positively to Jesus, its residents, just like the Nazareth congregation, misunderstand the scale of his true mission and "hope to limit his ministry to their own boundaries."[171] The desire for local prestige and benefit was widespread in the Roman Empire, and Nazareth and Capernaum were no exceptions. But such exclusiveness holds no place in Luke's vision of the reign of God, and so Jesus continues to expand his circle of work, from Nazareth to the rest of Galilee, and from Galilee to Judea (4:43-44). He is thus further established as a threat to the powers that be. As in Luke 4:14-15, he sparks further rumors and reports throughout the countryside (Luke 4:37), and the demons correctly identify him as the Holy One of God, Messiah, and the Son of God (Luke 4:34, 41).[172] The theology and worldview of the Lukan Jesus entail the dismantling of multiple forms of domination, whether perpetrated by the devil, the Roman Empire (under diabolic control, according to Luke 4:5-6), Rome's Jerusalem allies, or even the non-elite Galileans themselves.

As Jesus ministers in the Gospel of Luke, we read of further healings (for example, 5:12-16, 17-26), the calling of various disciples (5:1-11, 27-31; 6:12-16; 8:1-3), and more of Jesus' teaching, both through discussion with groups like the Pharisees, scribes, and John's disciples (for example, 5:33-39; 6:1-5; 7:18-23), and, most prominently, through the Sermon on the Plain (6:20-49). The status reversals and the hidden transcript proclaimed at Nazareth continue to be fleshed out and developed in Jesus' interactions with an ever-widening variety of people. Of particular interest is the eventual appearance in the narrative of those who have a higher social status than Jesus. The Pharisees, scribes, and teachers of the law were retainers who served the needs of the elite and therefore had more status and wealth (ES5 at minimum, perhaps ES4 for some) than their non-elite counterparts, although typically they were still well below the elites to whom they were loyal.[173]

By definition and necessity, retainers, in various ways and to different degrees, supported the system of domination that the Nazareth proclamation

---

171. Green, *Gospel of Luke*, 220.

172. Cf. the discussion of spirit possession as a source of the subordinates' hidden true feelings in Scott, *Domination*, 141–42.

173. Anthony J. Saldarini, *Pharisees, Scribes and Sadducees in Palestinian Society: A Sociological Approach* (Wilmington: Michael Glazier, 1988), 42. See also Lenski, *Power and Privilege*, 243–48.

sought to reverse in favor of equality for all people. Luke 20:45—21:4, for example, warns the people and the disciples against the exploitative practices of the scribes and seems to characterize them as higher status retainers. The Pharisees, on the other hand, are frequent debate partners for Jesus, as in Luke 5:17 (together with the teachers of the law),[174] 5:30 (with their scribes), 6:2, and 6:7 (again with scribes), to name only a few. Anthony Saldarini writes, "The Gospel of Luke charges that the Pharisees, as patrons of the people, are failing in their duties, and it claims that Jesus, acting as an intermediary with God, fulfills the role of patron in a new and more effective way."[175] But, consistent with the nuanced hidden transcript revealed in the examples of Elijah and Elisha, Jesus does not completely discount these upholders of the status quo; instead he repeatedly illustrates for them his "new and more effective way"—including the intimacy of table fellowship with them (7:36-50; 11:37-54; 14:1-24)—in the hope that they too will embrace this vision of a time truly acceptable to and worthy of the Lord, a time marked by justice for all the Lord's people.[176]

At the same time, Jesus continues to push through all types of barriers, reaching out not only to insiders like the Pharisees, but also to those considered outsiders by everyone from the highest of elites down to the artisans, peasants, and other "respectable" non-elites such as those of the Nazareth congregation. He performs signs, not to prove his identity and increase his own personal honor, as the Nazarenes had hoped,[177] but to reintegrate those designated on some level as unacceptable and expendable[178] back into full social standing in the community: lepers (as in Luke 5:12-16; 17:11-19), persons with physical disabilities (as in 13:10-17; 14:1-6), the possessed (as in 4:33-37; 8:26-39), Gentiles (as in 4:25-27; 7:1-10), and even unpopular and despised retainers like the tax collectors Levi and Zacchaeus (5:27-31; 19:1-10; cf. 18:9-14). Often in Luke, those on the fringes of Palestinian society are the first to recognize Jesus' true identity and give glory (δοξάζω) to God. For example, the central commandments to worship God and to love one's neighbors are demonstrated most prominently by two Samaritans: the grateful healed leper of Luke 17:11-19, and the hero of the parable in Luke 10:25-37.[179] With

---

174. Luke 5:17 specifically notes that these retainers had come "from every village of Galilee and Judea and from Jerusalem," indicating that Jesus' reputation had already extended to the center of power in Palestine.

175. Saldarini, *Pharisees*, 58.

176. For further discussion of the Pharisees in the Gospel of Luke, see the discussion in chapter 5 below.

177. Falcetta, *Call of Nazareth*, 71–74.

178. See Lenski, *Power and Privilege*, 280–83.

the beatitudes and woes at the start of the Sermon on the Plain, Luke also gives central place in Jesus' teaching to the social inversion of bipolar status reversals between the poor and the rich, the hungry and the full, the weeping and the laughing, and those with low social standing and those with high (Luke 6:20-26). The rest of the sermon's teaching continues to overturn social conventions of imperial society like patronage, kinship loyalty, and reciprocity, through commands such as "Love your enemies, do good to those who hate you, bless those who curse you, pray for those who abuse you" (6:27-28); "Give to everyone who begs from you; and if anyone takes away your goods, do not ask for them again" (6:30); "But love your enemies, do good, and lend without expecting anything in return" (6:35a); and "Be merciful, just as your Father is merciful" (6:36).

Commands such as these are equally challenging to elites and non-elites alike. As we have seen with the Nazareth proclamation, the Gospel of Luke espouses a nontraditional version of status reversal and social transformation, one that critiques not only the dominants' supposedly natural or God-given right to rule over the subordinated, but also the non-elites' insular assumption that they alone should receive God's gifts of salvation and release. This suggests that the author of Luke-Acts was to some extent an outsider to both the elite and the non-elite groups, likely someone who had contact with both groups and who experienced some level of status inconsistency.[180] It is conceivable, perhaps even likely, that the third evangelist functioned for at least some of his reading communities as what Lenski calls a "rebellious intellectual." Such a person was an important figure in any attempt at social reform because of his or her ability to formulate a new system of ideas to challenge and replace the old worldview, the one who provided "the catalytic agent, the counterideology, which is necessary for every successful social revolution."[181]

The Nazareth proclamation acts as an introduction to the newly proposed ideology, as a caution about the difficulties it might face, and as an invitation to those dissatisfied with their current social system to join the communities seeking to follow Jesus in this mission.[182] While it finds little resonance in

---

179. John R. Donahue, "Who Is My Enemy? The Parable of the Good Samaritan and the Love of Enemies," in *The Love of Enemy and Nonretaliation in the New Testament*, ed. Willard M. Swartley (Louisville: Westminster John Knox, 1992), 146–47.

180. Scott, *Domination*, 15.

181. Lenski, *Power and Privilege*, 70–71. See also Stephen L. Dyson, "Native Revolts in the Roman Empire," *Historia* 20 (1971): 267–73, particularly his conclusion that most revolts against Rome were led by one or a small group of strong native leaders who usually had had a relatively high level of Roman contact and education (242–44, 251, 255, 264–65, 267).

Nazareth, we can imagine greater interest and a more open response among the socially, ethnically, and religiously mixed congregations of Jesus-followers in the cities of Asia Minor. They needed elite members or those with an ES4-level surplus willing to offer their homes as meeting places, their financial resources to help the poorest community members, and their social status and influence to advocate for their Christian sisters and brothers. But those same community members were also the ones whose wealth and power created and sustained the Roman-ruled hierarchy that caused the poverty and powerlessness of many members of the Jesus movement. The Gospel of Luke offers one way to approach navigation of this very difficult terrain.

With such deeply ingrained concepts of social status and long-held beliefs and emotions regarding people in other social groups, any proposed compromise, such as the Gospel of Luke makes, is likely to be fraught with differing opinions and possible inconsistencies. Immediately after the Sermon on the Plain, in which Jesus overturns multiple accepted societal norms, Luke narrates several events that bear a striking similarity to 4:16-30. Echoing the story of Elisha and Naaman, Jesus heals the servant of a Roman centurion in Capernaum (Luke 7:1-10), and immediately afterwards, he goes to the town of Nain and raises a widow's only son from the dead, as did Elijah (Luke 7:11-17). Then, in response to a question from John the Baptist and his disciples, Jesus characterizes his mission with the same focus on reversal and Jubilee release that he proclaimed at Nazareth: offering sight to the blind, good news to the poor, and cleansing for the lepers, as well as healing for the deaf and renewal of life for the dead (7:18-22).[183] This shows a consistency in the core of Jesus' message and ministry as presented by the third evangelist.[184] The chapter concludes with a lengthy story (7:36-50) that focuses on the concept of release so central to the Nazareth proclamation pericope, embodied in a parable about the forgiveness of debts. The parable is designed to rebuke Jesus' Pharisee host for his lack of generosity (7:40-43). But it also serves to highlight the extravagant love shown to Jesus by a sinner[185] who anoints his feet (7:37-38), and the release from sin that is extended to her (7:44-50). Thus in a single tightly woven chapter, Jesus

---

182. Cf. Falcetta, *Call of Nazareth*, 23–27, in which he characterizes Luke 4:16-30 as an unsuccessful call story, in which the Nazarenes decline to acknowledge Jesus as God's true messenger and refuse to participate in his inclusive ministry.

183. Both of these lists of eschatological activity bear a remarkable similarity to a list from one of the Dead Sea Scrolls, found in 4Q521 (Messianic Apocalypse), lines 8, 12-13. Like Luke 4:18-19 and 7:22, the Scrolls author also draws from Isa. 35:5 and 61:1, as well as Ps. 146:7-8. This seems to indicate that such works of status reversal were associated in both traditions with the activity of God and his anointed one(s) in the last days. For further discussion, see Brooke, "Shared Intertextual Interpretations," 44–46.

184. Brown, *Unexpected News*, 94.

teaches, interacts with, and offers healing to a Roman centurion and his slave, a Jewish widow, members of an apocalyptic movement, a local retainer, and a woman deemed socially unacceptable.

Jeffrey Siker has arranged these parallels between Luke 4:18-30 and 7:1-23 into a semichiastic structure centered around acceptance of Jesus and acceptance of outsiders (in his argument, mainly Gentiles). The focal themes include the signs of the in-breaking reign of God, as prophesied in Isaiah 61 (Luke 4:18-19; 7:21-22); the question of Jesus' identity (4:22; 7:18-20); a reference to Capernaum (4:23; 7:1); the raising of a widow's son (4:25-26; 7:11-17); and a healing carried out on behalf of a Gentile soldier (4:27; 7:1-10). Both pericopes end with a strong statement about the socially threatening nature of these acts of acceptance: the Nazarenes reject Jesus to the point of attempted violence (Luke 4:28-30), while in chapter 7, he offers the beatitude, "Blessed are those who do not take offense at me" (Luke 7:23).[186] The author of the Gospel seems aware that this messianic mission may be difficult for some to accept, particularly the aid offered to Gentile military elites—the beneficiaries of the examples given at the central points in the chiasm (Naaman and the centurion), and a group whose members had perpetrated much oppression and injustice against those with less power and status than themselves. But at the same time, the evangelist is pushing for this acceptance despite the challenge.

It is easy to see the difficulty a Jewish peasant or a Hellenistic artisan might have in embracing this aspect of the Christian mission. Certainly Jesus' closing comment to the centurion in Capernaum ("I tell you, not even in Israel have I found such faith," Luke 7:9) would have been shocking and offensive to many of his fellow Jews in the crowds. As we see in Luke 4:25-30, the inclusion of Gentiles in the reign of God proved disturbing to the status quo, but such a move can hardly be avoided in a movement that not once, but twice calls its followers to love their enemies and do good to all, even those who hate them (6:27, 35). The picture becomes even murkier when we consider the reaction of a slave or freedperson upon hearing the story of Jesus healing the centurion's servant.

In Luke 7:1-10, Jesus is approached by the elders of Capernaum, bearing a local centurion's request for Jesus to heal his highly valued or esteemed

---

185. The nature of her sin is not specified in the text, merely that she is ἁμαρτωλός (Luke 7:37). Because of the social stigma seemingly attached to her sin (see Simon's inner monologue in 7:39), it is possible that she was a prostitute of some kind, or in another profession that was deemed necessary but socially unacceptable. See Lenski's discussion of what he calls the "unclean and degraded classes" in Lenski, *Power and Privilege*, 280–81.

186. Siker, "'First to the Gentiles,'" 86–89.

(ἔντιμος, 7:2) slave. The centurion is professed by the elders (likely local elites or retainers) as deserving of such help because of his service to the people (7:4-5), and he himself recognizes Jesus' authority and its apparent superiority to his own, stating that he is not worthy to host Jesus in his house (7:6-8). In response, Jesus commends the centurion's faith and heals the slave (7:9-10). It is possible to interpret this story as a disconcerting portrayal of Jesus upholding the social hierarchy and perpetuating the domination of the Roman centurion and the subordination of his slave.[187] This reading would point to a significant inconsistency in Luke's call for release and freedom, as proclaimed at Nazareth—or perhaps a realistic but still disturbing compromise or oversight made by the evangelist in his eagerness to offer hope to the retainers as well as the peasants and artisans among his readers. But the centurion can also be understood as a lower-status elite or a retainer who is breaking with the public transcript to seek the help of Jesus, thereby acknowledging Jesus' authority and power as greater than that of Rome, particularly in the area of healing and release from disease and the demonic forces generally believed to be its cause. An important theme in these two parallel chapters of Luke is "the acceptability (chapter 4) and the recognition (chapter 7) of Jesus as the one in whom people meet the inaugural celebration of God's reign."[188] The centurion seems to be a positive, if somewhat surprising, example of this acceptance and recognition in the Lukan narrative.

Questions arise, however, in audiences both ancient and modern, whether the inclusion of this example is harmful or helpful to the proclaimed Christian mission of status reversal and social justice for all. Should Jesus have healed the slave for the benefit of the master, so that this retainer might continue to profit from an unjust system? If that was the end result, perhaps not. But if the faith that Jesus recognized in the centurion was indicative of a true understanding of Jesus' identity and mission, then we might expect a Zacchaeus-like transformation (either in the past or in the wake of the centurion's encounter with Jesus). The story in Luke 7:1-10, in keeping with almost all the canonical stories of Jesus' teaching and healing (for example, the rich man in Luke 18:18-25), does not tell us one way or the other; Zacchaeus (Luke 19:1-10) is

---

187. One author argues that the relationship between the centurion and his slave was of a sexual nature, noting the common practice of pederasty between older elites and their young male slaves. See Donald Madder, "The Entimos Pais of Matthew 8:5-13 and Luke 7:1-10," in *Homosexuality and Religion and Philosophy*, ed. Wayne R. Dynes and Stephen Donaldson, *Studies in Homosexuality* (New York City: Garland, 1992), 223–35. He reads Luke as uncomfortable with this intimation because of the abuses often involved (229).

188. Ringe, *Jesus, Liberation*, 48.

the exception in that we are given an initial glimpse into the concrete changes that he makes in his life due to his interaction with Jesus. The open-ended nature of the centurion's story forces audiences to wrestle with the difficult questions we have been discussing here: how much acceptance and grace should be offered to oppressors who indicate their commitment to a changed social system, how their sincerity can be verified, and what role they should play in the Jesus movement.

Zacchaeus was not ordered to implement the economic redistribution that he undertakes; it is a voluntary response to the acceptance and fellowship that Jesus offers him. Luke may have included the centurion's story with hope for a similar act of release, for the centurion to manumit his healed slave, but we are given no information about what happened after the healing. Perhaps the narration of a manumission operating outside the usual requirements of minimum age, payment, and continuing social debt to the master was too inflammatory for Luke to risk. Or perhaps he did not condemn the institution of slavery in order to avoid alienating certain members of his reading communities. Luke declines, as he often does, to issue a direct command or make a binding judgment on this matter, instead encouraging readers to tease out the implications of his stories and voluntarily participate, as each individual's situation dictates, in the love and mercy of God's reign. We see this strategy yield good results in the story of Zacchaeus, but are left wondering about the centurion. These two stories illustrate the risk that such a rhetorical technique entails. Gracious gifts are not always returned in kind, particularly without an explicit command to do so. But at the same time, the hope of Jesus' work in the Gospel of Luke is that such redistributive gifts will, in time, be emulated by the recipients so that an alternative way of life is formed.

The texts considered in the above section are merely representative of many other Lukan pericopes that elaborate upon the Jubilee themes of 4:16-30.[189] The relationship between release from debt and release from sin, for example, surfaces again in the Lord's Prayer, a request for God's reign to be established in the world (Luke 11:1-4). The followers of Jesus are to participate in this reign both as those forgiven and as those who release their own debtors from repayment (11:4).[190] At the end of Luke (24:47), however, and throughout the book of Acts (for example, 2:38; 5:31; 10:43; 13:38; 26:18), as the work of Jesus and his followers moves out of Palestine and into the rest of the Greco-Roman world, ἄφεσις is used exclusively with reference to the forgiveness of sins. Is this a softening or a compromising of the message of holistic, concrete

---

189. For a more complete survey, see, e.g., Ringe, *Jesus, Liberation*, 50–64, 65–80, 81–90.

190. Ibid., 79.

reversal and release that the Gospel has espoused thus far? As the message of good news to the poor moves closer to the heart of the Roman Empire, we must look again at the context of Luke's first reading communities in the Hellenistic cities of Greece and Asia Minor and consider their reception of the Nazareth proclamation and its message of status reversal.

THE NAZARETH PROCLAMATION IN THE SOCIAL WORLD OF THE LUKAN COMMUNITY

As we move into the book of Acts, the message of the Nazareth proclamation is brought into the very regions where Luke's writings were first read and distributed. The Lukan communities of Jesus-followers would have been highly interested in the gospel message's early reception in cities like their own, or perhaps even cities that were their own. In Luke 4:21, Jesus proclaims that *today* the scriptural mandate to bring good news to the poor has been fulfilled, with the primary placement of the word σήμερον emphasizing the imminence of this salvific work. Certainly this refers to the symbolic start of Jesus' ministry in Nazareth, but as this story was read aloud by Christian communities in, for example, Ephesus, Thessalonica, or Philippi, another "today" would have presented itself for consideration, the present reality of the text's current audience.[191] What did the proclamation and fulfillment of Isaiah 61 and 58 mean for their time and place, in the Hellenistic cities of the Eastern Roman Empire, in the late first century CE? Salvation and Jubilee, as we have seen in the progression from Leviticus to Isaiah, then to Luke and beyond, are not static concepts, but rather liberating ideals to be fulfilled in multiple settings.[192] Admittedly, we will move in this section beyond what we know definitively from the work of the third evangelist, because we have no record of how the Lukan communities reacted to, interpreted, and enacted the Gospel. I will hold together what is known about life in the Roman Empire, what we have gleaned from our previous study, and clues from the book of Acts, in order to imagine in as informed a manner as possible how the alternative reign of God proclaimed by Jesus might have been embodied in Luke's congregations. The book of Acts will be a valuable tool in this task, as it includes several examples of the early disciples introducing the ideals of the Nazareth proclamation to the cities of Greece and Asia Minor, and the results of this preaching of the good news. These stories will provide a starting point for our discussion in this section, as we consider the earliest reading communities of the Gospel of Luke and their possible reactions to Luke 4:16-30.

191. Prior, *Jesus the Liberator*, 157–58.
192. Ringe, *Jesus, Liberation*, 98.

I have already noted one connection between Luke 4 and the story of Peter and the centurion Cornelius (Acts 10:1-48): the pivotal use of the adjective δεκτός in both Luke 4:19, 24 and Acts 10:35.[193] While the Acts story is set in Palestine, Caesarea Maritima was a Hellenistic city, built by Herod the Great and serving as the seat of Roman power in the region. Cornelius, as an officer, would have been an integral part of the imperial military machine (Acts 10:1), and probably a member of the status quo–supporting economic group of ES4. Yet he and all his household (probably including those from various social strata) are characterized as worshipping the God of Israel, and Cornelius in particular is noted for sharing his wealth with the people above and beyond the usual level (ἐλεημοσύνας πολλὰς, 10:2). Peter's sermon in Cornelius's household (10:34-43) connects with the Nazareth proclamation at many points beyond the shared use of the adjective δεκτός: the anointing of Jesus with the Spirit, the mention of Nazareth as his hometown, and his ministry of preaching good news and caring for the oppressed.[194] Peter concludes with a promise of forgiveness (ἄφεσις) of sins, leading to a possible argument that Luke has spiritualized the earlier message of salvation as social, economic, and political, as well as spiritual.

But there is still status reversal in this story, and there is still release from oppression and captivity, not only spiritual forgiveness. We must not miss the astonishing picture of a Roman centurion who falls at the feet of a Galilean fisherman and does obeisance to him (Acts 10:25), as clear a redefinition of honor and social status as one might wish. The definition of acceptability to God (10:34-35), newly understood by Peter but present in the Lukan narrative since the Nazareth proclamation itself, is also significant. God does not judge based on ethnicity or any other external marker of identity or favor; rather, God accepts any person, no matter their status, if he or she reveres (φοβούμενος) God and actively works for justice (ἐργαζόμενος δικαιοσύνην).

The holistic nature of salvation is not, then, eliminated as it moves into the Roman world, even if it is diminished in explicit reference. The author and the earliest Lukan communities may have felt it pragmatic to emphasize the "forgiveness" aspect of ἄφεσις rather than the meaning of "release," in order to camouflage at least some of its ramifications that threatened the economic practices and social hierarchies of the imperial system. The status reversal that was proclaimed relatively openly at Nazareth needed at times to take on the

---

193. It is worth noting another, albeit minor, connection between Acts 10 and Luke 4:16-30 (and to some extent, Luke 7). Before interacting with the Gentile military officer, Peter, like Elijah and like Jesus, raises someone from the dead in Acts 9:36-43. See Falcetta, *Call of Nazareth*, 80.

194. Ibid., 30–31.

protection of ambiguity, double meaning, and spiritual cover, and never more so than at the beginning of its implementation in the presence of Roman power.[195] The difficulty of finding a balance between survival and resistance in a system of domination can hardly be overestimated, and the Lukan communities had to try to implement their alternative values in this hostile imperial reality that remained in power. Even in in the areas where idealism gave way to realism, the ideal of a changed social world is still, significantly, given a central place in Luke's narration of the life of Jesus. It remains a core value and the ultimate goal toward which the Gospel's readers are urged to strive.

Cornelius is one of the first examples in Luke-Acts of a paterfamilias, someone with enough material resources and social status to support a household (Acts 10:2), all of whom he can influence to accept the salvation offered by Jesus (cf. 11:14). Others include the wealthy merchant Lydia (16:11-15) and Crispus, a Jewish synagogue official (18:8), both of whom are said to have joined the Christian movement together with their entire households. Such households (*domus* or οἶκος) included a wide variety of people: the householder, his or her spouse, children both young and grown, their spouses and children (all of whom would be at least ES5, and more likely ES4), as well as lower status slaves, servants, clients, and extended family.[196] Although Luke does not explicitly mention it, this consideration reveals another possible effect of allowing and even encouraging retainers and elites to join the Jesus movement if they fear God and practice justice (10:35). If such a person experiences divine mercy and healing, as did Jesus' example of Naaman (Luke 4:27), he or she may respond with sincere commitment to the social justice proclaimed at Nazareth and enacted in Jesus' ministry, and the actions resulting from that commitment could benefit numerous people in the household who had previously been afforded little consideration, power, or social status. Such "household conversion" is also a possible factor contributing to the highly mixed composition that we have postulated for the earliest Lukan reading communities, and to the need for a Gospel that addresses how they could all eat and worship together as a single community of faith.

As we imagine the reactions of Christian communities in the cities of the Greek East to the Nazareth proclamation and the rest of Luke's Gospel, we must also consider the ramifications of masters and slaves and everyone in between reading this celebration of Jubilee release *together* in the early house churches.[197] Luke 4:18-19 quotes Isaiah in order to define Jesus' Spirit-inspired mission

195. See Scott, *Domination*, 152–54.

196. Garnsey and Saller, *Roman Empire*, 127–28.

197. Horsley, "Slave Systems," 59.

as one proclaiming good news to the poor, release for the captives and the oppressed, and healing for the blind. The Torah legislation that this text echoes offers even more specificity for the community members familiar with it: the freeing of slaves (Lev. 25:39-43; Deut. 15:12-15), the restoration of the people's land (Lev. 25:13-17), and the remission of debts (Deut. 15:1-6). Commitment to such a mission would have radically redefined social relationships within the Christian communities. The manumission of select slaves was a common practice in the Roman Empire, unusually common, in fact, for a slaveholding society. But the ultimate benefits of the practice generally accrued much less to the freed slave than they did to the owner, who was paid by the slave in money, future labor, and client loyalty. The owner also gained honor and a reputation for generosity at very little cost,[198] or indeed, no cost at all if the manumission was made in his or her will and only enacted upon the death of the owner or the owner's heirs.[199] Freed slaves did gain some improvement in honor, status, and perhaps eventually wealth and citizenship for their children, but these gains were always accompanied by strong status inconsistency.[200] They faced great difficulty in overcoming the stigma of slavery to find some measure of acceptance among freeborn non-elites.[201]

In contrast, the freedom offered in the Nazareth proclamation has its roots in a tradition that advocated manumission accompanied by systemic changes to restore a level of social equilibrium. Greco-Roman manumission, like the practices of benefaction and almsgiving, served ultimately to uphold and strengthen the current social hierarchy, rather than transform or abolish it. But the conception of justice inherent in Luke 4 does not simply sustain the poor in their poverty; it seeks a substantive change in their circumstances, so as to move them out of poverty.[202] The solutions offered in Leviticus, such as returning families to their ancestral lands in Palestine, would not have been possible in the Roman provinces. But the Gospel of Luke still issues a call for Christian communities to explore similarly creative solutions to address the root causes of social inequalities present within their own settings. In the first century, this meant that at the very least the relationships between masters and

---

198. Bradley, *Slaves and Masters*, 81; Horsley, "Slave Systems," 52–53; and Wessels, "Letter to Philemon," 155–58.

199. See Bradley, *Slaves and Masters*, 91, where he calls this practice a type of "social ostentation" that was common to Roman and provincial elites as they built up their public honor and reputation through luxurious consumption.

200. Horsley, "Slave Systems," 49–50.

201. Bradley, *Slaves and Masters*, 81; and Horsley, "Slave Systems," 57.

202. Ringe, *Jesus, Liberation*, 93–94.

slaves, patrons and clients, and elites and non-elites would have had to undergo radical transformation. Slaves, for example, even in the supposedly "benign" and "milder" Roman system, faced extreme objectification and other forms of abuse at the hands of their owners and by the entire worldview of slavery.[203] For their part, slave holders displayed some insecurity and fear of their slaves as seen, for example, in the common saying, "The number of one's slaves equals the number of one's enemies."[204] Such statements indicate at least some knowledge among slave owners (both elite and non-elite) that slaves did not appreciate or accept the mistreatment inherent in slavery, despite public-transcript justifications of the system. Significant social transformation would have been required to allow the formation of peer or fictive sibling relationships between slaves, who no doubt resented their daily humiliation at the hands of their owners, and slave owners, who feared that very anger and resentment as a threat to their safety and well-being.

Another episode in the Acts narrative with parallels to the Nazareth proclamation is Paul and Silas's stay in Thessalonica and Beroea (Acts 17:1-15). Like Jesus in his hometown, Paul, accompanied by Silas, goes to the synagogue on the Sabbath "as was his custom" (κατὰ τὸ εἰωθός, Acts 17:2; cf. Luke 4:16), teaches about Jesus using the Hebrew Scriptures (Acts 17:2-3), and arouses anger and resentment in the local community (17:5). This eventually results in punishment for local Jesus-followers (17:6-9) and the flight of Paul and Silas to another city, where they are received more warmly (for a time, anyway; 17:10-13).[205] We find here a concrete example of the mixed Lukan community proposed in earlier chapters of this dissertation: in Thessalonica and Beroea alike, Jews, Greeks, men, and women, of both elite and non-elite status, come to believe in Jesus as the Messiah (17:4, 12). This social manifestation of Luke's theology becomes, as it was in Nazareth, one of the causes of exceedingly angry reactions by some in the Jewish community.[206] It also leads directly to charges of Christians turning the world upside down and proclaiming another king besides Caesar (17:6-7). These charges are significantly not refuted as false in the narrative. Jason (Paul and Silas's host) and the other Jesus-followers are released on bail, but never exonerated, perhaps because the charges are true at least in part. Certainly the author of Luke does not seek to place Jesus upon Caesar's throne, but, in the words of C. Kavin Rowe, "the accusations are true . . . in that the Christian mission entails a call to another way of life, one that

---

203. Wessels, "Letter to Philemon," 158.
204. Quoted in Horsley, "Slave Systems," 36–37.
205. Falcetta, Call of Nazareth, 30.
206. Rowe, World Upside Down, 93.

is—on virtually every page of the Acts of the Apostles—turning the world upside down."[207]

The communities first reading the work of Luke could hardly fail to notice the extensive social, political, and economic ramifications of their dedication to a low-status Galilean artisan who proclaimed good news for the poor and release for the oppressed. These effects were evident in Thessalonica, Beroea, and almost certainly in the daily lives of Luke's community members. Luke does not attempt to hide the dangers of this commitment; status reversal threatens the current beneficiaries of the established social hierarchy and provokes their resistance to it, as we see playing out in Nazareth and in Thessalonica.[208] No doubt many in the urban Christian communities of Greece and Asia Minor had in the past dealt with—or more likely were still dealing with—their own struggles to accept the hidden transcript of Jesus that welcomed former oppressors, destabilized the status quo, and thereby upset any benefits that the Roman hierarchy allowed to trickle down to them as retainers and the non-elites classified as the "good poor." Almost everyone, in all societies, claims some level of privilege on the basis of age, gender, ethnicity, religion, or something else, and Jesus' message at Nazareth and throughout Luke-Acts demands that *all* such claims to privilege be given up.[209]

The nuanced hidden transcript revealed in the Nazareth proclamation challenges readers from all social levels to consider their various roles as both victims of and participants in social stratification. The Christian communities first reading Luke and Acts could identify with these roles particularly well. The provinces of the Hellenistic East, on many levels, adapted quite well to Roman rule and enjoyed increased wealth and status—for at least the local elites and certain non-elites like retainers and urban artisans—as a result of their subordination to Rome.[210] But at the same time, Greeks often felt a sense of cultural superiority to the "less civilized" Romans and struggled to maintain their unique identity in the face of brute imperial force.[211] Thus the early

---

207. Ibid., 101–2.

208. Brown, *Unexpected News*, 97.

209. Ringe, *Jesus, Liberation*, 59–60.

210. Kelly, *Roman Empire*, 44–47; and Paul Trebilco, "Asia," in *The Book of Acts in Its Graeco-Roman Setting*, ed. David W. J. Gill and Conrad Gempf, *The Book of Acts in Its First Century Setting* (Grand Rapids: Eerdmans, 1994), 299–300.

211. Craige B. Champion, ed., *Roman Imperialism: Readings and Sources, Interpreting Ancient History* (Malden, MA: Blackwell, 2004), 268–70; Janet Huskinson, "Élite Culture and the Identity of Empire," in Huskinson, *Experiencing Rome*, 98, 116; and Kelly, *Roman Empire*, 71–72. For a more detailed discussion of this issue, see chapter 2 above.

Christians in Hellenistic cities were able to identify on some level with the angry mobs of Nazareth and Thessalonica, who felt their comfortable world and long-held assumptions being turned upside down by the new worldview of Jesus and the reign of God. But at the same time, they could identify also with Jesus, and with Jason and the other arrested Christians, as fellow members of a socially and ethnically mixed community of faith that offered a degree of equality and full acceptance not available in the competition-driven world around them.

We can imagine, then, that the readers' reactions were likely complex, and left them contemplating the dramatic change in their daily lives that was the natural outgrowth of a continued dedication to the God of Israel and the mission of Jesus of Nazareth. Such a reorientation is not overtly in revolt against the Roman Empire, but it will noticeably alter their lives socially, ethically, and economically, in ways that question and deny traditional Greco-Roman and imperial assumptions. Rowe writes,

> Against all spiritualizing tendencies, Luke narrates the salvation that attends the Christian mission as something that entails necessarily the formation of a community, a public pattern of life that witnesses to the present dominion of the resurrected Lord of all. If . . . we have trouble grasping this point, we would do well to remember that the ancient pagans did not: the community of Jews and gentiles gathered around a new pattern of life is the sociological presupposition both of the ability to scapegoat/persecute the *Christiani* (from Nero on) and of the fact that in Acts the missionaries are perceived not so much as religious quacks as harbingers of deep cultural problems.[212]

One final story from Acts will offer us insight into the possible effects and reactions that the Nazareth proclamation might have elicited from its earliest readers in the cities of Greece and Asia Minor. Acts 19 narrates Paul's years of ministry in the prominent city of Ephesus, a center of provincial trade and administration and the third largest city in the empire (after Rome and Alexandria).[213] A major source of local Ephesian pride, prestige, and revenue was the great Temple of Artemis, one of the traditional "wonders of the world," along with the worship and trade it generated. Artemis was considered

---

212. Rowe, *World Upside Down*, 154.

213. For more information on the city of Ephesus in the late first century CE, see Trebilco, "Asia," 304–38; and, with a focus on Rome's presence in the city and reactions to it, Warren Carter, *John and Empire: Initial Explorations* (London: T&T Clark, 2008), 58–81.

the patron deity of the city, and the Roman emperors had made it a point to align themselves and the imperial cult with the goddess, so as to share in the honor and history associated with her and her favored city.[214] Luke narrates a variety of episodes from Paul's ministry in Ephesus: an encounter with believers who had not yet received the Holy Spirit (Acts 19:1-7); Paul's standard practice of teaching in the synagogue and performing miracles, and the people's reactions to them (19:8-12); and the problematic results of people presumptuously invoking Jesus' name in exorcism and magic (19:13-20).

The stories of the apostles' ministry in Acts, however, continue to follow the pattern first laid out in Jesus' visit to Nazareth (Luke 4:16-30), and Paul in Ephesus is no exception. The narrative of Acts 19 culminates with a riot that drives Paul out of town, just as Jesus was forced to leave Nazareth because of his alternative version of the hidden transcript. One particularly interesting connection is the people who listen (ἀκούω) to a speaker (Jesus in Nazareth, the silversmith Demetrius in Ephesus) and as a result are filled with rage (θυμός; Luke 4:28 and Acts 19:28). In both instances, either sympathetically or hostilely, the extensive cultural ramifications of Jesus' mission are delineated, and one of the most prominent of these is the threat to local prestige.[215] Demetrius the silversmith is a prosperous artisan (probably ES5 at least) whose situation mirrored that of the more comfortable non-elites in Luke's communities, who benefitted from Roman-supported custom and benefaction, even as they resented the limits that Rome's system of domination placed upon them. Demetrius presciently articulates in Acts 19:25-27 what many in Luke's communities likely felt or intuited about the social, economic, and political challenges inherent in the act of commitment to the reign of God (as exemplified by the status reversals of the Nazareth proclamation). He makes his fellow artisans aware that a commitment to one God will radically alter their lives, from their personal finances to their city's prestige. The people, perhaps understandably, riot in support of their patron goddess, their city, and their way of life, thereby posing a danger to Paul, his traveling companions, and some local Jews, and eventually forcing Paul to leave for Macedonia (Acts 19:28—20:1). Stories such as this one "demolish the possibility . . . that . . . the Christian mission was in its essence culturally innocuous," and they also "exhibit the far-reaching and profoundly troubling effects of Christianity for pagan culture."[216]

---

214. Kelly, *Roman Empire*, 23–25; Perkins and Nevett, "Urbanism and Urbanization," 219–20; and Trebilco, "Asia," 322–24.

215. Johnson, *Gospel of Luke*, 80; and Rowe, *World Upside Down*, 45.

216. Rowe, *World Upside Down*, 51.

People like Demetrius, non-elites who had adapted relatively well to their subordination by the imperial system, were certainly present in the Lukan communities and among the neighbors, friends, and family of these early Christians. They would, perhaps, have been less surprised than modern readers often are at the rejection of Jesus by his Nazarene neighbors. They likely understood the radical nature, even the possible danger, of following Jesus on this path that involves both ministering to and alongside the resented elites and participating in status reversals that would threaten even the small benefits that some non-elites were allowed by the imperial system. The Gospel of Luke and the book of Acts do not hide these challenges, nor do they offer easy or universally applicable solutions. But the author does make it clear from the first public declaration of Jesus in Nazareth that these challenges are part of the identity, mission, and heritage of Christian disciples. The communities reading Luke's words, and the words of Isaiah and Jesus as proclaimed at Nazareth, likely had a multitude of reactions that ran the gamut of fear, anger, inspiration, motivation, hope, and everything in between. For despite the novelty and difficulty of Jesus' version of resistance to inequality and domination, the entire narrative of Luke-Acts shows that it could indeed be proclaimed and its implementation imagined even in Rome, at the center of power itself (Acts 28:11-31).

Conclusion

In the Nazareth proclamation, Jesus elaborates upon the themes of status reversal that have been a part of his life and identity from the very beginning. He picks up the refrain of his mother's Magnificat, that God has begun and continues to act in the world so that the lowly and humble might be lifted up, while the rich and powerful are brought down (Luke 1:46-55, especially verses 51-53). But he also carefully nuances the definition of status reversal as total inversion and schadenfreude at the downfall of the elite, both so common to the non-elite hidden transcript of resistance. Instead, Luke 4:16-30 lays out a different form of resistance, one that poses a formidable challenge for non-elite listeners in first-century Nazareth and Asia Minor, and for many twenty-first-century readers as well. This story narrates Jesus' call for status reversal, but it is status reversal in the tradition of the Year of Jubilee, a festival designed to restore social equality rather than simply to reverse the dominant and subordinate groups. The ramifications of this alternative hidden transcript play out in the rest of Luke and in the book of Acts, particularly in the presence of communities in which people who usually have little or no social interaction with one another are called to eat, worship, and work together as equals.

The foundational beliefs that underlie the Jubilee Year legislation and the oracle of Isaiah 61 are reinterpreted by the third evangelist for his own time and place. The Nazareth pericope and the proclamation that stands at its center challenge readers in all times and places to do the same, facing their own practices that hurt others and working alongside the converted whose power was once used to hurt: "What the poor can with justification require is that Christians use their power in [the poor's] favor. Modern Christians true to the picture presented by Luke are invited to subvert, rather than underpin, those cultures which produce poverty and ignore the plight of the poor."[217] The Nazareth proclamation calls even non-elites to take an active role in this task of helping the poor and eliminating systems of domination; this is one of the particular challenges of this pericope. We must also look, however, at the considerable onus that the Gospel of Luke, with its version of resistance and social transformation, places upon the wealthy, elite, and powerful who have been the foremost perpetrators and beneficiaries of domination and oppression. They are, as the Nazareth proclamation has illustrated, to be offered God's gift of holistic salvation and accepted into the community of faith, but they must also face considerable challenges in order to participate in the reign of God. Thus we turn our attention in the next chapter to the parable of Lazarus and the rich man, and its message for those with great wealth, power, and influence.

217. Prior, *Jesus the Liberator*, 194. See also Ringe, *Jesus, Liberation*, 98.

5

The Parable of Lazarus and the Rich Man: Reversal Now or Later

We move, in this chapter, from the beginning of Jesus' ministry in the Gospel of Luke to its very heart, in the midst of the travel narrative, as Jesus makes his way to Jerusalem followed by friends, seekers, and foes alike. Between the Nazareth proclamation (Luke 4:16-30) and the parable of Lazarus and the rich man (16:19-31), the beatitudes and woes of Luke's Sermon on the Plain (6:20-26) deal with the now familiar theme of status reversal between rich and poor, powerful and lowly, in a straightforward, explicit declaration. But after that, the Gospel makes a move toward practical instruction—not just declaring status reversal, but also trying to work out the implications of Jesus' unique ministry and interpretation of Torah for the daily life of his followers. As he comes closer to Jerusalem, Jesus' teachings seem to intensify, and the parable of Lazarus and the rich man is a part of that process. Of the three texts discussed in this project, the status reversals here in chapter 16 are the clearest example of total inversion, with little hint of leveling and with no chance of repentance or change after a certain, apparently imminent, point. There is a sense of urgency, a recognition that the Pharisees to whom the parable is directed, and the real-world elites represented by the parable's rich man and his brothers, are running short on time to change their lives and participate in the reign of God.

We have considered thus far in this study a song centered on status reversal (chapter 3), and a sermon exploring that theme further (chapter 4). In this chapter, we will look at a parable that embodies the reversal between rich and poor, hungry and fully sated (cf. Luke 6:20-21, 24-25), in a story about two men: "a certain rich man" and "a certain poor man named Lazarus" (16:19-20). This comparative set-up is a common element of Greco-Roman rhetoric, although it is unusual to name either character.[1] It is also a common set-up for other Lukan parables about "a certain man" (cf. 10:30; 12:16; 14:16; 15:11; 16:1; 19:12; 20:9). Often these parables are read and interpreted as spiritual allegories for God and the reign of God, and it is relatively easy to do so. But this practice alone, without further exploration, shortchanges the complexity of life and of Jesus' message. Certainly there is spiritual truth in the parables, but in keeping with the argument throughout this project, spiritual truths and relevance cannot and should not be separated from political, economic, and social realities.

According to Luke, Jesus was crucified as a political threat to the local elites of Palestine and to the Roman Empire. It is therefore unlikely that his parables and actions were simply spiritual in nature.[2] Even when his teachings speak of the afterlife, as Luke 16:19-31 does, they do so with a message intended to make a difference in the present world. The parables of Jesus in Luke typically employ an element of surprise in the midst of familiar settings in order to challenge the audience and push them into deeper thought and positive action in response to a new reality.[3] We shall follow William Herzog in our approach to the parable of Lazarus and the rich man, in acknowledging that such parables "were not earthly stories with heavenly meanings, but earthy stories with heavy meanings, weighted down by an awareness of the working of exploitation in the world of their hearers. . . . The parable was a form of social analysis every bit as much as it was a form of theological reflection."[4] The interconnectedness of social and theological issues and proposed solutions is indispensable to our study of Lazarus and the rich man, as it has been throughout this study.

A common understanding of this parable is that the rich man is sinful and therefore condemned to hell, while the pious poor man Lazarus is taken to heaven as a reward for his righteousness.[5] This reading can be seen, for example, in a modern-day African retelling of the parable, where the rich man is depicted as horribly immoral and abusive in every way imaginable: ignoring a young girl begging for food, wasting money to impress his sycophantic friends, divorcing a faithful wife simply from boredom, picking up a prostitute, and then killing them both in a car crash. In the same story Lazarus is represented not only by

1. Frank W. Hughes, "The Parable of the Rich Man and Lazarus (Luke 16.19-31) and Graeco-Roman Rhetoric," in *Rhetoric and the New Testament: Essays from the 1992 Heidelberg Conference*, ed. Stanley E. Porter and Thomas H. Olbricht, JSNTSup 90 (Sheffield: Sheffield Academic Press, 1993), 36–37, 40.

2. William R. Herzog, *Parables as Subversive Speech: Jesus as Pedagogue of the Oppressed* (Louisville: Westminster John Knox, 1994), 27.

3. Greg W. Forbes, *The God of Old: The Role of the Lukan Parables in the Purpose of Luke's Gospel*, JSNTSup 198 (Sheffield: Sheffield Academic Press, 2000), 36–37.

4. Herzog, *Parables*, 3. See also David B. Gowler, "'At His Gate Lay a Poor Man': A Dialogic Reading of Luke 16:19-31," *PRSt* 32 (2005): 260.

5. Ronald F. Hock, "Lazarus and Micyllus: Greco-Roman Backgrounds to Luke 16:19-31," *JBL* 106 (1987): 453–54.

the beggar, but also by a good Christian housewife who is propositioned by the rich man; instead of giving in to his promise of worldly riches and status, she remains faithful to her husband and family and witnesses to the rich man about the salvation offered by Jesus.[6] While this view of the parable is meaningful, it is not entirely reflective of the nuances of the Lukan text, such as the fact that the rich man is not presented as particularly evil outside of his wealth, nor is Lazarus presented as notably pious or moral (cf. Luke 16:25).

An exclusively moralistic reading of this pericope can also lead to more harmful interpretations, such as David Cowan's conclusion that the rich man's only problem was not following Scripture. The excessive wealth he enjoys would have been fine, Cowan argues, as long as he gave some to the poor and some toward "prayer . . . and sustaining a vibrant congregation."[7] As Ronald Hock points out, such views of the parable shortchange the complexity of the text and its place in the Gospel of Luke. He describes this common approach to the parable as "unusually stable, uniform, and one might almost say, self-satisfied."[8] A more nuanced interpretation is needed.

Morality in the Gospel of Luke cannot be separated from the role wealth plays in one's life and one's living out of repentance, and this tenet comes to the fore in Luke 16. Joel Green writes, "Even though 'dishonest wealth' is a reality of the present age, one's use of this wealth can either be 'dishonest' (i.e., determined by one's commitment to the present world order) or 'faithful' (i.e., determined by the values of the new epoch)."[9] In this chapter, we will explore the nuances and complexities of this countercultural perspective on status, wealth, and power. In the first section, we will consider other fables from Luke's era about social relations and afterlife reversal, the implied morals of each, and how they compare to Jesus' characterization of Lazarus and the rich man. The second section, as in previous chapters, will explore the status reversals of Luke 16:19-31 in more detail and with particular attention to the presence of Scott's hidden transcripts of resistance. Then, in the final section, we will consider the ways in which the various groups of Luke's Gospel, both within the narrative and within the earliest Christian communities reading it—elites,

6. Ernst R. Wendland, "Mwini-Chuma ('Owner-of-Wealth'): A Dramatic Radio Contextualisation of the Lukan 'Rich Man' Parable in Nyanja," *Neot* 37 (2003): 318–19.

7. David Cowan, *Economic Parables: The Monetary Teachings of Jesus Christ* (Colorado Springs: Paternoster, 2006), 157–59.

8. Hock, "Lazarus and Micyllus," 447.

9. Joel B. Green, *The Gospel of Luke*, NICNT, ed. Gordon D. Fee (Grand Rapids: Eerdmans, 1997), 596.

retainers, and non-elites alike—are encouraged to reject imperial values and participate in the status reversals that are so critical a part of God's coming reign.

INTERTEXTUALITY: TALES OF REVERSAL AND THE AFTERLIFE

The parable of Lazarus and the rich man is unique among the biblical parables not only because it names the poor man, but also because it presents a vivid, explicit description of the afterworld and the characters' fates there. But this vision of the world after death, specifically including the reversal of status between a poor man and a rich man, was a relatively well-known theme in ancient literature across cultures, including Egyptian, Greek, and Roman. Luke's cultural environment offers significant parallels to 16:19-31 that are often cited by scholars, particularly the Egyptian legend of Setne and his extraordinary son Si-Osire and the writings of the Cynic philosopher Lucian (second century CE).[10] These share with each other and with our parable two major folkloric themes: the narration of status reversal in the afterlife, and the suggestion of a dead person's return with a message for the living.[11] Similarities to a wide variety of other literary texts both before and contemporaneous with Luke are also evident. The Jewish book of *1 Enoch*, for example, depicts the afterworld much like the parable of Luke 16 does, including a separation of the righteous from the unrighteous, and suffering for those whose sins were not punished on earth (*1 Enoch* 22:9-13; Luke 16:23-26).[12] From Roman literature, Virgil's *Aeneid* describes Tartarus, a place where punishment is meted out after death to "those who sat tight on the wealth they had won, setting none aside for their own kin."[13] The Lukan parable, of course, also implies that part of the rich man's problem is that he was not faithful to the demands for social justice present in the Law and Prophets (Luke 16:27-31; cf. 16:16-17), although the difference between Luke 16 and Virgil's Aeneid is notable. Whereas Virgil condemns those who do not share resources with their *kin*, Luke advocates a sharing that transcends familial and status boundaries, extending even to the lowest of beggars, usually deemed by society as expendable.

Closer consideration of several parallels will illuminate the biblical parable of Lazarus and the rich man, particularly where it connects with and departs

---

10. For an overview of the arguments, see Richard Bauckham, "The Rich Man and Lazarus: The Parable and the Parallels," *NTS* 37 (1991): 225–46.

11. Ibid., 225.

12. Larry Kreitzer, "Luke 16:19-31 and 1 Enoch 22," *ExpTim* 103 (1992): 141.

13. Book 6, 535–627, especially 608–11. See Outi Lehtipuu, *The Afterlife Imagery in Luke's Story of the Rich Man and Lazarus*, NovTSup 123 (Leiden: Brill, 2007), 82–83.

from the wider cultural traditions about status reversal in the afterworld. Such millennial imagery of inversion, in which the subordinated will receive justice for their sufferings after death, is at home among the folk themes of hidden resistance.[14] But it can also easily be employed to sustain rather than subvert domination, by persuading non-elites and slaves to bear their burdens bravely in the knowledge that they will be rewarded after death. The following comparison of Luke 16:19-31 with the fables of Aesop, the Egyptian story of Setne and Si-Osire, and Lucian's *Gallus* and *Cataplus* will make it clear that Luke's parable argues against rather than in support of the status quo.[15]

AESOP'S FABLES

We will begin with a brief study of the collection of fables traditionally attributed to the sixth century BCE slave Aesop. Their main connection with the parable of Lazarus and the rich man is the similarity in form, as all are short, symbolic stories that point to a moral, ethical, or spiritual truth beyond themselves. Whoever Aesop was historically, the fables that bear his name remained well-known and in widespread use well into the time of the Roman Empire and beyond. Lucian of Samosata, whose work will be addressed in some detail below, is one author who referenced the fables with some regularity; examples can be found in *Timon the Misanthrope*, *A True Story*, and two stories dealing with wealth and poverty, *Gallus* and *Cataplus*.

The fables use symbolic animal characters, unlike the humans we find in the Gospel parables, but both use a twist in the story to impart their message. The Aesop tradition, however, tends to use this twist to reinforce pragmatic, common-sense wisdom, while the Jesus traditions often overturn or transform it. In the fables, there is a strong push to be happy in one's given place, however humble, and not strive for something more. A donkey, for example, is portrayed as perfectly (and admirably) happy eating thistles, even while he is carrying the provisions for an elaborate feast, in "The Ass Eating Thistles."[16] Similarly, in "The Jackdaw and Peacocks," the titular crow is rejected not only by the elegant

---

14. James C. Scott, *Domination and the Arts of Resistance: Hidden Transcripts* (New Haven: Yale University Press, 1990), 167, 199.

15. It is unnecessary for this project to choose, as much previous scholarship on the issue has done, one story as the "correct" influence or parallel for Lazarus and the rich man. A summary of such scholarly debates can be found in Hock, "Lazarus and Micyllus," 448–55. He concludes this section by arguing for his own preferred parallel (the work of Lucian). I am not attempting to posit direct influence, but instead to compare the Lukan parable with literature contemporaneous to Luke that is similar in theme, form, or both. The robust cultural exchange and integration that characterized first-century Asia Minor supports such a dialogic approach, as noted by Gowler ("'At His Gate,'" 259).

peacocks whom he ambitiously tries to join, but also by his own peers when he attempts to rejoin them after his failure with the fancier birds. His fellow crows berate him for this ambition: "If, friend, you could have been contented with our station, and had not disdained the rank in which Nature had placed you, you had not been used so scurvily by those upon whom you intruded yourself, nor suffered the notorious slight which now we think ourselves obliged to put upon you."[17]

An interest in maintaining the status quo comes across clearly in these and similar fables. Such a focus marks the most significant difference between Aesop and the social upheaval and reform envisioned by the Lukan texts of status reversal, including the parable of Lazarus and the rich man. Like other proverbs and non-elite wisdom sayings, the fables assumed a world of hostility and power inequality, and tried to offer wisdom for surviving as well as possible.[18] But the vision of the Gospel of Luke and other early Christian sources was more idealistic; they "showed that the people were capable of imagining a new social order . . . a potentially threatening message . . . to create a new social space where it had freedom to express itself."[19]

A few of Aesop's fables narrate a profitable exchange of help between those of different status, similar to the commands in Luke 16 and elsewhere to share one's wealth. In "The Dove and the Ant," a merciful dove provides a drowning ant with a branch, the means for the ant to save itself and return to dry land; later the ant repays the dove by biting the fowler's heel just as he is about to trap her.[20] In another story, a lion and a mouse exchange similar favors, as the lion decides not to eat the mouse, and the mouse then frees the lion from the hunter's net.[21] There is an exhortation in these tales to care for those lower than oneself, for they may at some point be in a position, however lowly, to return the favor. There is a limit to such relationships, however, as a companion fable to "The Lion and the Mouse" makes clear. In "The Fatal Marriage," the lion offers his mouse savior a favor. The mouse "did not . . . consider what was proper for him to ask," which turned out to be his undoing: when he asked to marry the lion's royal daughter, the enthusiastic bride crushed and killed the tiny groom under her paw.[22] The encouragement to help one another in Aesop,

16. Aesop, *The Fables of Aesop, with a Life of the Author* (Boston: Houghton, Mifflin, and Company, 1865), 49.

17. Ibid., 156–57.

18. Jerry Toner, *Popular Culture in Ancient Rome* (Cambridge, MA: Polity, 2009), 36–37.

19. Ibid., 174.

20. Aesop, *Fables of Aesop*, 305.

21. Ibid., 95–96.

then, comes with a strong caution never to forget one's proper place, while the Lukan status reversals challenge the very definitions of "proper place" and the qualifications that should determine one's status.

Although the fables' pragmatic wisdom generally counsels each person to make the best of his or her current situation, there are also a few examples that express dissatisfaction with the status quo in ways that are right at home in Scott's hidden transcript of the non-elite. Considering their likely origin in non-elite circles, this is not surprising, although it is certainly not the dominant theme either. Also not surprising is the fact that these particular fables show the closest connections between the Aesop collection and the reversal parable of Luke 16:19-31. "The Tunny and the Dolphin" is a classic case of schadenfreude in such expressions of resistance to the status quo, particularly with those who have oppressed the speaker in the past.[23] The fish of the fable is chased by the dolphin until both are fatally washed ashore. About to perish, the fish's last words are as follows: "Well . . . I must die, it is true; but I die with pleasure, when I behold him who is the cause of it involved in the same fate."[24] Similar celebrations of the downfall of the powerful can be found in the Gospel of Luke, specifically in the Magnificat (1:51-53); the woes of the rich, laughing, and well-regarded (6:24-26); and the author's narration of the rich man's fate after death (16:23-25).[25]

The last fable that we will consider, "The Horse and the Ass," is the strongest example of status reversal in Aesop's collection, and thus offers the most interesting comparison with Lazarus and the rich man. In this story, a noble and arrogant warhorse meets a humble donkey hauling a heavy burden and haughtily demands that the donkey make way for him to pass. Later, the two meet again, but now circumstances have changed dramatically, for the horse was injured in battle and thus experienced a sharp decline in status, being sold to a common carter. The donkey, in his own show of schadenfreude, spitefully points out that the horse's pride had set him up for just such a fall.[26] We have here the well-known idea that arrogance and excessive pride (or hubris) are often punished by the gods or fate with a downward reversal.[27]

22. Ibid., 97–98.

23. Scott, Domination, 41–42.

24. Aesop, Fables of Aesop, 292.

25. It is worth noting, however, that we receive no information or insight into the feelings of Lazarus himself about his newly elevated existence in Hades. We do not know whether he experienced schadenfreude at the rich man's tortured downfall. This question will be explored further in the final section of this chapter.

26. Aesop, Fables of Aesop, 70–71.

27. See examples and the discussion of this topic in chapter 3 above.

Certainly the proud and elaborately clothed warhorse is a symbol of the elite warrior who would have ridden upon him, and the donkey can be correlated with the non-elite laborer who rejoices at the elite's humiliation. The fable's one-way downward reversal, with no corresponding upward swing (as there is in our focal text), illustrates the reality that social hierarchies in stratified societies like that of Rome often created steep downward mobility, while upward mobility was rare and incremental at best.[28]

While both this fable and the Lukan parable use status reversal to make their case against arrogance and disregard for others, differences exist as well. Most notably, the parable of Lazarus and the rich man is more hopeful, in that it envisions an upward reversal for the beggar Lazarus that is just as great as the rich man's fall. This inversion, however, is delayed until after death, in the next world, while the donkey gets to rejoice in the horse's humiliation on earth. There is also a different tone to the narration of the downfall of the powerful party. In both "The Horse and the Ass" and "The Tunny and the Dolphin," the "lesser" animal seems to relish the more powerful animal's demise, while the Gospel of Luke, as I will show in the later sections of this chapter, tempers the schadenfreude to some degree. The Lukan parable offers no insight into Lazarus's personal feelings (positive or negative) about either his reversal or that of the rich man. Abraham, who does comment on the situation in Hades, explains the reasoning behind the reversal without commenting on his own feelings or those of Lazarus (Luke 16:25-31). If anything, it is possible to interpret Abraham's familial address of the rich man as "child" in 16:25 as a hint of sympathy toward his predicament.

The fables of Aesop, although similar in form to parables like Lazarus and the rich man, are quite different in their worldview and perspective on social change. The fables express a hope for cooperation between those of different status and allow for a measure of satisfaction in seeing the downfall of an arrogant or greedy elite, but that is as far as they go. In the end, the power structure remains unchanged and the hearer is urged to accept his or her lot in life with as much grace as possible. Luke's ambitions appear to be more radical than this, as the evangelist repeatedly narrates a vision of a world turned upside-down, one that challenges the status quo and its distribution of power, wealth, and social status. Whether this vision can become even partially a reality before the afterlife inversion narrated in Luke 16:19-31 remains an open question, and one that we will continue to explore in this study.

---

28. Gerhard E. Lenski, *Power and Privilege: A Theory of Social Stratification* (1966; repr., Chapel Hill: University of North Carolina Press, 1984), 290.

THE EGYPTIAN PARABLE OF SETNE AND SI-OSIRE

The extant manuscript of this story, in late demotic, is from the late first century CE, but it is likely based on an older tale, since the priest who is a main character, Setne Khamwas, lived in the thirteenth century BCE.[29] Si-Osire is a reincarnated magician, miraculously born to Setne and his wife Mehusekhe, so that he might save Egypt from the Nubians.[30] The text narrates several miraculous actions and teachings from his boyhood, before he fulfilled his destiny at the age of twelve and then "vanished as a shadow" from the presence of his father, the pharaoh, and the court.[31] Among these stories of Si-Osire are pronouncements that show wisdom beyond his young years, and he quickly surpasses his tutor and takes his place as an equal with the scribes in the temple of Ptah.[32] The general motif of extraordinary circumstances surrounding a hero's birth is shared between Si-Osire and Luke's portrayal of Jesus (cf. Luke 1–2), as is the more specific theme of the child unexpectedly distinguishing himself among religious scholars at a young age (cf. Luke 2:41-52).

The episode in the story of Si-Osire that concerns us here begins with his father Setne's observation of two burials: that of a rich man buried with full honors and much (perhaps professional) wailing, and that of a poor man wrapped in a mat and carried to the cemetery with no one to mourn him. The following dialogue ensues:

> Setne [said]: 'By [Ptah, the great god, how much happier is the rich man who is honored] with the sound of [wailing] than the poor man who is carried to the cemetery- – – – – –.' [Si-Osire said to his father: 'May it go with you in the netherworld] as it will go with this poor man in the netherworld! [May it not go with you as it will go with this rich man] in the netherworld!'[33]

This unexpected and unexplained statement of reversal naturally upsets Setne, who feels that his beloved son has wished upon him eternal dishonor and low status. This reaction is perhaps a rough approximation of how Jesus' beatitudes and woes might have been heard by elites in the audience hearing the Sermon on the Plain (Luke 6:20-49), or by persons of high status among Luke's earliest

---

29. Bauckham, "Rich Man and Lazarus," 225.

30. Ibid., 225–26.

31. For the text, in English translation, see Miriam Lichtheim, *The Late Period*, vol. 3 of *Ancient Egyptian Literature: A Book of Readings* (Berkeley: University of California Press, 1980), 138–51.

32. Ibid., 139.

33. Ibid.

readers. Like Si-Osire, Jesus makes an abrupt proclamation of status reversal with little to no explanation, one that would have seemed almost a curse to those of high status: "Favored are the poor, for yours is the reign of God. . . . But woe to you who are rich, for you are now receiving your consolation in full" (Luke 6:20b, 24). Both Jesus and Si-Osire eventually elaborate on the reasoning behind their respective reversals, focusing at least partially on the status of rich and poor in the afterlife. In the tale of Setne, however, this explanation comes almost immediately, while the audience of Luke must wait ten chapters, until the parable of Lazarus and the rich man enacts in graphic detail the first beatitude and its corresponding woe.

Through a supernatural journey to the underworld, Si-Osire shows that the wish for his father to follow the path of the poor man rather than the rich man is in reality a blessing. They journey through seven "halls," and in the final one they observe a scene of judgment and discover the fates of the two men whose burials Setne had witnessed on earth. The text identifies three standard fates in the afterlife, all based explicitly on the morality of one's actions: if a person's evil deeds during life outweigh the good deeds, he or she is destroyed by "the Devourer"; if the good and evil deeds are equal in weight, one remains in the underworld as an "excellent spirit" who serves Sokar-Osiris; and if one's good deeds outweigh the evil, then that one "is taken in among the gods of the tribunal of the lord of the netherworld, while his ba [i.e., soul and personal identity] goes to the sky together with the august spirits."[34]

Both the poor man and the rich man receive one of these judgments, but interestingly, neither one receives an entirely typical compensation for that judgment. Si-Osire identifies for his father the poor man, who has now changed almost beyond recognition. He was found to have more good than evil deeds, and therefore received the royal burial garments of the rich man and a place of honor near Osiris, the ruler of the underworld. He is also, however, said to serve Sokar-Osiris, which the text previously designated as the fate of those whose misdeeds and good deeds were equal. This curious change in his fate is not explained or commented upon, although there is a hint that the slight demotion might be due to his low status on earth. The story states that his good deeds were more numerous than his evil deeds "in relation to his life span . . . and in relation to his luck on earth."[35] Perhaps less was expected in the way of good deeds from one with so few resources, and at the same time less was given in reward. The fate of the rich man is less ambiguous, but still not the conventional punishment. His evil deeds are identified as more numerous than the good, but

34. Ibid., 140.
35. Ibid.

instead of total destruction, he is imprisoned in the netherworld with a doorpost stuck in his eye, to lament over his torture forever.[36] The final lesson to Setne is clear in its "golden rule" morality: "He who is beneficent on earth, to him one is beneficent in the netherworld. And he who is evil, to him one is evil. It is so decreed [and will remain so] for ever."[37]

Obviously there is a strong parallel to the parable of Lazarus and the rich man in this afterlife status reversal between a rich man buried with great panoply and a poor man buried with none. A Jewish version of this same folkloric motif is found in the Palestinian Talmud, and it expands the description of the two main characters to include their professions, as a rich tax collector and a poor Torah scholar.[38] This addition emphasizes the already clear moral lesson of the story, that it is a person's actions for good or evil, rather than his or her wealth, that matter most after death. Luke also adds more details about the earthly lives of the rich man and poor man—including, significantly, a name for the poor man—but he does so in a way that shifts the focus back to wealth versus poverty, rather than good deeds versus evil deeds. This is, in fact, the major difference between Luke and the parallels discussed here: reversal in the Lukan parable is based solely on one's circumstance of poverty or wealth, rather than righteousness and unrighteousness.[39] Luke 16:25, after all, has Abraham say, "Child, remember that you received your good things during your lifetime, and Lazarus in the same way received evil things; so now he is being comforted here, and you are being tormented." Richard Bauckham emphasizes this point, arguing that using these parallels to read conventional morality into Luke 16:19-31 is a fallacy based on modern discomfort with such a stark reversal text.[40]

Instead of casting the characters in stereotypically honorable and dishonorable professions, as does the Talmud, Luke's description of their lives underscores, to an almost satirical degree, the extreme poverty of Lazarus and the extreme wealth of the rich man in a way that extends far beyond their burials, or lack thereof, in the case of the poor man (16:19-21).[41] The physical proximity of Lazarus and the rich man during their lifetimes makes the contrast in their circumstances all the more shocking, unlike the Egyptian story where

36. Ibid., 141.

37. Ibid.

38. Bauckham, "Rich Man and Lazarus," 227.

39. Lehtipuu, *Afterlife Imagery*, 300–301.

40. Bauckham, "Rich Man and Lazarus," 230.

41. The exact descriptions of and form taken by this text's status reversals will be discussed in greater detail in the second section of this chapter below.

the two men had no connection except the coincidence of being buried on the same day.[42] It is difficult, however, to deny that Luke's discussion of the two men's connection on earth highlights the ignorance, apathy, or selfishness (or all three) that characterize the rich man's practice of conspicuous consumption. Luke therefore does cast judgment on the rich man, due to his neglect of a lowly neighbor in need when persons of such low status are of special concern to God,[43] and due to a general cultural understanding that great wealth was often gained through corrupt business practices and accompanied by personal immorality.[44] The final section of the Lukan parable, particularly its command to the rich man's brothers (and on another level, the rich and elite hearers of the parable) to listen to Moses and the Prophets (Luke 16:29), also contributes to this implication of at least some moral failing.

I agree with Bauckham that modern readers should not try to soften the text's stark reversal based on economic status, but at the same time, it is not possible to claim that the rich man's neglect of Lazarus and misuse of his wealth is irrelevant to the Gospel parable. The comparison of Luke 16:19-31 with the clear, simple lesson of Si-Osire for Setne (that deeds, rather than social status, determine one's ultimate fate) again reveals how carefully the third evangelist has nuanced his stories of reversal. The audience must work out the rich man's failings through induction, a much more effective way to convince those who are possibly resistant to the message than a straightforward command or explicit explanation. The Egyptian and Lukan parables also share another important observation: this status reversal in the afterlife is apparently supposed to be self-explanatory to the living. Setne told no living person about his lessons from the underworld,[45] and Abraham states twice that the living have already been given sufficient warning about the fate of the rich and poor (Luke 16:29, 31).[46] In each case, this silence clarifies people's responsibility to do good in the present world by "directing attention away from an apocalyptic revelation of the afterlife back to the inexcusable injustice of the coexistence of rich and poor."[47]

---

42. Bauckham, "Rich Man and Lazarus," 231.

43. Lehtipuu, *Afterlife Imagery*, 164–65.

44. Gowler, "'At His Gate,'" 259. This fact will be seen even more clearly in the next parallel to be discussed, from the work of the Cynic philosopher Lucian.

45. Lichtheim, *The Late Period*, 142.

46. Bauckham sees this refusal to send a messenger from the dead back to the living as distinguishing the Lukan parable from its contemporary parallels ("Rich Man and Lazarus," 244–45). I think, however, that this distinction is exaggerated. The main revelation of the afterlife to the living in the tale of Setne, the story *Cataplus* by Lucian, and the parable from Luke 16 seems to be the telling of the stories themselves.

47. Bauckham, "Rich Man and Lazarus," 246.

CATAPLUS AND GALLUS, BY LUCIAN OF SAMOSATA

Lucian was a Cynic philosopher, rhetorician, and author in the second century CE. Obviously his works postdate the Gospel of Luke, but they are a valuable object of comparison nonetheless. They reveal another nearly-contemporary take on the issue of wealth, poverty, and reversal, and confirm the rhetorical practice of using an extreme comparison of a rich man and a poor man. So we can posit that the parable of Lazarus and the rich man was working with a well-established theme in rhetorical declamation, both before and after the late first century CE.[48] In the work of Lucian, the character parallel to Lazarus is a poor artisan, a shoemaker named Micyllus (perhaps ES6 on the Economy Scale), who appears in two different texts, both times contrasted with a rich man. In *Gallus* ("The Cock, or the Dream"), Micyllus is introduced in his humble life, and in *Cataplus* ("The Downward Journey, or the Tyrant"), we meet him again on his way to the afterworld. The latter story has the clearest plot parallels with our biblical text, but a brief consideration of *Gallus* will also prove fruitful.

In *Gallus*, Lucian introduces his readers to Micyllus on the night that Micyllus had experienced a rare taste of the luxurious elite lifestyle. Eucrates, a local rich man, invited Micyllus to one of his banquets at the last minute, to replace a sick guest. After reveling in the feast, Micyllus goes to bed and dreams of inheriting Eucrates's wealth and throwing his own extravagant parties. He is awakened from this fantasy, much to his chagrin, by the crowing of a rooster, which turns out to be a reincarnated Pythagoras who engages Micyllus in a lengthy discourse on wealth, poverty, and happiness.

A few aspects of the discourse need to be considered here. The temporary venture into the realm of the elite, wealthy, and powerful, we learn, exacerbates Micyllus's already considerable envy at the fate of a fellow cobbler, Simon. After inheriting wealth from a distant relative, this former colleague styled himself as the aristocratic "Simonides" and refused to acknowledge any acquaintance with the "pauper" Micyllus. Such treatment elicits bitterness from Micyllus, who observes acidly, "What blessings gold is able to bestow, when it transforms ugly people and renders them lovely."[49] The rooster listens to this tale of woe from Micyllus, then promptly informs him that, in all his many lives over the centuries, "I have never seen anyone leading a happier life than you."[50] The two then proceed on a survey of various rich men and their activities that evening,

---

48. Hock, "Lazarus and Micyllus," 457. Hughes points to the presence of this tactic in the work of Quintilian, Seneca, Libanius, and Cicero ("Parable," 36–38).

49. Lucian, "The Dream, or the Cock (Gallus)," in *Lucian*, vol. 2, ed. and trans. A. M. Harmon, LCL 54 (1915; repr., Cambridge: Harvard University Press, 1953), 201.

50. Ibid., 203.

so that the philosophical rooster can demonstrate to Micyllus the dreadful burdens of wealth and power. The rich must worry about their property in times of war, pay taxes on it, and defend it through military service;[51] their wealth puts them at the disposal of the public who demand baths and other public amenities, and must be courted during elections;[52] it also entices them into intemperance and excess in eating, drinking, and sexual immorality.[53] Worst of all, claims the rooster, is the terrible burden of responsibility, the constant threat of envy, and the resultant mortal danger to the wealthy and elite, particularly rulers. Being poor, he argues, is much preferable.[54] Micyllus resists even these arguments, but finally concedes the point after the rooster shows him the newly enriched Simon worrying about losing all his goods, and Eucrates and his wife both sleeping with their servants. He declares in the end, "To the deuce with your gold and your dinners; two obols is a fortune to me in comparison with being an easy mark for the servants."[55]

A few observations must be made in comparison with the story of Lazarus and the rich man in Luke 16. First of all, Micyllus as an exemplar of poverty is not entirely comparable to Lazarus. Lazarus is clearly an expendable from ES7—diseased, abandoned, and left for dead in the street (Luke 16:20-21)—while Micyllus is an artisan, albeit a poor one, mostly likely ES6, or ES5 at the highest.[56] Ronald Hock claims that they are similar in social status at the "margins among the poor townspeople,"[57] but this is, I think, an exaggeration. Earlier in the article, Hock himself acknowledges the difference, but downplays it, noting instead that both characters live near their rich neighbors and desire to join their banquets.[58] The difference is significant, though; Micyllus lives at subsistence level with no extras, but with much more security than someone like Lazarus would have had. It is perhaps more conceivable to gain peace with an artisan lifestyle, as *Gallus* urges, than with the hopeless misery of life as a beggar.

Regarding the subject of status reversal, there is certainly no status inversion in Lucian's *Gallus*, and no real leveling either. It bears the closest resemblance to the fables of Aesop, which urge satisfaction with one's current

---

51. Ibid., 217.
52. Ibid.
53. Ibid., 219.
54. Ibid., 225.
55. Ibid., 233, 237, 239.
56. See Lenski, *Power and Privilege*, 278–84.
57. Hock, "Lazarus and Micyllus," 463.
58. Ibid., 457–58.

place in the social hierarchy. Its overall effect is patronizing toward the poor. The rooster explains, for example, that no matter how many comforts and luxuries the elites have, they have to work so hard for them, and the poor would surely not want to have to deal with all that complicated responsibility. So they should just leave it to the elites, and enjoy their impoverished but "free" lives. Such thinking is a strong part of the public transcript endorsed by the dominant group, which above all must insist that the elites rule on behalf of the subordinates and with their best interests at heart.[59] The parable of Lazarus and the rich man espouses a much more subversive point of view, born out of the hidden rather than the public transcript. Lucian hints at this type of status reversal in his other story involving Micyllus, to which we will now turn our attention.

Cataplus, like the Egyptian parable and Luke 16:23-31, is set in the underworld, as Hermes brings a group of the deceased to be ferried to Hades. Lucian first introduces the "rich man" half of the comparison, Megapenthes. His protests and tantrums at the indignity of dying delay the entire group and mark him clearly, in the view of Hermes, as "a king or a tyrant, to judge from his lamentations . . . in which he makes out that he has had great happiness taken away from him."[60] Indeed, Megapenthes is almost a caricature of the worst stereotypes of a rich and powerful man. He was killed by his cousin Megacles, who will now take possession of all his riches; ironically, Megapenthes initially gained his wealth in the same way, by murdering a rich man and all his heirs.[61] He continued such corruption to the end of his life on an even greater scale, buoyed by stolen power and resources: falsely accusing and convicting people so that he could confiscate their possessions, ruling his city as a tyrant, eating and drinking in shameful excess, and murdering anyone who disagreed with him or tried to stop his evil actions.[62] His evil nature is characterized by how he used his great wealth—for hedonism, sexual depravity, and murder.[63] Now, after death, Megapenthes is still attempting to bribe, coerce, and barter with underworld beings like Clotho (one of the Fates) to get his own way. Here it is possible to see a connection with the rich man of the Lukan parable, who also makes several requests of Abraham (Luke 16:24, 27, 30).[64]

---

59. Scott, *Domination*, 18.

60. Lucian, "The Downward Journey, or the Tyrant (Cataplus)," in Harmon, *Lucian*, 7.

61. Ibid., 16–19.

62. Ibid., 51.

63. Hock, "Lazarus and Micyllus," 460.

64. Ibid., 459.

Only later, after extensive theatrics on the part of Megapenthes, does the text reveal that the poor cobbler Micyllus is also present in this group of the deceased. As Lazarus begged near the rich man's estate, Micyllus had in life been a neighbor of Megapenthes, close enough that "the savour of the dishes prepared for his dinner drove me to distraction," along with his luxurious purple clothes and goods.[65] Micyllus is at first somewhat piqued that even in death the poor person (himself) is the last to get on Charon's ferry, but at the same time he observes that he is facing death more bravely than is the rich tyrant.[66] Indeed, he celebrates his changed status:

> By heaven I see already that everything is splendid here with you,
> for that all should have equal rank and nobody be any better than his
> neighbour is more than pleasant, to me at least. And I infer that there
> is no dunning of debtors here and no paying of taxes, and above
> all no freezing in winter or falling ill or being thrashed by men of
> greater consequence. All are at peace, and the tables are turned, for
> we paupers laugh [γελάω] while the rich are distressed and lament.[67]

Micyllus's declaration is particularly noteworthy because of its combination of both types of status reversal, total inversion as well as leveling. In one respect, death is regarded here as "the great leveler" that erases status distinctions ("all should have equal rank"), but there is also a clear moral judgment made on the rich and excessively evil Megapenthes, particularly in the judgment scene to come.[68] The final line in the above quotation, interestingly, closely resembles Luke's third beatitude-woe set, another significant status reversal text: "Blessed are you who are weeping now, for you shall laugh [γελάσετε]. . . . Woe to you who are laughing [οἱ γελῶντες] now, for you shall mourn and weep" (Luke 6:21b, 25b). Apparently this sentiment, as well as the characterization of the rich through their clothing and banquets,[69] was not uncommon in the imperial world, particularly in connection with this poor man-rich man dichotomy.

The status-leveling aspect of the afterlife (Micyllus notes that good looks and fancy clothes mean nothing in a place so dark that they cannot be seen)[70] only lasts for a short time, however, for soon each person faces judgment by

65. Lucian, "Cataplus," 32–35.

66. Ibid., 28–31.

67. Ibid., 33.

68. Bauckham, "Rich Man and Lazarus," 235; and Lehtipuu, *Afterlife Imagery*, 173–74.

69. Hock, "Lazarus and Micyllus," 458.

70. Lucian, "Cataplus," 43.

Rhadamanthus. It is here that the final act of status inversion in *Cataplus* takes place. The philosopher Cyniscus is sent to the "Isle of the Blest" because he atoned for his sins through philosophy, while Micyllus, unmarked by wicked deeds, receives the same reward.[71] Megapenthes, however, receives a unique punishment for his wickedness; instead of being put in the river of burning fire or fed to Cerberus, he is forbidden to drink the water of Lethe that is offered to all the dead so that they might forget their earthly lives.[72] That way, his prosecutor Cyniscus notes, "he will pay a bitter penalty . . . by remembering what he was and how much power he had in the upper world, and reviewing his life of luxury."[73] Like the rich man of Luke 16, Megapenthes is left painfully aware of how his circumstances have changed and of any regrets he might have about his earthly actions.[74] He is also faced with the insincerity of his relationships during his lifetime; after his death, his wife will dishonor his name by revealing publicly her sexual relationship with the slave Midas. Clotho remarks scathingly, "What friend did you have, and how did you make him? Don't you know that all those who bowed the knee and praised your every word and deed did so either from hope or from fear, being friends of your power, not of you, and keeping their eyes on the main chance?"[75]

This judgment scene, with its image of status inversion rather than leveling, is a strong parallel to the Hades portrayed in Luke 16:19-31. In both scenes the rich man is left alone in torment, with no real friends upon whom he might call. In the Lukan parable, the rich man has only Lazarus to ask for help, and he discovers that even his ethnic connection with "Father Abraham" is empty because he ignored the Law and the Prophets (16:29). We also see in both of the poor men a perhaps surprising lack of exceptional virtue. Lazarus is an entirely passive character; the only active verb of which he is the subject is a participle that denotes his longing for the crumbs of the rich man's feasts (ἐπιθυμῶν, Luke 16:21). Micyllus is not regarded as particularly good or pious, either; he is rewarded not for virtue or philosophy (as is Cyniscus), but seemingly because his poverty never allowed either the opportunity or the means to engage in the evils of hedonism and corruption.[76] Hock feels that

71. Ibid., 46–49.

72. Ibid., 55.

73. Ibid., 57.

74. Note also the example of Tantalus in the Odyssey, who is condemned to stand thirsty in a pool of water that he is never allowed to drink. See Michael J. Gilmour, "Hints of Homer in Luke 16:19-31?" *Did* 10 (1999): 29.

75. Lucian, "Cataplus," 22–25.

76. Hock, "Lazarus and Micyllus," 461.

this connection with *Cataplus* should govern our interpretation of the Lukan parable, and thereby concludes that Lazarus was saved because his poverty prevented immorality and that the rich man was judged and abandoned to torture for his hedonism, corrupt wealth, and general immorality.[77] In short, Hock uses the Lucian parallel to flesh out the details that the Lukan parable leaves out.

This approach is, in my view, problematic. The above exploration of Egyptian and Greco-Roman parallels to the parable of Lazarus and the rich man does not "fill in the gaps" of the biblical text. Instead, it highlights the similarities in the pattern and, even more so, the significant places where Luke departs from the pattern discerned in the other stories. Both the story of Setne and Si-Osire and Lucian's character Megapenthes make it clear that wealthy people were often regarded as corrupt, immoral, and deserving of punishment. Luke, on the other hand, is much more subtle in his condemnation, and yet more radical. As Bauckham points out, Luke departs from the form of these parallels and states the reason for the status reversal in stark terms of wealth and poverty and nothing more (16:25), thereby "serving primarily to express and highlight the intolerable injustice of the situation where one enjoys luxury and another suffers want."[78] The parable of Lazarus and the rich man condemns the wealthy simply for being wealthy when others are poor, which sounds on one level exceedingly harsh. But at the same time, an elite reader would perhaps be less alienated by Luke's version of the story because she or he is not portrayed as disgustingly and irredeemably evil. There is no doubt that the parable of Luke 16:19-31 is unrelenting about the eternal consequences of wealth and poverty, but Luke leaves the door to redemption cracked just a little with the command to the living brothers to heed Moses and the prophets (16:29), even as he feels that time to repent is running short (cf. 12:54—13:9). As one might expect after the previous chapters, Luke carefully and subtly nuances the status reversal traditions to fit his own community and context. It is those status reversals in Luke 16:19-31 and their relationship to the hidden transcript of resistance that we will now consider.

SOCIOLOGICAL ANALYSIS: HARSH CONSEQUENCES AND URGENT WARNINGS

In some ways, the parable of Lazarus and the rich man is the clearest example of status reversal, specifically total status inversion, in the Gospel of Luke. Lazarus

---

77. Ibid., 462.

78. Bauckham, "Rich Man and Lazarus," 233.

is very poor in this world and the rich man is very rich; then in the afterlife their positions are switched specifically because, in the words of Abraham to the rich man, "You received your good things during your lifetime, and Lazarus in the same way received evil things; so now he is being comforted here, and you are being tormented" (Luke 16:25). It is a parabolic enactment of the Nazareth proclamation's "good news for the poor" (4:18), the Magnificat's celebration of good things for the hungry and emptiness for the rich (1:53), and the Sermon on the Plain's declaration of the favored state of the poor and hungry compared to the woes meted out to the currently rich and satiated (6:20-21, 24-25). This enactment, particularly of the beatitudes and woes, is usually connected to the first part of the parable, verses 19-26, and divided from the more "theological" discussion of verses 27-31.[79]

In this section, I shall unpack the presentation, discussion, and immediate context of the parable's narration of status reversal, using the lens of hidden transcripts of resistance. Although it is indeed an acting out of previous declarations of inversion and leveling, this pericope is not without its own nuancing. Rather than separate the parable into "social" (verses 19-26) and "theological" (verses 27-31) sections, I will follow Alan Culpepper's view of the parable as two tableaux, one of this world's reality and one of the next world's reality, followed by a dialogue about the pictured reversal.[80] Thus I will discuss the role of hidden transcripts and status reversal in the situational reversal portrayed in the two tableaux (16:19-23), the dialogue between Abraham and the rich man (16:24-31), and the impetus behind Jesus' address of the parable to some Pharisees identified as "lovers of money" (16:14-18).

HIDDEN TRANSCRIPTS IN THE SITUATIONAL REVERSAL (LUKE 16:19-23)

The parable immediately sets the scene with an elaborate description of an earthly reality: the enormous divide in the Roman imperial world between the rich and the poor. Much of the language is reminiscent of other Lukan discussions of social status and economic issues. It begins, for example, by introducing ἄνθρωπος δέ τις πλούσιος, a certain rich man (also in Luke 12:16 and 16:1; cf. 14:16 and 15:11)—a generally ambiguous figure both in the Gospel (for example, the selfish "rich fool" of 12:16-21, the indecisive rich ruler of 18:18-23, and the repentant and reforming Zacchaeus in 19:1-10) and

---

79. R. Alan Culpepper, "The Gospel of Luke: Introduction, Commentary, and Reflections," in *NIB*, ed. Leander E. Keck, vol. 9 (Nashville: Abingdon, 1995), 318; Joseph A. Fitzmyer, *The Gospel According to Luke X–XXIV*, AB 28A (New Haven: Yale University Press, 1985), 1127; and Luke Timothy Johnson, *The Gospel of Luke*, SP 3, ed. Daniel J. Harrington (Collegeville, MN: Liturgical, 1991), 252.

80. Culpepper, "Gospel of Luke," 316–17.

in many other Greco-Roman texts. Seneca, for example, in the first century CE describes the "archetypal rich man" as one who farms land in all provinces. He and his contemporaries such as Pliny and Columella criticized some elites as degenerate, neglectful of their many tracts of land, and exploitative of both slaves and free citizens.[81] These views perhaps influenced what type of person Luke's community members pictured when they heard these parables about rich men.

Other examples of shared vocabulary connect this parable with the status reversals proclaimed elsewhere in Luke, and at the same time demonstrate the extreme differences between Lazarus and the unnamed rich man. The term πτωχός, particularly in contrast with πλούσιος (as in Luke 6:20, 24; cf. 1:53), is the preferred Lukan term for the poor and lowly of society, ES6–7 individuals with even less status and wealth than the poor-but-surviving members of ES5 (sometimes described with the term πένης).[82] Lazarus, the πτωχός (poor man), had been placed (ἐβέβλητο) by some unnamed person at the elaborate entryway (πυλῶνα; see BDAG, 897) of the rich man's estate,[83] perhaps in the hope that such a wealthy household might share some of its largesse. The rich man, the parable states, had the best of everything available to the rich and the elite: luxurious purple and white linen clothing, and sumptuous feasts and celebrations—and not just occasionally, but every day (16:19). Readers familiar with the Roman imperial system, however, would have known that a beggar like Lazarus had little chance of receiving any type of benefaction or patronage, because he had no value as a client.[84] And indeed, the rich man appears to subscribe to this same value system. While the food is literally dripping off his table, Lazarus lies right outside longing for these scraps, yearning to be made full as was promised to the hungry in Jesus' beatitudes (χορτάζω, 6:21 and 16:21).

The contrast between opulent luxury and disgusting poverty, with dogs licking Lazarus's sores (6:20-21), seems exaggerated in its extremity. But it presents a more realistic picture than the sensibilities of those of us who live

---

81. Peter Garnsey and Richard Saller, *The Roman Empire: Economy, Society and Culture* (Berkeley: University of California Press, 1987), 66–67.

82. The term πένης does not appear in Luke, or any of the Gospels for that matter. Its only occurrence in the New Testament is 2 Cor. 9:9. Πτωχός, on the other hand, is used frequently by the third evangelist: Luke 4:18; 6:20; 7:22; 14:13, 21; 16:20, 22; 18:22, 19:8; 21:3.

83. The Greek word πυλῶνα is customarily used for a palace or temple rather than a simple home, indicating further the grandeur of the rich man's lifestyle. See BDAG, 897.

84. Garnsey and Saller, *Roman Empire*, 117–18; and C. R. Whittaker, "The Poor," in *The Romans*, ed. Andrea Giardina (Chicago: University of Chicago Press, 1993), 294–95.

in comfort and plenty today would prefer to acknowledge. William Herzog classifies Luke 16:19-31 as a parable that is intended to codify an oppressive system for its victims.[85] Presenting these two characters side by side emphasizes the injustice in a way that real life, which often separated those of different status, was not able to do.[86] Luise Schottroff also argues that the parable's extreme depiction of wealth and poverty is realistic, citing, for example, mosaics that depict the waste of elite banquets as including pieces of bread that have been used as napkins. She writes, "Luke 16:19-21 sketches a fictional picture of a reality that was omnipresent in the cities of the Roman Empire. That the wealth of the rich is connected to the poverty of the poor is not explained with the aid of economic analyses, but with the literary means of antithetical parallelism."[87] Coming from the cultural tradition of the non-elites, the parable plays its own role in the hidden transcript of resistance. It shows that they were indeed aware of their domination and the injustice of their situation, even despite the seeming inevitability and ubiquity of the imperial hierarchy and values system.[88]

True to form, this tale of resistance does not leave the situation as it is. A hint of the coming radical reversal is present from the very start. As one might expect from the parabolic practice of the Lukan Jesus, he introduces the rich man in 16:19 as he does other parable characters, as a nameless figure. Lazarus, however, is a different case. He is presented as passive and living an almost subhuman existence, yet he is given a name—the only named character (apart from Abraham) in the canonical parables, in fact.[89] This small detail hints that not all is as it seems in the parable, or at least that it will not remain so for long. The meaning of *Lazarus*—Hebrew for "My God helps"—is also perhaps significant in that God does indeed come to the aid of this Lazarus in a most dramatic way. Thus Lazarus, through his name, is presented as a full human being, while the rich man, despite all his luxuries, is not.[90] The reversal begins with the deaths of the two men in Luke 16:22. On one level, the difference in status continues, as the rich man receives everything that signifies human

85. Herzog, *Parables*, 51, 77.

86. Ibid., 120.

87. Luise Schottroff, *The Parables of Jesus*, trans. Linda M. Maloney (Minneapolis: Fortress Press, 2006), 167.

88. Scott, *Domination*, 79–80.

89. Green, *Gospel of Luke*, 605–6.

90. Herman Hendrickx, *The Third Gospel for the Third World*, vol. 3B (Collegeville, MN: Liturgical, 2000), 229. Cf. Benson O. Igboin, "An African Understanding of the Parable of the Rich Man and Lazarus: Problems and Possibilities," *AJT* 19 (2005): 261, 266. He outlines the extreme implications of being nameless in African culture.

honor and status through his burial. In the Roman world, burial practices were an important means to cement one's social status both on earth and in the view of the gods, as evidenced partly by the proliferation of burial clubs and funds in trade guilds and other non-elite associations,[91] and by the tombs and memorials displayed outside of first-century cities such as Pompeii.

But on another level, in the view of the God of Israel, the opposite is true. It is Lazarus, presumably buried anonymously in a mass grave with other destitutes (if he was buried at all), who receives elaborate divine attention, being carried away by angels to the bosom of Abraham. The rich man, for all his earthly goods, ends up separated from God and tormented in Hades (Luke 16:23). The bosom of Abraham is undoubtedly a place of highest honor for the beggar Lazarus, now regarded as a valued guest at the heavenly banquet (cf. Luke 14:7-24),[92] and the word κόλπος (bosom) has additional connotations of protection and security.[93] All this combines to convey the appropriateness of the reversal in the Lukan worldview, for honor and status are valued quite differently by God than they are by humans (cf. Luke 16:15). At this point in the Gospel of Luke, such an assertion should not come as a surprise to an alert reader, who is by now familiar with the "ever-present Lukan theme" of status reversal on the basis of honor and wealth in this world.[94] Alan Culpepper aptly calls this parable "the capstone of Luke's prophetic critique of wealth."[95]

Lazarus and the rich man demonstrate the clearest and starkest example of total inversion of all the texts considered in this study, and, it could be argued, in the entire Gospel of Luke. The rich man is not just taken down from his high status or stripped of his excessive material privileges to create a more equal footing for the marginalized, as we saw in the Magnificat (explicitly) and the Nazareth proclamation (implicitly). Here, he is condemned to separation and torment without any possible recourse (as becomes clear in the following dialogue, which we will discuss in the next section), and without any apparent relation to morality; Schottroff calls it "an uncompromising and radical text."[96] There is no hint of leveling in the reversal of Luke 16:19-23. Rather, unnuanced inversion of status and fortune is the theme, with little ambiguity and plenty of the schadenfreude that is entirely consistent with the reversals of hidden transcripts of subordinated peoples[97]—although it is interesting that there is no

---

91. Whittaker, "The Poor," 287.

92. See BDAG, 556–57. Also Lehtipuu, *Afterlife Imagery*, 234.

93. Hock, "Lazarus and Micyllus," 456; and Forbes, *God of Old*, 188–89.

94. Gowler, "'At His Gate,'" 255.

95. Culpepper, "Gospel of Luke," 315.

96. Schottroff, *Parables of Jesus*, 168.

character explicitly mocking the rich man's downfall, as we saw, for example, in the treatment of Megapenthes in Lucian's *Cataplus*, or the fallen warhorse mocked by the donkey in Aesop's fable. The speaking of the Lukan parable, either in Palestine or in the Hellenistic cities of Greece and Asia Minor, amounts to a public refutation of the beliefs, values, and domination of the Roman Empire and its wealthy hierarchy.[98]

Even as this parable is in one sense a stronger declaration of reversal (inversion rather than leveling), it is also in another sense a much weaker, or at least more cautious, declaration than previous status-reversal texts. In these earlier passages, Jesus espoused a present or impending timeline, as seen, for example, in the emphasis at Nazareth on fulfillment "today" (Luke 4:21), and in the combination of present and future fulfillment in the beatitudes and woes (6:20-26). But the reversal for Lazarus is set firmly in the afterlife, deferring the change to the next world rather than this one. This shift lessens the radical nature of the message at first glance. It also, however, provides a layer of protection that the hidden transcript needs if it is to survive safely on the public stage. The millennial belief that the end of the world, and therefore of subordination, is near has long been common among oppressed groups; it allows them to publicly express their hope for a transformed social system, but attributing the change to God's action rather than their own is less dangerous.[99] It is, in fact, relatively safe because the dominating group is concerned with material appropriation and ideological subordination during this lifetime, and therefore cares little for threats to their status in the next world, at least as long as they do not threaten their public reputation and domination in the present.

One important question, then, is whether the parable of Luke 16:19-31 urges any action in the present that might challenge, harm, or subvert Rome's system of hierarchy, appropriation, and domination. The second part of this section will focus on the afterworld dialogue between the rich man and Father Abraham, to see what it has to say about status and reversal in this world. It will give, I suggest, a resounding yes in answer to the previous question. The whole of Luke 16 has a strong eschatological component. In the end God will reverse the human-dictated values of the world, and that fact matters urgently for human actions in the present. In the words of Dennis Ireland: "In short, eschatology is to have an influence on ethics, specifically on stewardship of material possessions."[100]

---

97. Scott, *Domination*, 41–42.

98. Ibid., 172.

99. Ibid., 148.

HIDDEN TRANSCRIPTS IN THE DIALOGUE (LUKE 16:24-31)

Before we proceed to exploration of the dialogue between Abraham and the rich man that makes up the rest of this parable, an observation about the character of Lazarus will be illuminating. He is a remarkably passive character, particularly in light of the fact that he is the only named character in any of Jesus' parables. Lazarus is the subject of no active verbal form except the participle ἐπιθυμῶν in 16:21—the only thing he does of his own accord is long to eat the rich man's table scraps. He is carried to the gate, carried to the bosom of Abraham, and discussed as an object lesson in the conversation between the rich man and Abraham. Certainly he shows no particular righteousness, piety, or exemplary moral behavior. The rich man is the central figure who acts and talks.[101] One of the likely effects of this characterization is that the elites in the Lukan communities would have felt particularly targeted by this parable. That effect might have been heightened by the fact that the rich man is nameless and therefore, from a literary perspective, easier for readers and hearers to identify with.[102]

But even with this passive, almost objectified role, the character of Lazarus has resonated over the centuries with many poor and oppressed populations reading the Gospel of Luke. The Nicaraguan peasants of Solentiname, for example, quickly identified Lazarus as one of their own. In their view, this story is "very simple" in its justice and reversal, and their discussion of it is brief.[103] Notably, however, they do not recommend using the parable to encourage the poor to endure their present hardships stoically, nor to condemn the rich to eternal torture; rather, they want it to help foment economic reform in the here and now.[104] Similarly, a modern retelling of this parable in an African context portrays Lazarus as a young street urchin begging in Malawi and, less directly, as a Christian housewife who tries to witness to the corrupt rich man—familiar figures from the lives of the people, the non-elites.[105] Finally, Cheryl Townsend Gilkes reminds us of the popular representations of Lazarus in the stories of enslaved and marginalized African-Americans. His fate, for example, is the hope

---

100. Dennis J. Ireland, *Stewardship and the Kingdom of God: An Historical, Exegetical, and Contextual Study of the Parable of the Unjust Steward in Luke 16:1-13*, NovTSup 70 (Leiden: Brill, 1992), 138–39.

101. Duck-ho Oh, "Faith and Wealth: A Literary-Historical Study of Luke 16" (Ph.D. diss., Union Theological Seminary in Virginia, 1996), 309–10.

102. Green, *Gospel of Luke*, 606.

103. Ernesto Cardenal, *The Gospel in Solentiname*, trans. Donald D. Walsh, rev. ed. (Maryknoll, NY: Orbis, 2007), 422–24.

104. Ibid., 423.

105. Wendland, "Mwini-Chuma," 318–19, 331.

and goal of enslaved people in the spiritual "Rock-a My Soul in the Bosom of Abraham."[106] After the American Civil War, "Po' Lazarus" appeared in secular song as a Southern Black oppressed by the unjust system of sharecropping and debt and killed by a violent sheriff "because he resists being a victim."[107] Thus we will need to keep in mind both the elite and the non-elite members of Luke's congregations, and how they might have heard and responded to this parable and to both of its main characters.

The reversal that was narrated in Luke 16:19-23 presents its message of status reversal clearly, but the parable has more to add to it. The dialogue in Hades between Abraham and the rich man proves enlightening, particularly for the elite reader of Luke's Gospel. Two main questions are addressed: why Lazarus and the rich man received their respective fates, and whether there is any hope for other wealthy people to avoid such a bleak outcome.[108] The rich man initiates the conversation, appealing for mercy to Abraham as his father and requesting the aid of Lazarus (16:24). The irony in this single statement is immense. The rich man first relies on a familial connection with his ancestor Abraham, but John the Baptist has already made it clear that such a relationship is worthless in God's reign unless it is accompanied by "fruits worthy of repentance" (Luke 3:8). Abraham himself acknowledges the truth of the relationship in his address of the rich man as "child," offering perhaps a glimmer of recognition and connection.[109] But it is still not enough; the injustice of the extreme inequality between the rich man and his destitute neighbor had to be remedied through status reversal (16:25).

The rich man requests from his ancestor Abraham two things, mercy and the services of Lazarus, thereby further exposing his own lack of both mercy and service to others. Mercy (ἔλεος, ἐλεέω) in the Gospel of Luke is exhibited by crossing status boundaries: in God's gifts to the barren Elizabeth (Luke 1:58), to those who revere God (1:50), and to the *servant* Israel (1:54); and also in the barrier-breaking aid given by a parabolic Samaritan to his (presumably Jewish) *neighbor* (10:37). The rich man's actions on earth and the attitude behind them showed his complete lack of the mercy that he now seeks. In the tableaux of Luke 16:19-23, the audience was made aware of the status and economic chasm between Lazarus and the rich man. But the rich man's

106. Cheryl Townsend Gilkes, "Resurrection in Prophetic Context: 'Poor Man Lazarus' and Christian Agency," in *Engaging the Bible: Critical Readings from Contemporary Women*, ed. Choi Hee An and Katheryn Pfisterer Darr (Minneapolis: Fortress Press, 2006), 6–7.

107. Ibid., 10.

108. Oh, "Faith and Wealth," 357.

109. Culpepper, "Gospel of Luke," 317.

request in verse 24 indicates that he, too, was aware of his destitute "neighbor" and, more significantly, did nothing about it. Not only does he recognize Lazarus in Hades, but he even knows his name. Nevertheless, he still treats him like a lower-status servant, showcasing his stubbornness by holding to an elite mindset and maintaining the social primacy of other elites, even in the midst of torture. He would order Lazarus to provide him with the same hospitality that he had refused to offer Lazarus on earth.[110] The rich man is unable, even in Hades, to understand the incompatibility between the public transcript values of the imperial elite and the attitude required to participate in the reign of God. Gilkes writes, "Jesus wanted his listeners to understand that their refusal to see and hear poor people in this world absolutely contradicted God's will."[111] Luke does not use a prosecutor or judge to condemn his rich man, as did Lucian and the author of the Egyptian tale of underworld reversal. Instead, the rich man in this story is condemned by his own words, which reveal the serious flaws in his mindset, values, and conduct.

Abraham's response to the rich man's revealing reaction to misfortune is in many ways the crux of the parable. It outlines the status reversal at its starkest and most permanent: "Child, remember that you received your good things during your lifetime, and Lazarus in the same way received evil things; so now he is being comforted here, and you are being tormented. Even with all this, between us and you a great chasm has been firmly set, so that those who want to go over from here to you cannot, nor can they cross over from there to us" (Luke 16:25-26). This statement contains several more vocabulary connections to Luke's theme of status reversal. On earth, the rich man received τὰ ἀγαθά, but the Magnificat allocates these "good things" to the hungry while the rich are "sent away empty" (1:53). In the same way, Jesus' "woe" to the rich in 6:24 proclaims that they have already received their παράκλησις (comfort); thus after death Lazarus is comforted (παρακαλεῖται) while the rich man is tormented (16:25).

Abraham's pronouncement of status reversal also places the parable even more firmly in the category of total inversion, with no hint of status leveling. It is unique among the parallels discussed in the first section of this chapter because the reasons Abraham supplies for the reversal do not include morality, righteousness, or piety in any way. The parable of Lazarus and the rich man highlights simply "the injustice of gross material inequality."[112] Richard Bauckham rightly pushes affluent readers to avoid glossing over this statement

---

110. Green, *Gospel of Luke*, 608; and Hendrickx, *Third Gospel*, 235.

111. Gilkes, "Resurrection," 15.

112. Hendrickx, *Third Gospel*, 225.

too quickly; it appears irrelevant whether the rich man misused his wealth, acquired it unjustly, or neglected the poor man at his gate.[113] According to Luke 16:25-26, the main problem is the basic injustice that the rich man received good things during his life while someone else received only evil. This idea of eschatological reversal springs from the folk culture of poor, ordinary, non-elite people.[114] But here it is presented to a rich man straight from the mouth of God's representative, and by extension to the elites, retainers, and prosperous artisans of Luke's congregations.

While taking Bauckham's statement to heart, it is also necessary to acknowledge that the parable does in fact elaborate upon the earthly injustice that caused the status inversion in Hades. True to Lukan practice, these nuances are subtle details of the story itself, rather than explicit commands or condemnations. Indeed, Greg Forbes points out that the parable of Lazarus and the rich man with its implications provides at least as much (and perhaps slightly more) reason for status reversal as do other texts like the Magnificat and the beatitudes and woes.[115] This factor, along with the permanence of the eternal consequences, heightens the intensity of the narrative's warning to the wealthy and elite.

One necessary consideration is the initial perception of the rich man in relation to his wealth. Duck-ho Oh points out that one strand of conventional wisdom would see wealth as indicative of the rich man's righteousness being rewarded by divine blessings, but he also acknowledges that divinely given wealth came with the responsibility to use it ethically.[116] Many other scholars, however, argue that the possession of excessive wealth is somewhat of a judgment in and of itself, because such conspicuous consumption could (and can) only be gained and maintained through oppression and exploitation of the poor.[117] The existence of a person as destitute as Lazarus and other members of ES7 could also be viewed as an indictment of the elite for not following God's commands to share resources in such a way that none are in true want in Israel.[118] And indeed, this is exactly where the dialogue of the rich man and Abraham ends up, with a command (the only command given in this pericope) to hear and obey Moses and the Prophets (Luke 16:29). Even though there is no

---

113. Bauckham, "Rich Man and Lazarus," 232.

114. Ibid., 233; and Scott, *Domination*, 166–82.

115. Forbes, *God of Old*, 196.

116. Oh, "Faith and Wealth," 314–15.

117. Herzog, *Parables*, 128. See also Hendrickx, *Third Gospel*, 204–5; and Schottroff, *Parables of Jesus*, 167–68.

118. Dieter H. Reinstorf, "The Rich, the Poor, and the Law," *HvTSt* 60 (2004): 344–45.

overt moral judgment in the reversal (16:25), the ensuing dialogue does indicate a moral failing on the part of the elite to live up to God's vision for the world (16:29).[119]

The final section of this parable (Luke 16:27-31), including its only imperative, has often been seen as more "theological," referring to disbelief persisting in both Christian and Jewish communities, despite Jesus' resurrection.[120] Certainly Abraham's comment in Luke 16:31 contains an implicit allusion to the resurrection of Jesus, but it is far from the main point of these verses and much less the main point of Luke's presentation of the entire parable. The theological "flavor" of this final piece of dialogue may have provided another level of protection for the hidden transcript message, in that it offers a less challenging "spiritual" interpretation of the subversive status reversals.

The rich man seems to accept the inevitability of his fate, but asks (again) for Lazarus's services as an errand boy, this time to be sent to his five brothers, who are, presumably, just as wealthy and neglectful of the poor as he was (Luke 16:27). This request refocuses the audience's attention away from Hades and back onto this world and its concerns, and makes the parable relevant to the present as well as the future.[121] It also no doubt drove home the point to the rich man's elite "brothers [and sisters]" in the Lukan communities that they were in very real danger of sharing his fate. Herzog actually characterizes this final exchange in 16:27-31 as an attempt by the author of Luke to "educate the oppressor,"[122] and indeed that seems to be the case.

Luke is, as we have seen in the other status reversal texts examined in this study, reluctant to give direct commands. The one he does issue, however, is important, coming in response to the rich man's request on his brothers' behalf. In 16:29, Abraham says (λέγει), rather abruptly, "They have Moses and the Prophets. They must listen [ἀκουσάτωσαν, third person plural imperative] to them!" This command is foregrounded slightly by the (historical) present tense of λέγει,[123] rather than Luke's more customary aorist, and offers the parable's one hint of reprieve for the elite and wealthy. This command is why I cannot agree with Luke Timothy Johnson that the parable of Lazarus and the rich man is a *final* rejection and judgment of the Pharisees and the wealthy.[124] It is harsh,

119. Johnson, *Gospel of Luke*, 256.

120. E.g., Fitzmyer, *Luke X–XXIV*, 1128.

121. Forbes, *God of Old*, 184.

122. Herzog, *Parables*, 126.

123. For other examples of the historical present in Luke, see, e.g., 16:7, 23; 19:22.

124. Johnson, *Gospel of Luke*, 256.

certainly, and it sounds an urgent warning, certainly; but it does leave open the slim possibility of repentance through obedience to Torah and the Prophets. In Luke, this repentance of the rich and elite must be made manifest through practices that are liberating and dignity-enhancing for the marginalized and oppressed.[125] The parable of Lazarus and the rich man does not present a bright outlook for the elite, the wealthy, and those who support them, but it does offer them one last chance to embrace "a mode of vertical generalized reciprocity . . . a redistribution from the advantaged to the disadvantaged with the expectation of nothing in return."[126]

The final two verses of dialogue in the parable are an exchange of conditional statements. The rich man seems to believe that there is indeed a possibility that his brothers might be saved if they receive a message from beyond the grave—in 16:30, he uses the subjunctive mood and ἐάν, the particle of possibility, if the right conditions are met. But Abraham responds with a stronger first-class conditional, stating unequivocally that if the rich brothers do not listen to Moses and the Prophets, they will not repent even in the face of a resurrection. He emphasizes again the connection between the Law and the Prophets and the work of social justice and status reversal. This strategy of persuasion would have hit home with "sincere elites," those who believed that the public transcript of following the Mosaic Law gave the best life possible to all the people, elite and non-elite alike.[127]

Luke issues a stern warning, but with hope for a change of heart, one that can be exhibited, even at this late date, through elite readers' use of possessions to provide for the needs of the poor. This option for repentance is a hallmark of Luke's parables. We see, for example a similar pairing of impending judgment and the call for repentance in the sequence of teachings found in Luke 12:54—13:9. Of particular note is the parable of the barren fig tree, where the vineyard owner allows the gardener one more year to coax the tree into bearing fruit before cutting it down (13:6-9). Much like the implicit warning to the rich man's brothers in 16:27-31, this parable makes clear that there is still time to repent, but only if immediate action is taken. Forbes writes, "In contrast to the other Synoptics, Luke certainly has a strong emphasis on repentance, and . . . is keen to underline the necessity of a changed lifestyle as a result, particularly with respect to the use of wealth and possessions. All these features are prominent in the Lukan parables."[128]

---

125. Forbes, *God of Old*, 244; Herzog, *Parables*, 124–25; and Walter E. Pilgrim, *Good News to the Poor: Wealth and Poverty in Luke-Acts* (Minneapolis: Augsburg, 1981), 118–19.

126. Gowler, "'At His Gate,'" 256.

127. Scott, *Domination*, 104–5.

The onus of responsibility for instigating this move toward social justice and status change is placed, in the parable of Lazarus and the rich man, upon the elite and wealthy.[129] Lazarus was apparently saved merely because he was poor; but the rich man, or more accurately his still-living brothers (and sisters as well, among Luke's readers), must change their values and their practices of conspicuous consumption now, in this world, if they are to join in the work of God's reign, and so have a future part in its inheritance. It is the responsibility of the rich to reach out and help the poor in their midst, and not the other way around. Gilkes writes that Jesus in this parable "reminds us that the resurrection is meaningless if we do not address the sufferings of those who are 'laid at our gate.' . . . The resurrection is meaningless if we do not live out the commands of the prophets: 'do justice, love mercy, and walk humbly with thy God.'"[130] She picks up on the christological overtones of the reference to the rich not being convinced even by a resurrection from the dead (presumably that of Jesus). This sentiment is echoed in Jesus' sayings about the difficulty of the rich entering the reign of God (Luke 18:24-25); the task is daunting for both the elites themselves and those trying to convince and welcome them, but it is not impossible with God's help (18:26-27).

In summary, the parable of Lazarus and the rich man is part of the hidden transcript of resistance and its use of status reversals, yet at the same time it opens the door at least a crack to sincere elites in Luke's congregations. Its main thrust is a sharp warning to those elites, that they must share their resources now, or suffer eternal consequences. Undoubtedly, this is a harsher and more urgent message than the Nazareth proclamation, and even than the Magnificat. The non-elite hope of afterlife inversion is adopted by the third evangelist not only to give them comfort (which it still does), but even more so to pressure elites into ending their exploitation and oppression of the non-elite population and creating at least a partial reversal now, in this world. According to Luke 16:19-31, the poor non-elites will receive favor from God simply because they are poor and have suffered much in this world. In the same manner, elites, with their power, status, and wealth, will be judged by a God who cares for the lowest of society. But speaking on behalf of this same God, Luke offers, in this parable, one last chance, in hopes that the congregations hearing it will start to resemble the reign of God in this world, not just in the next.

128. Forbes, *God of Old*, 245.

129. Green, *Gospel of Luke*, 608; Hendrickx, *Third Gospel*, 236; and Pilgrim, *Good News*, 119.

130. Gilkes, "Resurrection," 10.

Hidden Resistance in the Framing Narrative (Luke 16:14-18)

Now that we have studied the parable and its themes of status reversal in some detail, we must take one step back and consider the framing narrative in which the third evangelist places this pericope. The whole of chapter 16 pivots around the theme of status, wealth, and power, found prominently not only in Lazarus and the rich man, but also in the opening parable of the dishonest steward and its accompanying collection of aphorisms on money and possessions (Luke 16:1-13). Between these two parables, Jesus engages in a somewhat confusing discourse with the Pharisees, who are accused by Luke of being lovers of money and sneering at Jesus' teachings (16:14). This verse, with its accusation of loving money and human status more than God, is seen by Dennis Ireland as the hinge of chapter 16.[131] Jesus sharply rebukes his Pharisee detractors for valuing human honor over divine, and labels that human honor, and those who seek it, as an abomination (βδέλυγμα) in God's view (16:15). Several obscure reflections follow in verses 16-18, covering the diverse topics of John the Baptist, the continuing claim of Law and Prophets, the reign of God, and the issue of divorce and remarriage. It is this exchange, or rather this short speech by Jesus, that prompts the telling of our focal parable, and also reveals more dimensions to imperial negotiation in the Gospel of Luke.

Before we go further, we must briefly discuss in more detail the Pharisees, with attention mainly to their literary portrayal as characters in Luke's narrative.[132] In the travel narrative (Luke 9:51—19:27), Luke tends to be specific about the audiences for Jesus' various teachings, as he is here,[133] and it is important to understand how this stated audience influences the telling and interpretation of the parable. Jesus and the Pharisees are set against each other in the Gospel of Luke in that, among other areas of disagreement, they seem to have had differing views on how best to negotiate the Roman Empire. Saldarini identifies the Pharisees as retainers, according to Lenski's social stratification for agrarian empires.[134] In the Third Gospel, they are portrayed as "local leaders

---

131. Ireland, *Stewardship*, 123–24.

132. For a full treatment of the Pharisees' literary profile in Luke-Acts, see, e.g., John T. Carroll, "Luke's Portrayal of the Pharisees," *CBQ* 50 (1988): 604–21; John A. Darr, *On Character Building: The Reader and the Rhetoric of Characterization in Luke-Acts* (Louisville: Westminster John Knox, 1992), 85–126; and David B. Gowler, *Host, Guest, Enemy, and Friend: Portraits of the Pharisees in Luke and Acts*, Emory Studies in Early Christianity 2 (New York: P. Lang, 1991).

133. Gowler, "At His Gate,'" 252.

134. Anthony J. Saldarini, *Pharisees, Scribes and Sadducees in Palestinian Society: A Sociological Approach* (Wilmington: Michael Glazier, 1988), 38. See also Lenski, *Power and Privilege*, 243–48, 284.

who are engaged in a contest with Jesus for influence and control in Galilean society."[135] Saldarini elaborates,

> The Gospel of Luke charges that the Pharisees, as patrons of the people, are failing in their duties and it claims that Jesus, acting as an intermediary with God, fulfills the role of patron in a new and more effective way. . . . It is very likely that the emergence of identifiable, voluntary associations, which struggled for control of Jewish society, disagreed over how Judaism was to be lived, and reacted to the activities of foreign rulers differently.[136]

Halvor Moxnes points out a further source of conflict, in that the Pharisees are presented in Luke as village leaders trying to protect community boundaries, while the Lukan Jesus displays particular concern for those who live on or outside such social boundaries.[137] In the framing story of the Lazarus parable (16:14-18), Jesus is attempting urgently to convince the Pharisees to convert to his more faithful reading of Torah and his vision of the in-breaking reign of God.

This apparent conflict between equals is narrated in Luke over and over again, particularly in Galilee. Luke 16 is merely one of many examples. The Lukan portrayal of the Pharisees is, of course, written from a perspective sympathetic to Jesus, and also one that is concerned with relevance to the late-first-century urban gatherings of Hellenistic Jesus-followers (much more than with accurate representation of the historical setting of early-first-century Palestine). The Third Gospel, like Matthew and Mark, records many arguments or debates between Jesus and the Pharisees, but it also—uniquely—presents indicators of social-status equality and even friendship. Significantly, the Pharisees are not involved in any way in the Lukan Passion narrative, although they are Jesus' most prominent debate partners during his ministry (for example, Luke 5:17-26, 27-33; 6:1-5, 6-11; 7:36-50; 11:37-54; 12:1-3; 14:1-6; 15:1-10).[138] Jesus eats with Pharisees in their homes, evidently as a social equal (7:36-50; 11:37-52; 14:1-24); they warn him of a threat from Herod (13:31); and Jesus observes that the reign of God is already "among" or "within" the Pharisees (17:20-21). Condemnations of the Pharisees in Luke (for example,

---

135. Saldarini, *Pharisees*, 178.

136. Ibid., 58–60.

137. Halvor Moxnes, *The Economy of the Kingdom: Social Conflict and Economic Relations in Luke's Gospel*, OBT (Philadelphia: Fortress Press, 1988), 54–55.

138. Ibid., 18–19.

11:37-54; 16:14-15; 18:9-14) exist alongside calls to repentance (for example, 14:14; 15:3-32; and, I will argue, here in 16:14-31).[139] The author of Luke apparently has not entirely given up on the possibility of the Pharisees repenting and joining Jesus' movement to invoke the reign of God.

It seems probable that any retainers and wealthier (ES4-5) artisans within Luke's urban congregations would have identified with the Pharisees as he has presented them. Many of them, like the Pharisees, were likely open to significant accommodation to and acceptance of certain parts of Roman domination,[140] and would have gained a measure of status and wealth through this negotiation strategy. Luke's slightly more sympathetic representation of this group may have provided an opening for such partial adherents to the status quo to find a place in the alternative Christian communities—although not, of course, without significant realignment of their values and social practices, as the parable of Lazarus and the rich man makes clear. With these observations about the Pharisees in history and especially in the Gospel of Luke, let us then consider Luke 16:14-18 as it sets up our focal pericope.

In response to Jesus' summative aphorism that no one can serve both God and wealth (Luke 16:13), some Pharisees, listening in on these teachings directed at the disciples (16:1), are identified by the narrator as φιλάργυροι, greedy or lovers of money, and as such sneer derisively at these sayings (16:14). This label was a common Greco-Roman polemical term, identified variously as the root of social ills,[141] and as a designation for false teachers and those not fit to rule because of their reliance on empty human praise.[142] This epithet, provided by the narrator in 16:14, sets up the first challenge leveled at this group. Their valuing of human honor and status over divinely given worth leads to Jesus' declaration of a harsh, negative reversal: "For what is exalted by humans is an abomination in the sight of God" (16:15b). This exclusively negative inversion is almost the exact opposite of the Nazareth proclamation's focus on positive reversals and leveling (4:18-19, 25-27). Thus the Pharisees become here almost the personification or representation of the social and economic values of the imperial system, and those who adhere to them. The attempt to "justify yourselves in the sight of human beings" (16:15a) is a clear

---

139. Gowler, "'At His Gate,'" 252.

140. Bruce W. Longenecker, *Remember the Poor: Paul, Poverty, and the Greco-Roman World* (Grand Rapids: Eerdmans, 2010), 332.

141. Juvenal, *Sat.* 14, especially 14.173-78. See also Johnson, *Gospel of Luke*, 250.

142. Philo, *Spec.* 4.65; Dio Chrysostom, *Socr.* (Or. 54.1). See also Moxnes, *Economy of the Kingdom*, 6–8.

indication of concern on the part of the Pharisees for status as defined by human cultural norms (cf. 18:9, 14).

Luke 16, then, warns not only elite Christians like the rich man of verses 19-31, but also the retainers and other ES4–5 non-elites who have bought into the elites' public transcript. Like Jesus' message at Nazareth, discussed in chapter 4 of this study, the introduction to this parable in 16:14-18 is another unusual example of the hidden transcript critiquing domination within the non-elite group itself. In Scott's model, adherence to the social values and hierarchy of the subordinated group is usually critical to survival; it is required to sustain the collective interest of the non-elite group, even as it hurts the interests of some individuals.[143] In that way, the hierarchy among the subordinated group is similar to, almost a microcosm of, the elite-sponsored public transcript. In this area, Lukan resistance breaks significantly with the standard non-elite hidden transcript as identified by Scott. The parable of Lazarus and the rich man shows the consequences of the elite's over-valuation of wealth and power, but Jesus' rebuke to the Pharisees also implies that the non-elites who support this set of values and associated social practices will face these consequences as well. The use of the word βδέλυγμα (abomination or detestable thing)[144] to describe the love of money and desire for human status connects these values with idolatry, the highest offense against God (for example, Deut. 7:24-25; 1 Kgs. 11:5; Dan. 9:27).[145] Ireland writes, "Love of money ([Luke 16:]14) and the resultant neglect of the poor are an abomination in God's eyes. This point, implicit in vv. 14-15, is graphically illustrated in the rich man's fate."[146]

The final three disparate verses of this section make for an ambiguous transition to the parable of Lazarus and the rich man, as they are some of the most confusing in the Gospel. Their main topic is the Law and the Prophets, which anticipates the final section of the parable in which Abraham urges the rich man's brothers, and others "overhearing" this story, to hear and obey Judaism's sacred writings (Luke 16:29-31). Jesus is insistent that he is preserving the Law (16:17), but it must be understood in light of God's inclusive reign rather than with other interpretations that do not offer hope to the poor, lowly, and marginalized. In an effective image, Joel Green identifies wealth as the "melody" in Luke 16, with interpretation of Scripture as its "countermelody."[147]

143. Scott, Domination, 130–31.

144. BDAG, 172.

145. Oh, "Faith and Wealth," 287. The concept of abomination also provides a possible connection between the seemingly disjointed topics covered in Luke 16:14-18, as discussed below.

146. Ireland, Stewardship, 135.

147. Green, Gospel of Luke, 599–600.

Even as Jesus challenges the Pharisees' dismissal of his teachings, he meets them on their own ground through a discussion of the Law and the afterlife, two topics important to Pharisaic beliefs.[148] But he argues that they must be viewed through the even more important issue of the proper use of wealth and the proper definition of status in the reign of God. The Law and the Prophets remain in force even now, after John's time (16:16a), but they are in service to the reign of God that is being proclaimed as good news (εὐαγγελίζεται)—good news that elsewhere is the Gospel is specifically directed to the poor (4:18; 7:22) and to all people (2:10; 3:18; 20:1; cf. 4:43).

Jesus' focus on maintenance of the Law even in the reign of God is relatively clear in Luke 16:16-17, but the final clause of verse 16 presents a challenge in translation and intention. The NRSV translates καὶ πᾶς εἰς αὐτὴν βιάζεται as "and everyone tries to enter it by force." This rendering tries to preserve the nuance of violence or (negative) force that is usually implied by the verb βιάζω.[149] Commentators on this passage, however, generally prefer a translation using a positive connotation, something along the lines of "everyone is strongly urged to enter it [the reign of God]."[150] This is a strong possibility, particularly as the use of πᾶς, "all" or "everyone," picks up on the Pharisees' resistance in Luke 15 to Jesus' extending salvation to all people.[151] In this way, such a translation fits into the ongoing debate between Jesus and the Pharisees about how best to negotiate Roman imperial domination of the Jewish people—by making the circle smaller and the requirements stricter, or by opening it up to many. But this rendering also uses βιάζω in a way that differs from its typical use. It construes the verb as a positive rather than a negative use of force and, moreover, puts it in the passive voice, rather than the middle deponent that is "nearly always" used.[152]

I propose another possible translation, while acknowledging that it is almost impossible to know which is most accurate because of the ambiguity of these verses as a whole. If both the middle deponent voice and the usual negative connotation of βιάζω as inflicting violence are retained, the following translation is commended: "And everyone is using violence against it [the reign of God]," or more loosely, "everyone is trying[153] to dominate it by force." In this case, Luke 16:16b would recognize that various groups want to make

148. Ibid., 599.

149. BDAG, 175.

150. See, e.g., Fitzmyer, *Luke X–XXIV*, 1114–16; Green, *Gospel of Luke*, 603; Hendrickx, *Third Gospel*, 213; and Johnson, *Gospel of Luke*, 251.

151. Green, *Gospel of Luke*, 603.

152. BDAG, 175.

God's reign fit with their own ideas of what it should look like, and thus end up misusing and perverting it (and the Law and Prophets), that is, doing violence to it. This argument would fit nicely with our above conclusions that the Pharisees are characterized by Luke as community members who have adopted dominant, elite-sponsored values and practices for their own gain, at the expense of fellow non-elites (those for whom the reign of God is meant to advocate). Such attitudes and actions follow a path typical of non-elite leaders who are granted a measure of power over their fellow subordinates; they then seek to maintain the system of domination because they have a vested interest in it.[154] Jesus in this passage, especially with this translation of 16:16b, is presented as trying urgently to bring such non-elite leaders and retainers back to the side of the subordinated and oppressed, and to incorporate them into his own vision of the reign of God.

The final verse of this section needs a brief note, as well. Luke 16:18 reads as an essentially random inclusion in which Jesus espouses a strict view against divorce, or more specifically divorce followed by remarriage. It is perhaps connected to the desire to bolster Jesus' claim to stringent adherence to the law in 16:17, and also a continuation of the idea that faithfulness to God should be reflected in faithfulness in other areas of one's life (here in Luke 16, including money, marriage, and care for the poor and lowly).[155] Green argues that this rigorous application of the Law to divorce also emphasizes another Lukan theme, in that it equalizes and protects women from the financial and social losses that divorce could bring them.[156] One interesting proposal is Johnson's observation that βδέλυγμα is applied not only to idolatry (of which greed is an example) as discussed above, but also to financial misdealing (Deut. 25:13-16) and a divorced man living with his former wife (Deut. 24:4).[157] Perhaps, then, the relatively unusual word βδέλυγμα was the catchphrase that stitched these ideas in 16:14-18 together.

One further observation is pertinent. Multiple divorces and remarriages were common in the Roman Empire, particularly among elites and higher-status non-elites. An Augustan epitaph lauds a deceased couple's "long marriage ended by death, not broken up by divorce" as a rare occurrence, and Pliny's letters demonstrate that most marriages were made primarily for family status

153. Reading the present tense with a conative nuance here; see Daniel B. Wallace, *Greek Grammar Beyond the Basics: An Exegetical Syntax of the New Testament* (Grand Rapids: Zondervan, 1996), 534–35.

154. Scott, *Domination*, 27n13.

155. Culpepper, "Gospel of Luke," 313–14.

156. Green, *Gospel of Luke*, 603.

157. Johnson, *Gospel of Luke*, 255.

and advancement.[158] Such unions were often used to make further alliances and enhance the status, power, wealth, and connections of each family. This practice likely would have come to mind when 16:18 was read by the Lukan audiences. It is, in some sense, another form of the conspicuous consumption on display in the parable of Lazarus and the rich man, and vigorously opposed throughout the Gospel of Luke as incompatible with participation in God's reign and its earthly Christian communities. It is certainly portrayed as a moral failing of the rich man in the African dramatization of this parable discussed earlier. He is shown kicking his fourth wife out of the house, bragging that he never stays with the same woman for longer than three years. He then tries to coerce a young Christian woman into divorcing her husband and marrying him instead, and proceeds to hire a prostitute when the housewife refuses his advances.[159] The authors of this modernization seem to have regarded cavalier treatment of marriage and personal relationships as yet another immoral luxury with which elites indulged themselves. It seems likely that members of the Lukan audience may have drawn similar conclusions from their own observation of the imperial world, perhaps especially from the perspective of higher-status (or at least wealthy) women like those who appear repeatedly in the work of Luke (for example, Luke 8:1-3; Acts 16:11-15; 17:1-4, 10-12).

CONTEXTUALITY: LAZARUS AND THE RICH MAN IN THE HELLENISTIC CHURCHES

The first two status reversal texts studied in this work, the Magnificat and the Nazareth proclamation, are inaugural texts, placed at the beginning of Jesus' life and at the beginning of his ministry, respectively. The parable of Lazarus and the rich man comes much later, toward the end of Jesus' earthly ministry. Just a few chapters later, the long Lukan travel narrative will come to an end as Jesus encounters Zacchaeus, a rich man who finally "gets it" and responds with an act of economic redistribution (19:1-10); after that Jesus will enter Jerusalem for his trial and crucifixion (19:28-44). So it is worth exploring how the depiction of status reversals and their place in the hidden transcript of resistance might have changed or evolved over the course of the Gospel narrative, and how this narrative might have impacted the Greco-Roman audiences first hearing the parable of Lazarus and the rich man.

---

158. Both referenced by Garnsey and Saller, *Roman Empire*, 133. For their larger discussion of marriage and family, see 126–47.

159. Wendland, "Mwini-Chuma," 318–19.

LAZARUS AND THE RICH MAN IN THE SWEEP OF THE LUKAN NARRATIVE

The first related text that we must discuss is also the closest in proximity: the first parable of Luke 16, often regarded as one of Jesus' most confusing. Here in verses 1–13, we find a story of yet another "certain rich man" (16:1), but the pericope actually focuses on his dishonest steward or manager (οἰκονόμος)—a fitting choice since the direct audience for the parable is Jesus' non-elite disciples. This parable provides a positive (if ambiguous) example of using wealth and possessions appropriately to secure one's future, while the parable of Lazarus and the rich man completes the picture by offering a negative or inappropriate example.[160] To summarize: the rich master receives reports that his steward was "squandering" the master's property, and therefore fires him (16:1-2). This is perhaps an example of non-elites' practical strategies to limit material appropriation by their masters, such as pilfering and skimming off the top.[161] In response to his firing, this ES4–5 level slave or freedman seeks desperately for a way to preserve his status and avoid a precipitous social fall (16:3), to the place of a poor day laborer (ES6) or even an expendable beggar (ES7). He decides to use his last moments of status and power to make friends who will support him when he loses his position, namely by using his still-intact authority to reduce greatly the massive debts owed to his master (16:4-7). In the end, the master commends the manager for his "shrewd" actions (16:8), and Jesus exhorts his hearers to "make friends for yourselves by means of dishonest wealth" in order to assure their eternal welcome (16:9). A collection of sayings about money, wealth, possessions, and their relationship to God concludes the section (16:10-13), and clarifies that the parable's commendation of shrewdness does not extend to dishonest use of one's God-given resources.

A plethora of explanations has been offered for why Jesus would use someone so obviously dishonest as an exemplar. It has been proposed, for example, that the manager was not actually dishonest at all, but instead eliminated his own commission or unlawful interest from the debts in an attempt to make amends for past injustices.[162] But why, then, is he regarded, even at the end of the parable, as dishonest (τὸν οἰκονόμον τῆς ἀδικίας; 16:8)? Luise Schottroff regards him as an unambiguously negative figure, a "cheat" who unwittingly models the Christian praxis of forgiving debts and therefore building friendship.[163] A related interpretation is that the manager's dishonesty is not what Jesus' hearers are to emulate, but rather his shrewdness and quick

---

160. Forbes, *God of Old*, 180; and Hendrickx, *Third Gospel*, 156.

161. Scott, *Domination*, 188.

162. Fitzmyer, *Luke X–XXIV*, 1098.

163. Schottroff, *Parables of Jesus*, 158–60.

thinking in a crisis (which followers of Jesus in the midst of the Roman Empire were sure to face).[164] Indeed, it is most likely that the manager is depriving his rich master of part of the profits from these loans, while at the same time gaining some goodwill with the debtors. He cleverly creates a situation where the rich lord must uphold this generosity or risk public loss of face. In that sense, the manager has pleased the debtors, set himself up nicely whether he keeps or loses his job, and given his master at least the benefit of enhanced honor to assuage the lost income.[165]

J. Albert Harrill's study of this parable in light of stock characters in ancient theater is unusual and enlightening. He reads the dishonest steward as an example of the "clever slave" who outsmarts the rich to get himself out of a sticky situation. He "impersonates authority figures, misleads about his authorization to act as an agent of others, and forms alliances with social betters," always in the end gaining pardon from his master.[166] Harrill argues, then, that the dishonest steward was such a character and would have been a familiar and humorous figure to audiences, drawing them in to prepare for the more serious story of Lazarus and the rich man.[167] He also insists, however, that there is no challenge to authority or subversion of the status quo in this outsmarting of the rich by the lowly—simply an attempt by the author of Luke to promote generous support of the poor by his rich patrons.[168] Such generous support of the truly poor, however, by its very nature would subvert the Roman social hierarchy and practices of benefaction, as we have discussed multiple times in this study.

More importantly, Harrill's "clever slave" figure is only one form of the "trickster" who is often encountered in the folk tales of subordinated peoples.[169] This folk hero, such as Brer Rabbit in North American slave traditions, constantly outwits his stronger and more powerful adversaries through guile, cunning, and cleverness. Yet stories featuring such characters could be told in public settings as "innocuous" children's tales—in short, ideal vehicles for speaking a part of the hidden transcript in the face of power.[170] The Roman

164. Forbes, *God of Old*, 159–61; Hendrickx, *Third Gospel*, 181; and Johnson, *Gospel of Luke*, 247.

165. Herzog, *Parables*, 257–58; and Bruce J. Malina and Richard L. Rohrbaugh, *Social-Science Commentary on the Synoptic Gospels*, 2nd ed. (Minneapolis: Fortress Press, 2003), 293.

166. J. Albert Harrill, *Slaves in the New Testament: Literary, Social, and Moral Dimensions* (Minneapolis: Fortress Press, 2006), 72–73.

167. Ibid., 82–83.

168. Ibid., 74, 83.

169. Scott notes the Malay mouse-deer Sang Kanchil, the spider stories of West Africa, and the Brer Rabbit tales of North American slaves, among others (*Domination*, 163).

170. Ibid., 162–64.

version was found in the cunning lead character of the *Aesop Romance*, "a small, agile trickster who can use his intelligence to wriggle out of almost any predicament," and who embodied traits seen as valuable and admirable by the non-elite.[171] The dishonest manager of Luke 16 seems, in many ways, to be such a trickster figure. As a household manager he was most likely a slave or freedperson (albeit a relatively high-ranking one), and when threatened he outwits his elite master and saves himself, with the side benefit of helping a few fellow clients along the way. Certainly the rich man who is outsmarted would not have been viewed sympathetically either, as the rich seldom are in Luke's Gospel. Schottroff notes a West African reading of this parable by Justin S. Ukpong that views the manager as a non-elite hero—someone poor and powerless who did his best to help small farmers in need.[172] A similar view is taken by the peasants of Solentiname, who regard the manager as a "clever thief" who takes the rich man's money, which was stolen from the workers in the first place, and offers it back to others.[173] As much as Harrill would deny it, stories like that of the dishonest steward flourish and are preserved among oppressed non-elites because they are meaningful and hope-giving in their resistance to domination.

Nevertheless, the dishonest steward, as portrayed in Luke, is not a non-elite moral exemplar. For one thing, the amounts of the reduced debts (one hundred jugs of olive oil, and a hundred containers of wheat; Luke 16:6-7) are huge (perhaps subjected to typical Lukan hyperbole), more suited to commercial wholesalers or merchants than small-holders or tenant farmers.[174] The steward is not helping the poorest of the poor here, nor is he, as the household manager for an evidently very wealthy master, located among the lower non-elites himself. Particularly if the manager was a slave or freedperson, he likely experienced significant status inconsistency, as can be seen in his disdain for any suggestion that he might lose status and take the lowly position of a laborer or beggar (16:3-4). Additionally, and perhaps most significantly for this Lukan context, the manager helps the debtors with the express expectation of personal gain and in order to create through his patronage *clients*, rather than friends and equals. The goal of his benefaction is to secure his own future, not to help the less fortunate. In this way, the dishonest steward is an imperfect analogy, an ambiguous role model.[175] Earlier in Luke, for example, Jesus commands

---

171. Toner, *Popular Culture*, 28–29.

172. Schottroff, *Parables of Jesus*, 162–63.

173. Cardenal, *Gospel in Solentiname*, 395.

174. Culpepper, "Gospel of Luke," 308; Green, *Gospel of Luke*, 592–93; and Herzog, *Parables*, 240–41, 249–50.

his audience to "love your enemies, do good, and lend, expecting nothing in return" (6:35). The real lesson, then, is to be like the manager, but to go even further, to use whatever status, power, or wealth one has in this world to help others, but with an eye to pleasing God and seeking eternal reward (16:9), rather than one's own personal comfort, social status, or secure economic future.

Luke has, it seems, adopted an example of the classic trickster-type folktales, which are usually focused on individual triumph, and adapted it to his own more community-oriented view through the sayings of 16:9-18 and the parable of Lazarus and the rich man (16:19-31). The clever slave folk hero pairs nicely with the theme of status reversal to emphasize the hidden transcript of resistance as a strong influence in the Third Gospel. Non-elite audience members, like the disciples who are the direct addressees within the narrative, would recognize the clever ways of the manager and feel emboldened to use such familiar, creative methods of resistance even though they might seem unethical or unorthodox, and (most importantly) to use them to benefit the community rather than themselves. The elite and their supporters, meanwhile, would overhear this story and either scoff at it (as did the Pharisees) or seriously consider the possibility that they need to make unexpected friends through wise use of their own wealth. Such an appeal continues the theme of Luke 14–15, that "table fellowship [is] an appropriate means for including such outsiders as toll collectors and sinners in the community of the lost-but-found."[176] It also looks ahead to the parable of Lazarus and the rich man, which demonstrates exactly how one should make friends with wealth and issues a strong warning of the consequences of failing to do so.[177] The two parables of Luke 16, taken together, thus offer a clear message that the role of worldly wealth in the reign of God is primarily to welcome more outsiders into the community of faith, specifically those who are usually overlooked because of their inability to reciprocate.[178]

Let us now widen our focus even more, beyond the sixteenth chapter of Luke to the rest of the Gospel. As mentioned previously, the parable of Lazarus and the rich man, with its message advocating the use of wealth to aid persons of lower status, builds on previous Lukan texts of status reversal. After the Magnificat's claim that rulers shall be thrown down, the rich sent

---

175. Green, *Gospel of Luke*, 594.

176. Ibid., 587–88; and Hendrickx, *Third Gospel*, 157.

177. Ireland, *Stewardship*, 138.

178. See Green, *Gospel of Luke*, 587: "Wealth should be used to welcome another cluster of outsiders, the poor who are incapable of reciprocating with invitations of their own or of helping to advance one's own status."

away empty, and the hungry filled with good things (Luke 1:51-53), we should hardly be surprised at the fate of Lazarus and the rich man.[179] Indeed, the parable is almost an exact embodiment of the beatitudes and woes that Jesus proclaimed in 6:20-26. Including the Nazareth proclamation (4:16-30), the Gospel of Luke narrates three explicit declarations of status reversal in the first six chapters, but then there is a gap of ten more before the story of Lazarus and the rich man in Luke 16. This observation raises the question of whether the third evangelist is perhaps "softening" his stance on status reversal as the Gospel goes on. A closer look will prove that this is not the case; the Lukan Jesus does not abandon status reversal, but does continue to nuance his approach to the theme according to the realities and complexities of everyday life in the heart of the Roman Empire.

The development of the theme of status reversal in the Lukan narrative progresses overall from the agenda of God to transform the world (Luke 1:46-55), through Jesus' divinely inspired mission and public pronouncements of reversal (4:16-30; 6:20-26), to the implicit appeal of Luke 16 (and the following chapters) to reorient both values and practice in the light of God's coming reign. The Magnificat and the Nazareth proclamation in particular lay out the ideals of the reign of God in Luke, but they do not offer practical instruction on how to carry out those ideals. The Sermon on the Plain opens with clear status reversals in blessing the poor, hungry, weeping, and shamed, while proclaiming woe for the rich, full, laughing, and honored (6:20-26). But the rest of the sermon (6:27-49) also offers some thoughts on how to carry out this vision in the present world, in a manner applicable to the lives of people from all status groups. These commands are equally radical and disrupting to the status quo no matter what one's particular place in it—loving enemies, not judging others, and offering generosity without expectation of any personal gain are countercultural to almost anyone's worldview.

In these early chapters of the narrative, Luke is making a forceful argument that God, through the work of Jesus, is on the side of justice and equality, particularly for the poor, the lowly, and those who have been oppressed and marginalized by the imperial social system. But as the Gospel narrative continues, the evangelist, having established God's particular concern for the poor and lowly, turns to practical matters of how this should be lived out—not only by the lowly who no doubt welcomed much of this message, but also by those of higher status (or those of lower status, yet loyal to the prevailing system) for whom it posed a threat. And as Luke considers the real-life implications, he must deal with the complexities that result when the norms, roles, expectations, practices, and social structures of everyday life—especially within mixed-status

---

179. Oh, "Faith and Wealth," 405.

Christian communities in the provinces of Greece and Asia Minor—are reoriented according to the reign of God.

The travel narrative (Luke 9:51—19:27), of which our focal parable is a part, demonstrates these complexities with its images of Jesus' ministry challenging existing boundaries—especially those defined in terms of social status, wealth, and power—and the consequent intensification of conflict between Jesus and both elites and their retainers. In this section of the narrative, Jesus instructs his faithful followers on discipleship, and provokes and invites those who are not yet followers to join his company even if the message he proclaims is uncomfortable and challenging.[180] Moreover, we find a change in audience. Much of the travel narrative is addressed to persons of some status who are opposing Jesus' work and teaching (for example, 10:25-37; 11:37-54; 13:14-17, 31-35; 14:1-24; 15:1-32; 16:14-31; 17:20-21; 18:18-24; 19:1-27), and this affects Luke's approach as well. If the bold declarations of status reversal found in the early chapters of the Gospel are "softened," it seems to be because Luke is trying to make a place for the nonlowly, too, to find hope in the status-inverting reign of God, despite the fact that it will diminish their own status, power, and wealth. The Gospel does not abandon status reversal in these later chapters, as the very presence of Luke 16 indicates. As Joel Green has put it, discipleship in Luke "requires reconstruction of the self within a new web of relationships, a transfer of allegiances, and the embodiment of new dispositions and sensibilities. . . . Such a 'conversion' . . . requires resocialization in the new community being formed around Jesus."[181]

The basic guidelines for this "resocialization" are established early in the travel narrative, as Luke 10:25-37 identifies the most important part of the Law and Prophets in Jesus' understanding: "You shall love the Lord your God with all your heart, and with all your soul, and with all your strength, and with all your mind; and your neighbor as yourself." Jesus commends the lawyer for this "right answer" and says, "Do this, and you will live" (10:27-28, NRSV). But the parable of the compassionate Samaritan that follows (10:29-37) adds the transformative note that this love is to be much more widely inclusive than prevailing societal hierarchies and ethnic divisions would indicate.[182] The parable of Lazarus and the rich man fleshes out both of these themes: the Law and Prophets are to be interpreted in a way that puts love of God and love of others at the forefront, irrespective of status or wealth, thereby overturning the reigning social order—or any hierarchy, really. Those who have refused to do

180. Green, *Gospel of Luke*, 395–96.
181. Ibid., 397.
182. Oh, "Faith and Wealth," 411.

so, like the rich man, are offered a chance to change, but will have to face the consequences if they fail to do so.

The travel narrative also addresses the issue of how to define honor in the reign of God (Luke 11:37-52; 12:4-12, 22-34; 14:7-24; 18:9-30)—namely, through honoring Jesus as Lord, living according to the law of love laid out in the Law and the Prophets (even to the point of loving one's *enemies* [6:27, 35]), and actively participating in God's radical transformation of the world by helping the less fortunate with no expectation of reciprocal increase in human honor.[183] The rich man in our parable claims Abraham as his father and is acknowledged as "child" (16:24-25). But these traditional ethnic markers of identity and status in Judean society are not applicable in the reign of God (cf. 3:8). Traditional patron–client or familial connections are not valued by God as they are by humans (cf. 16:15).[184] We have only to look at the surrounding chapters to discover the true "children of Abraham": a woman marginalized for years through her disability, whose healing by Jesus is protested by the local synagogue leader (13:10-17, especially verse 16); and Zacchaeus, rich like the man in our parable, who spends his wealth extravagantly not on banquets for his elite friends, but on helping the poor and making recompense for his past financial misdeeds (19:1-10, especially verse 9).[185]

The reversal of human markers of status is also found in another parable that, like that of Lazarus and the rich man, is narrated in the later part of the travel narrative, where Luke's warnings increase in intensity. The parable of the Pharisee and the tax collector (Luke 18:9-14) ends with a classic bi-polar reversal saying: "All who exalt themselves will be humbled, but all who humble themselves will be exalted" (18:14; cf. 14:11; 16:15). The pride of the Pharisee in this short tableau and his sense of superiority continue the themes of Luke 16:14-31 and deal yet another blow to conventional ideas of honor. Again Luke makes it clear that the values of the current social hierarchy are not in line with those of God's reign.

In these later chapters of Luke, then, it seems that the third evangelist is attempting a careful balancing act as he envisions and interprets status reversal in the lives of higher-status Jesus-followers and within the Lukan communities. Acceptance of the "lost" and "sinners," both rich and poor, is advocated in Luke 15, but chapter 16 follows quickly to clarify that this is not a cheap grace; rather, it is one that requires transformation and a deep responsibility to care materially

183. Gowler, "'At His Gate,'" 263.

184. Frederick W. Danker, *Luke*, 2nd ed., Proclamation Commentaries, ed. Gerhard Krodel (Philadelphia: Fortress Press, 1987), 51.

185. Hendrickx, *Third Gospel*, 241.

for *all* of one's neighbors.[186] René Krüger sees Luke as attempting to "convert" wealth in the arc of his narrative, through two steps. Luke begins with the conventional idea of wealth as divine blessing and poverty as punishment, and shows first that wealth is actually a power ranged against humankind to corrupt and isolate people from one another. Then, through the work of Jesus, wealth is transformed yet again, back into a positive force, but only when it is used to help the poor and needy and thereby offer salvation to the rich and powerful.[187] The parable of Lazarus and the rich man falls neatly into this final step of transforming readers' perspective on the true value of wealth and status. Some compromise must be made with the strict inversion of status reversal, to be sure, but in the end this teaching of the Gospel of Luke attempts a reconciliation between persons of differing status that is so difficult to achieve that many never even try.

LAZARUS AND THE RICH MAN IN THE SOCIAL WORLD OF THE LUKAN COMMUNITY

We will turn our attention in this final section to those groups of differing status who worshipped God and read Luke's Gospel together. As we have considered literary parallels to the parable of Lazarus and the rich man, its meaning in light of Scott's models of hidden resistance, and the relation of Luke 16 to the rest of the Gospel, what remains is to place this text into the real life of the Lukan communities. How might its story of a rich man's shame and a poor man's honor have resonated with diverse groups in late-first-century Hellenistic cities of the Roman Empire? Bauckham and Scott both establish that the image of status reversal—not just leveling, but also total inversion—is most at home in the texts, traditions, and folklore of the common people, such as peasants, slaves, laborers, beggars, and artisans, among others.[188] Yet as it is presented in the Gospel of Luke, narratively, the non-elites are not meant to be the primary audience for this parable. Instead, Luke presents this story of reversal and resistance to elites and retainers. But as with so much in Luke, it is meant to be overheard by all the people and groups in the recipient Christian communities. Luke 16:1-13 is aimed at the disciples (non-elites faithful to Jesus), but overheard in 16:14 by the Pharisees (retainers who support elite values). Jesus responds to their scoffing with some choice words aimed directly at this

---

186. Oh, "Faith and Wealth," 433–34.

187. René Krüger, "Conversion of the Pocketbook: The Economic Project of Luke's Gospel," in *God's Economy: Biblical Studies from Latin America*, ed. Ross Kinsler and Gloria Kinsler (Maryknoll, NY: Orbis, 2005), 196.

188. Bauckham, "Rich Man and Lazarus," 233; and Scott, *Domination*, 80–81, 168.

group caught in the middle (16:14-18), and finishes with a parable that places a rich man and his wealthy family and friends at the center of the action (16:19-31). We shall try to unravel the strands of how such different groups might have reacted to this Gospel chapter.

The tableau envisaged by the first lines of the parable, a shockingly poor man lying in the alley next to the luxurious estate of an elite rich man (Luke 16:19-21), would have been familiar to anyone living in the Greco-Roman world, no matter his or her status. Such a contrast "would have been commonplace within the walls of every preindustrial city."[189] The speaking of the parable would have drawn attention to this sight and how each person listening played a role in the imperial culture and economy that created people like Lazarus, and people like the rich man. William Herzog offers an imaginative but informed possible scenario for the way in which Lazarus might have ended up in the street, starving and covered in sores. He may have been a small farmer who got deep into debt, or a younger son of a peasant or artisan family; either way there was no land for him, and his only choice was to try to make it in the city as a day laborer. Unfortunately, when he fell sick, that already-unstable source of income dried up completely, leading to a downward spiral of sickness and poverty, until he became the sad figure described in Luke 16:20-21.[190]

Such a story was likely common in the first-century cities of the Roman Empire, and perhaps resembled the story of some members of the Lukan churches. Downward mobility was much more common than status enhancement in agrarian societies, and was an ever-present danger particularly for non-elites living at or near the subsistence level.[191] Other members of differing socioeconomic status played their own roles in the story proposed by Herzog. An artisan or peasant might have been the oldest son who did inherit the land or workshop rather than his brothers. The wealthy woman in whose home a Christian gathering met might pay for her home and the meal served to her Christian group with income from that repossessed farm. A freedperson in the congregation may have chosen which laborers to hire for the day, or driven the family off their land when they could not pay their debts, on behalf of his

---

189. Malina and Rohrbaugh, *Social-Science Commentary*, 295.

190. Herzog, *Parables*, 119.

191. Lenski, *Power and Privilege*, 289–91. See, however, Valerie Hope, "Status and Identity in the Roman World," in *Experiencing Rome: Culture, Identity, and Power in the Roman Empire*, ed. Janet Huskinson (London: Routledge, 2000), 145–46. She makes the argument that status and membership in the Roman orders was rarely revoked, nor was Roman citizenship. This level of status security, though, seems more relevant to those of higher status than to provincial non-elites.

master and patron. And every member of the community would have walked by multiple beggars like Lazarus in the course of their daily routines. The elite-dominated system of appropriation and exploitation created this tableau, but all participated in it in some way.[192] The parable urges each group to particular action.

One of the more interesting aspects of this parable, as noted above, is that it is a standard status reversal text, part of the hidden transcript, but one that is directed primarily at the elites whom it would seek to depose. Such a promise of afterlife reversal (rather than present) could be used positively, to comfort and encourage the poor, or negatively, to entice them into submission with the hope that their suffering would be recompensed after death—similar to the way that the fables of Aesop, discussed in the first section of this chapter, advocated acceptance of one's given (and proper) role in life. Instead, the message in Luke 16 is almost the opposite. Its exhortation to the rich to care for the poor and oppressed "emphasizes the seriousness of the present. What really matters is what we do right now."[193] The onus of responsibility is placed on the rich and elite in this text, and it is difficult to imagine those members of the Lukan communities missing this point, whether they liked it or not. Lazarus is not pious or moral, but is saved. The rich man plays an active role in the parable as in life, as money gave the elite more control and choice in their lives, yet finds nothing but condemnation and a command (too late to heed) to listen to God's word through Moses and the prophets. He throws banquets to enhance his honor with other elites as he was expected to do; he converses and barters with Abraham; and he maintains his elite worldview even after death. His request that his brothers receive fair warning of the torture that awaits them, along with others who act like typical elites, could be seen as an example of his care for others. But more likely, it is another manifestation of the elite mindset, that the rich man is worried first and foremost about his own rich family and seeks special, privileged knowledge for them.[194]

Elites hearing this story were most likely to identify with the rich man and even more so with his still-living brothers.[195] Herman Hendrickx says of this subset of the audience, "According to Abraham, they have all the knowledge needed, but they lack the wanting to act: nobody or nothing is going to be able to persuade them; 'they will not listen.'"[196] Certainly it would have been

192. Gowler, "'At His Gate,'" 264.

193. Hendrickx, *Third Gospel*, 245–46.

194. Ibid., 244; Herzog, *Parables*, 124; and Malina and Rohrbaugh, *Social-Science Commentary*, 295.

195. Culpepper, "Gospel of Luke," 319; and Oh, "Faith and Wealth," 326–27.

196. Hendrickx, *Third Gospel*, 243.

extremely difficult for these wealthier Jesus-followers to give up the trappings of status to which they had been accustomed for most of their lives. Like the rich man after death, they likely struggled with understanding the change in their circumstances in the alternative Christian communities that were to reflect God's view of status and value. We can easily imagine the elite taking offense at how they were viewed and treated in the parable and in the early house churches, but there was also perhaps guilt and a desire to change, particularly among those who had already found meaning in Jesus' life and the reign of God he proclaimed. The parable of Lazarus and the rich man would have provided a literary prompt for them to repent by using their wealth to secure honor not for themselves, but for the poor and others who could not reciprocate.[197]

This redefinition of honor posed a challenge to the system of benefaction, charity, and almsgiving that was already in place. Elites in the cities of Asia Minor and Greece engaged in this practice regularly and enthusiastically, but it was designed to maintain the status of the benefactors rather than transform the lives of its recipients—yet another way to gain honor, create clients, and use wealth to enhance one's status and power even further.[198] The parable of Lazarus and the rich man, along with the banquet parables of Luke 14 and Jesus' sermon in Luke 6, urges that life-changing charity be given to the lowliest and most desperate ES7 individuals, like Lazarus, who could never enhance the giver's status in any way. This is, again, a stark challenge and a harsh message for elite community members, portrayed through a hidden-transcript critique of their entire socioeconomic system. Yet that is the message that Luke conveyed in his Gospel through this parable of status reversal.

While the parable itself deals with the fate of a rich man and a poor man, the Gospel narrative applies it also to Pharisees who have been accused of being "lovers of money" (Luke 16:14-18). I suggested above that the label "money lovers" indicates that these retainers, though non-elite, have adopted elite values as their own and have thus misplaced their loyalties, in Luke's opinion. Jesus' struggle to convince the Pharisees to participate in God's reign was likely mirrored in the struggle of early Christian converts or potential converts who had ES4–5 level wealth as prosperous artisans or merchants, Roman soldiers, or high-ranking slaves and freedpersons with powerful patrons. The guilds and burial associations of these groups, for example, mimicked the larger social hierarchy and usually sought to increase their members' honor and status, rather than their actual material security.[199] The parable of Lazarus and the rich

197. Lehtipuu, *Afterlife Imagery*, 231.

198. See Anthony D. Macro, "The Cities of Asia Minor under the Roman Imperium," in *ANRW* 2.7.2, ed. Hildegard Temporini and Wolfgang Haase (Berlin: Walter de Gruyter, 1980), 684–85.

man, together with the whole of chapter 16, would pose a challenge to these assumptions, as it reveals the true fate of the elites in whom these retainers were putting their trust. Cheryl Townsend Gilkes sums up the situation in this way: "The story itself stands as a challenge to all who are, or wish to be, rich. What happens when people are confronted with a human need and possess the power to help?—they become the targets of divine judgment."[200] The most interesting and important aspect of Gilkes's reading is the inclusion of those who "wish to be" rich along with those who actually are. Such a desire, according to the Lukan status reversals, reflects a kind of idolatry and abomination, expressed in the belief that one must seek status and wealth at the expense of helping other people. Luke 16 does not exempt anyone from participating in the life-giving work of God's alternative community, and our parable argues that simply ignoring social and economic inequalities in the world and colluding with those who have created them could put one on the wrong side of the status reversals.

Finally, we must consider the possible reactions of lower-status, non-elite community members upon hearing the parable of Lazarus and the rich man, which after all seems to be good news for them. Certainly we could expect them to feel vindication and even delight at the harsh fate of the rich man, but perhaps also discouragement because the reversal of circumstance was apparently being put off until the next world. This paradox bears some similarity to the celebration of death in the Roman arena by Christian martyrs in the first few centuries CE. The fact that they welcomed death as a gateway to paradise seemed ridiculous to many at the time, but it also offered its own challenge to the Roman social hierarchy; when they should have been dreading the shameful death that Rome assigned them, they were instead welcoming it as God's will, not that of the emperor.[201] In such a context, martyrdom can be regarded as an act of resistance, but it still comes at the cost of death—an ambiguous blessing at best. Might there have been some desire on the part of non-elite followers of Jesus for retribution this side of the grave, and was less than enthusiastic if they perceived that Luke was offering this tale as a warning to the rich, rather than as a pure condemnation?

Outi Lehtipuu raises an intriguing question in her monograph on the afterlife imagery of this parable. She maintains that Luke, unlike *1 Enoch* and other reversal texts of the time, always allows a slim possibility for the wealthy

199. Ramsay MacMullen, *Roman Social Relations: 50 B.C. to A.D. 284* (New Haven: Yale University Press, 1974), 76–77.

200. Gilkes, "Resurrection," 13.

201. Christopher Kelly, *The Roman Empire: A Very Short Introduction* (Oxford: Oxford University Press, 2006), 85–86; and Toner, *Popular Culture*, 175.

to repent and be saved even in the harshest of warnings. Commenting on Abraham's statement in Hades that the chasm separating Lazarus from the rich man is in place so that even "those who want to go over" from Abraham's bosom to the place of torment are not able to (Luke 16:26), she wonders if this verse implies that Lazarus (or others with him in Abraham's company) would have been willing to help if possible.[202] This observation by Lehtipuu raises other pertinent questions. Would Lazarus have wanted to help the rich man if Abraham had allowed it? Would he have felt compassion because of his own sufferings, or a reluctant sense of duty, or simply satisfaction because justice had been done and the rich man had gotten what he deserved? The same questions, I imagine, might have run through the minds of non-elite hearers of this parable in the first century as well. Even the beneficiaries of status reversal would likely have appreciated the complexity of the situation and experienced mixed feelings about it.

Ivoni Richter Reimer offers a suggestive scenario that effectively captures this experience, a retelling of the story of Zacchaeus's transformation (Luke 19:1-10) from the perspective of a poor woman from Jericho, one of many who had suffered injustice at Zacchaeus's hands for years.[203] Richter Reimer describes the initial anger of this woman, and her peers, that Jesus chose to minister first to "that thief" Zacchaeus, rather than to their own more pressing needs that were, after all, caused by the Romans and their local allies for whom Zacchaeus worked: "We women felt frustrated, deceived. Was that the Jesus who came to liberate oppressed, marginalized people? And now he's going into the house of such an oppressor?"[204] But when the woman and her neighbors heard Zacchaeus's proclamation that he was planning to give half of his wealth to the poor and would pay back any whom he had defrauded four times over, their anger turned to astonishment and disbelieving joy. Richter Reimer envisions their conflicting emotions thus:

> We couldn't believe it! Could it be that this was why Jesus had to go into the house of Zacchaeus? So that Zacchaeus, after the arrival of Jesus and Jesus' acceptance of him, would analyze his life and change his behavior? . . . We realized that the salvation that took place in the house of Zacchaeus would have consequences in our concrete, daily life as well. The conversion, redemption, and liberation of Zacchaeus

202. Lehtipuu, *Afterlife Imagery*, 180–81.

203. Ivoni Richter Reimer, "The Forgiveness of Debts in Matthew and Luke: For an Economy without Exclusions," in Kinsler and Kinsler, *God's Economy*, 164–67.

204. Ibid., 165.

did not take place only spiritually, but rather it had socioeconomic repercussions in the lives of impoverished children, women, and men, because he was the chief of the tax collectors. . . . Jesus, entering the house of Zacchaeus, did not do it to legitimize the corrupt practice of a sinner, but to make him just through the experience of grace. And we rejoiced, because we could feel the lifting of the weight of corruption and, as a result, we could begin to organize our lives in a form that was more worthy and just.[205]

Although obviously an imagined scenario, this retelling conveys some of the struggles that non-elite Christians would have had with Luke's nuanced treatment of status reversal and social change. Even the poor who were lifted up were challenged to change in some ways.

The most dangerous aspect of any status reversal imagery, but particularly in Luke where it is so carefully nuanced, is the temptation to become enamored or proud of one's place in any hierarchy, whether humanly constructed or divine. The result is a degree of instability in the Lukan theme of status reversal. In the stories, texts, songs, and parables that proclaim this inversion or leveling, outsiders become insiders in a positive upward reversal, but immediately they are in danger of getting too comfortable as insiders, and again becoming outsiders, if they stop relying on God and living out the grace of their reversed position.[206] In truth, no one of any status level should allow him- or herself to feel entitled or superior based on position. In the true view of things, that defined by the reign of God, neither the situation of Lazarus nor the situation of the rich man is a good option for anyone to live out his or her life. As Felipe, one of the peasants of Solentiname, observes:

What I think is that neither the rich nor the poor ought to suffer the fate of those two guys in the Gospel. The rich man damned for having squandered selfishly, the poor man screwed all his life even though afterwards he's saved. Which means there shouldn't be rich or poor, nobody would be screwed in this life, nobody should be damned in the next life. All people ought to share the riches in this life and share the glory in the next one.[207]

205. Ibid., 165–66.

206. Forbes, *God of Old*, 247.

207. Cardenal, *Gospel in Solentiname*, 422.

CONCLUSION

In this chapter we have studied the parable of Lazarus and the rich man as a text of status reversal that resists the dominant values of Roman imperial society and how it defined wealth, status, and human worth. The standards of the reign of God, according to the Gospel of Luke, are such that their true application to daily life should critique and reform all social systems and those living at all levels of earthly hierarchies.[208] The parable of Lazarus and the rich man departs from other tales of reversal in Luke's cultural milieu, in that it bases the reversal on social justice and inequality much more than it does on piety. Its reversals illustrate the gross injustice of such a system and the responsibility of all to change it. In the words of Herman Hendrickx,

> Luke 16:19-31 is not simply a story about the fates of a rich man and a poor man. It is much more. It depicts the oppressive structures of society in Jesus'—and Luke's and our—time that allow a person to live in utter poverty. . . . The story points out that God holds the rich responsible for their lifestyles and that their response to the poor has eternal consequences.[209]

In so doing, the parable continues the lengthy and complex process of discerning how to enact the realities of God's reign in the midst of the world and responding to its demands, addressing the need for status reversal in the lives of all members of the Lukan communities.

In Luke 16:19-31, Jesus tells a tale that embodies the blessedness of the poor and hungry and the woefulness of the rich and sated—a graphic personification of earlier declarations of reversal, such as the Magnificat (1:46-55), the beatitudes and woes (6:20-26), and the Nazareth proclamation (4:16-30). But instead of telling this tale only to the poor, for whom this hope for inversion was familiar, the Gospel of Luke addresses the parable's message to the elites and their retainers—"a challenge to all who are, or wish to be, rich," as Gilkes puts it.[210] In this way, this status-reversal pericope provides an important counterbalance to the other two passages on which we have focused. The Magnificat, voiced by the peasant girl Mary, introduced the unexpected theme of status reversal with almost martial language at the beginning of Luke's Gospel. Then Jesus, at the beginning of his earthly ministry, picked up the theme, but carefully nuanced it in a way that challenged the non-elite (usual)

208. Gowler, "'At His Gate,'" 265.
209. Hendrickx, *Third Gospel*, 245.
210. Gilkes, "Resurrection," 13.

beneficiaries of status reversal, perhaps even more than the elites who are normally threatened by such texts. Then finally, in the parable of Lazarus and the rich man, Luke directs the message of status reversal back upon the rich and elite, in an urgent warning to change now before their chance at reform and voluntary reversal is gone. As this theme develops throughout the Gospel, it campaigns for a new social order that leaves no person or group unchanged or unchallenged.

6

Conclusion

We have now considered all three of our chosen status-reversal texts in some detail, specifically through the interrelated spheres of intertextuality, sociological analysis, and contextual interplay. This exploration has proven fruitful on many levels, but most especially it has revealed clear evidence of resistance to the imperial status quo in the Gospel of Luke. The values and practices of the reign of God, as envisioned and proclaimed by the Lukan Jesus, are at odds with the values and practices of the Roman Empire, and this conflict is part of the imperial negotiation tactics of the third evangelist and his earliest reading communities. This concluding chapter will summarize the arguments and findings of the project, spell out its contributions to the scholarly conversation about status reversal and imperial negotiation in the work of Luke, and identify potential areas for further study on this and related topics.

CONCLUSIONS AND CONTRIBUTIONS

The introduction and first chapter oriented us to status reversal texts in the Gospel of Luke, and to the relevant research in prior scholarship. In order to build on the recent recognition that the perspective of Luke-Acts on the Roman Empire is more nuanced and complex than previously assumed, I proposed a socio-rhetorical study of three prominent status reversal texts that are unique to the Third Gospel. Status reversal is a major theme in Luke, with significant ramifications for the question of imperial negotiation. Central to this project's task of bringing status reversal and imperial negotiation into conversation with each other has been the identification by James C. Scott of status-reversal imagery as part of subordinated groups' "hidden transcript of resistance." Through this connection, my work in this project argues that the prevalence of reversal texts in Luke's Gospel is yet another indicator of its multivalent relationship with the Roman Empire, particularly of its oft-ignored subversive aspects. Earlier perspectives on this topic most often maintained a view of Luke as political apology, either to Rome for the church,[1] or to the church for the empire.[2] Recent studies, however, have expanded and nuanced this approach to incorporate the whole of the Lukan text and the many methods of imperial negotiation at work within it,[3] and this project continues such work.

Chapter 1 examined in much more detail the relevant sociological and anthropological models of Scott, Gerhard Lenski, and John H. Kautsky; the specific evidence for the heuristic power of these models in describing and explaining important features of the Roman world; and the use of such models (that of Scott in particular) in Gospel studies thus far. This survey chapter demonstrated the great potential that Scott's work holds for enhancing our understanding of the prevailing attitude toward Rome of both the author and the audiences of the Gospel of Luke.

Chapter 2 completed the foundational material of this project with an in-depth description of the sociocultural and historical milieu of the earliest audiences of Luke's Gospel. Although the exact location of Luke and his Christian communities has proven difficult to pinpoint with any certainty,[4] even the Gospel's general setting in Greek-speaking provinces controlled by the Roman Empire (the topic of the first half of chapter 2) offers insight into the ways in which the work of the third evangelist might have been heard and interpreted in the late first century. Status competition was an ever-present facet of daily life in the Roman Empire, and ambivalence toward imperial

---

1. Henry J. Cadbury, *The Making of Luke-Acts*, 2nd ed. (Peabody, MA: Hendrickson, 1999), 308–16.

2. Paul W. Walaskay, *"And So We Came to Rome": The Political Perspective of St. Luke*, SNTSMS 49 (Cambridge: Cambridge University Press, 1983). See also Philip Francis Esler, *Community and Gospel in Luke-Acts: The Social and Political Motivations of Lucan Theology*, SNTSMS 57 (Cambridge: Cambridge University Press, 1987), who argues that Luke's Gospel sought to show Roman Christians how they could maintain their position in Roman administration and their faith in Jesus.

3. E.g., David Rhoads, David Esterline, and Jae Won Lee, eds., *Luke-Acts and Empire: Essays in Honor of Robert L. Brawley*, PTMS (Eugene, OR: Wipf & Stock, 2011); C. Kavin Rowe, *World Upside Down: Reading Acts in the Graeco-Roman Age* (Oxford: Oxford University Press, 2009); Rowe, "Luke-Acts and the Imperial Cult: A Way Through the Conundrum?" *JSNT* 27 (2005): 279–300; Gary Gilbert, "Luke-Acts and Negotiation of Authority and Identity in the Roman World," in *The Multivalence of Biblical Texts and Theological Meanings*, ed. Christine Helmer and Charlene T. Higbe, SBLSymS (Atlanta: Society of Biblical Literature, 2006), 83–104; Gilbert, "Roman Propaganda and Christian Identity in the Worldview of Luke-Acts," in *Contextualizing Acts: Lukan Narrative and Greco-Roman Discourse*, ed. Todd Penner and Caroline Vander Stichele, SBLSymS (Atlanta: Society of Biblical Literature, 2003), 233–56; and Steve Walton, "The State They Were In: Luke's View of the Roman Empire," in *Rome in the Bible and the Early Church*, ed. Peter Oakes (Carlisle: Paternoster, 2002), 1–41.

4. See, e.g., Luke Timothy Johnson, "On Finding the Lukan Community: A Cautious Cautionary Essay," in *SBLSP* 1979, vol. 1, ed. Paul J. Achtemeier (Missoula, MT: Scholars, 1979), 87–100.

domination and Roman superiority characterized the attitude of the Greek East in particular. The second part of the chapter focused more closely on the Lukan communities themselves, specifically the likely diversity of status, occupation, ethnicity, and wealth among their members. I concluded that the earliest audiences of the Third Gospel probably included people from various areas of Roman provincial life, from retainers and maybe a few lower elites, through artisans and merchants, to the lowliest day laborers, beggars, and expendables. Thus it becomes necessary to consider how the status reversal texts addressed and affected not just one of these groups, but all of them individually and, even more significantly, as an interdependent community of Jesus-followers.

With the book's methods, models, and context properly introduced, chapters 3–5 proceeded to analyze the Lukan pericopes themselves. Chapter 3 explored one of the first status reversal texts presented in the Gospel, the Magnificat (Luke 1:46-55). As sung by a pregnant Mary, this poem is a strong opening declaration that God will radically alter the prevailing order and values of this world. It hints, too, that not only will the status quo be changed, but the usual means for achieving that social and spiritual change will also undergo transformation. The intertextual comparison of the Magnificat and other songs of victory and reversal from the Hebrew Bible, Apocrypha, Pseudepigrapha, and Greco-Roman literature revealed that the Lukan text moves a few steps—but only a few—away from the military battles and harsh downward reversals celebrated in most of the parallel songs. The lens of Scott's hidden resistance established the Magnificat even more firmly as a text that publicly questions the status quo in order to ignite hope for change among non-elite hearers, yet not so explicitly as to invite retaliation from the elites in control of the situation. The Magnificat represents Luke's opening argument, developed further in the rest of the Gospel, for the coming reign of God that will turn upside down the world of elite and non-elite alike. Such a song, sung together in socially diverse Christian communities and in praise of a king and savior who willingly died a traitor's death, would have made a powerful statement about the imperial world.

Chapter 4 of this study explored another major proclamation of status reversal, specifically in the opening act of Jesus' public ministry, set in the Nazareth synagogue (Luke 4:16-30). In many ways, this event mirrors the Magnificat's reversals as introduced before Jesus' birth, but it also departs from them in significant respects. For example, the reversals in the Nazareth proclamation, carefully chosen from the Hebrew Bible, are all upward reversals in favor of the afflicted—including a foreign elite (4:27) who is helped by the

God of Israel, along with the more usual beneficiaries: the poor, oppressed, captive, and widowed (4:18-19, 25-26). This surprising twist on the conventional hidden transcript of resistance supports the major conclusion of chapter 4, namely that the Lukan Jesus critiqued the imperial status quo and its unjust domination of non-elites, but also sought to disrupt social divisions and prejudices among the subordinate groups themselves. Luke takes this critique even to the point of advocating for the inclusion of foreigners and repentant elites within the reign of God and its representative Christian communities on earth. Coupled with its intertextual connections with the Year of Jubilee, this pericope reveals a tendency toward social leveling rather than total inversion in its proclamation of status reversal. Thus chapter 4 demonstrates how carefully nuanced was the Lukan approach to imperial negotiation, in its attempt to find a balance between resistance and survival in the Roman Empire, particularly as exhibited by a willingness to challenge the non-elite, too, to make reforms.

The final status reversal text, studied in chapter 5, is the parable of Lazarus and the rich man (Luke 16:19-31), situated in Luke's narrative toward the end of Jesus' ministry. As in his opening proclamation at Nazareth, this later teaching of the Lukan Jesus centers around status reversal between the rich and well fed and the poor and hungry (cf. 1:52-53; 4:18-19; 6:20-21, 24-25). The intertextual section of this chapter revealed that the parable of Lazarus and the rich man is unique among contemporaneous stories of a similar afterlife reversal, in that it explicitly attributes the reversal to the characters' socioeconomic status rather than their morality or piety (16:25). But even while highlighting the basic injustice of the Roman social hierarchy, the third evangelist reaches out to elites and retainers with a harsh warning *and* an urgent call to repent and to transform their wealth and power by using them to provide honor and material comfort to others, rather than to increase their own status. Thus even the stark inversion of the parable functions rhetorically to offer a glimmer of hope for the repentance of its Lukan audience (if not to the parable characters; see 16:27-31). It also, implicitly in Luke 16 and explicitly in conversation with the rest of the Gospel (e.g., 4:16-30 as discussed in chapter 4), continues to exhort the non-elite to accept such gifts and their elite benefactors not as enemies, but as fellow participants in the dawning reign of God. The final section of this chapter explored the possible reactions of elite, retainer, and non-elite readers, and confirmed once again that resistance to the status quo, as proclaimed in the Gospel of Luke, issues challenges to Jesus-followers from all levels of social status.

Overall, the results of the above study of the Magnificat, the Nazareth proclamation, and the parable of Lazarus and the rich man support the argument that Luke had a complex and multifaceted relationship with the Roman Empire. It was neither entirely resistant nor entirely complicit and conciliatory, but rather accepting (for now) of imperial dominance, while also determined to proclaim and enact the radically different values and practices of God's reign in the midst of the opposing Roman status quo.[5] I have focused in this study on the subversive or resistant elements of Luke's Gospel, specifically the status reversals, because they are more often downplayed in favor of the aspects that seem conciliatory. Close attention to such resistance texts, however, particularly in light of their predominance in the traditions and history of subordinated groups, demonstrates that Luke and his audiences were well aware and presumably supportive of the resistant overtones of this "world-upside-down" imagery.

Scott's study of the subtle resistance of oppressed non-elite groups to their domination, and, in particular, the role of status reversals in such resistance, played an important role in the above contributions. I have applied Scott's models to the Gospel of Luke more systematically and more extensively than previous studies. This task has proven illuminating for Luke, which has so often been regarded as the most "pro-Roman" of the canonical Gospels. This is not to say that Scott's work proves that Luke is *unambiguously* against the Roman Empire; imperial negotiation of Rome or any other dominating system is seldom that clear-cut. But it has helped us a great deal in revealing the nuances of the imperial negotiation techniques that would have been considered by the earliest communities reading the Gospel of Luke. Of particular importance is the conclusion, borne out through the sociological analysis of all three focal texts, that Luke's nuancing of hidden resistance and status reversals involved challenges and exhortations not only for elites and other beneficiaries of the imperial system, but also for retainers and non-elites who had their own hierarchies and values that were not entirely in line with Luke's envisioning of the reign of God. This discovery may contribute important nuance to the changing conversation in Lukan studies: it is not an "either-or" question of whether Luke is conciliatory or resistant to Rome, but must, instead, become a "both-and" exploration of the complexities of Lukan imperial negotiation.

Suggestions for Further Study

The results of this study of three Lukan texts featuring status reversal have answered some questions about the role of such texts in the Gospel of Luke

---

5. Cf. Rowe, *World Upside Down*, 149–51. See also Gilbert, "Luke-Acts and Negotiation," 104; Rowe, "Luke-Acts," 298; and Walton, "State," 33–35.

and in shaping its audiences' relationships with one another and with their Roman context. But it has also, inevitably, raised additional questions that are suggestive for future projects. First, there are many other status-reversal texts in Luke that could be profitably examined using the various lenses employed in this book, particularly the lens of sociological analysis using Scott's work of differentiating modes of resistance to the status quo on the part of subordinated groups. This is not an exhaustive list by any means, but prime pericopes for such a study include the beatitudes and woes in Luke's Sermon on the Plain (6:20-26); the anointing of Jesus at the house of Simon the Pharisee (7:36-50); Jesus' teachings on meal practices, honor seeking, benefaction, and hospitality at the Pharisee's banquet (14:1-24); and the parable of the Pharisee and the tax collector (18:9-14).[6] In light of the discussion (in chapter 5) of the parable of Lazarus and the rich man as told to scoffing Pharisees, the setting of two of these additional reversal texts in scenes of meal fellowship between Jesus and a Pharisee is particularly intriguing. Study of these pericopes might further strengthen the argument that the author of Luke was seeking to persuade elites and retainers among his audiences, rather than simply to condemn them. Future work might also consider the development of the theme of status reversal, both as leveling and as total inversion, in the book of Acts.

There is also a need for studies that address the sociological issues of hidden resistance and imperial negotiation in the Gospel of Luke beyond the status reversal texts. This work would fall into two main areas, the first being consideration of Luke's nonresistant tactics of imperial negotiation, such as mimicry and conciliation, alongside the subversive ones represented in this project, for there are clearly treatments of Rome in Luke-Acts that seem conciliatory or placating. For example, Roman military officers such as Cornelius (Acts 10–11), the Capernaum centurion (Luke 7:1-10), and the centurion at the crucifixion (Luke 23:44-47) are portrayed as well-disposed toward Judaism and responsive to the person or message of (or about) Jesus. Likewise, comparisons of the Synoptic passion accounts show that Luke has emphasized the role of the Jerusalem authorities in Jesus' trial and crucifixion over that of Pilate and the Romans, and made the ultimate responsibility as ambiguous as possible by using an unspecified "they" throughout much of the crucifixion account (Luke 23:1-5, 13-43).

---

6. A brief treatment of all these texts as reversal imagery can be found in John O. York, *The Last Shall Be First: The Rhetoric of Reversal in Luke*, JSNTSup 46 (Sheffield: Sheffield Academic Press, 1991), 56–62, 74–75, 119–26, 133–45. Many of the other pericopes discussed in York's broad survey would also be profitable objects of study.

Granted, these are not wholly positive depictions of the Roman Empire; Luke's portrait of Pilate as one swayed by the crowd to condemn an innocent man to death (23:13-25) is not complimentary of his strength as a Roman administrator (cf. 13:1), nor is his depiction of later procurators Felix and Festus as involved in bribes and favors (Acts 24:24-27; 25:9). It could also be argued that there was obviously something wrong with the system if even those heavily invested in enforcing Roman rule, such as centurions, were attracted to this new movement of Jesus-followers. Detailed discussion of these seemingly conciliatory pericopes was beyond the scope of this project, but they certainly deserve focused attention in future studies in order to elucidate the full complement of imperial tactics used in the Gospel of Luke—resistant, conciliatory, and everything in between.

The second area of Lukan studies that would profit from further examination in light of imperial sociological models, particularly that of Scott, is the exploration of other hidden resistance techniques (beside status reversal) that are evident in Luke-Acts. Jesus, for example, repeatedly acts as a trickster-hero in dealing with the local elites of Jerusalem. In the final few days before his crucifixion, he employs multiple hidden transcript techniques: when the scribes try to trap him into revealing his resistance to Roman domination, he counters by trapping them into either revealing their own agenda or losing face by not answering (Luke 20:1-8); he tells a parable against the Jerusalem elite that is fraught with double meaning (20:9-19); he subtly resists Rome's idolatrous domination of Israel (20:20-26);[7] and he continues his proclamation of disturbing status reversals by praising the miniscule gift of a penniless widow and in the process gives a backhanded rebuke to the leaders, specifically the scribes, who "devour the homes" of such widows (20:45—21:4).[8]

We might take, as one more example of hidden resistance in Luke, the intriguing and uniquely Lukan parable about a widow and an unjust judge (Luke 18:1-8). The very expression κριτὴς τῆς ἀδικίας (18:6)—a judge who does not know justice—has a certain irony to it, and renders an indictment of a political system that places those who do not know their job in positions of

---

7. For a reading of the Markan parallel to this passage, using Scott's hidden resistance model, see William R. Herzog, "Onstage and Offstage with Jesus of Nazareth: Public Transcripts, Hidden Transcripts, and Gospel Texts," in *Hidden Transcripts and the Arts of Resistance: Applying the Work of James C. Scott to Jesus and Paul*, ed. Richard A. Horsley, SemeiaSt (Atlanta: Society of Biblical Literature, 2004), 52–59.

8. See Blake R. Grangaard, *Conflict and Authority in Luke 19:47 to 21:4*, Studies in Biblical Literature 8, ed. Hemchand Gossai (New York: Peter Lang, 1999), 65–173, for an extensive treatment of this segment of Luke.

power. This parable also picks up another theme of hidden resistance, that of God and Jesus as the true benefactors, the ones who truly provide what earthly rulers only claim to provide.[9] According to the public transcript, the dominants rule mainly on behalf of and for the benefit of their subordinates.[10] This often involves provision of safety, security, productive work, food, shelter, and other basic survival necessities.[11]

The Lukan Jesus, however, asserts that the true provider of these things is not the elites, especially considering that they do not share their wealth with the peasantry and the poor (12:13-21; 18:18-25). It is instead God who fulfills the public transcript claims upon the elite by providing food, clothing, and other needs (12:22-31), and then goes beyond it: God is compared to a master who will not only eat with but even serve his faithful servants (12:37), and Jesus exhorts a questioning ruler to emulate God in giving all that he possesses so as to provide for the poor (18:22). Thus it becomes obvious, even from the two brief examples given here, that there is much potential work still to do in the study of Luke-Acts and the early Christian imperial negotiation techniques revealed in these two books.

Final Thoughts

At the end of his book *The Roman Empire and the New Testament: An Essential Guide*, Warren Carter observes that discussions of imperial negotiation in the late-first century have significant contemporary applications that are sometimes overlooked. In the modern world, the United States, with its broad reach of global power, has aptly been described as an "empire," as have been national and multinational corporations that are deemed "too big to fail." In light of this, Carter raises the question, "How might Christians—whether they live at the center of the world's most powerful empire ever, or who know the impact, reach and power of such empires—engage these realities?"[12] In modern-day communities of faith, a self-understanding of believers as participants of varying social status in the imperial systems of today's world makes the tactics of imperial negotiation employed by Luke and the other New Testament authors much more relevant than they might otherwise seem. As well as being part of

9. Cf. the myth of the Russian Deliverer-Czar in James C. Scott, *Domination and the Arts of Resistance: Hidden Transcripts* (New Haven: Yale University Press, 1990), 98.

10. Ibid., 18.

11. John H. Kautsky, *The Politics of Aristocratic Empires* (Chapel Hill: University of North Carolina Press, 1982), 111.

12. Warren Carter, *The Roman Empire and the New Testament: An Essential Guide* (Nashville: Abingdon, 2006), 137.

our Christian heritage, they are also examples that people of faith can continue to reflect upon and learn from.

The conclusions reached in the course of this study about the Gospel of Luke should encourage churches to consider their relationship with the values of the dominant culture today, specifically where those values conflict with the values and practices that mark God's reign. In North America, many church communities are composed of middle- and upper-class members with more status and wealth than many of our fellow citizens, and *much* more than the great majority of people around the world. In Luke's vision of the reign of God, it is our responsibility to dedicate these resources to status reversal and improving the lives of others. It is scary to think of ourselves on the receiving end of a downward reversal like that faced by the rich man in Luke 16:19-31, and it is easy to argue that we do not live any more extravagantly than our peers, that we are actually modest by the standards of today's culture. But the first-century lower elites, retainers, and prosperous non-elites most likely would have felt the same; they, too, lived reasonably within their culture's norms. The status reversals of Luke remind us that the in-breaking of God's empire into the empire of this world should compel us to be different from today's systems of power and domination—not only in individual morality (a prominent and sometimes exclusive emphasis in many Christian communities), but also in social and economic practices. Finding myself at the end of a book such as this, I find it nearly impossible to ignore the central importance that the biblical texts assign to such holistic and communal transformation.

This study of Luke's imperial negotiation techniques, particularly those that seem to originate from subordinated groups and resist or question the status quo, can also make us more aware of the times and ways in which we are on the giving and receiving ends of prejudice and oppression. The Lukan reversals remind us to listen carefully to those who have a different experience in our own stratified societies, whether because of race, socioeconomic status, or other identity markers, and to examine the boundaries that Jesus' vision in the Gospel of Luke would call us to cross and break down. How to emerge fully from oppression and discrimination, without engaging in similar acts of injustice and exploitation oneself, is an ongoing issue with which communities, groups, and nations continue to struggle, even in the present day. In the Gospel of Luke, the evangelist and his reading communities were wrestling with similar questions, and some of their answers we may like more than others. The conclusions drawn in the preceding chapters do not necessarily offer definitive answers, but they do call us to consider both how injustice can be stopped, and how (or if) those who perpetrated the injustice can be reintegrated into community with those whom they used to oppress.

While I was writing chapter 4 on the Nazareth proclamation, news broke that Osama bin Laden had been killed. I observed (and cautiously participated in) the ensuing frenzy of opinions, Facebook posts, conversations, celebrations, and riots, but with mixed feelings. From one perspective, justice had been served, as someone responsible for the deaths of many was now dead himself. But at the same time, it did not feel right to celebrate death of any kind when we worship a God of life and resurrection, and are to be participating in God's work of bringing "the year of the Lord's favor" (Luke 4:18-19) into reality for all people, even elites and other (former) oppressors. What is the proper response to domination, oppression, and violence, from a faith perspective? This question is closely related to the debate between inversion and leveling in the imagery of status reversal, and it is, I think, one without a definitive answer that can be applied to all situations. We saw in the Lukan texts studied here examples of both inversion and leveling, but the search for the right balance between the two seems to be an ongoing one in the Gospel of Luke, in the life of the earliest communities reading Luke, and in the life of those of us reading it today. Luke and his status reversals offer one more theory, and one more attempt at addressing these questions—not a perfect theory, perhaps, but a carefully considered one with much wisdom to offer us today.

Bibliography

Abogunrin, Samuel O. "Jesus' Sevenfold Programmatic Declaration at Nazareth: An Exegesis of Luke 4.15-30 from an African Perspective." *Black Theology* 1 (2003): 225–49.

Ackerman, Susan. "Household Religion, Family Religion, and Women's Religion in Ancient Israel." In *Household and Family Religion in Antiquity*, edited by John Bodel and Saul M. Olyan, 127–58. The Ancient World: Comparative Histories. Malden, MA: Blackwell, 2008.

———. "Why Is Miriam Also Among the Prophets? (And Is Zipporah Among the Priests?)." *Journal of Biblical Literature* 121 (2002): 47–80.

Aesop. *The Fables of Aesop, With a Life of the Author*. Boston: Houghton, Mifflin, and Company, 1865.

Ahn, Yong-Sung. *The Reign of God and Rome in Luke's Passion Narrative: An East Asian Global Perspective*. Biblical Interpretation 80. Leiden: Brill, 2006.

Alderink, Larry J., and Luther H. Martin. "Prayer in Greco-Roman Religions." In Kiley, *Prayer from Alexander to Constantine*, 123–27.

Alexander, Loveday. "Ancient Book Production and the Circulation of the Gospels." In Bauckham, *The Gospels for All Christians*, 71–111.

———, ed. *Images of Empire*. Journal for the Study of the Old Testament Supplement Series 122. Sheffield: Sheffield Academic Press, 1991.

———. *The Preface to Luke's Gospel: Literary Convention and Social Context in Luke 1.1-4 and Acts 1.1*. Society for New Testament Studies Monograph Series 78, edited by Margaret E. Thrall. Cambridge: Cambridge University Press, 1993.

Anderson, Janice Capel. "Mary's Difference: Gender and Patriarchy in the Birth Narratives." *Journal of Religion* 67 (1987): 183–202.

Bailey, Kenneth E. "The Song of Mary: Vision of a New Exodus (Luke 1:46-55)." *Theological Review* 2 (1979): 29–35.

Balch, David L. "Rich and Poor, Proud and Humble in Luke-Acts." In *The Social World of the First Christians: Essays in Honor of Wayne A. Meeks*, edited by L. Michael White and O. Larry Yarbrough, 214–33. Minneapolis: Fortress Press, 2005.

Barton, Stephen C. "Can We Identify the Gospel Audiences?" In Bauckham, *The Gospels for All Christians*, 173–94.

————. "Historical Criticism and Social-Scientific Perspectives in New Testament Study." In *Hearing the New Testament: Strategies for Interpretation,* edited by Joel B. Green, 61–89. Eugene, OR: Wipf & Stock, 1995.

Bauckham, Richard, ed. *The Gospels for All Christians: Rethinking the Gospel Audiences.* Grand Rapids: Eerdmans, 1998.

————. "Introduction." In Bauckham, *The Gospels for All Christians: Rethinking the Gospel Audiences,* 1–7.

————. "The Rich Man and Lazarus: The Parable and the Parallels." *New Testament Studies* 37 (1991): 225–46.

Bemile, Paul. *The Magnificat within the Context and Framework of Lukan Theology: An Exegetical Theological Study of Luke 1:46-55.* Regensburger Studien Zur Theologie 34. Frankfurt: Peter Lang, 1986.

Birley, Anthony R. *Hadrian: The Restless Emperor.* London: Routledge, 1997.

Blenkinsopp, Joseph. *Isaiah 56–66.* The Anchor Bible 19B. New York: Doubleday, 2003.

Boff, Leonardo. *The Maternal Face of God: The Feminine and Its Religious Expressions.* Translated by Robert R. Barr and John W. Diercksmeir. San Francisco: Harper & Row, 1987.

Bovon, François. *Luke 1: A Commentary on the Gospel of Luke 1:1—9:50.* Translated by Christine M. Thomas. Hermeneia: A Critical and Historical Commentary on the Bible, edited by Helmut Koester. Minneapolis: Fortress Press, 2002.

————. *Luke the Theologian: Fifty-Five Years of Research (1950–2005).* Translated by Ken McKinney. 2nd rev. ed. Waco, TX: Baylor University Press, 2006.

Bowe, Barbara E. "Prayer Rendered for Caesar? 1 Clement 59.3—61.3." In *The Lord's Prayer and Other Prayer Texts from the Greco-Roman Era,* edited by James H. Charlesworth, Mark Harding, and Mark Kiley, 85–99. Valley Forge: Trinity, 1994.

Bradley, K. R. *Slaves and Masters in the Roman Empire: A Study in Social Control.* New York: Oxford University Press, 1987.

Breasted, James Henry. *The Nineteenth Dynasty. Vol. 3 of Ancient Records of Egypt.* Chicago: University of Chicago Press, 1906.

Brent, Allen. "Luke-Acts and the Imperial Cult in Asia Minor." *Journal of Theological Studies* 48 (1997): 411–38.

Bright, John. *A History of Israel.* 4th ed. Louisville: Westminster John Knox, 2000.

Brooke, George J. *The Dead Sea Scrolls and the New Testament.* Minneapolis: Fortress Press, 2005.

————. "Shared Intertextual Interpretations in the Dead Sea Scrolls and the New Testament." In *Biblical Perspectives: Early Use and Interpretation of the Bible in Light of the Dead Sea Scrolls*, edited by Michael E. Stone and Esther G. Chazon, 35–57. Leiden: Brill, 1998.

Brooten, Bernadette J. "Early Christian Women and Their Cultural Context: Issues of Method in Historical Reconstruction." In *Feminist Perspectives on Biblical Scholarship*, edited by Adela Yarbro Collins, 65–91. Biblical Scholarship in North America 10. Chico, CA: Scholars, 1985.

Brown, Francis, S. R. Driver, and Charles A. Briggs, eds. *The Brown-Driver-Briggs Hebrew and English Lexicon: With an Appendix Containing the Biblical Aramaic*. Peabody, MA: Hendrickson, 2001.

Brown, Raymond E. *The Birth of the Messiah: A Commentary on the Infancy Narratives in the Gospels of Matthew and Luke*. New updated ed. New York: Doubleday, 1993.

Brown, Robert McAfee. *Unexpected News: Reading the Bible With Third World Eyes*. Philadelphia: Westminster, 1984.

Brunt, P. A. "Laus Imperii." In Champion, *Roman Imperialism*, 163–85.

Buth, Randall. "Hebrew Poetic Tenses and the Magnificat." *Journal for the Study of the New Testament* 21 (1984): 67–83.

Byrne, Brendan. *The Hospitality of God: A Reading of Luke's Gospel*. Collegeville, MN: Liturgical, 2000.

Cadbury, Henry J. *The Making of Luke-Acts*. 2nd ed. Peabody, MA: Hendrickson, 1999.

Caesar Augustus. *Res Gestae Divi Augusti*. Edited and translated by Frederick W. Shipley. Loeb Classical Library. London: William Heinemann, 1924.

Callahan, Allen Dwight. "The Arts of Resistance in an Age of Revolt." In Horsley, *Hidden Transcripts and the Arts of Resistance*, 29–40.

Campbell, Jonathan G. *The Exegetical Texts*. Companion to the Qumran Scrolls 4. London: T&T Clark, 2004.

Cardenal, Ernesto. *The Gospel in Solentiname*. Translated by Donald D. Walsh. Rev. ed. Maryknoll, NY: Orbis, 2007.

Carey, Greg. "Symptoms of Resistance in the Book of Revelation." In *The Reality of Apocalypse: Rhetoric and Politics in the Book of Revelation*, edited by David L. Barr, 169–80. Society of Biblical Literature Symposium Series 39. Atlanta: Society of Biblical Literature, 2006.

Carroll, John T. "The God of Israel and the Salvation of the Nations: The Gospel of Luke and the Acts of the Apostles." In *The Forgotten God:*

Perspectives in Biblical Theology, edited by A. Andrew Das and Frank J. Matera, 91–106. Louisville: Westminster John Knox, 2002.

———. "Luke's Portrayal of the Pharisees." *Catholic Biblical Quarterly* 50 (1988): 604–21.

Carter, Warren. "Evoking Isaiah: Matthean Soteriology and an Intertextual Reading of Isaiah 7–9 and Matthew 1:23 and 4:15–16." *Journal of Biblical Literature* 119 (2000): 503–20.

———. "James C. Scott and New Testament Studies: A Response to Allen Callahan, William Herzog, and Richard Horsley." In Horsley, *Hidden Transcripts and the Arts of Resistance*, 81–94.

———. *John and Empire: Initial Explorations*. London: T&T Clark, 2008.

———. *Matthew and Empire: Initial Explorations*. Harrisburg, PA: Trinity, 2001.

———. *The Roman Empire and the New Testament: An Essential Guide*. Nashville: Abingdon, 2006.

———. "Singing in the Reign: Performing Luke's Songs and Negotiating the Roman Empire (Luke 1–2)." In *Luke-Acts and Empire: Essays in Honor of Robert L. Brawley*, edited by David Rhoads, David Esterline, and Jae Won Lee, 23–43. Princeton Theological Monograph Series. Eugene, OR: Wipf & Stock, 2011.

Cassidy, Richard J. *Jesus, Politics, and Society: A Study of Luke's Gospel*. Maryknoll, NY: Orbis, 1978.

Cassidy, William. "Cleanthes—Hymn to Zeus." In Kiley, *Prayer from Alexander to Constantine*, 133–38.

Catchpole, David R. "The Anointed One in Nazareth." In *From Jesus to John: Essays on Jesus and New Testament Christology in Honour of Marinus de Jonge*, edited by Martinus C. de Boer, 231–51. Journal for the Study of the New Testament Supplement Series 84. Sheffield: JSOT Press, 1993.

Champion, Craige B., ed. *Roman Imperialism: Readings and Sources*. Interpreting Ancient History. Malden, MA: Blackwell, 2004.

Champion, Craige B., and Arthur M. Eckstein. "Introduction." In Champion, *Roman Imperialism*, 1–15.

Charlesworth, James H. "Ode of Solomon 5: Praise While Contemplating Persecutors." In Kiley, *Prayer from Alexander to Constantine*, 273–79.

———, ed. *The Scrolls and Christian Origins*. Vol. 3 of The Bible and the Dead Sea Scrolls: The Second Princeton Symposium on Judaism and Christian Origins. Waco, TX: Baylor University Press, 2006.

Cloud, Duncan. "Roman Poetry and Anti-Militarism." In *War and Society in the Roman World*, edited by John Rich and Graham Shipley, 113–38. New York: Routledge, 1993.

Collins, John J., and Devorah Dimant. "A Thrice-Told Hymn: A Response to Eileen Schuller." *Jewish Quarterly Review* 85 (1994): 151–55.

Conzelmann, Hans. *The Theology of St. Luke*. Translated by Geoffrey Buswell. London: Faber and Faber, 1960.

Cook, Edward M. "A Thanksgiving for God's Help (4Q4343 II-III)." In Kiley, *Prayer from Alexander to Constantine*, 14–17.

Cowan, David. *Economic Parables: The Monetary Teachings of Jesus Christ*. Colorado Springs: Paternoster, 2006.

Crawford, Michael H. "Rome and the Greek World: Economic Relationships." In Champion, *Roman Imperialism*, 96–107.

Croatto, José Severino. "From the Leviticus Jubilee Year to the Prophetic Liberation Time: Exegetical Reflections on Isaiah 61 and 58 in Relation to the Jubilee." In Kinsler and Kinsler, *God's Economy*, 89–111.

Crossan, John Dominic. *The Birth of Christianity: Discovering What Happened in the Years Immediately after the Execution of Jesus*. New York: HarperCollins, 1998.

Crossan, John Dominic, and Jonathan L. Reed. *In Search of Paul: How Jesus's Apostle Opposed Rome's Empire with God's Kingdom*. New York: HarperCollins, 2004.

Culpepper, R. Alan. "The Gospel of Luke: Introduction, Commentary, and Reflections." In *The New Interpreter's Bible*, edited by Leander E. Keck, vol. 9, 1–490. Nashville: Abingdon, 1995.

Danker, Frederick William. *Luke*. 2nd ed. Proclamation Commentaries, edited by Gerhard Krodel. Philadelphia: Fortress Press, 1987.

Danker, Frederick William, Walter Bauer, W. F. Arndt, and F. W. Gingrich, eds. *A Greek-English Lexicon of the New Testament and Other Early Christian Literature*. Chicago: The University of Chicago Press, 2000.

Darr, John A. *On Character Building: The Reader and the Rhetoric of Characterization in Luke-Acts*. Louisville: Westminster John Knox, 1992.

Donahue, John R. "Who Is My Enemy? The Parable of the Good Samaritan and the Love of Enemies." In Swartley, *The Love of Enemy and Nonretaliation in the New Testament*, 137–56.

Downing, F. Gerald. "Theophilus's First Reading of Luke-Acts." In *Luke's Literary Achievement: Collected Essays*, edited by C. M. Tuckett, 91–109.

Journal for the Study of the New Testament Supplement Series 116. Sheffield: Sheffield Academic Press, 1995.

Duling, Dennis C. "Empire: Theories, Methods, Models." In Riches and Sim, *The Gospel of Matthew in Its Roman Imperial Context*, 49–74.

Duncan-Jones, Richard. *Money and Government in the Roman Empire.* Cambridge: Cambridge University Press, 1994.

Dyson, Stephen L. "Native Revolt Patterns in the Roman Empire." In *Aufstieg und Niedergang der römischen Welt: Geschichte und Kultur Roms im Spiegel der neueren Forschung* 2.3, edited by Joseph Vogt, Hildegard Temporini, and Wolfgang Haase, 138–75. Berlin: Walter de Gruyter, 1975.

———. "Native Revolts in the Roman Empire." *Historia* 20 (1971): 239–74.

Edwards, Douglas R. "Surviving the Web of Roman Power: Religion and Politics in the Acts of the Apostles, Josephus, and Chariton's Chaereas and Callirhoe." In Alexander, *Images of Empire*, 179–201.

Elliott, John H. "Temple versus Household in Luke-Acts: A Contrast in Social Institutions." In Neyrey, *The Social World of Luke-Acts*, 211–40.

Elliott, Susan M. "Hidden Transcripts and Arts of Resistance in Paul's Letters: A Response." In Horsley, *Hidden Transcripts and the Arts of Resistance*, 157–71.

Esler, Philip Francis. *Community and Gospel in Luke-Acts: The Social and Political Motivations of Lucan Theology.* Society for New Testament Studies Monograph Series 57. Cambridge: Cambridge University Press, 1987.

Evans, Craig A. "The Function of the Elijah/Elisha Narratives in Luke's Ethic of Election." In Evans and Sanders, *Luke and Scripture*, 70–83.

Evans, Craig A., and James A. Sanders. "Gospels and Midrash: An Introduction to Luke and Scripture." In Evans and Sanders, *Luke and Scripture*, 1–13.

———. *Luke and Scripture: The Function of Sacred Tradition in Luke-Acts.* Minneapolis: Fortress Press, 1993.

Falcetta, Alessandro. *The Call of Nazareth: Form and Exegesis of Luke 4:16-30.* Cahiers de la Revue Biblique 53. Paris: Gabalda, 2003.

Fanon, Frantz. *The Wretched of the Earth.* Translated by Richard Philcox. 1963. Reprint, New York: Grove, 2004.

Farris, Stephen. "The Canticles of Luke's Infancy Narrative: The Appropriation of a Biblical Tradition." In Longenecker, *Into God's Presence*, 91–112.

———. *The Hymns of Luke's Infancy Narratives: Their Origin, Meaning, and Significance.* Journal for the Study of the New Testament Supplement Series 9. Sheffield: JSOT Press, 1985.

Fears, J. Rufus. "The Cult of Jupiter and Roman Imperial Ideology." In *Aufstieg und Niedergang der römischen Welt: Geschichte und Kultur Roms im Spiegel der neueren Forschung* 2.17.1, edited by Hildegard Temporini and Wolfgang Haase, 3–141. Berlin: Walter de Gruyter, 1981.

Fitzmyer, Joseph A. *The Gospel According to Luke I–IX*. The Anchor Bible 28. Garden City, NY: Doubleday, 1981.

———. *The Gospel According to Luke X–XXIV*. The Anchor Bible 28A. Garden City, NY: Doubleday, 1985.

Flanders, Henry Jackson Jr., Robert Wilson Crapps, and David Anthony Smith. *People of the Covenant: An Introduction to the Hebrew Bible*. 4th ed. New York: Oxford University Press, 1996.

Fless, Friederike, and Katja Moede. "Music and Dance: Forms of Representation in Pictorial and Written Sources." In Rüpke, *A Companion to Roman Religion*, 249–62.

Flusser, David. *Judaism and the Origins of Christianity*. Jerusalem: Magnes, 1988.

Forbes, Greg W. *The God of Old: The Role of the Lukan Parables in the Purpose of Luke's Gospel*. Journal for the Study of the New Testament Supplement Series 198. Sheffield: Sheffield Academic Press, 2000.

Ford, J. Massyngberde. *My Enemy is My Guest: Jesus and Violence in Luke*. Maryknoll, NY: Orbis, 1984.

Foskett, Mary F. "Miriam/Mariam/Maria: Literary Genealogy and the Genesis of Mary in the Protevangelium of James." In Good, *Mariam, the Magdalen, and the Mother*, 63–74.

Foster, Ruth Ann. "Mary's Hymn of Praise in Luke 1:46–55: Reflections on Liturgy and Spiritual Formation." *Review and Expositor* 100 (2003): 451–63.

Fredriksen, Paula. "Did Jesus Oppose the Purity Laws?" *Bible Review* 11, no. 3 (1995): 18–25, 42–47.

Friesen, Steven J. "Poverty in Pauline Studies: Beyond the So-Called New Consensus." *Journal for the Study of the New Testament* 26 (2004): 323–61.

Garnsey, Peter, and Richard Saller. *The Roman Empire: Economy, Society and Culture*. Berkeley: University of California Press, 1987.

Gerstenberger, Erhard S. *Psalms Part I, With an Introduction to Cultic Poetry*. Forms of the Old Testament Literature 14, edited by Rolf Knierim and Gene M. Tucker. Grand Rapids: Eerdmans, 1988.

Gilbert, Gary. "Luke-Acts and Negotiation of Authority and Identity in the Roman World." In *The Multivalence of Biblical Texts and Theological Meanings*, edited by Christine Helmer and Charlene T. Higbe, 83–104. Society of Biblical Literature Symposium Series. Atlanta: Society of Biblical Literature, 2006.

————. "Roman Propaganda and Christian Identity in the Worldview of Luke-Acts." In Penner and Vander Stichele, *Contextualizing Acts*, 233–56.

Gilkes, Cheryl Townsend. "Resurrection in Prophetic Context: 'Poor Man Lazarus' and Christian Agency." In *Engaging the Bible: Critical Readings from Contemporary Women*, edited by Choi Hee An and Katheryn Pfisterer Darr, 1–19. Minneapolis: Fortress Press, 2006.

Gill, David W. J. "Achaia." In Gill and Gempf, *The Book of Acts in Its Graeco-Roman Setting*, 433–53.

————. "Macedonia." In Gill and Gempf, *The Book of Acts in Its Graeco-Roman Setting*, 397–417.

Gill, David W. J., and Conrad Gempf, eds. *The Book of Acts in Its Graeco-Roman Setting*. The Book of Acts in Its First Century Setting 2, edited by Bruce W. Winter. Grand Rapids: Eerdmans, 1994.

Gill, David W. J., and Bruce W. Winter. "Acts and Roman Religion." In Gill and Gempf, *The Book of Acts in Its Graeco-Roman Setting*, 79–103.

Gilmour, Michael J. "Hints of Homer in Luke 16:19-31?" *Didaskalia* 10 (1999): 23–33.

Gingrich, Andre. "When Ethnic Majorities Are 'Dethroned': Towards a Methodology of Self-Reflexive, Controlled Macrocomparison." In *Anthropology, by Comparison*, edited by Andre Gingrich and Richard G. Fox, 225–48. London: Routledge, 2002.

Good, Deirdre, ed. *Mariam, the Magdalen, and the Mother*. Bloomington, IN: Indiana University Press, 2005.

————. "The Miriamic Secret." In Good, *Mariam, the Magdalen, and the Mother*, 3–24.

Goodman, Martin. "Opponents of Rome: Jews and Others." In Alexander, *Images of Empire*, 222–38.

Gottwald, Norman. *The Hebrew Bible: A Socio-Literary Introduction*. Minneapolis: Fortress Press, 1985.

Gowler, David B. "'At His Gate Lay a Poor Man': A Dialogic Reading of Luke 16:19-31." *Perspectives in Religious Studies* 32 (2005): 249–65.

————. *Host, Guest, Enemy, and Friend: Portraits of the Pharisees in Luke and Acts*. Emory Studies in Early Christianity 2. New York: Peter Lang, 1991.

Grangaard, Blake R. *Conflict and Authority in Luke 19:47 to 21:4*. Studies in Biblical Literature 8, edited by Hemchand Gossai. New York: Peter Lang, 1999.

Green, Joel B. *The Gospel of Luke*. The New International Commentary on the New Testament, edited by Gordon D. Fee. Grand Rapids: Eerdmans, 1997.

———. "The Social Status of Mary in Luke 1,5–2,52: A Plea for Methodological Integration." *Biblica* 73 (1992): 457–72.

———. *The Theology of the Gospel of Luke*. New Testament Theology, edited by James D. G. Dunn. Cambridge: Cambridge University Press, 1995.

Griffiths, J. Gwyn. "Cross-Cultural Eschatology with Dives and Lazarus." *The Expository Times* 105 (1993): 7–12.

Grimshaw, Jim. "Luke's Market Exchange District: Decentering Luke's Rich Urban Center." *Semeia* 86 (1999): 33–51.

Gutiérrez, Gustavo. *A Theology of Liberation: History, Politics, and Salvation.* Translated by Caridad Inda and John Eagleson. Rev. ed. Maryknoll, NY: Orbis, 1988.

Hahn, Frances Hickson. "Performing the Sacred: Prayers and Hymns." In Rüpke, *A Companion to Roman Religion*, 235–48.

Hamel, Edouard. "Le Magnificat et le Renversement des Situations: Réflexion théologico-biblique." *Gregorianum* 60 (1979): 55–84.

Hansen, G. Walter. "Galatia." In Gill and Gempf, *The Book of Acts in Its Graeco-Roman Setting*, 377–95.

Hardwick, Lorna. "Concepts of Peace." In Huskinson, *Experiencing Rome*, 335–68.

Harrill, J. Albert. *Slaves in the New Testament: Literary, Social, and Moral Dimensions.* Minneapolis: Fortress Press, 2006.

Hays, Richard B. *Echoes of Scripture in the Letters of Paul*. New Haven: Yale University Press, 1989.

Hendrickx, Herman. *The Third Gospel for the Third World*. Vol. 3B. Collegeville, MN: Liturgical, 2000.

Hertig, Paul. "The Jubilee Mission of Jesus in the Gospel of Luke: Reversals of Fortune." *Missiology: An International Review* 26 (1998): 167–79.

Herzog, William R. *Jesus, Justice, and the Reign of God: A Ministry of Liberation.* Louisville: Westminster John Knox, 2000.

———. "Onstage and Offstage with Jesus of Nazareth: Public Transcripts, Hidden Transcripts, and Gospel Texts." In Horsley, *Hidden Transcripts and the Arts of Resistance*, 41–60.

———. *Parables as Subversive Speech: Jesus as Pedagogue of the Oppressed.* Louisville: Westminster John Knox, 1994.

Hiebert, Theodore. *God of My Victory: The Ancient Hymn in Habakkuk 3.* Harvard Semitic Monographs 38, edited by Frank Moore Cross. Atlanta: Scholars, 1986.

Hobbs, T. Raymond. "The Political Jesus: Discipleship and Disengagement." In Stegemann, Malina, and Theissen, *The Social Setting of Jesus and the Gospels*, 251–81.

Hock, Ronald F. "Lazarus and Micyllus: Greco-Roman Backgrounds to Luke 16:19–31." *Journal of Biblical Literature* 106 (1987): 447–63.

Hope, Valerie. "The City of Rome: Capital and Symbol." In Huskinson, *Experiencing Rome*, 63–93.

———. "Status and Identity in the Roman World." In Huskinson, *Experiencing Rome*, 125–52.

Hopkins, D. Dombrowski. "The Qumran Community and 1Q Hodayot: A Resassessment." *Revue de Qumran* 10 (1981): 323–64.

Hopkins, Keith. "Conquerors and Slaves: The Impact of Conquering an Empire on the Political Economy of Italy." In Champion, *Roman Imperialism*, 108–28.

Horgan, Maurya P., and Paul J. Kobelski. "The Hodayot (1QH) and New Testament Poetry." In *To Touch the Text: Biblical and Related Studies in Honor of Joseph A. Fitzmyer*, edited by Maurya P. Horgan and Paul J. Kobelski, 179–93. New York: Crossroad, 1989.

Horsley, Richard A. "The Dead Sea Scrolls and the Historical Jesus." In Charlesworth, *The Scrolls and Christian Origins*, 37–60.

———, ed. *Hidden Transcripts and the Arts of Resistance: Applying the Work of James C. Scott to Jesus and Paul*. Semeia Studies. Atlanta: Society of Biblical Literature, 2004.

———. "Introduction: Jesus, Paul, and the 'Arts of Resistance': Leaves from the Notebook of James C. Scott." In Horsley, *Hidden Transcripts and the Arts of Resistance*, 1–26.

———. *Jesus and Empire: The Kingdom of God and the New World Disorder*. Minneapolis: Fortress Press, 2003.

———. *The Liberation of Christmas: The Infancy Narratives in Social Context*. New York: Crossroad, 1989.

———. *Oral Performance, Popular Tradition, and Hidden Transcript in Q*. Semeia Studies. Atlanta: Society of Biblical Literature, 2006.

———. "The Politics of Disguise and Public Declaration of the Hidden Transcript: Broadening Our Approach to the Historical Jesus with Scott's 'Arts of Resistance' Theory." In Horsley, *Hidden Transcripts and the Arts of Resistance*, 61–80.

———. "The Slave Systems of Classical Antiquity and Their Reluctant Recognition by Modern Scholars." *Semeia* 83–84 (1998): 19–66.

Howard-Brook, Wes. *"Come Out, My People!" God's Call out of Empire in the Bible and Beyond*. Maryknoll, NY: Orbis, 2010.

Hughes, Frank W. "The Parable of the Rich Man and Lazarus (Luke 16.19-31) and Graeco-Roman Rhetoric." In *Rhetoric and the New Testament: Essays from the 1992 Heidelberg Conference*, edited by Stanley E. Porter and Thomas H. Olbricht, 29–41. Journal for the Study of the New Testament Supplement Series 90. Sheffield: Sheffield Academic Press, 1993.

Hughes, Julie A. *Scriptural Allusions and Exegesis in the Hodayot*. Leiden: Brill, 2006.

Huskinson, Janet. "Élite Culture and the Identity of Empire." In Huskinson, *Experiencing Rome*, 95–123.

———, ed. *Experiencing Rome: Culture, Identity, and Power in the Roman Empire*. London: Routledge, 2000.

———. "Looking for Culture, Identity and Power." In Huskinson, *Experiencing Rome*, 3–27.

Igboin, Benson O. "An African Understanding of the Parable of the Rich Man and Lazarus: Problems and Possibilities." *Asia Journal of Theology* 19 (2005): 256–69.

Ireland, Dennis J. *Stewardship and the Kingdom of God: An Historical, Exegetical, and Contextual Study of the Parable of the Unjust Steward in Luke 16:1-13*. Supplements to Novum Testamentum 70. Leiden: Brill, 1992.

Isaac, B. "The Limits of Empire: The Roman Army in the East." In Champion, *Roman Imperialism*, 283–92.

James, Paula. "The Language of Dissent." In Huskinson, *Experiencing Rome*, 277–303.

Johnson, Luke Timothy. *The Gospel of Luke*. Sacra Pagina 3, edited by Daniel J. Harrington. Collegeville, MN: Liturgical, 1991.

———. *The Literary Function of Possessions in Luke-Acts*. Society of Biblical Literature Dissertation Series 39, edited by Howard C. Kee and Douglas A. Knight. Missoula, MT: Scholars, 1977.

———. "On Finding the Lukan Community: A Cautious Cautionary Essay." In *Society of Biblical Literature Seminar Papers* 1979, vol. 1, edited by Paul J. Achtemeier, 87–100. Missoula, MT: Scholars, 1979.

Jones, Douglas. "The Background and Character of the Lukan Psalms." *Journal of Theological Studies* 19 (1968): 19–50.

Kautsky, John H. *The Politics of Aristocratic Empires*. Chapel Hill: University of North Carolina Press, 1982.

Kelber, Werner H. "Roman Imperialism and Early Christian Scribality." In *Orality, Literacy, and Colonialism in Antiquity*, edited by Jonathan A. Draper, 135–53. Semeia Studies. Atlanta: Society of Biblical Literature, 2004.

Kelley, Nicole. "Deformity and Disability in Greece and Rome." In *This Abled Body: Rethinking Disabilities in Biblical Studies*, edited by Hector Avalos, Sarah J. Melcher, and Jeremy Schipper, 31–45. Semeia Studies. Atlanta: Society of Biblical Literature, 2007.

Kelly, Christopher. *The Roman Empire: A Very Short Introduction*. Oxford: Oxford University Press, 2006.

Kiley, Mark, ed. *Prayer From Alexander to Constantine: A Critical Anthology*. London: Routledge, 1997.

Kim, Heerak Christian. *Intricately Connected: Biblical Studies, Intertextuality, and Literary Genre*. Lanham, MD: University Press of America, 2008.

Kim, Seyoon. *Christ and Caesar: The Gospel and the Roman Empire in the Writings of Paul and Luke*. Grand Rapids: Eerdmans, 2008.

Kinsler, Ross, and Gloria Kinsler, eds. *God's Economy: Biblical Studies From Latin America*. Maryknoll, NY: Orbis, 2005.

Kraybill, Donald B., and Dennis M. Sweetland. "Possessions in Luke-Acts: A Sociological Perspective." *Perspectives in Religious Studies* 10 (1983): 215–39.

Kreitzer, Larry. "Luke 16:19-31 and 1 Enoch 22." *The Expository Times* 103 (1992): 139–42.

Kristeva, Julia. "Word, Dialogue and Novel." In *The Kristeva Reader*, edited by Toril Moi, 34–61. New York: Columbia University Press, 1986.

Krüger, René. "Conversion of the Pocketbook: The Economic Project of Luke's Gospel." In Kinsler and Kinsler, *God's Economy*, 169–201.

Labahn, Michael, and Jürgen Zangenberg, eds. *Zwischen den Reichen: Neues Testament und Römische Herrschaft*. Texte und Arbeiten zum Neutestamentlichen Zeitalter 36. Tübingen: Francke, 2002.

Lehtipuu, Outi. *The Afterlife Imagery in Luke's Story of the Rich Man and Lazarus*. Supplements to Novum Testamentum 123. Leiden: Brill, 2007.

Lenski, Gerhard E. *Power and Privilege: A Theory of Social Stratification*. 1966. Reprint, Chapel Hill: University of North Carolina Press, 1984.

Levine, Amy-Jill. *The Misunderstood Jew: The Church and the Scandal of the Jewish Jesus*. New York: HarperCollins, 2006.

Lichtheim, Miriam. *The Late Period*. Vol. 3 of *Ancient Egyptian Literature: A Book of Readings*. Berkeley: University of California Press, 1980.

———. *The New Kingdom*. Vol. 2 of *Ancient Egyptian Literature: A Book of Readings*. Berkeley: University of California Press, 1976.

Longenecker, Bruce W. "Exposing the Economic Middle: A Revised Economy Scale for the Study of Early Urban Christianity." *Journal for the Study of the New Testament* 31 (2009): 243–78.

———. *Remember the Poor: Paul, Poverty, and the Greco-Roman World.* Grand Rapids: Eerdmans, 2010.

Longenecker, Richard N., ed. *Into God's Presence: Prayer in the New Testament.* Grand Rapids: Eerdmans, 2001.

Lucian. *Lucian,* vol. 2. Edited and translated by A. M. Harmon. Loeb Classical Library 54. 1915. Reprint, Cambridge: Harvard University Press, 1953.

Lust, Johan, Erik Eynikel, and Katrin Hauspie, eds. *Greek-English Lexicon of the Septuagint.* Stuttgart: Deutsche Bibelgesellschaft, 2003.

MacMullen, Ramsay. "Romanization in the Time of Augustus." In Champion, *Roman Imperialism,* 215–231.

———. *Roman Social Relations: 50 B.C. to A.D. 284.* New Haven: Yale University Press, 1974.

Macro, Anthony D. "The Cities of Asia Minor under the Roman Imperium." In *Aufstieg und Niedergang der römischen Welt: Geschichte und Kultur Roms im Spiegel der neueren Forschung* 2.7.2, edited by Hildegard Temporini and Wolfgang Haase, 659–97. Berlin: Walter de Gruyter, 1980.

Madder, Donald. "The Entimos Pais of Matthew 8:5-13 and Luke 7:1-10." In *Homosexuality and Religion and Philosophy,* edited by Wayne R. Dynes and Stephen Donaldson, 223–35. Studies in Homosexuality. New York City: Garland, 1992.

Malina, Bruce J. *The New Testament World: Insights From Cultural Anthropology.* 3rd ed. Louisville: Westminster John Knox, 2001.

Malina, Bruce J., and Jerome H. Neyrey. "Conflict in Luke-Acts: Labeling and Deviance Theory." In Neyrey, *The Social World of Luke-Acts,* 97–122.

Malina, Bruce J., and Richard L. Rohrbaugh. *Social-Science Commentary on the Synoptic Gospels.* 2nd ed. Minneapolis: Fortress Press, 2003.

Mallen, Peter. *The Reading and Transformation of Isaiah in Luke-Acts.* Library of New Testament Studies 367. London: T&T Clark, 2008.

Martínez, Florentino García, and Eibert J. C. Tigchelaar. *The Dead Sea Scrolls Study Edition.* 2 vols. Grand Rapids: Eerdmans, 2000.

Mattern, Susan. "Rome and the Enemy: Imperial Strategy in the Principate." In Champion, *Roman Imperialism,* 186–200.

McKinnon, James. *Music in Early Christian Literature.* Cambridge Readings in the Literature of Music. Cambridge: Cambridge University Press, 1987.

McVann, Mark. "Rituals of Status Transformation in Luke-Acts." In Neyrey, *The Social World of Luke-Acts*, 333–60.

Meadors, Gary T. "The 'Poor' in the Beatitudes of Matthew and Luke." *Grace Theological Journal* 6, no. 2 (1985): 305–14.

Meeks, Wayne A. *The First Urban Christians: The Social World of the Apostle Paul*. 2nd ed. New Haven: Yale University Press, 2003.

Meyers, Carol. *Households and Holiness: The Religious Culture of Israelite Women*. Facets. Minneapolis: Fortress Press, 2005.

———. "Miriam, Music, and Miracles." In Good, *Mariam, the Magdalen, and the Mother*, 27–48.

———. "Mother to Muse: An Archaeomusicological Study of Women's Performance in Ancient Israel." In *Recycling Biblical Figures*, edited by Athalya Brenner and Jan Willem van Henten, 50–77. Studies in Theology and Religion. Leiderdorp: Deo, 1999.

Miles, Richard. "Communicating Culture, Identity and Power." In Huskinson, *Experiencing Rome*, 29–62.

Miller, Colin. "The Imperial Cult in the Pauline Cities of Asia Minor and Greece." *Catholic Biblical Quarterly* 72 (2010): 314–32.

Miller, Merrill P. "The Function of Isa 61:1-2 in 11Q Melchizedek." *Journal of Biblical Literature* 88 (1969): 467–69.

Montserrat, Dominic. "Reading Gender in the Roman World." In Huskinson, *Experiencing Rome*, 153–81.

Moore, Stephen. *Empire and Apocalypse: Postcolonialism and the New Testament*. Sheffield: Sheffield Phoenix, 2006.

Moreland, Milton. "The Jerusalem Community in Acts: Mythmaking and the Sociorhetorical Function of a Lukan Setting." In Penner and Vander Stichele, *Contextualizing Acts*, 285–310.

Mowinckel, Sigmund. *The Psalms in Israel's Worship*. Translated by D. R. Ap-Thomas. 2 vols. Oxford: Basil Blackwell, 1962.

Moxnes, Halvor. *The Economy of the Kingdom: Social Conflict and Economic Relations in Luke's Gospel*. Overtures to Biblical Theology. Philadelphia: Fortress Press, 1988.

———. "Patron-Client Relations and the New Community in Luke-Acts." In Neyrey, *The Social World of Luke-Acts*, 241–68.

———. "The Social Context of Luke's Community." In *Gospel Interpretation: Narrative-Critical and Social-Scientific Approaches*, edited by Jack Dean Kingsbury, 166–77. Harrisburg, PA: Trinity, 1997.

Moyise, Steve. *Evoking Scripture: Seeing the Old Testament in the New*. London: T&T Clark, 2008.

Nardoni, Enrique. *Rise Up, O Judge: A Study of Justice in the Biblical World*. Translated by Seán Charles Martin. Peabody, MA: Hendrickson, 2004.

Newsom, Carol A. *The Self as Symbolic Space: Constructing Identity and Community at Qumran*. Leiden: Brill, 2004.

Neyrey, Jerome H. *Give God the Glory: Ancient Prayer and Worship in Cultural Perspective*. Grand Rapids: Eerdmans, 2007.

————, ed. *The Social World of Luke-Acts: Models for Interpretation*. Peabody, MA: Hendrickson, 1991.

————. "The Symbolic Universe of Luke-Acts: 'They Turn the World Upside Down.'" In Neyrey, *The Social World of Luke-Acts*, 271–304.

Nitzan, Bilhah. *Qumran Prayer and Religious Poetry*. Translated by Jonathan Chipman. Leiden: Brill, 1994.

Nogueira, Paolo Augusto de Souza. "Ecstatic Worship in the Self-Glorification Hymn (4Q471B, 4Q427, 4Q491C): Implications for the Understanding of an Ancient Jewish and Early Christian Phenomenon." In *Wisdom and Apocalypticism in the Dead Sea Scrolls and in the Biblical Tradition*, edited by Florentino García Martínez, 385–93. Leuven: Leuven University Press, 2003.

Nolland, John. "Classical and Rabbinic Parallels to 'Physician, Heal Yourself' (Lk 4:23)." *Novum Testamentum* 21 (1979): 193–209.

————. "Impressed Unbelievers as Witnesses to Christ (Luke 4:22a)." *Journal of Biblical Literature* 98 (1979): 219–29.

————. *Luke 1—9:20*. Word Biblical Commentary 35a. Dallas: Word, 1989.

Noorda, S. J. "'Cure Yourself, Doctor!' (Luke 4,23): Classical Parallels to an Alleged Saying of Jesus." In *Logia: Les Paroles de Jésus—The Sayings of Jesus*, edited by Joël Delobel, 459–67. Bibliotheca Ephemeridum Theologicarum Lovaniensium. Leuven: Leuven University Press, 1982.

Oakes, Peter. "A State of Tension: Rome in the New Testament." In Riches and Sim, *The Gospel of Matthew in Its Roman Imperial Context*, 75–90.

Oakman, Douglas E. "The Countryside in Luke-Acts." In Neyrey, *The Social World of Luke-Acts*, 151–79.

Oh, Duck-ho. "Faith and Wealth: A Literary-Historical Study of Luke 16." PhD diss., Union Theological Seminary in Virginia, 1996.

Osiek, Carolyn, Margaret Y. MacDonald, and Janet H. Tulloch. *A Woman's Place: House Churches in Earliest Christianity*. Minneapolis: Fortress Press, 2006.

O'Toole, Robert F. *The Unity of Luke's Theology: An Analysis of Luke-Acts.* Good News Studies 9, edited by Robert J. Karris. Wilmington: Michael Glazier, 1984.

Page, Christopher. *The Christian West and Its Singers.* New Haven: Yale University Press, 2010.

Penner, Todd. "Contextualizing Acts." In Penner and Vander Stichele, *Contextualizing Acts*, 1–21.

Penner, Todd, and Caroline Vander Stichele, eds. *Contextualizing Acts: Lukan Narrative and Greco-Roman Discourse.* Society of Biblical Literature Symposium Series 20. Atlanta: Society of Biblical Literature, 2003.

Perkins, Phil. "Power, Culture and Identity in the Roman Economy." In Huskinson, *Experiencing Rome*, 183–212.

Perkins, Phil, and Lisa Nevett. "Urbanism and Urbanization in the Roman World." In Huskinson, *Experiencing Rome*, 213–44.

Perry, Menakhem. "Literary Dynamics: How the Order of a Text Creates Its Meanings." *Poetics Today* 1 (1979): 35–64, 311–61.

Phillips, Thomas E. *Reading Issues of Wealth and Poverty in Luke-Acts.* Lewiston, NY: Edwin Mellen, 2001.

Pilgrim, Walter E. *Good News to the Poor: Wealth and Poverty in Luke-Acts.* Minneapolis: Augsburg, 1981.

Price, S. R. F. *Rituals and Power: The Roman Imperial Cult in Asia Minor.* Cambridge: Cambridge University Press, 1984.

Prior, Michael. *Jesus the Liberator: Nazareth Liberation Theology (Luke 4:16-30).* Sheffield: Sheffield Academic Press, 1995.

Quasten, Johannes. *Music and Worship in Pagan and Christian Antiquity.* Translated by Boniface Ramsey. 1930. Reprint, Washington, DC: National Association of Pastoral Musicians, 1983.

Reimer, Ivoni Richter. "The Forgiveness of Debts in Matthew and Luke: For an Economy without Exclusions." In Kinsler and Kinsler, *God's Economy*, 152–68.

Reinstorf, Dieter H. "The Rich, the Poor, and the Law." *Hervormde teologiese studies* 60 (2004): 329–48.

Rich, John. "Fear, Greed, and Glory: The Causes of Roman War Making in the Middle Republic." In Champion, *Roman Imperialism*, 46–65.

Richard, Pablo. "Now Is the Time to Proclaim the Biblical Jubilee." In Kinsler and Kinsler, *God's Economy*, 43–58.

Riches, John K. "The Synoptic Evangelists and Their Communities." In *Christian Beginnings: Word and Community from Jesus to Post-Apostolic Times*, edited by Jürgen Becker, 213–41. Louisville: Westminster John Knox, 1993.

Riches, John, and David C. Sim, eds. *The Gospel of Matthew in Its Roman Imperial Context*. Journal for the Study of the New Testament Supplement Series 276. London: T&T Clark, 2005.

Ringe, Sharon H. *Jesus, Liberation, and the Biblical Jubilee: Images for Ethics and Christology*. Overtures to Biblical Theology 19. Philadelphia: Fortress Press, 1985.

Ringgren, Helmer. "Luke's Use of the Old Testament." In *Christians among Jews and Gentiles*, edited by George W. E. Nickelsburg and George W. MacRae, 227–35. Philadelphia: Fortress Press, 1986.

Rives, James. "Religion in the Roman Empire." In Huskinson, *Experiencing Rome*, 245–75.

Robbins, Vernon K. "Luke-Acts: A Mixed Population Seeks a Home in the Roman Empire." In Alexander, *Images of Empire*, 202–21.

———. "The Social Location of the Implied Author of Luke-Acts." In Neyrey, *The Social World of Luke-Acts*, 305–32.

———. "Socio-Rhetorical Criticism: Mary, Elizabeth, and the Magnificat as a Test Case." In *The New Literary Criticism and the New Testament*, edited by Elizabeth Struthers Malbon and Edgar V. McKnight, 164–209. Journal for the Study of the New Testament Supplement Series 109. Sheffield: Sheffield Academic Press, 1994.

Rohrbaugh, Richard L. "Ethnocentrism and Historical Questions about Jesus." In Stegemann, Malina, and Theissen, *The Social Setting of Jesus and the Gospels*, 27–43.

———. "The Pre-Industrial City in Luke-Acts: Urban Social Relations." In Neyrey, *The Social World of Luke-Acts*, 125–49.

Rowe, C. Kavin. "Luke-Acts and the Imperial Cult: A Way Through the Conundrum?" *Journal for the Study of the New Testament* 27 (2005): 279–300.

———. *World Upside Down: Reading Acts in the Graeco-Roman Age*. Oxford: Oxford University Press, 2009.

Horace. *Odes and Epodes*. Edited and translated by Niall Rudd. Loeb Classical Library 33. Cambridge: Harvard University Press, 2004.

Rüpke, Jörg, ed. *A Companion to Roman Religion*. Blackwell Companions to the Ancient World. Malden, MA: Blackwell, 2007.

Saldarini, Anthony J. *Pharisees, Scribes and Sadducees in Palestinian Society: A Sociological Approach*. Wilmington: Michael Glazier, 1988.

Sanders, James A. "From Isaiah 61 to Luke 4." In Evans and Sanders, *Luke and Scripture*, 46–69.

———. "Isaiah in Luke." In Evans and Sanders, *Luke and Scripture*, 14–25.

Schottroff, Luise. "Das Magnificat und die älteste Tradition über Jesus von Nazareth." *Evangelische Theologie* 38 (1978): 298–313.

———. *The Parables of Jesus*. Translated by Linda M. Maloney. Minneapolis: Fortress Press, 2006.

Schowalter, Dan. "Written in Stone: A Prayer to Augustus." In Kiley, *Prayer from Alexander to Constantine*, 159–64.

Schuller, Eileen M. "A Hymn from a Cave Four Manuscript: 4Q427 7 i+ii." *Journal of Biblical Literature* 112 (1993): 605–28.

———. "Prayer in the Dead Sea Scrolls." In Longenecker, *Into God's Presence*, 66–90.

Scott, James C. *Domination and the Arts of Resistance: Hidden Transcripts*. New Haven: Yale University Press, 1990.

———. *Weapons of the Weak: Everyday Forms of Peasant Resistance*. New Haven: Yale University Press, 1985.

Scott, James M. "Luke's Geographical Horizon." In Gill and Gempf, *The Book of Acts in Its Graeco-Roman Setting*, 483–544.

Seccombe, David Peter. *Possessions and the Poor in Luke-Acts*. Linz: Studien zum Neuen Testament und Seiner Umwelt, 1982.

Siker, Jeffrey S. "'First to the Gentiles': A Literary Analysis of Luke 4:16-30." *Journal of Biblical Literature* 111 (1992): 73–90.

Sloan, Robert Bryan Jr. *The Favorable Year of the Lord: A Study of Jubilary Theology in the Gospel of Luke*. Austin: Schola, 1977.

Sölle, Dorothee. *Revolutionary Patience*. Translated by Rita Kimber and Robert Kimber. Maryknoll, NY: Orbis, 1977.

"A South African Example: Jesus' Teaching at Nazareth–Luke 4.14-30." In *Voices from the Margin: Interpreting the Bible in the Third World*, edited by R. S. Sugirtharajah, 423–30. Maryknoll, NY: Orbis, 1991.

Stegemann, Wolfgang, Bruce J. Malina, and Gerd Theissen, eds. *The Social Setting of Jesus and the Gospels*. Minneapolis: Fortress Press, 2002.

Swain, Simon. *Hellenism and Empire: Language, Classicism, and Power in the Greek World, AD 50–250*. Oxford: Clarendon, 1996.

Swartley, Willard M., ed. *The Love of Enemy and Nonretaliation in the New Testament*. Louisville: Westminster John Knox, 1992.

———. "Luke's Transforming of Tradition: Eirēnē and Love of Enemy." In Swartley, *The Love of Enemy and Nonretaliation in the New Testament*, 157–176.

Tannehill, Robert C. "The Magnificat as Poem." *Journal of Biblical Literature* 93 (1974): 263–75.

———. "The Mission of Jesus according to Luke iv 16–30." In *Jesus in Nazareth*, edited by Walther Eltester, 51–75. Beihefte zur Zeitschrift für die neutestamentliche Wissenschaft und die Kunde der älteren Kirche, 40. Berlin: Walter de Gruyter, 1972.

Toner, Jerry. *Popular Culture in Ancient Rome*. Cambridge, MA: Polity, 2009.

Trebilco, Paul. "Asia." In Gill and Gempf, *The Book of Acts in Its Graeco-Roman Setting*, 291–362.

Trible, Phyllis. "Bringing Miriam out of the Shadows." *Bible Review* 5, no. 1 (1989): 14–25, 34.

Turner, Victor W. *The Ritual Process: Structure and Anti-Structure*. Chicago: Aldine, 1969.

Van der Horst, Pieter W. "Abraham's Bosom, the Place Where He Belonged: A Short Note on ἀπενεχθῆναι in Luke 16:22." *New Testament Studies* 52 (2006): 142–44.

Verhey, Allen. *The Great Reversal: Ethics and the New Testament*. Grand Rapids: Eerdmans, 1984.

Versnel, H. S. *Transition and Reversal in Myth and Ritual: Inconsistencies in Greek and Roman Religion II*. Studies in Greek and Roman Religion 6. Leiden: Brill, 1993.

Viljoen, Francois P. "Song and Music in the Early Christian Communities: Paul's Utilisation of Jewish, Roman and Greek Musical Traditions to Encourage the Early Christian Communities to Praise God and to Explain His Arguments." In *Zwischen den Reichen: Neues Testament und Römische Herrschaft*, edited by Michael Labahn and Jürgen Zangenberg, 195–213. Texte und Arbeiten zum neutestamentlichen Zeitalter 36. Tübingen: Francke, 2002.

Walaskay, Paul W. *"And So We Came to Rome": The Political Perspective of St Luke*. Society for New Testament Studies Monograph Series 49. Cambridge: Cambridge University Press, 1983.

Wallace, Daniel B. *Greek Grammar Beyond the Basics: An Exegetical Syntax of the New Testament*. Grand Rapids: Zondervan, 1996.

Walton, Steve. "The State They Were In: Luke's View of the Roman Empire." In *Rome in the Bible and the Early Church*, edited by Peter Oakes, 1–41. Carlisle: Paternoster, 2002.

Watts, James W. *Psalm and Story: Inset Hymns in Hebrew Narrative.* Journal for the Study of the Old Testament Supplement Series 139. Sheffield: Sheffield Academic Press, 1992.

Watts, John D. W. *Isaiah 34–66.* Word Biblical Commentary 25. Nashville: Thomas Nelson, 2000.

Wendland, Ernst R. "Mwini-Chuma ('Owner-of-Wealth'): A Dramatic Radio Contextualisation of the Lukan 'Rich Man' Parable in Nyanja." *Neotestamentica* 37 (2003): 312–45.

Wessels, G. Francois. "The Letter to Philemon in the Context of Slavery in Early Christianity." In *Philemon in Perspective: Interpreting a Pauline Letter*, edited by D. Francois Tolmie, 143–68. Beihefte zur Zeitschrift für die neutestamentliche Wissenschaft und die Kunde der älteren Kirche 169. Berlin: Walter de Gruyter, 2010.

Westermann, Claus. *Praise and Lament in the Psalms.* Translated by Keith R. Crim and Richard N. Soulen. Atlanta: John Knox Press, 1981.

Whittaker, C. R. "The Poor." In *The Romans*, edited by Andrea Giardina. 272–99. Chicago: University of Chicago Press, 1993.

Williams, Margaret. "Jews and Jewish Communities in the Roman Empire." In Huskinson, *Experiencing Rome*, 305–33.

Woolf, G. "Becoming Roman: The Origins of Provincial Civilization in Gaul." In Champion, *Roman Imperialism*, 231–42.

Yamazaki-Ransom, Kazuhiko. *The Roman Empire in Luke's Narrative.* Library of New Testament Studies 404. London: T&T Clark, 2010.

Yang, Seung Ai. "Luke 1:46-55 the Magnificat." In Kiley, *Prayer from Alexander to Constantine*, 216–21.

York, John O. *The Last Shall Be First: The Rhetoric of Reversal in Luke.* Journal for the Study of the New Testament Supplement Series 46. Sheffield: Sheffield Academic Press, 1991.

Zerbe, Gordon M. "Economic Justice and Non-Retaliation in the Dead Sea Scrolls: Implications for New Testament Interpretation." In Charlesworth, *The Scrolls and Christian Origins*, 319–55.

Zorilla, C. Hugo. "The Magnificat: Song of Justice." In *Conflict and Context: Hermeneutics in the Americas*, edited by Mark Lau Branson and C. René Padilla, 220–37. Grand Rapids: Eerdmans, 1986.

Index